"A fascinating investigation into the development of economic thought from David Ricardo's era to the present day—and its impact on real lives and livelihoods. Wide-ranging and carefully researched, this book shows the temptations and dangers of assuming away too much of reality in the pursuit of elegant economic models. A heartfelt and reasoned call for a more human economics."
Erica Thompson, author of *Escape from Model Land*

"A wonderful achievement bursting with humanity. As important for how we study international economic affairs today as it is in reappraising nineteenth-century imperial trade."
Matthew Watson, University of Warwick

"This important and lucid book skewers—in delightful detail—the false gods of the profession that has wreaked so much modern havoc around the globe."
Nicholas Shaxson, author of *Treasure Islands* and *The Finance Curse*

"Nat Dyer's gripping, page-turning exposé of the Neverland of economic models, thriving at the crippling expense of the real world, is simply brilliant."
Patrick Alley, co-founder Global Witness and author of *Very Bad People* and *Terrible Humans*

"Brilliant and erudite ... This pioneering deep dive into Ricardo's intellectual and social universe is a revelation for those interested in history, economics, science, and their rich interaction at the dawn of the modern world."
Jacob Soll, University of Southern California, author of *Free Market: The History of an Idea*

RICARDO'S DREAM

How Economists Forgot
the Real World and Led Us Astray

Nat Dyer

BRISTOL
UNIVERSITY
PRESS

First published in Great Britain in 2025 by

Bristol University Press
University of Bristol
1–9 Old Park Hill
Bristol
BS2 8BB
UK
t: +44 (0)117 374 6645
e: bup-info@bristol.ac.uk

Details of international sales and distribution partners are available at
bristoluniversitypress.co.uk

British Library Cataloguing in Publication Data
A catalogue record for this book is available from the British Library

ISBN 978-1-5292-2550-1 paperback
ISBN 978-1-5292-2551-8 ePub
ISBN 978-1-5292-2552-5 ePdf

Cover design: blu inc
Front cover image: blu inc/GettyImages-1337172638

Bristol University Press uses environmentally responsible
print partners.

Printed and bound in Great Britain by CPI Group (UK) Ltd,
Croydon, CR0 4YY

FSC
www.fsc.org
MIX
Paper | Supporting
responsible forestry
FSC® C013604

To Sarah, who made it possible

History, including economic history, is the
essential corrective for intellectual hubris.

Susan Strange (1923–1998)

Contents

PART II: Death

PART III: Rebirth

List of Figures and Tables

Figures

Table

Acknowledgements

I'm grateful for the work of all the researchers and writers on which *Ricardo's Dream* builds. I owe much to Matthew Watson in particular, whose article first alerted me to the enormous gap between the myth and reality of the iconic trade in English cloth and Portuguese wine. Matthew has been exceptionally kind and supportive at various stages of the project. The work of Avner Offer and Gabriel Söderberg was crucial too in introducing me to the 'Ricardian Vice' and its connection to recent economics. This book began as a marriage of these two insights. Many of my other intellectual debts can be seen in these pages.

Paul Stevens at Bristol University Press took the seed of an idea and generously gave his time to nurture and shape it to maturity. My thanks too to Isobel Green, Kathryn King, and the rest of the BUP team—and to Polly Chester from Bourchier—for helping to create the book and get it out into the world. I'm grateful too for the anonymous reviewers of my proposal and draft text who helped sharpen my ideas and for the diligent copy editing of Jane Entrican. I would have become stuck attempting to wrestle the lines into shape without the guidance of freelance editor Jonathan Cobb. Jonathan gave great encouragement and gently pointed out the difference between the book I thought I'd written and the words on the page. *Ricardo's Dream* is much richer for his broad-minded critique.

I've also had support from numerous subject area experts too many to mention here. Their often generous and enthusiastic responses to my requests for information or for feedback on my writing have been heart-warming, saved me from many errors, and fed my research. I'd like to particularly thank Julian Baggini, Leonor Freire Costa, Patricia Fara, Randall Germain, Terry Peach, Reinhard Schumacher, and Laura J. Snyder for engaging with my work. They are, of course, not responsible for the errors that remain in the text. Three people read my entire draft manuscript and provided invaluable feedback: Jag Bhalla, Roger Tooze, and Erica Thompson. Jag has, from the beginning, been a steadfast believer in the contemporary relevance of the book and my ability to deliver it. Jag and the rest of the Philosophy Zoom group—Adam, Dave, and Mia—have sustained me with their deep interest in new ideas and spirited defence of their own thinking.

My research would not have been possible without the dedication of librarians and archivists, such as those at the British Library, the UK National Archives, the Bank of England Archive, and the Smithsonian's National Numismatic Collection. Online archivists and knowledge sharers have been just as valuable, including, but not limited to: the Internet Archive, the History of Economic Thought Website, the Trans-Atlantic Slave Trade Database, and the Online Library of Liberty. I was also helped by the free research service, The Counter, run by SOMO—the Dutch non-profit Centre for Research on Multinational Corporations.

Museums and historical sites in London, Washington DC, Rio de Janeiro, and Minas Gerais allowed me glimpses of the past. Guides, notably Sadakne Baroudi, creator of the Afro-Rio Walking Tour, helped me better understand the history of Africans in Brazil. My thanks also to Laís, Sueli, Carlos and Tiago. In London, Terry Silvers and Susie Steed walked me through neglected aspects of the city's economic history.

My family and friends have helped in countless ways large and small during the three years of research and writing. I'm grateful for my parents, and for W. and E. for reminding me what life is really about. And, for Sarah—to whom the book is dedicated—without whose conversation, advice, and love it would not have been written.

Nat Dyer
March 2024

Introduction:
'As Certain as the Principle of Gravitation'

A sketch of the book's argument

As a deadly pandemic, originally from Asia, spread through English towns and cities, Cambridge University suspended all lectures, closed its buildings, and sent students home to isolate. One recent graduate retreated to his family home, in Lincolnshire, 60 miles north of the university. In the almost two years of lockdown, the 23-year-old would lay the groundwork for theories that revolutionized human understanding.

This was not COVID and the year was not 2020. It was 1665, the disease was bubonic plague, and the student was Isaac Newton, now celebrated as one of the world's greatest scientists. Late in his life, Newton told the famous story—perhaps clever self-promotion—of sitting by a tree, on a warm evening after dinner at his family farm, wondering why an apple fell directly down to the ground. From that seed, he said, came the idea for a *universal* law of gravity: one force that could explain both the apple falling to Earth and the Moon revolving around it. Everything in the universe, he proposed, was attracted to everything else through this stable, universal law.[1]

When the pandemic was over—leaving a fifth of Londoners dead—Newton returned to Cambridge and, over the next two decades, worked up his theories of motion and gravity. In 1687, aged 45, he published *Principia Mathematica*, revealing hidden regularities behind the chaotic appearance of nature. He described these laws of nature in precise mathematical formulas. Although we now know

1

Newton's laws break down in extreme conditions, they remain a master key for understanding the physical world and, almost three centuries later, helped humans get to the Moon.[2]

Newton's stunning success fell on fertile ground and set imaginations alight. Across Europe, Enlightenment thinkers reimagined society founded on reason and science. From that time to today, prominent intellectuals have dreamed of doing for the human and social world what Newton had done for the physical world: revealing hidden patterns and laws. Modern thinkers in this tradition have worked to produce clear, quantified, and often predictive theories of social science. The holy grail is a simple model that can nonetheless explain great things. 'Newtonian physics', the historian of ideas Isaiah Berlin wrote about this movement, 'understandably enough, hypnotised the entire intellectual world.'[3]

This book is about the most consequential attempt to create a kind of physics of society: economics. No other social science has so boldly aspired to capture mass human interactions and relationships in mathematical models. No other social science has matched its apparent success or its certain influence—on politics, the economy, and many other aspects of our collective lives—over the past 50 years. Much of its authority has come from a claim to be more rigorous or scientific than other social sciences, such as politics or anthropology. Mainstream economics has seen itself as a noble attempt to build a science of human behaviour without ideology or politics. It promised a method that would move so carefully from step to step that its conclusions would be indisputable.

Ricardo's Dream investigates the dark side of this intellectual trend. What gets excluded or ignored when you attempt to capture humans rather than atoms in logical, predictive models? How do we know that the invisible, hidden order is really in the world rather than in our minds? And, can the economics we've inherited deal with today's urgent global problems, from the ecological crash to rising inequality that threatens to rip democratic societies apart?

An economic law as certain as gravity

To shed light on these questions, I've found it useful to go back to one of the first people to consider economics to be, as he said, 'a strict science' like mathematics.[4] David Ricardo was born in London in 1772 and is considered one of the great classical economists; according to some, he is even more influential than 'the father of economics' Adam Smith. If you take financial and intellectual success together, Ricardo was among the most successful men who have ever lived. Aged 21, he was cut off by his family for marrying someone of a different religion but went on to co-found the London Stock Exchange and become one of the wealthiest men in the country. His skill on the financial markets allowed him to retire, aged 43, to a vast country estate after having helped finance Britain's victory over Napoleon's France. Ricardo then wrote *On the Principles of Political Economy and Taxation*, in 1817, which defined mainstream economics for a generation and casts a shadow today even on those who have never heard of it. He overcame his reticence at public speaking to become a Member of Parliament, in which setting he defended his economic ideas. These economic laws were like Newton's, he said, natural and universally true: 'as certain as the principle of gravitation'.[5]

David Ricardo is only one of many thinkers in history—from the mathematician Euclid in ancient Greece to the 'new classical' economist Robert Lucas in our time—who have inspired the belief that logical abstractions or equations can capture lasting truths about the human social world. Ricardo is unique, however, in giving us two intellectual traditions that have been hugely influential in the last half-century.

First, he produced the most influential theory of international trade ever written, one that, filtered and amended by later generations, justified the 'hyper-globalization' of the 1990s and 2000s. For this theory, called comparative advantage, Ricardo is known as the father of international economics. Second, and even more consequential, a good case can be made that Ricardo was the originator of economics' method of creating simple, abstract, numerical models to explain the social world. This method was fiercely challenged and fell from favour, after a social and political revolt, 60 years after he died. But it was reborn with a vengeance in the mid-twentieth century in North America. His intellectual ghost, Ricardo's Dream of guiding policy by highly abstract theory, still hovers over us two centuries after his death.

There is a paradox in the dream. What Ricardo and later imitators hoped to achieve was to strip society down to its essentials and reveal its mechanisms: as if it were an old-style pocket watch whose lid you could lift to expose its wheels and cogs. 'By building a model world, Ricardo gave the powerful tool of abstraction to economics,' wrote Robert Heilbroner in his best-selling history of economic thinkers, *The Worldly Philosophers*. It was a mixed blessing. From Ricardo's method of abstraction, Heilbroner says, 'we owe the claim of economics to be considered a science. Perhaps it is to this very penchant for oversimplification that we also owe its rather spotty record *as* a science.' How can we reconcile these two? Why does a method, which looks so scientific, often fail in practice? Heilbroner provides a clue when he says that the 'strength' of Ricardo's economic thinking lay 'in its very unreality'.[6] We will trace the 200-year intellectual battle over whether this unreality is a strength or weakness, a virtue or a vice. We will see the devastating consequences of unreal stories and how they erase other histories.

Making things disappear

The conventional story is that mainstream economics is all about understanding how society really works. It was most forcefully expressed by one of the intellectual giants of the twentieth century, the American economist Milton Friedman. In a highly influential 1953 paper, Friedman distinguished between investigating 'what is', which he called positive economics, and 'what ought to be', which he called normative economics. In his telling, his type of economics that became mainstream was positive economics: a clear-eyed look at what 'is'.[7] A similar idea was expressed by the most-read economics book of recent decades. Promising to reveal 'the hidden side of everything', the authors of *Freakonomics* told their millions of readers: 'Morality, it could be argued, represents the way that people would like the world to work, whereas economics represents how it actually does work.'[8]

The message is clear: mainstream economics investigates the real, while other, less rigorous, subjects give in to superficial or wishful thinking. That's why economics has often been described as exposing the 'harsh realities' of a situation. Thus, Friedman could write, with a silent hat-tip to locked-down student Isaac Newton: 'positive economics is, or can be, an "objective" science, in precisely the same sense as any of the physical sciences'.[9] *Ricardo's Dream* suggests a different narrative, a different history, which turns this distinction on its head. It recognizes that economists are visionaries, not just number crunchers, and that when they are trusted by society what they see, or fail to see, matters.

The book's argument is that in straining to peer through the chaos and confusion of the world to the underlying mechanisms, too much economic thinking, both in Ricardo's day and ours, mistook a small, unrepresentative sample as the whole picture. This has distorted the vision of generations. If your scientific ideal is a simple, logical model, there is a tendency to focus on those parts of reality that are more regular or can be easily counted. The awkward aspects more difficult to capture in formal laws or mathematics—the fact that humans are a diverse group of emotional and social primates, for example, or the natural, political, and legal contexts in which markets are born and function—tend to get filtered out, set apart, and eventually forgotten. One physicist-turned-financial modeller, Emanuel Derman, has compared the process of creating a model to forcing the ugly sisters' feet into Cinderella's glass slipper by cutting off the toes or heel (as in early versions of the tale). Whatever does not make it into the elegant slipper often disappears in the mind's eye and some begin to say it never existed at all.

The pay-off, once you've hacked these awkward parts off (and added some new features), is big. At the centre of this new theoretical world is an imaginary creature, known as a 'rational actor' or 'economic human', that has an order and regularity that is a scholar's dream.[10] You can ask your model all sorts of questions and if you've set it up correctly, it will give you amazingly precise answers. But too few economists have weighed carefully the costs and benefits of the approach.

The main cost, I want to convince you, is that the questions seeming being studied are quietly replaced with different, easier, less relevant ones. This problem-solving strategy is called 'substitution'.[11] There is nothing necessarily wrong with the method. If the easier problem incorporates the essential features of the more complex one, it can provide insight. Substitution can be used to create a quick, rough-and-ready answer to a difficult or even impossible question. (For example, asking a representative sample of 2,000 people their views to get a decent, but not perfect, gauge of national opinion.) The trouble begins, however, if the simpler world is not a good analogy for the real one. It is made worse if researchers fail to communicate clearly that a substitution or swap has been made and the answers are used uncritically to guide actions in the real world. It becomes most dangerous when people start to fall in love with the simple model and see it as the real, hidden truth behind the events of the world. This, as we'll see, is called the Pygmalion Syndrome. In the final stage, when events or actions violate the imaginary model, the true believer will keep faith with the substituted reality and try to alter the world to match it. This has happened time and again, often with disastrous consequences.

The method of getting clear-cut results to economic questions by piling on one huge assumption after another has been named after its originator, David Ricardo. The influential Austrian-American economist Joseph Schumpeter wrote, in the mid-twentieth century, that the method produced 'an excellent theory that can never be refuted and lacks nothing save sense'. He continued: 'The habit of applying results of this character to the solution of practical problems we shall call the Ricardian Vice.'[12]

Unfortunately, since the 1970s, we have been guided by economists who portrayed a similar method not as a vice but a virtue. The mainstream economics we have inherited has at its core the assumptions that people are calculating, self-interested, and all-knowing and that markets work perfectly. These are not the conclusions but often the starting points for research. These assumptions are known to be empirically false and yet scholars grip onto them tightly because they allow them to use standard mathematical techniques and produce precise answers. The result has been a tendency to investigate hypothetical or unreal worlds, to value reasoning over observing, and to prefer theoretical over empirical knowledge. This tendency is not just a right-wing, conservative phenomenon, but has been embraced by left-leaning, interventionist thinkers too.[13] There are other models produced by 'liberal' economists that acknowledge that people do not have perfect information, for example, or that prices are 'sticky' and do not adjust instantaneously, but they often only depart from the ideal tentatively: one assumption at a time. These timid steps towards reality have left the physics-like 'frame', as linguist George Lakoff would call it, at the centre of the discipline.[14] Only since the 2010s has this frame been seriously challenged within the mainstream.

The chasm between events and the models meant to describe these has been a defining feature of the last few decades of global politics. It was demonstrated most dramatically in the global financial crisis of 2008. A year later, *The Economist* magazine, not traditionally a venue for critiques of economics, summed up the tendency of economic theorists to look through the real world to a more beautiful, imaginary realm with a twist on the title of Robert Heilbroner's book. It called them: 'The other-worldly philosophers'.[15]

One way of thinking about this is to consider Oscar Wilde's only complete novel, *The Picture of Dorian Gray*, published in 1891. Dorian Gray, a vain young man, is granted his wish to remain young and beautiful while his portrait, which he locks away, ages and displays the signs of his sinful life. When he's 40, others marvel at the unblemished looks of a 22-year-old and how his appearance fails to match his ever more dishonest and illegal behaviour. I've come to think of Dorian Gray as an analogy for the mismatch between the mainstream vision of the economy and the real thing. In the most extreme cases, the economics we have inherited presents an idealized version, as beautiful as Dorian Gray's unchanging face. The actual economy, or at least large parts of it, are increasingly ugly like his portrait: marked by oligarchs and the underclass, the looting of poor countries, and the industrial-scale gobbling up of the living planet. To meet these challenges, we need to ditch the flattering, abstract painting of the economy and create a new, more realistic one. The analogy simplifies a complex issue, but simplifying, as modellers will tell you, can be useful if it focuses on the essentials.

Economists have a difficult job. The object of their study—humans interacting in a dynamic environment—is fiendishly complicated. PhD supervisors, politicians, and the media often want clear, simple, and precise answers. Too much modesty or open critical thinking about the limitations of the standard method are not ways to advance a career. Publishing in the most prestigious journals often requires conformity to orthodox methods and the ability to pump out papers quickly. The problem is often the system, not individuals.

My view is that applying the mindset of physics to society was deeply naive. Spurred on by broader societal trends and breakthroughs in computing power from the 1950s onwards too many researchers were told, and believed, that knowledge was 'cumulative': that they did not need to bother reading the old authors. Nobel-winning economist Ronald Coase summed this up in the 1980s when he said that an earlier generation of institutional economists 'had nothing to pass on except a mass of descriptive material waiting for a theory, or a fire'.[16] Without first-hand observation or a sense of history, the new researchers too often were led astray. Models were misused in more knowing ways too by powerful groups to reframe their self-interest as the general interest. Policy legitimated by these theories often comforted the rich and afflicted the poor. Ideas were shielded from democratic oversight by being presented in highly technical forms. It is, to borrow another line from Robert Heilbroner, 'an intellectual tragedy of the first order'.[17]

Where this book comes from

The origins of this book go back to at least the global financial crisis. In 2007, as the financial world imploded, I was in Edinburgh, finishing a Master's dissertation in global political economy. It focused on trade deals and the work of Susan Strange (1923–1998), a pioneering professor at the London School of Economics. In the 1970s, she had argued that neither economics nor politics alone provided an understanding of what was happening at the global level. She combined the two to help create a new discipline: global political economy.[18] In articles and books such as *Casino Capitalism* and *States and Markets*, Strange foresaw much of the global financial crisis of 2007/8 and its aftermath.[19] She unfashionably criticized Newtonian physics as an ideal in the social world: 'The ambition in the social sciences to imitate the natural sciences and to discover and elaborate "laws" of the international system, patterns so regular they govern social, political and economic behaviour, is and always has been a wild goose chase.'[20] Instead, she paid close attention to history, values, and power. She understood power to be structured at the global level, not just by military force, but also by productive capacity, finance, and knowledge. These four types of power are the ability to 'provide protection, make things, obtain access to credit, and develop and control authoritative modes of interpreting the world'.[21] This book has grown out of Susan Strange's capacious view of the world.

After Edinburgh, I saw first-hand the bleaker side of the twenty-first-century economy while working for over a decade for various non-governmental organizations (NGOs). At the Rainforest

Foundation UK, I saw the rich world's response to destruction of rainforests was to create a global market in forest credits—known as REDD—that was inspired by mainstream economic visions. In reality though, the scheme meant that forest and Indigenous communities risked getting kicked off their lands, to which they had no legal title. It may also have allowed more forests to be cleared, while heavy industries that bought the 'offsets' continued to spew pollutants into the air. Later, with Global Witness, I travelled often to the Democratic Republic of Congo, one of the poorest countries on earth (created by Western powers in 1885 as a central African free-trade zone known as 'Congo Free State' that became arguably the world's most brutal and murderous colonial regime).[22] Alongside colleagues, I helped expose how the country lost out on $1.5 billion between 2009 and 2012, through a series of corrupt mining and oil deals involving corporations listed on the London Stock Exchange and offshore tax havens such as the British Virgin Islands.[23] We also worked with investors and park rangers in Virunga, Africa's oldest national park and home to some of the world's last mountain gorillas, to resist attempts by a company listed on the London Stock Exchange to open the park to oil exploration with bribery and violence.[24] The companies and individuals concerned denied wrongdoing and tried to stop our reporting. I came to see these not as isolated incidents but part of a much broader corporate crime wave.

I grew more interested in exposing the deeper reasons why these systemic problems of environmental and economic justice and abuse of corporate power persist. And why there was a curious, and dangerous, narrowing of vision and imagination about how to counter them. I began researching and writing about Susan Strange again and discovered Mary Midgley, a British philosopher who rebelled against the abstract, analytical thinking of the mid-twentieth century and charted a new course inspired by the Gaia theory of the Earth as a self-regulating system. On the way, I worked for a small NGO, Promoting Economic Pluralism, where, in 2019, we used the 50th anniversary of the Bank of Sweden creating and funding the Nobel Memorial Prize in Economic Science—a majestic piece of public relations—to highlight the need to shake up economic thinking.[25]

Mary Midgley has a wonderful metaphor for exploring deeper structures and ideas: philosophical plumbing. The network of pipes and plumbing under your floorboards is invisible and mostly forgotten. Only if something begins to stink, and you can't find the source, do you think about them. If the blockage doesn't clear, the pavement or the floorboards may need to come up and the broken pipes repaired or replaced. The same is true, Midgley said, of the ideas and concepts that run underneath human society and can quietly distort and obstruct our thinking. They are important and often ignored.[26] Few in the 2020s can claim that they do not smell the stink. This book is my attempt to look under the floorboards and make sense of what's wrong with one part of our collective intellectual plumbing.

Mathematical models and abstract logic can be fantastically useful tools. I have come to think of models like the spotlight in a theatre, which, if pointed at the main action, can helpfully sharpen our focus and understanding.[27] Spotlights, however, plunge the rest of the scene into greater darkness. If they are pointed away from the essential elements, they can leave those trying to see by their light distracted and confused. Sometimes, in the theatre—and in economics—spotlights are used so that the audience doesn't notice things being moved around elsewhere on stage. Who directs the beam is important. Models, when used well in the right context, especially when describing human-made systems where we can control all the inputs, can provide an almost God-like insight into the past, present, and future. They are essential to much of what we take for granted in the modern, digital world. But they can lead us to blunder, when applied in the wrong context or trusted too much. My argument is that some of the most consequential economic models time and again have failed to focus the spotlight on what and where matter most. They have been weapons of mass distraction.

This is not a comprehensive or global history of economics. It picks a few important thinkers and strands in the Western, primarily English-speaking, tradition to illustrate the origin and development of a powerful way of seeing the world and its backlash. While I see the study of history, up to the present, as the surest route to economic knowledge, no history is totally neutral or impartial. The knowledge history produces is provisional and can always be improved, but it cannot be ignored. So, the history related here is not presented as 'reality' but to show how much has been excluded by dominant models.

The book is in three parts. Part I—Chapters 1 to 6—investigates David Ricardo's life and influence with a focus on perhaps the original, longest-lasting, and most venerated 'model' (or proto-model) in economics: his theory of comparative advantage, which is often illustrated with the example of England and Portugal both benefitting by trading cloth and wine. Building on the work of Warwick Professor of Political Economy Matthew Watson, I show that this common story is a facade.[28] Hidden behind it is another, rarely seen, history of naval power, slavery, and exploitation. It is a history that comes back to Isaac Newton in his less-known later life at the Royal Mint.

Part II—Chapters 7 to 10—tells the story of classical political economy created in Ricardo's mould and the raw capitalism associated with it. It describes how his way of doing economics fell out of favour in the mid-1800s and was criticized for the 'vice' of unreality. Here we see the link between Ricardo as a stockbroker and the self-interested 'economic human'. It profiles major economic thinkers, often excluded from the modern canon, whose analyses shine a light on the fate of ideas that lose contact with the world.

Finally, Part III—Chapters 11 to 14—describes what happened when unreality came to be seen as a virtue from the 1960s onwards: when highly abstract models were used to guide public policy. It brings the story up to the present and explores the tilt back to raw capitalism, financial crises, a timid response to climate change, and soaring inequality and its backlash. It shows how mainstream economics helped make huge and essential things, such as corporate power and the natural world, disappear conceptually—and how it is only in the last decade that there has been a partial turn back to looking at the world.

Together, the three parts chart the birth, death and rebirth of economics built on unrealistic assumptions and its practical consequences.

From single vision to polycrisis

There have been some excellent recent books critical of the influence of mainstream economics and its style of thinking on public policy, such as Binyamin Appelbaum's *The Economists' Hour*.[29] This book provides a deeper, historical context to these debates. It shows that many of the problems with contemporary economics were present close to its birth as a discipline.[30]

There are, of course, critics of the critics. British economist and author Diane Coyle says the 'unchanging criticism' of economics is 'deeply frustrating', as it is based on an outdated and misleading vision of the subject. Back in the 1980s, when she graduated, she admits that a 'neoliberal economics' that aspired to be like physics dominated. But by 2005, Coyle claimed, the profession had changed. Now, she says, it is much more 'soulful' and empirical, at the forefront of 'big data', with a greater appreciation of institutions and historical and political contexts.[31] She is right that there have been changes in economics, many of them for the better. My claim is not that *all* economics is blind to the real world. Many economists work away on specific areas—Coyle is a big fan of 'applied microeconomics'—that have little to do with the global 'macro' economics I focus on in this book. However, I cannot share her view that by 2005, or even 2024, orthodox economics had abandoned its envy of physics and that its authority was not often invoked to serve the interests of the wealthy. Many of the changes in economics have been too superficial and retained at their core the old orthodoxy.

In the last few decades, a large literature has developed on the philosophy of economics, which raises similar questions to this book.[32] On the whole, though, I've opted to tell the story with the words of economic thinkers themselves. This is because I'm interested in how economists have wrestled with different approaches to knowledge. I want to show that the questions I'm raising have always been part of a vibrant debate *within* the field. Many arch-insiders, including Nobel Prize winners, have claimed that too much of mainstream economics is blind to the real world and obsessed with meaningless models that are more like magic tricks than science. The pioneer of behavioural economics, Daniel Kahneman, called out 'theory-induced blindness' in economics. Princeton economist and former Vice Chair of the US Federal Reserve, Alan Blinder, critiqued his fellow economists for playing 'games with silly models that seem to have very little to do with what's going on in the real world'. Chicago-trained economist Paul Romer, winner of the 2018 Nobel in Economics, has written of his worry that presenting 'a model is like doing a card trick … Perhaps our norms will soon be like those in professional magic; it will be impolite, perhaps even an ethical breach, to reveal how someone's trick works.'[33] These economists will not agree with everything here, but a critique along these lines cannot be written off as irrelevant or ignorant.

The last two centuries have seen a stunning improvement in human material welfare. The average global life expectancy of only 32 years in 1820 rose to 73 years in 2020.[34] This improvement in human life, along with many others, would have been impossible without the Industrial Revolution and the vast new productive capacities unleashed by capitalism. However, broadly shared prosperity from the mid-twentieth century onwards would also have been impossible without social protests, revolts, the organization of labour, the break-up of European empires, and the desire of Western leaders to prevail over communism. Since the 1980s, however, Western countries have seen a fracturing of the social contract, with economic elites gaining a greater share of national income (and political power) and ordinary peoples' wages stagnating. Globally, hundreds of millions of people have been lifted out of poverty in this time but primarily in heavily interventionalist states such as China that flagrantly contravened Western economic ideals. We are increasingly aware of the damage to the rest of the living world, and our mental health, of today's economic and social system.

Ideas matter. In the 1990s and early 2000s, Western leaders, whether they were on the left or right, tended to see economic globalization—a deeper, tightly knit, and lightly regulated supranational market in goods, finance, and services—as an advantageous and almost natural phenomenon. A particular type of globalization was seen as the only possible mode for economic affairs to which people and their human-made laws needed to confirm. This political and intellectual belief was known in English as the Washington Consensus and in French as *la pensée unique* (the single vision). It was supported by the authority of economic science. The diverse opposition, from environmental groups to labour unions, were called anti-globalization protestors. It was largely a left-wing movement that announced itself by shutting down the World Trade Organization meeting in Seattle in 1999. Often, they were called stupid or dangerous or accused of reaching for the reverse gear of history. In 2005, Tony Blair, the centre-left British Prime Minister, told those who wanted to debate globalization: 'You might as well debate whether autumn should follow summer.'[35] Kofi Annan,

UN Secretary-General, said some world leaders saw questioning globalization 'like arguing against the law of gravity'.[36]

But if you listened to the most articulate campaigners, such as Lori Wallach, a trade lawyer with non-profit group Public Citizen, it was clear that she was not against more closely integrating people around the world with new technologies like the internet. The protestors themselves were multinational and relied on that technology. What they opposed were the specific set of laws and rules by which this global knitting was taking place and who got to hold the needles. They objected to new global rules that gave greater rights and power to large corporations, for example, allowing them to take democratic governments to court, extend lucrative copyright protections, and remove all barriers to financial flows. Wallach provocatively called this type of globalization a 'stealthy, slow-motion corporate coup d'état'.[37] The protestors argued that another type of globalization was possible and preferable. A more accurate term for the movement, then, is not anti- but alter-globalization.[38]

Skipping ahead to the 2020s, Tony Blair-esque confidence in hyper-globalization as a natural and positive force is on life support. We are not all alter-globalists yet, but more people now admit, especially in the US, that the elite common sense of recent decades was wrong and naive. The *Wall Street Journal* suggested that the era of 'free and unfettered trade with rivals, is looking more like a fad and less like the end point of a trend'.[39] The old Washington Consensus was pronounced dead by Jake Sullivan, US National Security Advisor, in a widely reported speech in April 2023. It had undermined the foundations of democracy, he said, so the 'project of the 2020s and the 2030s is different from the project of the 1990s'.[40]

The immediate cause lay in a series of events that could not be dealt with by the conventional economic wisdom. In March 2020, the COVID-19 pandemic showed the fragility of just-in-time global supply chains as countries scrambled to buy ventilators, masks, and other protective equipment. In January 2021, the US Capitol was stormed by supporters of President Donald Trump, stoking fears about the social and political instability of all Western democracies. In February 2022, Russia invaded Ukraine, putting a spotlight on Europe's overdependence on an autocratic state for oil and gas. These events happened alongside rising anxiety of ecological catastrophe and the widening gap between the super-rich and the rest, and

Western fears of China's new superpower status. The historian Adam Tooze, writing in the *Financial Times*, popularized a term for these simultaneous events: the polycrisis. It is a long way from the single vision. A few decades ago, it was possible to have 'believed that "the market" would efficiently steer the economy, deliver growth, defuse contentious political issues,' Tooze wrote, 'who would make the same claim today?'[41]

This book, then, investigates elite cultural beliefs that upheld the move back to a rawer form of capitalism. It brings into focus the societies and minds in which these ideas originated and tracks their results. It focuses on Ricardo's iconic story about the benefits of global trade as an example of an idea founded on unreality. It resurrects a long, almost unbroken tradition of thinking, within and outside economics, that warned of a turning away from the world and getting caught up in other-worldly models and speculations.

To help guide it through the twenty-first century, the world needs good political and economic thinkers who can confidently answer 'yes' to the question at the heart of this book: 'Got Reality?'

PART I

Birth

1

The Other Founding
Father of Economics

*How David Ricardo made a fortune on
the Stock Exchange, thanks to Napoleon
Bonaparte, and took up political economy*

Adam Smith is known as the founder of modern economics. His 1776 work *An Inquiry into the Nature and Causes of the Wealth of Nations* helped illuminate a newly emerging commercial world. He has been indelibly linked to the idea of the free market as an 'invisible hand', that is, if people follow their own self-interest, this will result in the greater good of society. More recently, his name and image were tied to the turn back to raw capitalism—often called neoliberalism—of the 1970s and 1980s, underpinned, as President Ronald Reagan put it, by a belief in 'the magic of the market place'.[1] Adam Smith ties were regularly worn by conservative economists in Washington, DC, during that time.[2] His name is used by a self-described 'neoliberal' think tank—the Adam Smith Institute—in the UK.[3] Since the early 1970s, historians and close readers of Adam Smith have been on a largely unsuccessful quest to show that the neoliberal image is a misreading of the works of the Scottish professor of moral philosophy, but the image persists.[4]

Less well known is that there were two founders of economics, or political economy as it was then known, Adam Smith and David Ricardo. Despite the vast influence of Adam Smith, economics of the past 50 years has, I will argue, followed more in the method of

Ricardo, a stockbroker turned politician, than Smith, a philosopher. Our current situation makes more sense when we acknowledge that the former has an equal claim to the title of father of economics.

Ricardo's influence can be felt, beyond any one idea, in the methods of orthodox economics. Ricardo was the first great builder of simple, abstract theories or models to explain economic affairs. He began the tradition of putting self-interested, knowledgeable, and calculating humans—an imaginary creature known as 'economic human'—in the centre of those models. As Mark Blaug, an expert in the history and methods of economics, wrote, 'Ricardo literally invented the technique of economics.'[5] That technique, in a sentence, is to take a problem, focus on two or three of its elements, ignore the rest, and build a logical framework or model to fit them together.

David Ricardo is something of an economists' economist, better known within the profession than outside it. In 2011, he came in second to Adam Smith in a poll of US economists for the greatest pre-twentieth-century economist.[6] He was considered the most influential economist of all time by giants of the field such as John Stuart Mill, Walter Bagehot, and John Maynard Keynes. One of the most well-known economic thinkers of the twentieth century, John Kenneth Galbraith, called Ricardo 'Adam Smith's only serious rival for the title of founding father of economics … an innovating force in both capitalist and socialist thought.'[7]

'Extraordinary quickness' on the Stock Exchange

Born in London in 1772, Ricardo came from a Sephardic Jewish family who had been driven out of Portugal generations before by the Inquisition. They had become refugees in the port of Livorno in Italy—where the family worked coral into jewellery and picked up their Italian-sounding surname—before settling in Holland and then finally moving to England. His father, Abraham Ricardo, decided early on that David would follow him in the family stock trading business. As a boy, David received little education besides reading, writing, and arithmetic but, according to his brother Moses, he 'showed a taste for abstract and general reasoning'.[8] His father sent him to Amsterdam between the ages of 11 and 13 to learn French and Dutch, which he largely refused to do. Then, in 1785, aged 14 and back in London, he went to work in the Stock Exchange alongside his father, uncles, and brothers, while exploring his interests in chemistry, geology, and mathematics.[9] But everything changed in his early 20s when he fell in love with the girl next door. The problem was, she was not Jewish, but a Quaker.

Priscilla Wilkinson is described as having pink cheeks, auburn hair, and hazel eyes. David Ricardo, who always had an independent streak, renounced his Jewish faith and married her, aged 21. Because he had abandoned the religion of his birth, his parents cut off all contact and disinherited the young David. He later attended Unitarian meetings. As far as we know David never saw, spoke, nor wrote to his mother again. Despite having to start again in business on his own, David used his skills and contacts in the London's nascent stock markets to become, by his mid-20s, richer than his father and recognized as a 'moneyed' man.[10] His sharp mind and trading skills rescued him when he needed it most. Only after his mother's death, eight years later, would he reconcile with his father.

Trading on stock markets around the globe today is often done by lightning-quick computer algorithms that exploit fleeting pricing quirks. One contemporary paints the young Ricardo as a proto-algorithmic trader, touting his 'extraordinary quickness' in seeing 'any accidental difference which might arise between the relative price of different stocks' and the self-control to 'realise a small percentage upon a large sum' rather than go in for more speculative bets.[11] He worked by gaining small profits on a much larger number of trades than most of his fellow traders. At the turn of the nineteenth century, it is estimated that the average trader of Consols—a form of government debt and one of the main products on the Exchange—bought and sold £30,000 to £40,000 per year. Even early in his career, Ricardo bought and sold more than £1 million a year (approximately £160 million today).[12] In his busiest year, 1813, Consols worth more than £3.7 million (£592 million today) passed through his hands.[13]

With his financial success, Ricardo bought vast estates and grand houses across southern England. These included Hadlow Estate in Kent, Pauntley Court in Gloucestershire, the fourteenth-century moated manor house of Brinsop Court and the grand Bromesberrow Place in Herefordshire near the Welsh border.[14] But his home was the 5,000-acre Manor of Minchinhampton, which came with Gatcomb (now Gatcombe) House, situated in the green hills of the English Cotswolds, 100 miles west of London (see Figure 1.1). Ricardo

Figure 1.1: An engraving of Gatcomb House, David Ricardo's country home, from 1825

Source: Rostron & Edwards

bought the estate in 1814 for £60,000 (around £9.6 million today). As he wrote, 'in this sweet place I shall not sigh after the Stock Exchange and its enjoyments'.[15] The house—which still conveys power and prestige—is now home to royalty: in 1976, Gatcombe was bought by Queen Elizabeth II. It was a gift for her daughter, Princess Anne, who still lives there.

Ricardo was friendly with the novelist Maria Edgeworth, sometimes called the Irish Jane Austen. She most vividly described his Gatcomb estate, arriving by carriage at night:

> We went down, down, down a hill—not knowing how it was to end or when or where the house would appear—that it was a beautiful place was clear however by moonlight. ... A dog began to bark loud and incessantly but we came within view of an excellent house—Hall with lamp and lights very cheerful—servants all ready on the steps—Mr. Ricardo happy to see us—beautiful hall—pillars—flowers but just seen in passing—into a most comfortable sitting room—family party—books open on the table.[16]

She also gave us the most human and warm image of the great economist relaxing at home with family and guests in the evening. 'We played charades last night,' Edgeworth wrote to her sister. Ricardo was 'very droll' strutting about as a dandy, then a monk 'with coloured silk handkerchiefs, as cowls, a laughable solemn procession' and finally 'Mr Ricardo as *monkey*'. She beamed: 'He is altogether one of the most agreeable persons, as well as the best informed and most clever, that I ever knew.'[17]

At Gatcomb alongside Priscilla, for nine short years, Ricardo would devote himself to 'the science of political economy' and would revolutionize the subject. After him, political economy would radically differ from Adam Smith's vision.[18]

Reading Adam Smith in Bath

Ricardo's interest in economics began years earlier, in 1799, after a family tragedy. He was already married to Priscilla and a father of three children. She became pregnant with a fourth, but then misfortune struck. The child, a girl, was stillborn. Priscilla fell into postnatal depression and, to aid her recovery, Ricardo took her to Bath. It was then a fashionable British spa town famous for its waters and Georgian architectural marvels like the Royal Crescent and the Pump Room; a few years later it would welcome its most famous resident, the novelist Jane Austen. It was in one of Bath's circulating libraries that Ricardo, in his late 20s, picked up Adam Smith's *Wealth of Nations*. After reading a page or two, he was hooked.[19]

Smith was a much more interesting and complicated thinker than the raw capitalist image suggests. He thought of himself as a moral philosopher; his style of work and approach have little in common with today's mainstream, rationalist approach of modern economics. Although he wrote about the 'natural' course of commerce and trade, he was not dogmatic: he rarely advanced a position without qualifying it. *The Wealth of Nations* is richly infused with history, ethics, human psychology, and politics.[20] He often advocated for the interests of the poor against the wealthy, writing, for example, 'No society can surely be flourishing or happy, of which the far greater part of the members are poor and miserable.' He harshly criticized the richest and most powerful multinational corporation of the day, the British East India Company, for monopolizing trade, impoverishing India, and becoming its rulers or 'sovereigns'.[21]

One of Smith's most famous examples, which featured until recently on the Bank of England £20 note, is about the benefits of the division of labour in a pin factory. This is how *The Wealth of Nations* starts. Smith showed how a skilled blacksmith trained in making nails can make up to 1,000 a day. But ten people working together, each trained in one simple, specific step such as cutting the metal or attaching the pinhead, can make 48,000 pins in a day, equivalent to 4,800 each. Thus, the cooperative division of labour allows unskilled workers, in this case, to produce almost five times more per person than a skilled blacksmith working alone.[22] The division of labour is often seen as the thread that ties all of Smith's thinking together. Trading allows workers to specialize more, and that in turn helps increase and spread wealth in society. However, as usual, Smith added caveats to this. He warns that the division of labour where workers are confined 'to a few very simple operations' can lead to intellectual and social 'corruption and degeneracy of the great body of the people', which should be countered by government education, a radical proposal for the time.[23]

Waterloo was won on the trading floors of the Exchange

We might never have heard of Ricardo were it not for Napoleon Bonaparte. It seemed like it was all over for the French Emperor in 1814, when he was captured and exiled to an island in the Mediterranean. But then he famously escaped, and within 100 days took back control of the French state and military and went on the attack.

On 18 June 1815, at around 11 am, Napoleon's 70,000 troops began their assault on the Duke of Wellington's force of British, German, and Dutch soldiers massed south of the village of Waterloo in present-day Belgium. French artillery tore through the British lines and infantry and cavalry charges weakened them further. By the afternoon, momentum appeared to be with the French. By 6 pm, Napoleon's troops captured a fortified farmhouse—La Haye Sainte—at the centre of the battlefield and sensed triumph. Victory, and the prize of the leading power in Europe, hung in the balance. So too did the price of stock.

Prices on the London Stock Exchange had swung wildly with British fortunes in the 23-year war with the French. In one famous fraud the year before Waterloo, men dressed as French soldiers had landed on the Kent coast and spread fake news that Napoleon was dead, causing stock prices to soar upwards, with some traders cashing out their holdings at the top of the market.[24] Financiers in London, therefore, were desperately waiting for credible news from Waterloo. To finance war—and pay its continental allies—the British government had raised taxes, introduced new ones (such as an income tax), cut the link between paper money and gold, borrowed heavily from the great banking houses of the day, and squeezed funds out of the Bank of England. In the later stages of the war, the government had turned to the new London Stock Exchange to raise funds. A contemporary called the Exchange 'a kind of standing miracle among foreigners' due to its ability to raise money.[25]

On 14 June, as Napoleon was approaching Belgium, 43-year-old David Ricardo, as one of the leading 'stock jobbers' of his age, went to the Treasury to sign a deal with the Governor of the Bank of England. Ricardo was described by *The Sunday Times* as 'the little plain man with the acute features and the keen eye'. A contemporary diarist, J.L. Mallet, wrote: 'his eye had a soft, beaming, intelligent and, at the same time, thoughtful expression'. His voice, Mallet says, 'although sweet and pleasing, was pitched extremely high'.[26] In a portrait by Thomas Phillips, painted a few years after these events, Ricardo captures the viewer with a direct, engaging look, and he is dressed in a black coat and white cravat, his hair greying above the ears (see Figure 1.2).

Ricardo was at the Treasury to agree the terms of the government's largest loan of the war: £36 million (around £5.7 billion today). He headed a consortium from the London Stock Exchange responsible for taking on and reselling to a subscribing public half the amount.[27] The other half of the debt was taken on by a consortium led by the Baring Brothers (whose eponymous bank would last until it was sunk by rogue derivatives trader Nick Leeson in 1995). When the government wanted to issue debt it would set out its terms, welcome sealed bids, and select the best deal.[28] Ricardo's group had first won part of the loan in 1807, and from 1812 he earned vast

Figure 1.2:
David Ricardo

Source: Engraving
by W. Hodgetts after
the painting by Thomas
Phillips. © National
Portrait Gallery, London

sums as the financiers avoided competition and cooperated to submit identical bids, which the government begrudgingly accepted.[29] Once the government bond was issued, the debt became tradable and all financiers' eyes would turn to the price of the 'Omnium'—a bundle of assets traded on the London Exchange—which would show if, and how much, money they would make from the deal. It is a quirk of history that Ricardo, one of the most strident advocates in the history of economics for governments to leave markets alone, made most of his money from trading in government debt.

For decades, shares in companies—such as the East India or South Sea Companies—had been traded in the coffee houses in Exchange Alley in the City of London. The small passageway, now called Change Alley, then connected the Post Office, where market-moving news arrived, and the Royal Exchange, where merchants exchanged goods. The registered address of Ricardo's father was for a long time Garraway's Coffee House on Exchange Alley.[30] But in 1802, the stockbrokers moved out of the coffee houses into a smart new headquarters, Capel Court, opposite the Bank of England. The new building—the first in London to be called 'The Stock Exchange'—closed its doors to the general public and was only open to paying members. This was the moment when the

London Stock Exchange came into being as a formal institution with rules, a full-time administration, and the ability to exclude undesirables.[31] An illustration from the time shows the inside of a tall, spacious, colonnaded room, like a church without the pews, where men with top hats and tails shouted, swapped gossip, and traded in small groups under the gaze of guards in tricorn hats and pikes.[32] Its ability to raise credit made it a key element of national power. David was on the founding committee and a dominant figure in its dealings.[33]

The Exchange had been Ricardo's saviour when his parents had cut him adrift, and he was now its master. His brother, Moses, a fellow trader, most completely described Ricardo's 'extraordinary powers' in the Stock Exchange:

> His complete knowledge of all its intricacies; his surprising quickness at figures and calculation; his capability of getting through, without any apparent exertion, the immense transactions in which he was concerned; his coolness and judgment, combined certainly with (for him) a fortunate tissue of public events, enabled him to leave all his contemporaries at the Stock Exchange far behind, and to raise himself infinitely higher not only in fortune, but in general character and estimation, than any man had ever done before in that house.[34]

The 'fortunate tissue' of events in June 1815 revolved around Wellington and Napoleon. As the French tried to capitalize on their dominance at Waterloo, a Prussian army arrived on the battlefield before night fell and turned the tide in Wellington's favour. In a last throw of the dice, Napoleon sent his elite French Imperial Guard, the most feared troops in Europe, against his enemies. When they were driven back by Wellington's men, French morale collapsed and its army fled. Wellington would later comment how close the battle had been, calling it 'the nearest run thing you ever saw in your life'.[35] Upwards of 50,000 men and thousands of horses were left dead or wounded. Napoleon was captured for a second time and exiled for good to the South Atlantic. Everyone who was invested in British government bonds would reap rich rewards, but first they needed to know the outcome of the battle.

'Bless us all! no body can tell *how* rich!'

London was oblivious for days. News of Napoleon's defeat could only travel as fast as horse and sail. Stock prices, which had yo-yoed wildly with the twists and turns of the war, were up a modest 3 per cent.[36] Ricardo and his friends were anxious for news. As the underwriter of the government debt, Ricardo had offered his acquaintances—such as John Murray, his and the poet Lord Byron's publisher—'a little of the loan' from which they could hope to make a profit.[37] Through Ricardo, Thomas Robert Malthus—another venerated classical economist—took £5,000 of the loan. This was a huge sum for Malthus as his annual teaching salary was £500 (around £80,000 today), itself far more than the average wage for an English labourer of £15–20 per year.[38]

Malthus wrote to Ricardo the day after the Battle of Waterloo, still oblivious of its result, speculating whether the 'Omnium' price would 'rise very considerably' with a British victory or see a panic-induced fall following a triumph by Napoleon.[39] The cautious Malthus asked Ricardo to sell his stock and made a modest profit of £150. Days after the battle, rumours began to circulate in London of a great victory but still there was no official news.[40]

A story frequently told suggests that Ricardo engaged in a dubious, perhaps illegal, scheme to profit from prior knowledge of the outcome of Waterloo. It comes from the person who did more than anyone else to revive, and push forward, the vision of economics as a mathematical science in our time: the American economics professor Paul Samuelson (1915–2009). According to Samuelson, Ricardo had a spy at the battlefield who galloped away to a ship, crossed the channel, and brought Ricardo news of the victory before anyone else in London. Ricardo went down to the Stock Exchange and rather than buying, he sold and sold again! His fellow traders, thinking Ricardo knew the British had lost, sold too and prices tumbled. Then, Ricardo about-turned, bought up the cut-price stock, and made a killing when it soared on official news of the victory. Ricardo illegally profited from 'spreading of false rumors', Samuelson wrote, and then retired in shame from the Exchange.[41]

The story is a fantasy. Ricardo's correspondence doesn't back up the myth. It's highly unlikely that a sole trader like Ricardo had a horse at the battle. Detailed contemporary newspaper listings of stock prices do not show a sharp fall before rising. Samuelson's tale likely stems from another story attributed to Ricardo's contemporary Nathan Rothschild, who did have a horse at the battle, which in an embellished form was later used by the Nazis for anti-Semitic propaganda.[42]

When official news of British victory was eventually received in London on 21 June, the Omnium jumped from 5 to 9 per cent up, and would hit a high of 19 per cent.[43] But, due to how the loans were structured, the profits were far higher than these percentages suggest. For each portion of the loan taken, the government required that only one tenth of the value be paid right away, the remainder to be paid once per month for the next nine months.[44] With this first payment, the government gave the owner an official paper called a 'scrip (short for subscription), which itself could be traded. So, the right to bonds worth £100 could be had by outlaying only £10. If the value of this £100 increased by 10 per cent, to £110, the 'scrip would now be worth £20: double the initial sum paid. With this system a 19 per cent rise meant almost tripling your money. So, even though Ricardo sold out his stake before the top of the market, he still made a killing. As he told Malthus: 'I have all my money invested in Stock, and this is as great an advantage as ever I expect or wish to make by a rise.'[45]

Ricardo was already a wealthy man in 1815, after nearly three decades of stock trading and having participated in seven previous government loans, including two in 1813, which totalled £49 million (£7.8 billion today). He had already agreed to buy the grand country estate of Gatcomb House in 1814, but his gains from the Waterloo loan were still, his biographer Piero Sraffa notes, 'the largest single profit he ever made'.[46] Ricardo himself wrote: 'Perhaps no loan was ever more generally profitable to the Stock Exchange.'[47] Ricardo's good friend, who would play an oversized role in his life, James Mill, the father of the philosopher John Stuart Mill, wrote to the trader: 'you are now—Bless us all! no body can tell *how* rich!'[48]

In the City of London, there's a large statue of the Duke of Wellington, riding his horse, on a stone plinth. It is cast from bronze, melted down from captured French cannon at the Battle of Waterloo. A few steps away, in the Bank of England's basement library, I was able to leaf through the enormous, original bound volumes (one is 22 cm deep, the thickness of ten regular-sized books) that record Ricardo and his fellow traders' transactions.[49] Flicking through page after page, year after year, you glimpse the extent of Ricardo's three decades of trading. But even with these it is impossible to put a figure on his total profit. Trading in 'scrips was not registered and neither were so-called time bargains, an early type of options trading that was officially illegal but tolerated.[50]

Ricardo's profits from Waterloo were exaggerated even in his own day. The *Sunday Times* reported that Ricardo made £1 million from the battle—equivalent perhaps to £160 million today—but the figure does not withstand scrutiny. The best estimate is that his total estate was worth £750,000 (or £120 million today).[51] This still made Ricardo one of the wealthiest people in the country. A contemporary comparison can be made with Jane Austen's *Pride and Prejudice*, published in 1813. In the novel, Mr Darcy has an income of £10,000 per year, which implies a fortune of £200,000 (£32 million today) as interest rates were around 5 per cent. Mrs Bennett, on learning about the match between her daughter Elizabeth and Mr Darcy, says 'Oh, my sweetest Lizzy! how rich and how great you will be! … Ten thousand a year, and very likely more! 'Tis as good as a lord!' By this comparison, Ricardo was almost four times as rich as Mr Darcy. He was the wealthiest of all the great economic thinkers.[52]

The *Principles*

'Even *you* must, by this time, be parched and panting for the Country; and impatient to turn your back upon the modern Babylon' and 'the anxieties and vexations of business,' wrote Ricardo's closest friend on the Stock Exchange a month after Waterloo.[53] Ricardo was, but even when he left the Stock Exchange physically, it stayed with him. The Exchange condenses all important information into a few numbers—stock prices—which move up or down. In casting his eyes towards the larger questions of society, he held a similar vision in which he saw behind the messy world a precise, quantified, and tightly controlled system. In his writings on the Bank of England, loans, and the Stock Exchange, subjects in which he had personal experience, Ricardo would, at times, display a mastery of facts and draw on official reports and statistics.[54] But the intense focus on prices that had helped him so much in the Stock Exchange would lead him astray as he broadened the scope of his economics. This has been called Ricardo's 'broker's myopia'.[55]

As Ricardo pushed his thinking further, towards subjects such as agriculture or foreign trade, his writing became more and more abstract and speculative. As we'll see, his thinking was attacked from the beginning as having lost contact with the real world. It is ironic that the economist who spent more time trading on markets than any other should be responsible for a turn towards unrealistic theory. But perhaps it was Ricardo's practical engagement and success in business that provided the overconfidence which fuelled his theorizing and gave it credibility. His economics did *not* float like a void completely cut off from reality. Usually, he had a real political aim connected to the big issues of the day, such as boosting foreign trade, or reducing welfare programmes or the power of the landed aristocracy. But he too often constructed his arguments with logic founded on assumptions rather than observable relations. This misled him, and many people since, into believing that his arguments were universal, holding everywhere, including, as we'll see, in the far reaches of the British Empire and among hunter-gatherer communities. This was a dangerous delusion.

Ricardo's sole book-length work of economics appeared in 1817, two years after he retired, following Waterloo. *On the Principles of Political Economy and Taxation* was the most complete work of economics published in Britain since Adam Smith's *Wealth of Nations* over forty years earlier. Compared to most books published, it was a barnstorming success.

John Maynard Keynes, perhaps the most influential economist of the twentieth century, penned some of the best lines about Ricardo's influence: 'Ricardo conquered England as completely as the Holy Inquisition conquered Spain. Not only was his theory accepted by the city, by statesmen and by the academic world. But controversy ceased; the other point of view completely disappeared; it ceased to be discussed.'[56] Keynes exaggerated. There was controversy, leading figures disagreed with Ricardo's doctrines, but his analytical mechanism provided the central framework for understanding economics for the next two generations, after which it would be dethroned. Keynes, nonetheless, had an acute insight into the appeal of the great stockbroker's style of economics to his society:

That it was adapted to carry a vast and consistent logical superstructure, gave it [Ricardo's theory] beauty. That it could explain much social injustice and apparent cruelty as an inevitable incident in the scheme of progress, and the attempt to change such things as likely on the whole to do more harm than good, commended it to authority. That it afforded a measure of justification to the free activities of the individual capitalist, attracted to it the support of the dominant social force behind authority.[57]

One area of economic life of particular interest to the dominant social force of the time, Britain's rising middle classes, was expanding foreign trade, which we turn to next.

2

'The Unshakeable Basis for International Trade'

*How Ricardo's theory of England trading
cloth for Portuguese wine became a 'beautiful
proof' of the benefits of globalization*

In the opening paragraph of *On the Principles of Political Economy*, David Ricardo argues that wealth is divided among three classes of society: landowners, stock owners, and workers, both agricultural and industrial. In Ricardo's system—and he was a man of systems—the wealth which each class receives goes by a different name: landowners gain *rent*, stock owners' *profit*, and workers' *wages*. The aim of political economy, he tells us, is to 'determine the laws which regulate this distribution' and the 'natural course of rent, profit, and wages'.[1] His system had great intellectual appeal as a story that connected these seemingly disparate phenomena—rent, profit, and wages—together in fixed, understandable relationships. As will become clear, Ricardo thought the class of his birth—middle-class stock owners—pushed society towards greater wealth, while the rent and wages of the other two classes were a drag.

Even though the language of the *Principles* is denser and more difficult than Adam Smith's writing, Ricardo's class-based theory of economics was hugely influential in the Britain of his day. Much of it, since, has been consigned to history by the mainstream, either because it was taken up by socialist critics of capitalism, such as Karl Marx, or because it came to be seen as a block to more widely shared prosperity. The most lasting elements of Ricardo's contribution to mainstream economics have been his method of abstraction (refined concepts that interact in almost mechanical ways) and his theory of international trade, which will be the focus here.

Ricardo's modern reputation as the father of international economics rests on one short chapter called 'On foreign trade'. The text has been described as 'ten pages that changed the world'.[2] It is the origin of the principle, or law, of 'comparative advantage', which is often claimed to be the intellectual foundation of the last 50 years of globalization—and, by some, the rationale by which powerful, wealthy countries have exploited poorer ones.

Ricardo built his theory of trade using elements he found in Adam Smith's work. Smith's case for free trade is often explained by the principle he saw operating in a pin factory: the increased productivity that comes with the division of labour. International trade is good because it gives access to a more extensive, global market and therefore more specialization and ultimately more wealth.[3] Countries trade goods for the same reason that most people buy their shoes, rather than make them, Smith tells us:

> It is the maxim of every prudent master of a family never to attempt to make at home what it will cost him more to make than to buy. ... What is prudence in the conduct of every private family can scarce be folly in that of a great kingdom. If a foreign country can supply us with a commodity cheaper than we ourselves can make it, better buy it of them with some part of the produce of our own industry employed in a way in which we have some advantage.[4]

It made no sense for his native Scotland to use heated greenhouses to make wine, Smith argued, at 30 times the cost of buying wine from abroad. Each nation should employ their workers in industries where they have 'some advantage over their neighbours' and buy whatever else they need with the proceeds.[5] This idea was called the principle of 'absolute advantage' in the twentieth century and associated with Adam Smith, even though his view of trade was more complex and dynamic.[6] Smith was writing to counter the ideas of what he called the 'mercantile system' (often associated with hoarding gold and reducing imports with high border tariffs), which, he argued, held back national prosperity.

As ever, Smith's account was not just theoretical but deeply historical. He devotes a whole chapter to a 1703 treaty between England and Portugal concluded by John Methuen, a diplomat, and celebrated Smith says, as 'a masterpiece of English commercial policy'.[7] The treaty binds Portugal to admit English cloth duty-free into its home market and England to give preferential tariffs to Portuguese wine compared to its competitors. (Some have seen it as one of the foundations for the material abundance of eighteenth-century British elites, see Figure 2.1.) Smith wanted to show why preferential treaties like the Methuen Treaty were *not* advantageous: he thought merchants would bend the rules in their favour and against the greater good. This discussion, read by Ricardo, contained the two countries and two goods that would later be associated with his most famous idea.

Figure 2.1: Detail from The Painted Hall, Greenwich, showing gold coins falling down on Britain's King George I, resting on a globe

Photo: Nat Dyer

Smith outlines exceptions and caveats to his general rule on international trade. As a broad-minded philosopher, he did not look at the world just through economic or commercial eyes. Britain was reliant on its ships and sailors for defence in the eighteenth century. The plentiful supply of these was ensured by the English Navigation Acts that gave British ships a monopoly on carrying trade in and out of the country. Smith knew these acts dampened foreign trade by excluding ships of other countries but he still supported them: 'As defence, however, is of much more importance than opulence, the act of navigation is, perhaps, the wisest of all commercial regulations of England.'[8] Similarly, he argued that it was not prudent to depend on foreign countries for the supply of products necessary for defence of society, for example, sailcloth and gunpowder in his day or semiconductor chips and critical minerals in ours.[9] In Smith's work there is an attempt to balance differing values, such as wealth and security, which has been lost in our time.

The science of political economy

Ricardo was a much more ambitious and, to his critics, narrow and dogmatic, theorist than Smith. While relying on *The Wealth of Nations* for many of his examples and starting points, Ricardo sought to bring the 'science of political economy' up to the level of certainty of mathematics. Smith and Ricardo breathed different air. For Smith, political economy was 'a branch of the science of a statesman or legislator'.[10] *The Wealth of Nations* is infused with observations of all kinds about the world, with dates, places, figures, and history that relate to a lived reality.[11] Ricardo's work is much more refined: conceptual investigations with an often-fragile connection to history and the real world. Ricardo cut the discipline's ties to politics and philosophy. He included far fewer caveats to his general principles and, unlike Adam Smith, explicitly claimed to be presenting economic 'laws'.[12] Ricardo's treatment of international trade is a good example. Many who have read Smith's description of free trade could see no rationale for trade between two countries if one could produce *every* product more cheaply than the other. Ricardo found one.

'To simplify the question' of international trade, Ricardo wrote in the *Principles*, he created a proto-model. He did not use the advanced mathematics or algebra common today, but still the simple numerical example was perhaps the original economic model. Ricardo imagines a world of 'trade between two countries to be confined to two commodities—to wine and cloth', the two countries being England and Portugal. The production in England of a certain quantity of cloth 'may require the labour of 100 men for one year' and a quantity of wine the labour of 120 men. (Women did not feature in Ricardo's model.) Meanwhile, Portugal is more efficient: it can produce the same quantity of wine with just 80 men and cloth with 90 men.[13] These four numbers—80, 90, 100, 120—like nearly all the figures in the *Principles*, were convenient inventions. Even when they are hypothetical, models can change the way people see and think, according to historian of science Marcel Boumans, as models 'are the economist's instruments of investigation, just as the microscope and the telescope are tools of the biologist and the astronomer'.[14]

In Ricardo's theoretical world, the value of goods is based solely on the amount of labour expended to create them (called the labour theory of value). Money is put to one side, at least initially, in his theory of international trade: so too are wages and how they might differ between countries. Workers are a cost, so the lower the number the better as fewer people are employed (and by assumption could be put to productive use elsewhere). In the example given, Portugal is more efficient at making both products: it has an absolute advantage over England in cloth and wine. Where is the incentive or justification for trade? Why should Portugal import goods it could produce more cheaply at home? And wouldn't free trade wipe out all jobs in English wine and cloth as domestic customers there could buy imported products more cheaply? Ricardo provided the answers.

The practical, political implications of questions of foreign trade in Ricardo's day were huge. Restrictions on trade, both agricultural and industrial, were central to discussions in the British parliament at the time Ricardo was formulating his theories. During the decades-long wars against the French, overseas commerce had been severely restricted. Napoleon had tried to impose a continental blockade to cut Britain off from valuable European markets. As the population in Britain had grown, and imports of grain from overseas had dwindled, the price of basic foods, such as bread, had skyrocketed. This meant that landowners grew rich while labourers faced starvation. At the end of the war, when grain prices fell again, the House of Commons, in which the landed gentry still held a majority, passed the 1815 Corn Law, which blocked imports of foreign (mainly North American) wheat and other grains. This locked in the economic power of landlords, enraged the rising capitalist class (as they had to pay higher wages so their factory workers could buy the more expensive bread) and led to rioting by the poor in London and elsewhere.[15]

Ricardo was not producing theory for its own sake. He developed his principles with a clear view on their real-world economic and political import. This has led some to argue that the view of Ricardo as an overly abstract thinker cut off from the realities of life is wrong. But this misses the point. The way in which Ricardo made his arguments, with a desire to construct 'laws' in the image of the physical sciences and with the use of hypothetical numerical examples meant that his work was anchored not in reality but in an ideal world. John Maynard Keynes spoke of this in the 1930s with an analogy from mathematics: 'The classical theorists resemble Euclidean geometers in a non-Euclidean world who, discovering that in experience straight lines apparently parallel often meet, rebuke the lines for not keeping straight.' (The true remedy for economists, Keynes, suggested was to accept that the lines meet and throw out the false assumption that they are parallel.)[16] Real-world politics motivated Ricardo's ideas, but he was other-worldly in how he arrived at his conclusions.

There is some controversy about who first came up with the theory of trade associated with Ricardo. Given the political salience of international trade others were also writing about the subject at the time. One of these, an economist and Royal Marine, Robert Torrens, claimed to have first described comparative advantage two years before Ricardo. Ricardo used the term 'comparative advantage' just once in his *Principles*, and the modern version of the theory was more fully set out by James Mill and his son, the philosopher and economist John Stuart Mill. Nonetheless, the theory—associated with Ricardo's name—swept his own day and ours. To understand its intellectual appeal, and how it answered the questions of the day, we need to do some simple sums.

'Four magic numbers'

Buried in Ricardo's prose, as mentioned, are the elements of a simple arithmetic rationale for trade. A formalized version has been taught to generations of students of economics, sometimes as their introduction to the subject. It is, according to one Ricardo scholar, 'the most frequently reproduced numerical example in the entire history of economics'.[17] That the result is counter-intuitive has added greatly to its appeal. To reveal how it works, you have to do some simple mathematics, starting with what American economist Paul Samuelson called Ricardo's 'four magic numbers': 80, 90, 100, and 120.[18]

Table 2.1: Ricardo's four magic numbers

Country/commodity	Cloth	Wine
Number of workers needed to labour for one year to produce a certain quantity		
England	100	120
Portugal	90	80

It is easier to think about the benefits of trade in this theory by considering how many workers each country would need to produce a set unit of cloth and wine with or without trade using Ricardo's numbers.

The case for less-efficient England trading with Portugal is easier to grasp. Without trade, it costs England 220 workers (100 plus 120) to produce one unit of cloth and one of wine. But with trade England can specialize in its comparative advantage—the product that it is relatively better at making—cloth. England can produce two units of cloth with 200 workers (100 times two). If it trades one unit of cloth with Portugal for one unit of wine, it would have a unit of each with a saving of 20 workers (220 minus 200).

Portugal can produce a unit of each product with 170 workers (80 plus 90). It has an absolute advantage. But, it is relatively more productive at making wine than cloth. If it follows this comparative advantage, Portugal can produce two units of wine with 160 workers (80 times two). If it then trades one of these units of wine for English cloth, Portugal has a unit of each with a saving of ten workers (170 minus 160) compared to the scenario with no trade. Generations of economists have marvelled at this beautiful, pro-trade result. It relies on the assumption that each country's workers are fully employed, so that these workers freed up from producing cloth and wine can be used in other parts of the economy and hence boost the total output and wealth of each country.[19]

Ricardo described how Portugal could save the labour of ten people with trade even though it was better at producing both products this way:

> This exchange might even take place, notwithstanding that the commodity imported by Portugal could be produced there with less labour than in England. Though she could make the cloth with the labour of 90 men, she would import it from a country where it required the labour of 100 men to produce it, because it would be advantageous to her rather to employ her capital in the production of wine, for which she would obtain more cloth from England, than she could produce by diverting a portion of her capital from the cultivation of vines to the manufacture of cloth.[20]

Essential for Ricardo is how each country can best use its limited resources of capital, which should be directed to the most efficient parts of the economy. According to this classic theory, when each country follows its comparative advantage this benefits everyone: total global output increases as what previously took 390 workers to make can be done by 360 workers with trade.

Ricardo's insight may be easier to understand with a story from today's best-selling economics textbook Greg Mankiw's *Principles of Economics*, which has sold 4 million copies since 1997.[21] It uses the hypothetical example of NBA star LeBron James (and in earlier versions the golfer Tiger Woods). James, we are told, is both a sport superstar and so efficient at mowing his lawn that he can do it faster than anyone including a paid gardener. James has an absolute advantage in both areas: does this mean he should cut his own grass? No, Mankiw answers: employing a gardener to mow his lawn, even if they don't do it as quickly, frees up James to specialize in his comparative advantage of being a highly paid sports star.[22]

In modern economics textbooks like Mankiw's, students are told that comparative advantage is 'the ability to produce a good at a lower opportunity cost than another producer'.[23] An opportunity cost is what you give up in order to get an item. To produce more, England would have to give up more working hours for wine than cloth. This means it has a lower opportunity cost—and hence comparative advantage—in cloth. The moral of this Ricardo-inspired story: every country and every person should focus on their comparative advantage and all would benefit. This is intuitive when thinking about how a team or family with different strengths can work better together, but as we will see it is not always so clear when it comes to global trade.

'Comparative advantage is a beautiful thing,' Don Boudreaux, Professor of Economics at George Mason University, wrote. 'No matter what my talents are I can still help you even if you are better at everything.'[24] In economic jargon, it pushes out the 'production possibility curve'. For proponents, the theory vindicates markets as working for the betterment of humanity. The message is: trade benefits everyone! Some have gone even further and claimed that trade is a moral and ethical goal as it ties people's interests together and leads to peace among nations.

Almost never mentioned by Ricardo or the subsequent literature is that when the classical economist penned his England and Portugal example in 1817, Portugal was effectively a British colony.[25] Its royal family, who had fled to Brazil a decade earlier, had yet to return, leaving the country under the military rule of the British general Lord Beresford. His regime was so harsh it would only be overthrown in a revolutionary uprising in 1820. On the power between the states, the comparative advantage model is silent. And power imbalances can make all the difference.

Two centuries and counting

Ricardo's wine and cloth example is clearly a hypothetical model that leaves out vast areas of the real-world to focus more clearly on what are claimed to be the essential elements. Ricardo makes no mention of differences in wage rates. The costs, both monetary and ecological, of transporting products across the globe are largely neglected. For an economist interested in the laws that regulate the distribution of wealth in society, Ricardo spends little time on who wins and who loses from trade within a country (and modern textbooks often skate over the question after noting that the winners could *theoretically* compensate the losers from trade but that is a separate political task). The theory assumes that trade will only happen if both sides benefit, so rules out from the start the worst forms of exploitation.[26]

And, yet curiously, perhaps due to the apparent solidity of the numbers—and the desire for industrialized countries to import cheap raw materials and export manufactured products—the story has retained an immense power, influencing how people see the world 200 years later. Ricardo's ideas, not Smith's, have been the root of subsequent theorizing about international trade. Orthodox economists have generalized Ricardo's theory and claimed that it still holds with many countries and many commodities. A common view is that Adam Smith's ideas on trade were second-rate and he failed to discover comparative advantage. Paul Samuelson's *Economics*, the best-selling textbook in the field for decades after it was first published in 1948, describes Ricardo's 'beautiful proof' as a 'simple principle [that] provides the unshakable basis for international trade'.[27]

Other trade theories are available. In the nineteenth century, the US and Germany particularly ascribed to the view that 'free trade' helped Britain maintain its position as the world's leading manufacturing power, while keeping other countries poor and agricultural. In the US, Alexander Hamilton (of musical fame) argued that domestic manufacturing was essential for national security.[28] Following his lead, by 1820 the US imposed average border tariffs of 40 per cent, behind which America's 'infant industry' grew to maturity. Friedrich List, who lived in Pennsylvania in the 1820s, brought Hamilton's theory to the Germanic states. List argued that the benefits of trade depend on the level of industrial development and critiqued free trade as a clever strategy by which a dominant power, when it has reached: 'the summit of greatness ... kicks away the ladder by which he has climbed up'.[29] The US and Germany, while embracing 'protectionism', surpassed Britain as a manufacturing power by the early twentieth century. High tariffs—it is often forgotten today—remained the blueprint for US economic policy until it emerged as the undisputed global manufacturing power during the Second World War and embraced 'free trade'.

During the second half of the twentieth century, other economic thinkers from South America and East Asia put forward theories to rival the new US promotion of 'free trade'. From the late 1940s, the Argentine economist Raúl Prebisch argued that the economic world was divided into an industrial 'core' (of the US and Europe) and a raw material-producing 'periphery'. Over time, he showed, the relative price of primary commodities had declined compared to manufactured goods. This school is known as 'dependency theory', as it argues that economies of countries in the periphery are dependent on the economic needs of the global 'core'. It promoted substituting imports with domestic goods and fell from favour following global economic crises in the 1970s.

Many East Asian countries, meanwhile, employed an active 'developmental state' to promote exports and shield industries from foreign competitors until they were able to hold their own. South Korea, for example, used high tariffs, state subsidies, and direct state control in key sectors such as banking and steel. Ha-Joon Chang, a leading institutional economist from South Korea, describes this model as 'a clever and pragmatic mixture of market incentives and state direction', avoiding both blind faith in the market or rejecting it, as in communist countries.[30] The spectacular economic development of Japan and China followed a similar policy mix. Following the collapse of communism in the late 1980s, however, this rich and diverse history of thinking and practice was either ignored or sidelined due to the belief that the only route to economic development was free trade.

In the 1990s, American economist Paul Krugman published an influential popular article, 'Ricardo's difficult idea', in which he invoked the classical economist's prestige to fight the trade policy battles of that decade. Krugman is a fascinating thinker. As a kid, he was entranced by Isaac Asimov's sci-fi trilogy *Foundation* and its fictional science, called psychohistory, which draws on history, psychology, and statistics to predict the behaviour of large groups of people centuries into the future with decimal-point accuracy. The closest equivalent he could find was the predictive power of economic models. 'I became an economist because I wanted to be a psychohistorian, saving civilization through the mathematics of human behavior,' he wrote in 2010.[31] He is a left-of-centre liberal (in the American sense), an advisor to the Democratic Party, and a thorn in the side of Republicans. He is so disliked by libertarian economic thinkers that a *Contra Krugman* podcast, which attempted to refute his *New York Times* columns one by one, ran to 225 episodes and even hosted several seven-day cruises for Krugman haters.[32] Even so, Krugman was one of the sharpest enforcers of a pro-globalization consensus in the 1990s.

In 'Ricardo's difficult idea', Krugman wrote that anyone who wants to speak knowledgeably about the global expansion of trade must wrap their 'mind around a difficult concept that was devised by a frock-coated banker 180 years ago!'[33] The banker was, of course, David Ricardo and the concept was comparative advantage. Krugman appeared to believe if only opponents of globalization could truly understand Ricardo, they would change their mind. He compared those who reject the teachings of economics to creationists and evolution deniers. Ricardo's great idea, he concluded, is 'utterly true, immensely sophisticated—and extremely relevant to the modern world'.[34]

The consensus on laissez-faire trade between countries was backed by a robust and deeply held expert consensus within mainstream economics. This can be seen by comparing Krugman's views with that of the prominent economist and textbook author Greg Mankiw. On domestic issues, they disagreed on many things. In the 2000s, Krugman used his *New York Times* column to assail the tax cuts for the rich in the George W. Bush presidency, while Mankiw worked as Bush's top economist. But, there was—for a long time—a happy agreement between them on international trade. Indeed, it became almost the hallmark of what it means to be a serious economist to believe in free trade, claiming an unbroken heritage of two centuries back to David Ricardo. As Krugman once memorably wrote, 'If there were an Economist's Creed, it would surely contain the affirmations "I understand the Principle of Comparative Advantage" and "I advocate Free Trade".'[35]

Greg Mankiw wrote that although economists over the years have broadened and refined Ricardo's theory 'the central argument for free trade has not changed much in the past two centuries ... [and] is still based largely on the principle of comparative advantage'.[36] It is taught in all the textbooks of international trade—often as the first and most important lesson. When asked in a podcast in 2021 how he would make the case for globalization, Mankiw responded:

> 'When I teach basic economics, I make comparative
> advantage—which is Ricardo's theory of why trade can
> make both trading parties better off—I make that the
> very centre of the course … I think it's really central to
> economics. The basic theory of comparative advantage
> explains not only why we trade with other countries. It's
> why we trade with other people. It's why we don't grow
> our own food and make our own clothes.'[37]

There have been a few critics, even within the mainstream. Harvard
Economics Professor Dani Rodrik, who has argued courageously
since the late 1990s against 'hyper-globalization', has praised the
theory of comparative advantage as: 'one of the very first (and most
successful) uses of models in economics'.[38] But he's also written that
some of the reason that 'economists' analytical minds turn to mush
when they talk about trade policy in the real world' is 'to do with
the idea of comparative advantage being the crown jewel of the
profession. It is too painful to let go of.'[39]

Other critics of the mainstream have lined up in support of
Ricardo's great idea. Chicago-trained economist Deirdre McCloskey,
who once wrote of the 'unspeakably sad fact' that the apparent
accomplishments of economics of the last 50 years were a fantastical
and pseudo-scientific 'game in a sandpit', felt strongly enough
in 2017 to write: 'The pattern of trade is determined solely by
comparative advantage.'[40]

Other critics argue that Ricardo's theory was once true but is
now obsolete due to changes in the global economy. This has some
merit. Ricardo wrote about the 'difficulty' with which capital moved
between countries, in his time, and implied that if money moved
easily across borders his example would break down: all the workers
and capital would go to Portugal, the most productive place. One
of the reasons this doesn't happen, Ricardo wrote are the patriotic
feelings of businessmen 'which I should be sorry to see weakened,
[that] induce most men of property to be satisfied with a low rate of
profits in their own country, rather than seek a more advantageous
employment for their wealth in foreign nations'.[41] In today's world
of instant global money transfers and multinational corporations and
executives with fewer ties to any one country, this reasoning is an
embarrassment to boosters of globalization.

Another critique along the same lines can be seen in Matthew Klein and Michael Pettis' *Trade Wars Are Class Wars* (2020). Klein and Pettis point to the fact that, in Ricardo and Smith's day, trade between countries was about raw materials and finished goods. Now, much international trade is in intermediate goods (electronic components or car parts, for example) and services (such as accountancy or advertising).[42] Although both points are true, the flaws in Ricardo's theory are even more fundamental, as the following chapters make plain. Ricardo's ideas never truly described trade in his day.

The story of Ricardo's magic numbers shows how theory can confuse the real and hypothetical and how a mathematical facade can screen off a bleaker, more complex story. The real story of England and Portugal's trade is one of empire, exploitation, slavery, and suffering amid plenty.[43] Ricardo, as a financial trader, would have been aware of the importance of the Portuguese trade to England. He had read about the real treaty between the two countries in cloth and wine in Adam Smith's work. Ricardo, elsewhere in the *Principles*, described Portugal as one of the 'most beggarly countries in Europe', but he never once in print or in parliament mentioned the real history of the trade between England and Portugal.[44]

To uncover the hidden history of comparative advantage, we have to go back to the early 1700s, more than a century before Ricardo first published a word.

3

Unequal Treaty

Why England and Portugal's real prizes
were neither cloth nor wine

All the essential elements of the standard story about England and Portugal's trade—retold in newspapers and textbooks as a parable of the benefits of globalization—are recognizable in a very special document drawn up 320 years ago. The document is kept under lock and key in the UK National Archives near Kew Gardens in south-west London. It is a Treaty of Commerce between Portugal and England—not Britain, as this was signed on 16 December 1703, a few years before the Act of Union with Scotland.[1] Its pages, rendered almost translucent with time, contain only three articles written in Latin. Attached by a frail string is a weighty, palm-sized red wax seal of Pedro II, King of Portugal.[2]

The first of the three articles obliges Portugal to admit freely 'the woollen cloths, and the rest of the woollen manufacturers' of the English. Article 2 obliges England 'to admit the wines of the growth of Portugal' at a tariff one third lower than French wines. Article 3 deals with ratifying the treaty (see Figure 3.1).[3] Compared to the hundreds of pages of modern free-trade agreements, it is almost laughably simple. But it includes the two countries and two products—England and Portugal, cloth and wine—of the most iconic and perhaps most influential model in economics.

The treaty reduced government tariffs and restrictions and trade boomed. English exports to Portugal of bays, a lighter type of woollen cloth, averaged £159,000 per year in 1706–1710 and rose

Figure 3.1: The three articles of the Methuen Treaty of Commerce between Portugal and England, concluded 16 December 1703

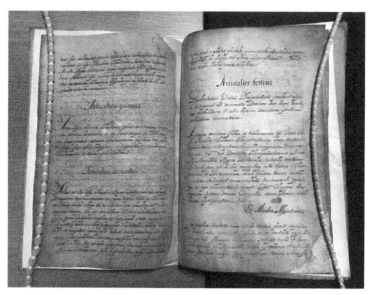

Source: © The National Archives. Photo: Nat Dyer

to £435,000 per year—approximately £157 million today—by the 1730s.[4] Portugal, despite its relatively small population, became by the mid-eighteenth century Britain's second largest commercial partner. Exports from England to Portugal consistently topped £1 million—around £360 million today—per year in those decades, accounting for almost 20 per cent of England's foreign trade. More than half of Britain's exports were textiles.[5] The English also grew to appreciate Portuguese wine, especially once merchants began adding grape brandy to preserve it on the sea voyage and created the fortified wine known as port. Portuguese exports to England —of which around 80 per cent was wine—doubled from the time before the treaty to the 1740s to £429,000 per year—around £154 million today.[6]

Port displaced French wine, which had to be bought with silver, from its top spot and became (with the accompanying gout) a cultural fixture of British middle- and upper- class life. Dr Johnson, the dictionary maker and most famous man of letters in eighteenth-century England, once refused French wine with the roar: 'Poor stuff! No, Sir, claret is the liquor for boys; port for men' (and added mischievously 'he who aspires to be hero must drink brandy').[7] The England–Portugal trade appears to be a win for both sides. This is as far as the history often goes. That's why Tim Harford, the *Financial Times*' 'Undercover Economist', was able to describe the Methuen Treaty in 2022 as 'one of my favourite trade deals'.[8]

Some readers may have noticed that the Portuguese imported significantly more from England than they exported. At the height of the bilateral trade, Portuguese imports were worth £1.3 million and exports were rarely above £0.4 million, leaving a trade imbalance in some years of one million pounds.[9] The way in which Portugal filled the gap, and paid England back, will became important later when we look at the missing products and countries in the standard model. As we expand our view to those who created the document, and to its economic and political impacts both in Europe and across the Atlantic, a radically different picture will emerge.

Secret payments

When I used to investigate corrupt natural-resources deals the first question to ask was: who was behind the agreement and did they have anything to gain personally? So, let us look at the men—and they were all men with the exception of the English Queen Anne— who brought the treaty into being. Often called the Cloth and Wine Treaty, it is also known as the Methuen Treaty after the English diplomat John Methuen (1650–1706). The English have frequently been accused—especially by French and Portuguese authors—of greasing the palms of Portuguese ministers and having a personal interest in the deal.[10]

John Methuen, then in his early 50s, was a lawyer and a long-time Member of the English Parliament. He was the English envoy to Portugal for a few years in the 1690s, and he provoked scandal when he started living with Sarah Earle, the wife of one of his colleagues. Methuen's son Henry was tragically killed in a Lisbon bar brawl. When Methuen was called back to London to sit on the new Board of Trade alongside philosopher John Locke, he left his other son, Paul, in Portugal as the English representative.[11] Portraits of John Methuen produced half a century after his death show a man with a small mouth, direct gaze, and a domed forehead. His contemporary, spy-chief John Macky, described him as 'a common lawyer' and 'a man of intrigue', physically tall and in 'complexion and manners much of a Spaniard'.[12] The author of *Gulliver's Travels*, Jonathan Swift, was even more scathing, calling him a 'profligate rogue, without religion or morals; but cunning enough, yet without abilities of any kind'.[13] Against this, John Methuen's voluminous letters, held at the British Library and National Archives, show a competent and informed diplomat, carrying out intricate business at the highest levels in English, Portuguese, and sometimes in code. He knew Portugal, its court, and, crucially, the King intimately. He was also born into the wool trade.

His father, also named Paul Methuen, was immensely rich and, according to a contemporary chronicler, 'the greatest cloathier [cloth maker] of his time'.[14] John's brother William took over the family cloth business in the Wiltshire town of Bradford-on-Avon in 1660s. He would have been one of the first winners from the immediate jump in cloth sales following the treaty. Annual exports of cloth from Bradford-on-Avon to Portugal numbered just 486 pieces when the treaty was signed, but rose in the following years to an average of around 3,000 pieces, a more than sixfold increase.[15] John Methuen had a family interest in wine too: he owned a vineyard in Portugal and his son-in-law was an importer of wines to England. Similarly, King Pedro and the Marquis of Alegrete, the Portuguese lead negotiator, owned vineyards.[16] But there is also more direct evidence of corruption.

Methuen performed eighteenth-century shuttle diplomacy, often making the nine-day sea crossing between Lisbon and the south coast of England and then taking post horses—the quickest form of travel—to the capital in order to keep both King Pedro and Queen Anne onside. On one of his London trips, in July 1703, records from the UK Treasury show that Methuen requested and received £2,000—worth perhaps £720,000 today—of 'secret service money'. To justify his expense, he said that 'I have by her Majesty's express command paid in Portugal for her Majesty's service and by her own immediate direction.'[17] I have found no record of those royal commands but French and Portuguese authors have long claimed he used the funds illegitimately. Again, in October, back in Portugal, John Methuen needed more funds quickly. He asked for and received 'two bills of exchange of £1,000 each' from his brother William back in Bradford-on-Avon. The evidence for this comes from the secret service accounts for November 1703, which show that William Methuen asked Queen Anne's Treasury to be reimbursed for monies he had sent to his brother, the Ambassador, for work performed at 'her Majesty's particular direction' in Portugal.[18] In December, the England–Portugal commercial deal was done.

Only rarely when investigating corruption have I found the receipts, and there is no record of how John Methuen used his 'secret' funds. But there is some evidence in his letters that he made private payments to Portuguese public officials. Writing to his boss, the Earl of Nottingham, English Secretary of State for the Southern Department, in January 1704, a month after the trade deal was signed, Methuen said: 'I have made the utmost use of all the money which I have had orders for to satisfy the P [Portuguese] ministers.'[19] This is the type of line a corruption investigator today would be very happy to find in an email. Methuen also gave a huge wedding present to the son of Portugal's chief negotiator, who married during the negotiations, and 'dowries for the nieces of the king's confessor', an influential person at court.[20] It seems very likely that the iconic England and Portugal trade deal was tainted from the start by corruption, which calls into question how much it was in the public interest of both sides. But a larger challenge to the textbook version comes when we further broaden our view and look at the political and military context of the deal.

An English victory over French tyranny

One aspect that disappears from view when you see the world through the comparative advantage model is power, especially state power. The graphs and equations to determine who should produce and trade what product are concerned with identifying the ideal trading outcome. Personal interest, or the power of one dominant country over another, are omitted from the calculations. There is an underlying, often unspoken and forgotten, assumption that both sides have equal power. History tells a different story. Nothing about the trade between English cloth and Portuguese wine makes sense without understanding the politics and military rivalries of the time. In fact, the commercial pact was only one of three treaties Methuen sealed with Portugal in 1703.

Methuen was working at the beginning of a period known by some historians as the Second Hundred Years' War that pitched Britain and its allies against France. It was a series of conflicts running from 1687 to Waterloo in 1815. Methuen's first posting to Portugal in the 1690s was during the first of these wars: the Nine Years' War, known as King William's War in North America. His second posting to Lisbon in 1702 came just as the Grand Alliance—of England, the Dutch Republic, and the Holy Roman Empire—was about to declare war on France in what became known as the War of Spanish Succession or Queen Anne's War. During the 15 years of that conflict, an estimated 400,000 people died in combat and many more from disease. Yet, it is little remembered in Britain today apart from the allied victory in Blenheim in present-day southern Germany—giving its name to Blenheim Palace, birthplace of Winston Churchill—and the English capture of Gibraltar in Spain. The elderly Spanish king had died childless and European powers were fighting over whether the crown would go to the nephew of the French Sun King Louis XIV or a rival supported by England and its allies. Portugal, important for its Atlantic ports and proximity to Spain, had sided with France at the outset. Methuen's task was to make Portugal's King Pedro II change sides in the war. 'How far I may from all this hope for success is very uncertain,' Methuen confessed in a letter home. He knew his only hope lay with the English Royal Navy.[21]

Within days of arriving in Portugal, the English diplomat had a private 90-minute audience with King Pedro II and frequent conversations with his chief ministers. Pedro had been on the throne since 1683, when he banished his brother, the former King to the Azores, and married his brother's wife. He was tall, with dark hair and eyes, physically strong, and reputedly a master of horseback bullfighting.

Methuen wrote to his superiors in London begging for an English fleet to be dispatched. It was essential, he argued, to demonstrate the English command of the ocean and the country's ability to protect Portugal. If a strong English fleet were to sail into Lisbon, he wrote, 'the effect of it may be more than could be imagined'.[22] Only then could Portugal be persuaded to quit the French alliance and side with England. Methuen returned to London himself to drum up support for the plan and then went to Portsmouth to meet with

Admiral George Rooke, who would lead the English fleet. All the while, he continued his advocacy, writing to the Secretary of State in London, 'our affairs in the Court of Portugal depend absolutely upon the coming of the fleet'.[23] And yet, when the Royal Navy came, disaster struck—twice.

First, Admiral Rooke's fleet attempted to capture Cádiz in southern Spain in August 1702. They failed utterly. Worse, a landing party of English troops plundered cellars full of wine and brandy and then looted and destroyed warehouses, convents, and churches. The drunk, riotous troops horrified the local Catholic population, whom the English admirals had hoped would rally to their side. The episode solidified the locals' prejudices against the heretical Protestants. Rooke and his men set sail for England in disgrace. Then, to make things even worse for Methuen's cause, French warships escorted the Spanish Treasure Fleet, laden with precious metals and other spoils from the Americas, safely across the Atlantic. They docked in the port of Vigo in north-east Spain and started to unload the cargo. It showed that the French could command the ocean and, Methuen was sure, they planned to channel some of the fleet's riches to Pedro II to keep him onside.[24] But here was a golden opportunity too. If Rooke's fleet could meet the French warships and Spanish galleons in battle, destroy them, and capture the treasure, everything would change.

Before Admiral Rooke's ships crossed the Bay of Biscay back to England, news reached him of the Spanish Treasure Fleet. Seventeen Spanish galleons, escorted by 18 warships, most of which were French, were anchored at the end of a narrow strait in Vigo Bay. They were safely protected, they believed, by a Spanish fort and cannon on either side of the strait and by a floating barrier in the harbour (a boom) made of masts, cables, and chains. Rooke launched a combined land and sea attack, in fog, on 12 October 1702. His men, together with their Dutch allies, stormed the fort and silenced the cannon, while his lead ship broke through the harbour chain and attacked the Franco-Spanish fleet at anchor. The Battle of Vigo Bay was a major victory for the English and Dutch. They did not lose a ship. The French and Spanish lost every one of theirs: either sunk, burnt, or commandeered by their enemies (see Figure 3.2).[25]

Rooke sent the two tonnes of silver and a little gold captured to the Royal Mint in London, which coined silver sixpences with

Figure 3.2: *The Battle of Vigo Bay* by Ludolf Backhuysen, *c.* 1702

Source: © National Maritime Museum, Greenwich, London

VIGO stamped under the head of Queen Anne. The impact of the events at Vigo on Portugal were not lost on the soldiers and sailors. The Duke of Ormonde, second-in-command, wrote to Admiral Rooke immediately after the battle: 'this success which I cannot but fancy will make him [the King of Portugal] entirely leave the French interest since he has now nothing to feare from them'.[26] Ormonde was right.

Overjoyed, John Methuen continued his 'private negotiations with the King which remain a perfect secret' from everyone, he wrote, including 'almost all the Portuguese ministers'.[27] All the details were hammered out by May 1703, and two military agreements—the first two Methuen Treaties—were signed. Portugal pledged to provide 28,000 troops for the war on France and her allies, and England and the Grand Alliance agreed to pay subsidies to maintain half of them. The treaties also gave the Grand Alliance access to Portugal's seaports. Methuen had succeeded! Portugal was firmly allied to the English. The threat of France dimmed.

Only after this did Methuen push his advantage by negotiating the commercial deal for wine and cloth, helped with the loan from his brother, which, as mentioned, would be reimbursed from Queen Anne's secret service funds. The Cloth and Wine Treaty was made possible by, and followed in the wake of, the military agreements. The military agreements also put in Methuen's hands the ability to disburse the English subsidies to the Portuguese military. It can be no coincidence that the first of these payments of 'five hundred thousand dollars', as Methuen relates, was made in December 1703, a few days after the commercial deal was signed by King Pedro II.[28] None of the agreements would have been finalized at all if it were not for the power and protection offered by the English Royal Navy.[29]

In the decades after Methuen sealed his deal, the drinking of Portuguese wine became not just a matter of taste or economics, but patriotism. As Jonathan Swift put it in the 1730s:

> Be sometimes to your country true,
> Have once the public good in view:
> Bravely despise champagne at court,
> And chose to dine at home with port.[30]

In the real world, global trade is 'the result of a complex and interlocking network of bargains that are partly economic and partly political', wrote the global political economist Susan Strange.[31] Power matters. So too do values. States have always balanced the economic benefits of greater trade against other values and concerns, such as security, freedom, and, at times, justice. The original example of comparative advantage David Ricardo used was a particularly unsuitable choice for prioritizing economic values above all others, Strange wrote in the 1980s:

> The freer exchange of British wool and woollen goods for Portuguese wine was acceptable to the Portuguese government only because it perceived an urgent need for the defensive protection of the Royal Navy. The Portuguese must have guessed that the result of the increased trade with England would be the ruin of many honest, hardworking Portuguese weavers. Yet the price had to be paid, because the treaty promised greater security for the state. It was not primarily a commercial agreement.[32]

Did the Methuen Treaties, then, ruin the Portuguese textile industry? What were its economic impacts?

'All their own manufactures … will be immediately laid down'

In the decades before the Cloth and Wine Treaty, Portuguese elites had made some strides in developing a domestic cloth manufacturing industry. Supply of wool was ample as the Iberian Peninsula was home to large flocks of merino sheep, which produce a thinner and softer type of wool that still commands a premium. Cloth workers were brought from England to teach Portuguese producers, and an energetic minister, the Count of Ericeira, set up some woollen-cloth factories. In 1677, King Pedro II banned the wearing of foreign cloth in order to boost domestic production, which hurt English traders.[33] This was classic 'infant industry' protectionism.

Methuen's trade deal with the Portuguese was designed to roll back these protectionist moves (although the English at the time were passing similar laws banning the sale of world-leading Indian cotton textiles, a 'crime' later punishable by death, while imitating Indian designs).[34] A few days before the commercial treaty was signed in December 1703, Methuen allowed himself to speculate on its impacts. He was clear-eyed: it was 'greatly advantageous to England' but would end Portugal's cloth industry. 'This agreement,' he wrote to the English Foreign Secretary, 'will have this consequence in Portugal. That all their own manufactures which at this time make a vast quantity of ill cloth and dear will be immediately laid down & totally discontinued. The cloth … of no other nations will be able to come in competition with those of England.'[35] This sounds more like securing a monopoly rather than free trade; more like win–lose than win–win.

Portuguese domestic cloth production did decline, although historians disagree as to what extent this was a direct result of the Methuen Treaty. The Portuguese Inquisition, which had kicked out David Ricardo's ancestors, harassed merchants and the Protestant cloth workers brought in to pass on their skills. The energetic Count of Ericeira, who suffered from depression, committed suicide in 1690. Further, the Portuguese elite were conservative landowners who feared the rise of an independent manufacturing and merchant class: producing agricultural wine for export suited their interests better.

Even if the English imports did cut Portugal's cloth industry to shreds this was not necessarily a negative from the point of view of comparative advantage. Methuen claimed—and he may have been correct—that the Portuguese cloth was poor quality ('ill') and expensive ('dear'). (This suggests that Ricardo's magic numbers, which show Portugal as more efficient at producing both cloth and wine, are not grounded in reality.) So, it would be more efficient and benefit both countries, according to the theory, for the English to specialize in cloth and the Portuguese in wine. They could both still gain as Portuguese textile workers could be employed in another, more productive industry. But that's where history departs from economic theory.

As Harvard global economic historian Sven Beckert shows in *Empire of Cotton*, out of the cloth industry time and again in England, continental Europe, and the US came the factory and an engine of industrial development.[36] In the 1700s, Portugal did continue to produce textiles, but mostly in private households for local clothing and footwear. The Portuguese state did attempt to create a silk industry and, later, set up many other types of factories, but these failed to alter the course of Portuguese economic development.[37] Portugal became stuck in a pattern of exporting raw materials in exchange for manufactured goods. By the 1790s, 87 per cent of England's exports were manufactured products while 78 per cent of Portugal's were wine or food.[38] Economic historians have estimated that the long-term trend of growing per capita income in Portugal continued up to the 1750s, but then stalled and began to fall back. By the 1850s, incomes were the same as they had been 300 years earlier! Portugal remained one of the poorest countries in Europe into the twentieth century.[39]

The British economist Joan Robinson argued: 'in real life Portugal was dependent on British naval support, and it was for this reason that she was obliged to accept conditions of trade which wiped out her production of textiles and inhibited industrial development, so as to make her more dependent than ever'.[40] David Birmingham, a historian of Portugal, wrote that in 'some respects the Methuen Treaty made Portugal a "neo-colonial" client of Britain'.[41] With the Methuen Treaty, he writes, Portugal was 'tied to Britain in a way which inhibited the broadening of the industrial base'.[42] The deal did have some economic benefits for Portugal, not least access to the English market for its wines. But even here, consider the names of the big port producers: Cockburn, Croft, and Graham. Not exactly traditional Portuguese names. That's because the Porto wine trade was, and still is to a large degree, controlled by English, Scottish, and Dutch families.[43]

The Methuen Treaty was not all negative for Portugal, but its win was political not economic. As Susan Strange reminds us, the treaty—like all free-trade deals—was a blend of politics and economics. Portugal's real prize, in its alliance with England, was English naval and military support to maintain its independence. King Pedro II had come to the throne at the end of a 30-year war against Spanish dominance. Spain and France attacked Portugal's land border time and again in the 1700s and early 1800s. Although we cannot know for certain, without British military and political support Portugal may not have remained an independent country. It could easily, like Catalonia, which also fought on the English side in the War of Spanish Succession, have been absorbed into a greater Spain. As a recent Brazilian historian put it: Lisbon bought protection, not just products, from London.[44]

Even with this broader political view, we do not yet have the full picture of this iconic free-trade agreement. We need to widen our focus once again, this time to include the world beyond Europe, to view the conflict and diplomatic wrangling in its global context. In doing so, we'll answer the million pound question of how Portugal met its massive annual deficits from the trade imbalance— the mismatch between its large imports from, and modest exports to, England.

Colonial riches

Portugal and Spain in the early 1700s were portals to another world. The two Iberian monarchies had been the first European countries to colonize parts of Africa, the Americas, and Asia more than 200 years earlier. Their empires were now declining in power, with navies unable to protect their commercial sea routes. New challengers came from the north of Europe. The rising maritime powers of France, England, and Holland used their mastery of the oceans in a desperate attempt to catch up and reap some of the benefits of the empire. The Dutch had already wrestled control of much of Portugal's empire—from present-day Sri Lanka in Asia to El Mina on the West African coast and, for a few decades, most of northern Brazil. The War of Spanish Succession was only partly about who would wear the Spanish crown. It was also about who would have access to Spain and Portugal's lucrative South American empires and the trade that brought Africans in chains across the Atlantic to work these. It was a fight for imperial dominance.

This missing extra-European element ties up many of the loose ends in the story of English cloth and Portuguese wine. Once in place, the colonial lens helps illuminates many things. King Pedro II had been lured to the French side at the beginning of the war, Methuen said, with a promise that France's Louis XIV would repay Pedro's disastrous personal investment in the slave trade and defend 'his Conquests in both Indias'.[45] The English and Dutch fleet under Rooke had launched the ill-fated attack on Cádiz in part because it was the city at the forefront of Spain's trade with the Americas. The English and Dutch naval power demonstrated at Vigo was so crucial because Portuguese royal wealth depended on the safe arrival of the annual fleet from their Brazil colonies carrying gold, tobacco, and timber. Portugal relied on the rising maritime powers of Europe for safe passage to its New World riches even if that meant undercutting its own industry. 'The preservation of our overseas colonies makes it indispensable for us to have a good intelligence with the powers which now possess the command of the sea,' the Portuguese minister in London, José da Cunha Brochado, said of the Methuen Treaty, 'the cost is heavy, but for us such an understanding is essential'.[46]

In an effort to entice his superiors in London to ratify the commercial treaty he was cooking up, John Methuen, a month before it was signed, predicted that the deal would change the balance of trade in England's favour 'above fifty thousand pounds a year and for some time near a hundred thousand pounds'.[47] He was wrong. It was much more. England's surplus in its trade with Portugal jumped by over £250,000 per year in the first decade of the 1700s. Methuen became a hero to some. A contemporary newspaper supportive of the Portugal trade wrote that 'he deserves to have his Statue erected in every Trading Town in Great Britain'.[48] By the 1730s, the trade imbalance rose another £250,000, and by the late 1750s it had peaked at over £1 million (£360 million today).[49] Historians continue to debate how much the Methuen Treaty represented a continuity or a break with previous trade patterns.[50] But one fact is uncontested: Portugal did not sell enough wine to England to make up for the vast quantities of cloth it imported.

It would have been impossible for Portugal to keep importing vast quantities of cloth for decades and decades unless it had a commodity other than wine to export back to England. Fortunately for King Pedro II, a fountain of wealth had been uncorked 250 miles north of Rio de Janeiro in the 1690s. Portugal had a trade deficit with England for almost the entire 1700s: it was made good by Brazilian gold.

The classic comparative advantage model features two countries and two products. It is conceptually sealed off from concerns of politics, power, or colonization. The iconic story of England and Portugal trade makes no sense without a third product and country: gold from Brazil. But, as will be explored in Chapter 4, the story does not end there. The Portuguese needed one more 'commodity' to colonize Brazil in the early 1700s and to extract, wash, and refine the gold from the rivers and hillsides of the interior. It's a product no longer legally traded: human beings. The vast majority of the enslaved were captured in, and transported from, West and Central Africa. Even stripped to its essentials, we should consider the iconic parable of international trade as a four-region and four-product model.

Those who still hold on to the old story of English cloth and Portuguese wine have the wool pulled over their eyes.

4

Black Gold

A history of Portuguese Brazil, its gold,
and the trade in captives from Africa

In a house on one of the graffiti-filled streets in Rio de Janeiro's old town in 2022, I stood peering down into a glass-covered hole in the floor. Below, the lit excavation pit revealed scattered bone fragments and then deeper, in one corner, a full human skeleton. You could make out the teeth and jaw twisted to the right, hard pressed against the dirt, and the ribcage and spine leading down to the pelvis. They were the remains of a woman: she was 20 years old, born in Africa, and taken against her will to Brazil, where her body was dumped in a pit.

The house belongs to the Guimarães family. While they were renovating it in the 1990s, they started to find human teeth and bones and called the police. The mother, Mercedes Guimarães, later said 'I was thinking that the previous owner killed his entire family.'[1] She was right that it was the scene of a massacre, but one that took place 200 years earlier. Back then, it was not against the law. The family had stumbled on one of the world's largest slave burial grounds. When the authorities failed to commemorate the site or build a museum, the Guimarães family did so themselves. The Cemitério dos Pretos Novos (Memorial of the New Blacks) stands as a rebuke to the erasure and rose-coloured view of slavery in Brazil.

Underneath my feet were the remains of tens of thousands—estimates vary from 20,000 to 60,000—young men, women, and children, who had been dumped in the ground. Analysis of their teeth showed they came from as far away as Sudan and Mozambique.[2] Whole skeletons like the 20-year-old woman are rare, as the site was also used as a rubbish dump, which was regularly burnt. Each of my footsteps on the smooth concrete around the glass-covered hole fell on a vast mass grave of mutilated bodies. The African cloth on the wall and the piped-in sounds of water evoke the land from which the dead were taken and their shackled voyage across the ocean. It was the most moving and powerful place I visited in Brazil, where one can begin to grasp some of the immense scale of human suffering caused by the transatlantic slave trade.

In popular Western imagination, the history of slavery is bound up with the US perhaps more than any other country. Images of the triangular trade across the Atlantic often show a line from Africa skirting the South American coast and terminating in the US or perhaps the Caribbean. The importance of Brazil to transatlantic slavery is often overlooked. In fact, slavers brought *ten times more* people from Africa to Brazil than to the US. Around 400,000 captives from Africa were landed on mainland North America (although more arrived through the intra-American trade) and an estimated 5 million in Brazil.[3] This means Brazil claims top spot on a lot of lists related to the slave trade. As well as being the country that received the largest number of enslaved Africans (only surpassed by the Caribbean states taken together), Brazil was the last country in the Americas to abolish slavery, keeping the system until 1888. Rio de Janeiro is likely the biggest slavery port in all of human history. Buried artefacts from that time keep appearing. In 2011, as the city was redeveloping its port region ahead of hosting the Olympic Games, workers uncovered the stone Valongo Wharf, just a ten-minute walk from the Cemitério dos Pretos Novos. Built two centuries earlier, upwards of half a million enslaved Africans passed through the wharf. It is now recognized as a World Heritage Site.

This is not just about the past. Today, 112 million Brazilians, 55 per cent of the population, identify as either Black or dual heritage.[4] This is, by some estimates, the second-highest Black population in the world, surpassing all African countries except Nigeria. The influence of Black Brazilians on Brazilian culture is immense, from samba to Carnival, capoeira and beyond, and yet Black Brazilians are much more likely to suffer poverty than their White compatriots. The murder of George Floyd in the US pushed issues of systemic racism and lack of representation into public conversations in Brazil.

Brazil's prominence in the slave trade is partly down to geography as it's closer to Africa than anywhere else in the Americas. It is explained in part too by the longevity of slavery in the country. It also reflects how essential African labour was for the commodities on which Brazil's economy floated and sank in various cycles: sugar, cotton, coffee, tobacco, and more. Most relevant to this book, the early stages of Brazil's slave trade were intimately tied to the gold rush that started in the hills north of Rio a decade before the Cloth and Wine Treaty.

'A proper enforcement of the bringing of them from Africa'

The common image of the economy of transatlantic trade in the 1700s is as a triangle. The top of the triangular trade lies in Europe and runs down to West Africa, carrying with it manufactured goods such as cloth and guns. Another side of the triangle shows enslaved people transported from West Africa to the Americas: the Middle Passage. Then, a final side of the triangle brings raw materials such as sugar, tobacco, or furs back from the Caribbean and North America to Europe, where it begins again. We need to add something to this image to account for the English and Portuguese trade, which was a significant appendage to, and facilitator of, the triangular trade. Imagine if you can two arrows coming from the top of the triangular diagram. One arrow takes cloth from England down to Portugal, the other takes wine and gold back up to England. In each case, Portugal was a gateway, an intermediary, to the real prize in Africa and South America (see Figure 4.1).

Much English cloth was sold to Portugal only to be re-exported to buy captured men, women, and children on the West African coast or to clothe them in Brazil. 'England after the Methuen Treaty of 1703 also dominated Portugal and its empire,' writes Hugh Thomas in *The Slave Trade*. He estimates that 'perhaps 85 percent' of English textile exports to Portugal were used for the Portuguese slave trade before 1750 and over 40 per cent during the following 20 years.[5] The story of English cloth and Portuguese wine is yet another subject where, in the words of British historian David Olusoga,

Figure 4.1: Map of English cloth and Portuguese wine as part of the transatlantic triangular trade

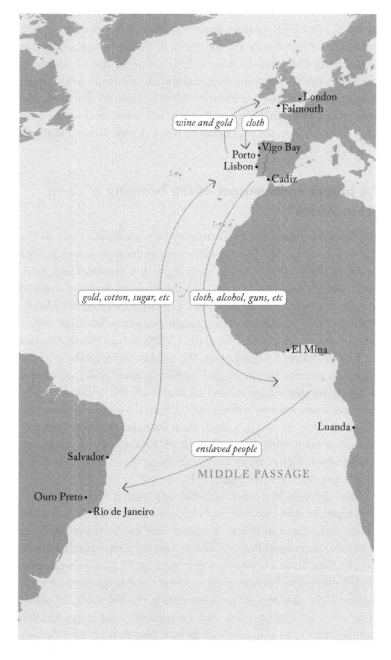

'events and phenomena that we think we know and understand contain within them lost or camouflaged connections to Africa, slavery and black history'.[6]

The link between England and Portugal's trade and the Atlantic triangular trade was not an unintended consequence. It was part of the original plan. John Methuen—England's cunning and talented diplomat in Lisbon—was steeped in the Portuguese world, English trade, and colonial relations. England, during Methuen's lifetime, founded the Royal African Company—state-owned slave traders— and overtook Portugal as the biggest transporter of captured and bound Africans across the Atlantic. John and Paul Methuen's letters tell of the diplomatic pressure they exerted to help English merchants transporting human captives across the Atlantic.[7] What's more, Methuen explicitly vaunts the connections between his trade deal, slavery, and empire in a pair of letters written to the English Foreign Secretary, the Earl of Nottingham, at the time he was finalizing the famous commercial agreement.

A number of historians have written about the period, and at least one has quoted from these letters, but to my knowledge this is the first time the quotations that follow have been printed.[8] On 26 November 1703, John Methuen wrote to the Earl of Nottingham. He set out the terms of the England and Portugal cloth and wine deal, told the Earl he was writing them up 'in the form of a Treaty' for Queen Anne's approval, and suggested a similar deal could be struck with the Spanish.[9] In any future agreement with the Spanish, Methuen said, it would be essential that 'the [English Royal] African Company is to take the Contract for furnishing the Spanish Indyes with blacks which is called Assiento'.[10] The *asiento*—or agreement— was a key prize of the War of Spanish Succession, as Spain, with vast territories in South America but none in Africa, relied on other European powers to provide enforced labourers. Britain would eventually get the Spanish *asiento* in 1713 and give it to its South Sea Company. As Methuen noted, the prize was not just the direct trade in humans, but also the trading opportunities that came with access to otherwise closed Spanish ports in the Americas.

Methuen continued on the same theme in a letter of 15 January 1704. His trade deal had been signed by the Portuguese but he was still eagerly anticipating news that it would be ratified by Queen Anne and the English parliament. Perhaps to entice his superiors, he sketched out a plan for the 'future Establishment' of a new commercial world after the war: 'The assiento of Negros if well established will be of great advantage to England.' Of course, he adds, there will be objections. These objections had nothing to do with the capture, transport, and forced labour of men, women, boys, and girls. Methuen anticipated the main barrier to adoption of his idea would be fear that 'the most usefull blacks may be carryed from our plantations to their great prejudice'. He was worried that an inter-American trade might harm *the English colonies in the Caribbean* if merchants took their best labourers and sold them to Spain. To get around this, he proposed the English parliament pass a law at its next session stipulating 'a proper enforcement of the bringing of them [enslaved labourers] from Africa' rather than English plantations. Methuen was advocating *for* the Middle Passage to be enforced by order of parliament.[11]

Transatlantic slavery was driven by many factors, notably the immense wealth generated by sugar plantations in the Caribbean, which in the 1700s drew in more enslaved Africans and, almost certainly, generated more wealth than Brazilian gold. Yet the stark fact remains that the two countries used in the classical example of comparative advantage—England and Portugal—were the dominant slave-trading powers of the age. In the 1700s, Britain would transport around 2.5 million enslaved people to the Americas and the Portuguese another 2.2 million. Portugal was the leading European slaver from the 1500s to the mid-1600s, at which time England—fighting off competition from the Dutch—took the top spot until the British parliament abolished its trade in 1807. After this time, Britain was replaced as the country importing most captives to the Americas by Portugal's junior partner: Brazil.[12] Together, Britain, Portugal, and their colonies were responsible for more than seven out of ten slave voyages.[13] Ricardo used the wine and cloth example in his *Principles*, just ten years after Britain abolished the slave trade. British dominance of the trade was well within living memory and slavery itself would still be legal in the British Empire for decades.

It was horrifying, at times, turning the yellowed pages of centuries-old letters in the quiet of the archives in London, to read the dispassionate description of a crime against humanity. Most shocking to me were the cold-blooded accounting of slave purchases for Humphry Morice, when he was Governor of the Bank of England in the 1720s. His papers include pre-printed, numbered receipts detailing the humans—one man and one girl in one, 'one large' boy in another—purchased in modern-day Ghana for various quantities of silk, cloth, gunpowder, and alcohol.[14] In a 1724 letter Morice instructed one of his slaving ships' captains to sell as many captives on the West African coast 'to the Portuguese and others for gold'.[15] John Methuen was not responsible for British slave-trading policy of the 1700s. There were more powerful individuals and forces at work. Yet the originator of the celebrated deal between England and Portugal in cloth and wine saw the arrangement as inextricably connected to England as a major transatlantic slave-trading power. There is barely a word on this in all the vast literature on comparative advantage. To begin recovering the history of these connections, we need to turn to the discovery of gold in Brazil and its impacts in West Africa.

The gold rush that forged Brazil

By the time Pedro II signed 'Petrus R' on the Cloth and Wine Treaty in 1703, he had been issuing orders related to gold in Brazil for almost a decade. In the 1680s, gold had been discovered by *bandeirantes*, small bands of explorers and fortune-hunters who had been searching the interior for Indigenous peoples to enslave. They had tried to keep it secret but rumours circulated. Pedro II decreed in 1694 that gold deposits would belong to those who find them—as long as they gave him 20 per cent, a payment known as the royal fifth. The decree worked: in the next few years, there were multiple, official discoveries of gold.[16] Then, in 1697, Pedro II got to feel the precious yellow metal with his own hands as the first shipments arrived in Lisbon. By 1700, as the immense scale of the discovery became clear, masses and celebrations were held in the Lisbon court, Brazilian historian Lucas Figueiredo tells us. Portuguese elites had reason to celebrate. Brazil had been in economic trouble since European plantations in the Caribbean had undercut its sugar trade. As Figueiredo writes: 'Portugal finally had its Eldorado.'[17] Gold would revitalize the whole economy, including commerce with England and the transatlantic slave trade.

An estimated 725 kg of Brazilian gold arrived in Lisbon in 1699; this rose to 4.35 tonnes, worth around £217 million in today's prices, in 1703.[18] Much more was to come. News of the finds had spread so widely by this time that large numbers of Portuguese left to seek their fortune in Brazil: it was the first modern gold rush. Methuen, so well connected with both the Portuguese political elite and English merchants, regularly updated his superiors on the 'very rich' annual 'Brasile fleets' arriving in Lisbon.[19] Although he does not explicitly mention Brazilian gold in correspondence, it is difficult to imagine that he would be unaware of it. He wrote, just a month after the Cloth and Wine Treaty was agreed upon, in the same letter as he discussed the slave trade: 'It is certain at Present that there never was so much ready money at any one time in America nor so great want of European goods.'[20]

The sheer scale of the Brazilian gold rush, which lasted almost a century, is hard to comprehend. The historian of Brazil's Golden Age, Charles Boxer, wrote: 'Nothing like it had been seen before and nothing like it was seen again until the California gold rush of 1849.'[21] The Governor of Rio de Janeiro wrote to King Pedro II in 1697 to tell him that reserves in just one mountain range 'extend in such a fashion' that the gold 'will last for a great length of time'.[22] Riverbeds turned up gold nuggets as big as potatoes: one was 1.3 kg in weight and had to be broken up using axes.[23] Portuguese Jesuit priest Antonil wrote in 1711, in a book that would later be banned for revealing colonial secrets: 'Every year a crowd of Portuguese and of foreigners come out in the fleets in order to go to the Mines. From the cities, towns, plantations, and backlands of Brazil, come Whites, Colored, and Blacks, together with many Amerindians.'[24] Deserters from the garrisons in the ports also flocked to the area. No one was immune from gold fever. Clergymen came, not to tend to the spirit, but to use their immunity from search to smuggle gold out of the region, sometimes in hollow wooden saints' images.[25]

The gold rush changed the shape of Brazil. When gold was discovered, Rio de Janeiro was a small colonial town of 8,000 people. The capital city of Portuguese Brazil was Salvador, on the coast closest to Africa. Most Portuguese stayed by the coast. In the 1710s and the 1720s there were more large gold strikes in what are now the Brazilian states of Mato Grosso and Goiás. Adding to the frenzy, around this time a rich seam of diamonds was discovered in what is now the town of Diamantina. Each new discovery pushed the

Portuguese border further out and brought death and destruction to Indigenous populations. The flow of gold and diamonds out to the coast, and then on to Europe, shifted the economic and political centre of Brazil to the south-west, with Rio de Janeiro replacing Salvador as the capital in 1763. New research by Portuguese economic historians estimate that Brazil legally exported more than 856 tonnes of gold from the 1720s to the 1800s, more than half of world gold production in that century.[26] Total production, including smuggled gold and pre-1720 exports, would be higher still.

The gold was still flowing in November 1768 when the British explorer Captain James Cook, on his first voyage to New Zealand and Australia, stopped in Rio de Janeiro for supplies. Cook's journal describes Rio as a flamboyant, despotically governed city with a White population one seventeenth, he estimated, of the Black population, 'many of whom are free'. On the local economy, he wrote: 'The riches of the place consist chiefly in the mines, which we supposed to lie far up the country, though we could never learn where.' Anyone caught on the roads leading to the mines by the troops who guarded them could be imprisoned or 'immediately hanged up upon the next tree'. He continued:

> Much gold is certainly brought from these mines, but at an expense of life that must strike every man, to whom custom has not made it familiar, with horror. No less than forty thousand negroes are annually imported on the king's account, to dig the mines and we were credibly informed, that the last year but one before we arrived here this number fell so short, probably from some epidemic disease that twenty thousand more were draughted from the town of Rio.[27]

Black gold

The chief town of Brazil's eighteenth-century gold rush—from which James Cook and all other foreigners were barred—was the town of Ouro Preto, literally 'black gold' (a name which comes apparently from the dark, steel-coloured gold). In the early 1700s, it was a potentially deadly four-to-six-week trek through thickly wooded, hostile terrain from Rio—before African labourers built a

1,600 km (1,000 mile) cobblestone route called the *Estrada Real* or Royal Road. You can still drive parts of the road and marvel at the enormous stones hauled into place to construct bridges. The first decade saw a famine as many miners took no time to plant crops or raise animals, a war between Portuguese miners and outsiders, and vast profits made by merchants selling cattle, tools, food, and enslaved workers to the miners. Finally, the Portuguese crown regained control of the gold trade and the royal fifth. In time, the makeshift mining camps of bare earth floors, walls of sticks and mud, and roofs of palms leaves or straw gave way to multistorey tiled houses with plastered walls and balconies.[28] By the 1730s, one eyewitness described the town of Villa Rica as the 'precious pearl of Brazil' and claimed that its chief merchants' trade 'incomparably exceed the most thriving of the leading merchants of Portugal'.[29] Although estimates vary, in the mid-1700s there were perhaps 30,000 people in Minas Gerais (literally 'General Mines', a Brazilian state), more than in North America's largest cities of Philadelphia and New York at the time.

Ouro Preto, once a wild El Dorado, is now a picturesque tourist town. Its baroque churches and red- and brown-tiled roofs are set on steep cobblestone roads and ringed by the mineral-rich hills. The jewellery shops sell gold, topaz, and other locally mined gems. Tourists, most of them Brazilian, come to the region for its renowned food—such as feijoada, a delicious black bean stew—and to explore the origins of Brazilian art, culture, and self-identity. Behind the beautiful art and architecture lies a bleaker story though, one that is still often hidden from today's tourists. Exploiting the Brazilian goldfields demanded vast numbers of manual labourers, the majority of whom came in chains from Africa. In the quarter of a century before 1700, 82,000 enslaved Africans were landed in Brazil; in the quarter of a century after 1700 it was almost three times that at 238,000.[30] Agricultural commodities, such as sugar, cotton, and tobacco, loom large in the history of Brazilian slavery. But so too does gold. The discovery of precious metals and stones in Minas Gerais was 'the decisive impetus' behind Brazil's booming slave trade of the eighteenth century, Laurentino Gomes, a popular Brazilian historian recently wrote.[31] The gold rush sucked in enslaved people from Africa and from Brazil's sugar, cotton, and tobacco fields, who were then replaced with fresh arrivals.

In trying to picture the early days of the Brazilian gold rush perhaps the closest we can get are the breathtaking images of Sebastião Salgado, from Minas Gerais, who photographed the gold frenzy in the Brazilian Amazon in 1986. His immense black-and-white images of the tens of thousands of muddy, barely clothed men carrying sacks of rock up 400-metre-high wooden ladders out of the open-pit mine look like they are from another time. In one image a muscular Black man, with only a cloth tied round his waist, grasps the barrel of a rifle pointed at him by a White soldier (see Figure 4.2).[32] The Brazilian gold rush also makes me think of the gold-mining town of Kamituga, in eastern Democratic Republic of Congo that I visited in 2014. The mine site—a short motorbike ride from town—was a vast, steep hillside that had been burrowed into by men and women, organized into small groups, using hand tools. The long tunnels were supported by frail wooden frames (one of these collapsed a few years later, leaving 50 miners dead).[33] Women and girls at the top of the hill crushed rocks with giant pestle and mortars all day in the hot sun. Armed Congolese soldiers illegally controlled the mineral washing station. Traders with small hand scales on the main street in town bought and sold gold dust, much of which was ultimately sold on to Dubai, Switzerland, and elsewhere.[34]

Figure 4.2: Serra Pelada Gold Mine, state of Pará, Brazil, 1986

Source: © Sebastião Salgado

In the heyday of Ouro Preto, there were perhaps 400 mines in the hillside and dozens are still open for visitors. At Mina St Rita, I walked along the narrow hand-dug passageway, now lit by electric lights, until the tunnel became too small for my six-foot frame. In these tiny, dark tunnels enslaved children as young as seven would dig away at the rock with picks and shovels. Jefferson, a 40-something African Brazilian and new father, showed me a whip topped with an armadillo tail used to keep order and a branding iron used to burn a symbol into the captives' skin. Brazil still wants to hide the link between gold and the 'tears, blood, and suffering' of the enslaved, he told me. In the artisanal market near the main square there is no plaque, but it is, according to Jefferson, where Africans were once sold.[35]

There is no place like Rio's Memorial of the New Blacks in Ouro Preto. The history of slavery is everywhere and nowhere. In the sturdy Casa dos Contos, an eighteenth-century tax collector's house, you can visit the basement slave quarters or *senzala*. As you enter, there is an eight-foot-high scale that, I only realized later, would have been used to weigh captives, who were sometimes sold by weight rather than by person. Elsewhere in Ouro Preto you can glimpse the history in the ecclesiastical bling of the Church of Nossa Senhora do Pilar, which is reputedly decorated with over 300 kg of gold. Or the Church of Saint Ephigenia—dedicated to a Black female saint from Ethiopia—believed to have been built from the proceeds of gold dust washed by Black women from out of their hair, under their nails, and inside tooth cavities.

The history of this corner of Brazil is only a small part of the transatlantic slave trade: the largest forced migration in human history. Of the 12 million men, women, and children transported, 2 million died on the middle passage. Millions more were killed in the interior of Africa by wars fuelled by the slave trade and forced marches to the coast.[36] Once in Brazil, the treatment of enslaved people was often particularly brutal. Jorge Benci, a Jesuit priest who lived in Brazil in the 1690s, wrote that some slaveholders 'for trifling offenses threw their slaves alive into furnaces, or killed them in various barbarous and inhuman ways'.[37] Other enslaved people would be tied to a cart and flogged, then cut with a razor and their 'wounds rubbed with salt, lemon juice, and urine'.[38] Work in the mines was so hard and dangerous that a slaveholder would only expect a young enslaved person to live for between seven to

12 years (although this was longer than the average seven-year life expectancy in sugar plantations).[39] Enslaved Africans often resisted by armed revolt or escaped to form self-governing communities known as *quilombo*, the most famous—the Quilombo dos Palmares, led by Brazilian folk heroes Zumbi and his wife Dandara—lasted for over eighty years before being conquered by the Portuguese in the decade the gold rush began.[40]

'A slave coast'

A lust for gold spurred European colonization from the beginning. The Portuguese explorers who travelled down the coast of Africa in the 1400s were searching for the source of the immense wealth controlled by the Malian Empire and transported across the Sahara. The Portuguese struck gold, literally, in 1470s, when they rounded the bulge of Africa and came to coastal villages in present-day Ghana, where the evidence of a booming trade in the precious metal was everywhere. The new sea route meant they could bring African gold into Europe directly, cutting out the intermediary. The Portuguese King, João II, ordered a fort be constructed in 1481, the first of its kind and a landmark in the history of imperialism, to protect the gold from rival powers and pirates. They called the region the Gold Coast and the fort El Mina, or The Mine.[41]

Similarly, the European conquest of the Americas was often driven by the search for precious metals. Christopher Columbus learned his trade in the 1480s along the coasts of West Africa and reached El Mina.[42] In Columbus' journal of his time in the Americas in late 1492, which covers about a hundred days, he mentioned gold, 'a metal most excellent above all others', at least 65 times.[43] The Spanish discovered rich silver deposits in the 1540s, much of which was exported to China, but little gold. Similarly, the Portuguese had continued to search in vain for the fabled golden El Dorado of the New World for the first 200 years of their occupation. This meant they were still reliant on the West African coast for gold.

Perhaps surprisingly, for most of the first two centuries, the Portuguese and Dutch—the leading early slave traders—discouraged slaving in Africa's Gold Coast. The reason is simple: it disrupted trade in the precious metal.[44] Compared to other parts of West Africa, very few captives were transported from the Gold Coast until the 1640s, and numbers remained relatively low until 1700. Then, in a few decades, the trade in humans shot up dramatically. It has been called a Slave Rush. The number of enslaved Africans taken from the Gold Coast across the Atlantic was three times higher in the first 25 years of the 1700s, rising to over 123,000 people, compared with the previous 25 years.[45] It was at this time, writes Howard French in *Born in Blackness*, that 'the Gold Coast went from being predominantly prized as a gold mine to being regarded above all as a slave mine'.[46] The Director of the Dutch West Indian Company wrote in 1705 that the area was 'changing completely into a slave coast, and the natives no longer concentrate on the search for gold, but make war on each other to acquire slaves'.[47]

The Gold Coast was transformed into a slave coast at about the same time as the Methuen Treaty was signed and the Brazilian gold rush began. The influx of Brazilian gold was a double blow for West Africa. First, West Africa became less important as a source of gold for European economies. Second, the high demand, and hence prices, for enslaved labour by miners and settlers in Minas Gerais boosted the slave trade.[48] It even led to a booming clandestine trade where ships left Rio with tobacco, rum, and gold to buy captives in West Africa: south–south trade cutting out Portugal.[49] (Such a slaving voyage from Brazil to Africa was the setting for English novelist Daniel Defoe's famous 1719 novel *Robinson Crusoe*, a story now frequently used to teach basic principles of economics!) These raids targeted Africans from El Mina as they were especially prized in Minas Gerais for having talent for finding and digging gold.[50] Slave raiders in West Africa helped to destroy trade in the Gold Coast, as it was not safe to travel with gold or dig, and gold exports plummeted. According to the historian of the Royal African Company, the English company that monopolized the African trade, gold takings in West African forts 'fell away to very little' around 1700 and never recovered.[51] The West African gold trade only really picked up again after the abolition of slavery—following revolts of enslaved peoples—in the nineteenth century.[52]

In total, perhaps 1 million of the 5 million Africans transported to Brazil worked in the mines. The Brazilian gold rush supercharged the transatlantic slave trade. It was with this slave-mined gold, which entered England unrecorded by Customs, that Portugal made good its debts to English cloth merchants.

When John Methuen died in Lisbon in 1706, his son Paul (later Sir Paul) took him to be buried in Westminster Abbey, the traditional resting place of Britain's kings, queens, and venerated poets, soldiers, and scientists, including, most prominently, Isaac Newton. To this day, the substantial marble memorial to John and Paul Methuen still stands. It is in a neglected aisle, I found out when I visited in 2022, and is usually roped-off when the Abbey is opened to tourists and used to store chairs. Nonetheless, it is in one of the most venerated buildings in English history, perhaps only 20 paces from the Cosmati Pavement in front of the high altar where King Charles III was crowned in 2023. One of the guides let me pass the black-and-gold rope barrier to see the Methuen memorial. Above a tribute to Methodist-founder John Wesley and directly under a large window are two baby angels either side of a handsome plaque with still clearly legible script: 'Near this place lies the body of John Methuen Esqr who died abroad in the service of his country.'[53]

I have thought time and again of the contrast between the resting place of Methuen—in 'a building that takes memory seriously' as the Abbey audio guide puts it—and that of the 20-year-old African woman in an unloved part of Rio, nameless and totally forgotten but for the care of one family. Two humans on different ends of the transatlantic slave trade, not even equal in death.

After Methuen's death, his diplomatic duties were taken over for a time by the British consul-general for Portugal, John Milner. In 1706, Milner wrote to his superiors in London to criticize John Methuen for not being firmer with the Portuguese in how they conducted the war, although he did praise his predecessor's commercial treaty:

> The great quantities of our wollen manufactures and other Commodities they [the Portuguese] take from England is a great advantage to us and a very beneficial trade to England, and itt may be no country even in peace in proportion to itts bigness takes such a quantity of our manufactures and this improves every day and will doe more as their country grows richer which itt must necessarily do if they can continue the importation of so much gold from the Rio [de Janeiro] every year.[54]

Modern economic historians, such as Leonor Costa from the University of Lisbon and her co-authors, strike a similar note, writing in 2016: 'The re-export of gold coin or bullion was a necessity to finance the [Portuguese] kingdom's deficit', two thirds of which was with Britain.[55]

Gold from Brazil and captives from Africa were essential elements in the English and Portuguese trade of cloth and wine. What remains to be seen is the impact of the influx of gold on Britain: a story that comes back to one of the most famous names in science and, eventually, to David Ricardo.

5

Newton's Mint

How Isaac Newton grew rich from Brazilian
gold and Ricardo's family came to London

Looking towards the central nave of Westminster Abbey is a monument to Sir Isaac Newton. Completed by the same sculptor (Michael Rysbrack) as the Methuen memorial a few paces away, it is far more prominent and imposing. A life-sized Newton, in a toga, rests on a pile of heavy books. Above him hangs a globe of the night sky. Underneath, a frieze of boys look through telescopes and prisms and—more relevant for us—feed a metal bar into a furnace and pour gold coins from a jar (see Figure 5.1). These speak to Newton's lesser-known later career at the Royal Mint, where he worked from 1696 to his death in 1727, for most of that time as Master of the Mint.

When the English and Dutch destroyed the Spanish Treasure Fleet at Vigo Bay in 1702, it brought the Portuguese back into the English sphere of influence, as we saw in Chapter 3. The Spanish silver and gold were sent to the Mint—then housed in ramshackle wooden buildings inside the walls of the Tower of London—to be catalogued and turned into English coins. The items seized at Vigo were weighed and assessed. A list—held in the British Library—describes objects more familiar in a pirate adventure: 'pieces of eight', 'Cup of Mother of Pearl', '148 Guineas', a silver 'spitting pott', 'four snuff boxes', and large treasure chests stamped with initials (also, bizarrely, a gold 'ear picker'). In the bottom right-hand corner of the list is the signature of the person overseeing the cataloguing of treasure from the Spanish Americas, applying the same meticulous detail as he gave to the movement of the stars, Isaac Newton.[1]

The gold standard

Cambridge historian of science Patricia Fara tells the often-overlooked story of Newton's time in London—where he lived longer than in Cambridge—in *Life after Gravity* (2021).[2] Newton immersed himself in the politics and economics of the day and grew wealthy from his role at the Mint. As the Lucasian Professor of Mathematics at Cambridge, he had earned £100 per year (equivalent to £36,000). As Master of the Mint he was paid five times as much and got an additional 'master's fee' for every coin minted.[3] The more gold that poured into the Tower of London, the richer he got. In 1702, Newton gave up the Cambridge professorship and a few years later was earning nearly £3,500 a year (£1.26 million today). At his death, Newton was worth £32,000—approximately £11.5 million today— and left a clutch of fine silver. These included, Fara writes, extravagant items such as two silver urinals or chamber pots for male guests to relieve themselves during dinner, apparently behind a screen.[4]

Newton's Mint turned the gold into guineas, coins about the size of a US quarter or British tenpence coin but heavier, at 8 grams. (These were dwarfed by the largest gold coins minted in Brazil that felt—when I got to hold them at the Smithsonian Museum in Washington DC—as heavy as an egg in my hand.) The guinea still evokes a quintessential, old-school British feeling associated with the novels of Charles Dickens and prestigious horse races like the Newmarket Guineas. The name, as historians such as David Olusoga have pointed out, comes from West Africa's Guinea Coast (a large area that includes the Gold Coast) where the first gold was sourced. But this has led to the mistaken idea that Britain was mainly minting African gold in the eighteenth century. The switch to minting guineas from Brazilian gold in the first decade of the 1700s is often overlooked even by experts.[5] Newton, according to Fara's biography, knew that England's wealth rested on the triangular trade in enslaved people. She wrote that he was minting gold 'dug up by Africans whose friends and relatives were being shipped across the Atlantic'.[6] When I presented Patricia Fara with evidence that Newton was actually minting gold dug up in Brazil by Africans

Figure 5.1: Detail from Isaac Newton's memorial in Westminster Abbey

Source: © Dean and Chapter of Westminster

who *had* been enslaved and shipped across the Atlantic, she told me she regretted not having known about the Brazilian connection earlier: 'this links Newton even more directly to the trade in enslaved peoples than I had realised'.[7]

Newton's own writing confirms the origin of the gold. In 1701, Newton wrote: 'We can have no bullion but from the West Indies [South and Central America] belonging to Spain and Portugal.'[8] In 1715, he wrote that the gold coined in the ten years from 1702 to 1712 'came from Portugal and some of it from Jamaica'.[9] And in a note to the Treasury in 1717, Newton recounted the history of West England: 'full of Gold' from Portugal. Its merchants 'did pour that Money in upon us' bringing 'into the Mint great Quantities of Gold'.[10]

During Newton's time as Master of the Mint, Britain took its first steps towards the gold standard: a money system based on a fixed value of gold. Many historians—and others such as David Ricardo—trace its origins to a 1717 report that Newton prepared for the Treasury.[11] From this time, Britain, in practice and later in law, adopted a gold standard, which it followed for most of the next 200 years (and was then continued by the US until 1971). Newton's report put forward a new estimate for the value of gold against silver. A gold guinea should be worth 21 shillings, he wrote, just over £1 at the time, and parliament accepted his suggestion. But, the standard story goes, Newton, the greatest mathematician of his generation, miscalculated. Gold was still valued too highly, meaning it flooded into the country while silver went overseas—much of it eventually to China—where it was worth more.[12]

But the difference in the price of gold between Britain and continental Europe was small. The French historian Pierre Vilar rejects the idea that the gold standard came from 'the small technical detail of a slight over-valuation of gold in terms of silver'. Instead, Vilar suggests, the influx of gold into England was due to a series of 'political, economic, maritime and colonial victories', including the Methuen Treaties with Portugal in 1703 and the English capture of the Spanish *asiento* in 1713—the contract to carry enslaved people to the Spanish Empire that John Methuen had written about to his superiors. This is the more convincing explanation.[13] A historian of gold in Britain, Timothy Alborn, writes of bullion imports from Brazil: 'Britain could never have established a sustainable gold standard without this gold, much of which remained in circulation, melted and reminted several times over, well into the nineteenth century.'[14]

What Newton recorded, as the horse-drawn coin presses of the Mint ran from 5 am to midnight turning Brazilian gold into British guineas, is confirmed by later studies.[15] Pierre Vilar calculated that in the 33 years between 1694 and 1727—a period that tallies with Newton's three decades at the Mint—England minted around £14 million in gold coin. That's almost as much gold as England minted (£15 million) in the 136 years before 1694. The spike in production Vilar puts down to: 'The constant surplus of England's trading balance with Portugal and Brazil [which] drained away gold [to London].'[16] The gold flows in Lisbon grew even more after

Newton's death, from an average of 8 tonnes a year in the 1720s to a peak of more than 11 tonnes a year in the 1740s. From there they slowly declined to the end of the century. Recent research by Nuno Palma, an economic historian originally from Portugal and now at the University of Manchester, suggests that the Brazilian gold rush doubled the amount of gold in Europe.[17] Portuguese economic historians estimate that 80 per cent of Brazil's gold production reached Portugal.[18] And others estimate that between half and three-quarters of the gold that arrived in Lisbon ended up in English hands.[19] Every gram was bound up in the Atlantic slave trade.

We know exactly how the English got their hands on the gold, because some of the merchants have left records and accounts. John Koster, a merchant from Liverpool, started trading Portuguese gold in London in 1772 before moving out to Lisbon. Over the next two decades, he wrote, 'I was in the habit of purchasing large quantities of gold bar and dust and exported it to England in his Majesty's packets and ships of war.'[20] These were the two main ways gold reached England. The 'packets' were five Post Office boats—originally set up by John Methuen's son—that went back and forth between Lisbon and Falmouth in Cornwall, the closest major English port to Portugal.[21] The 'ships of war' were navy vessels that docked in Plymouth in Devon or Chatham in Kent. The gold was then transferred to London in armed coaches or spent in the local economy. (The Cornish and Devon ports explain Newton's story about the West of England being full of Portuguese gold.) Both the Post Office and navy ships were heavily armed and had diplomatic immunity from searches by Portuguese customs.[22] It was technically illegal to export gold from Portugal, but as Koster explains, it was not too difficult. The gold, he wrote, was 'brought from the Brazils clandestinely, but it was done without much apparent risk, nor was there any great secrecy observed in the purchase of it at Lisbon: it seems as if it had been known to, but winked at by, the government'. Once in London, he sold most of his gold to the Bank of England.[23]

We also know about English merchants who moved from the more familiar trade in cloth and wine into gold. One was William Braund (1695–1774), who initially imported woollen textiles into Lisbon for port wine exports back to England. But when the devastating Lisbon earthquake of 1755—which left thirty to forty thousand people dead and shocked Europe—disrupted business, Braund started taking payment for wool in gold, became a bullion dealer, and did not look back.[24]

Several historians have pointed out the broad similarities between the quantities of gold Portugal received from Brazil, the Portuguese trade deficit with England, and the quantity of gold coins minted at the Tower of London. Between 1750 and 1769, for example, Lisbon imported an average of 8.8 tonnes of gold per year and the Mint coined an average of 5.2 tonnes per year.[25] By this analysis, England captured around 59 per cent of Portugal's colonial gold. The trade was no secret. Adam Smith, in a section of *The Wealth of Nations* that David Ricardo must have read, wrote that: 'Almost all our gold, it is said, comes from Portugal' and Portugal's from 'the Brazils'.[26] But the connections, and its implications, have been buried.

Britain's industrial and financial revolution

One story often told—in museums in Ouro Preto in Brazil or in references to the Brazilian gold rush—is that the gold made Portugal immensely rich. This is true. It produced Lisbon's baroque churches dripping with gilded wood and gold and fuelled grandiose projects. In the 1710s, King Pedro II's son, João V, started to build a small convent for 13 friars in Mafra outside Lisbon. The building project— on the back of the Brazilian wealth—ended up as the immense 1,200-room Palace of Mafra, with an 88-metre-long library and a basilica with six organs.[27] The rush inspired a new range of horse-drawn coaches in Portugal decorated in 'unparalleled magnificence' with gold-covered wooden sculptures, according to the historian Charles Boxer.[28] New heights of decorative bling in Portugal, however, were only part of the story.

As well as making one of the great figures in the history of science immensely wealthy, the influx of more than half of Brazil's gold to Britain in the eighteenth century helped balance British trade deficits, solidify London as a financial centre, and allow the country to fight expensive wars on the European continent. Brazilian gold was not *the* cause of Britain's rise to prominence in the eighteenth century: that is a much larger story, beyond the scope of this chapter, about the agricultural and industrial revolutions, Caribbean sugar plantations, the Atlantic slave trade, and Britain's empire in India, among other factors. But the wealth from Brazil was pushing in the same directions as these other forces and aided Britain's growing global power.

The quantity of gold coin circulating in England increased from £9.25 million in early 1701 to £26 million in 1780.[29] This was a great stimulus to economic activity, as in an era before the widespread use of paper money, increasing the number of coins in circulation was the only way to expand the money supply other than the trust-destroying practice of debasing coins (reducing the gold content while retaining their face value). These effects went far beyond London, as can be seen in the widespread use of gold in the West of England. In the 1730s in Cornwall, almost all tax payments were made in Portuguese bullion.[30] Britain also had a persistent trade deficit with the Baltics, where it got much of its timber for ship building, and East Asia, from where it imported spices, silk, and porcelain, among other items, in the early 1700s. Britain imported from these markets more than it exported, and thus had to pay the balance in hard currency and European merchants shipped silver to China where it was worth more. The inflows of gold from Brazil, via Portugal, were crucial to balance Britain's overall trading.

London's direct access to large quantities of gold from Brazil, via Portugal, gave it a strategically important place in the European financial market. When merchants in other European trading and financial centres like Amsterdam, Paris, and Hamburg wanted gold they had to get it second-hand from London. Adam Smith in *The Wealth of Nations* referred to this as the 'round-about trade'. He wrote: 'In facilitating all the different round-about foreign trades of consumption which are carried on in Great Britain consists the principal advantage of the Portugal trade.'[31] Still, Smith argued dubiously that direct trading was always a better use of capital than the round-about trade. The eighteenth century saw London overtake Amsterdam as the chief financial centre of Europe, creating great opportunities for bankers and other professions such as lawyers and accountants. The large and stable supply of Brazilian gold helped underpin and solidify this development.

According to the economic historian H.E.S. Fisher, 'without the expansion of Brazilian gold output on which so much else turned, English commercial, financial and industrial advance would have been even slower'. Along with others, Fisher judges that Brazilian gold helped to prepare the British economy for 'take off' in the Industrial Revolution.[32] It also had political and military impacts.

Joseph Ricardo of Amsterdam

The eighteenth century can be seen as a century-long conflict between Britain and France over how to divide up the world. When wars broke out on the European continent, Britain did at times commit troops to military combat but more often subsidized other European powers to fight for its interests. In this, British foreign policy often rested on Brazilian gold—the hidden foundation of the celebrated trade in English cloth and Portuguese wine—to pay allies. For example, when Britain entered the War of Austrian Succession in 1742, it looked to pay a subsidy to its Austrian allies. The leading London merchant and MP Thomas Gore wrote to the British Prime Minister that year offering to source the gold from Portugal: 'I can supply funds and credits at Lisbon sufficient to answer this service.'[33] Brazilian gold was also crucial for Britain during the Seven Years' War, the global conflict it fought against France and its allies in Europe, the Americas, and Asia in the 1750s and 1760s (known in North America as the French and Indian War). A small role in wartime gold trading was played by someone with a familiar name.

The British government maintained a network of financial agents scattered across the European continent, responsible for supplying money to pay for muskets, wagons of bread for the troops, fodder for the horses, and whatever else was needed for the Seven Years' War. They were managed by an official in London working for the Treasury. A letter from August 1758 survives from the London official to a banker in Amsterdam on the subject of '500 ducats' (the gold coin of the Netherlands). The gold was intended for the Prussian troops fighting on Britain's side against the French. The letter is written not in English or Dutch but in Portuguese. The person tasked with supplying the ducats was Joseph Ricardo, who retained the language of his ancestors expelled from Portugal centuries before.[34] (Although it cannot be proved, the Dutch gold may have come from Brazil as records of William Braund, the British wool-turned-gold trader, show he sent five shipments of gold to Amsterdam from Lisbon in warships in the early years of the war.[35])

Joseph Ricardo, one of the founders of the Amsterdam Stock Exchange, had a good war. In its first year, 1757, his business multiplied fivefold. As the war progressed, Dutch capitalists, Joseph among them, began investing heavily in British securities. By 1762, he had half of his money invested in Britain. Needing to keep a close eye on its management, Joseph sent his youngest son, Abraham, to London. Abraham Ricardo stayed and took up one of the 12 official broker positions then allocated to Jewish traders in the City.[36] He married Abigail, a member of the Portuguese-Jewish community, and started a family. Their third child, born in 1772, they named David Ricardo.[37] The future economist was born into a world and a profession shaped, at least in part, by the huge influx of gold from Brazil.

'The high price of gold'

We saw in Chapter 1 how David Ricardo was sent back to Amsterdam as a child, started working in the London markets at 14, broke with his family at 21 over his choice to marry outside the religion of his birth, and then used his trading skills to become wealthy and independent. We have seen how, when his wife gave birth to a stillborn girl, they went to the spa town of Bath to recover and Ricardo happened upon Adam Smith's *Wealth of Nations*. What we have not seen is how Ricardo first went from being a wealthy stockbroker to a renowned thinker on economics and how this too was connected to colonial gold.

Ricardo became a political economist in the context of Britain's economic tribulations during the long wars against the French, which broke out again in 1792, three years after the epoch-changing French Revolution. Five years into the war, Britain faced dwindling gold supplies and bank runs as the public feared French invasion. In response, the Bank of England issued for the first time £1 and £2 paper notes and an act of parliament decreed that these could no longer be convertible to gold. The bank abandoned the gold standard. A satirical cartoon (by James Gillray) from that year shows an old lady, with a dress made entirely of notes, sitting on a golden chest stamped 'Bank of England'. The Prime Minister, William Pitt the Younger, lunges forward, grasping her waist in one hand while reaching into her pockets with the other to pick out gold coins, while the lady shouts 'Rape! Murder!' (The title of the cartoon, 'The Old Lady of Threadneedle Street', gave the Bank of England its nickname.[38]) Ending the convertibility of paper notes to gold freed up the Bank of England to issue more notes but prompted fears that it was inflating prices.

Critics pointed to other causes of inflating prices such as failure of harvests, exchange-rate differences, and the decline to virtually nothing of the century-long gold flows from the Brazilian gold rush. John Koster, the Liverpool merchant who described how he smuggled gold out of Lisbon, wrote that in the 1790s 'the quantity of gold at the Lisbon market began sensibly to diminish' and 'to fall off gradually'.[39] This is confirmed by recent research by Portuguese economic historians, who show that authorities in Lisbon recorded 80 tonnes or more of gold imports every decade between 1720s and 1760s, before it fell to only 12 tonnes in the 1790s. In 1797, the year the Bank of England stopped converting notes into gold, just 0.1 tonnes of gold was recorded as entering Lisbon.[40] The lack of gold flow was due, in part, to Portugal finally having a trade surplus with England, as its Brazilian cotton flooded into the new factories in northern England, replacing supply cut off after the British loss in the American Revolutionary War in 1783. According to the great French economic historian Fernand Braudel: 'It is probably no accident that precisely when her trade balance with Portugal went into deficits, thus interrupting or slowing down the flow of Brazilian gold, England should have proceeded towards the next logical stage: that of paper money.'[41]

Inflation spiked again in 1809, which prompted Ricardo to publish his first article on economics, 'The high price of gold', in the *Morning Chronicle*. He blamed the Bank of England and other banks for issuing too many notes, which, he argued, had pushed up the market price of gold and other commodities. The article was a great success, sparking a parliamentary inquiry and reopening a national conversation. For Ricardo and his supporters the excess issue of notes was the sole cause of inflation and should be reduced.

The spike in gold prices in England that Ricardo had noticed may also be related to, if not fully explained by, interruptions in the supply of Brazilian gold. In 1806, Napoleon had imposed a continental blockade closing European ports and trade to the British. Just as in the time of Methuen, Portugal was the pawn caught in a great game of chess played by Britain and France. All of Europe fell into line with France except Portugal, which remained—in part thanks to the legacy of the Methuen Treaties—friendly to the British. Enraged, Napoleon launched his armies against Portugal. In November 1807, just days ahead of the French invasion, Portugal's Prince Regent João VI (the great-great-grandson of Pedro II), after crisis meetings at the Palace of Mafra, ordered the transfer of the entire royal court to Brazil, including the government offices, law courts, archives, treasure, and employees. As rumours of the voyage spread, more people flocked to the docks to join the exodus. Later that month, around 10,000 people, with their worldly possessions stuffed into bags and chests, loaded themselves onto a flotilla of 50 ships. In the confusion and panic some valuables were left behind: boxes of priceless books from the Royal Library, 14 cartloads of silver from the cathedral, and the royal carriages of 'unparalleled magnificence'. Four British warships escorted the Portuguese elite across the Atlantic, safe from Napoleon's troops.[42]

After 54 days of a cramped and dirty voyage—during which time ladies shaved off their hair due to an infestation of fleas—the Portuguese royal family arrived in Brazil. It was the first time a European monarch had set foot in the Americas and it would change the trajectories of both countries. For a while, it turned off the tap of gold from Brazil via Portugal to London. The Liverpool merchant John Koster wrote that the gold trade was 'a mere trifle for some years before the emigration of the Prince Regent [João VI] and the government, and since that epoch the supply [of gold] from thence has ceased totally and entirely'.[43] The detailed records of Portuguese imports of gold from Brazil simply end in 1807, as the court and its bureaucracy moved to Brazil.[44]

Ricardo's first article, which appeared two years after the Portuguese royal court fled Lisbon, does not ignore the South American origin of Britain's gold. He mentions 'the discovery of mines in America, which so greatly increased the quantity of money' in Europe. His stated ambition in the paper was to reform the monetary system, so that Britain's paper money, regardless of the demand from Europe or 'whatever supply might be poured in from the mines in America', would maintain its value 'as invariable as gold'.[45] Ricardo's plan was for the Bank of England to commit to converting notes into gold again, so as to crack down on excessive issuing of notes. He suggested that notes should only be convertible into large, unwieldy gold bars rather than coins, so that the Bank did not have to amass large quantities of gold. A few of these gold bars were created but the plan was never fully implemented.[46] Ricardo knew the Bank of England through his work and this essay is seen by some historians of economics as a high point of his thinking.[47]

Even when Ricardo was motivated by questions of real national importance, the way he answered them showed his tilt towards abstract theory. His first article claimed that 'the laws that regulate the distribution of the precious metals throughout the world' are the same as those for other commodities.[48] Notice how this framing of distribution by impersonal laws of the market sucks all power, politics, and history from transatlantic gold flows. There is no Royal Navy, no diplomacy, no slavery. Ricardo's article brought him the attention and friendship of fellow economist Thomas Robert Malthus. But when, in 1811, Malthus, in a letter, challenged Ricardo's theory on precious metals as too narrow and excluding other reasons for the flows, the stockbroker would not be deterred. The way Ricardo responded is very revealing. He distinguished between how countries act and how countries *would* act if they 'truly understood their own interest' and were 'alive to their advantage and profit'. The actual practice of countries, he dismissed as not worthy of attention: 'a question of fact and not of science'.[49] Ricardo had a very peculiar definition of science and a mind drawn to what would happen in an idealized world of his imagination.

Ricardo's first article on gold is the earliest reference in English, some historians of economics suggest, to 'laws' in economics in the sense of stable relationships between variables: laws that have been compared to Newton's physics and Euclid's geometry.[50] In the economic realm, the laws were reliant on stable and predictable traders. 'It is self-interest which regulates all the speculations of trade,' and only self-interest, Ricardo wrote, adding tellingly 'we should not know where to stop if we admitted any other rule of action'.[51] (This, to my mind, is the early 1800s version of 'greed is good'.) Ricardo's theoretical self-interested traders were modelled on the gold merchants of London, Amsterdam, Paris, and Hamburg, he said. Like him, they possessed excellent knowledge of the market and quickly responded to fluctuations in prices.[52] As later economic thinkers knew, and we have forgotten, these traders are the origin of 'economic human': the self-maximizing creature at the heart of later economic models that have shaped our time.[53] Ricardo's economic theories were birthed in the Stock Exchange.

The real history of the exchange of English cloth and Portuguese wine—which cannot be told without Brazilian gold and African labourers—has brought it us back to the originator of the story. We have seen that Ricardo's four magic numbers, believed by some to be the deepest truth in economics, are 'a mathematical façade behind which the actual historical social relations of production of the real England and Portugal are deliberately taken out of the equation' as Warwick's Matthew Watson described. These 'explicitly oppressive social relations of production based on slave labour and the imperial policing of national hierarchies' have conceptually disappeared in the orthodoxy.[54]

Perhaps that vanishing act is the real magic of Ricardo's four numbers.

6

The Empire of Free Trade

*The cost of British 'free' trade with India
and Brazil and why economics should
not be called the 'dismal science'*

The exchange of English cloth and Portuguese wine may be a terrible example of mutually beneficial trade, but, a sceptical reader might ask, what is the broader significance of its hidden history?

The history of other periods and places, it is true, could tell a much rosier story: of how trade has expanded peoples' worlds, created new languages and flows of news, provided a more diverse range of food and goods to ordinary people.[1] The sceptical reader might continue: the history told in the last three chapters is not relevant to the modern world as it relates to the 1700s when an imperialistic, exploitative, and gold-obsessed approach to economic matters was embraced in Britain. The ideas of Adam Smith and David Ricardo swept away that old 'mercantile system'.[2] Both men opposed slavery. They helped reorientate Britain towards genuine free trade, the argument might continue, that was anti-imperialist and anti-slave trade. Classical economics ushered in a period of peaceful and win–win trade. This chapter examines these counter-arguments.

As we saw, David Ricardo took the England–Portugal story from Adam Smith. The two classical economists, however, drew radically different lessons from the same trade between two countries. In Ricardo's hands it was an abstract, numerical argument for why trade between weaker and stronger economies benefitted both sides. In Smith's, it was a historical episode that showed the problems with the type of economics he wished to explode. Smith called the bad, old economics the 'mercantile system'.

Smith's argument went like this. The Methuen Treaty was *not* about free trade at all. It locked in a certain pattern of foreign trade that benefitted a few and disadvantaged the many. The few who benefitted were the British wool producers (such as John Methuen's brother) and those in the Portuguese wine trade. The many who lost out were the 'great body of the people' in Britain who had to pay more for wine from France and could not 'buy whatever they want of those who sell it cheapest'.[3] The Cloth and Wine Treaty, he argued, served the jealous, small-minded, and nationalistic interests of a few merchants. *The Wealth of Nations* was published in the same year as the US Declaration of Independence and married this advocacy for trade free from merchant control with an anti-imperial stance. European countries, Smith argued, should let their colonists become politically and economically free.[4]

It was David Ricardo, however, who became the fountainhead of international trade theory, and he had a very different take on imperialism and power. He was part of a generation of European 'liberal' thinkers who came to believe that the alleged superior rationality of Europeans justified their overseas empires.[5] Smith, part of the earlier generation, had placed his writing on economics in a world profoundly warped by public and private power. About a third of *The Wealth of Nations* is about empire. It argued that private interests, such as the British East India Company, had 'intimidated' parliament and confounded common sense to enrich themselves while exploiting their home countries and the colonies. Governments, Smith argued, should take 'an extensive view of the general good' and ignore the clamour of merchants and manufacturers whose interests were often 'directly opposite to that of the great body of the people'.[6] By contrast, Ricardo mostly avoided writing about empire or the nefarious intent of businesspeople.[7] His two closest economist friends—James Mill and T.R. Malthus—were both long-term employees of the East India Company, as was James' son, John Stuart Mill. Only occasionally did Ricardo tear himself away from abstractions and make some brief asides on the overseas trade with India and Brazil of his day.

When British elites embraced free trade, they did not reject empire but created a new kind of 'free-trade empire'. The sheer power of Britain, with its industrial and technological advantages and world-beating navy, allowed it to access a vast new labour force and areas of fertile soil in the Global South without the expense and complications of governing these directly.[8] This was an informal empire that complemented the formal empire under direct control. Between the formal and informal empires was the special case of India, ruled by a privately held British corporation.

How Britain underdeveloped India

During David Ricardo's most active years as a political economist, British factories were flooding India with cheap machine-made cotton goods. This triumph for British industry was the result of over a century of government support and protection. In 1700, two years before the Methuen Treaty with Portugal, the English parliament outlawed the import of superior, printed cotton cloth from India and eventually criminalized selling Indian cottons.[9] Protected from competition from India, cotton cloth production in Britain was revolutionized by technological improvements such as the flying shuttle, the spinning jenny, and the spinning mule in the mid-eighteenth century. The labour-intensive weaving in northern England of slave-grown cotton produced the factories that would ultimately be at the centre of the world's first industrial revolution (see Figure 6.1). Never before had so many products been produced so quickly or cheaply. These new factories allowed a Manchester mill worker to be 400 times more productive than an Indian weaver. Their machine-made products would eventually eliminate both British and Indian handweavers.[10]

After decades of petitioning from mill owners, in 1813 the British parliament ended the East India Company's monopoly of trade with India. In the next 20 years, British cotton exports to India increased more than fifty times. It destroyed what had been India and the world's richest area of textile manufacturing in Bengal. Harvard historian Sven Beckert, in *Empire of Cotton* (2014), describes this episode as 'the world's most rapid and cataclysmic deindustrialization'.[11] According to one estimate, the population of Dhaka, the city at the centre of cloth production, fell from 150,000

Figure 6.1: Cotton, at the centre of global trade in the 1800s

Photo: Karl Wiggers on Unsplash

in the 1810s to 20,000 by 1840.[12] As Europe and North America boomed, India's share of global industrial production declined, from 25 per cent in 1750 to just 2 per cent by 1900.[13] In the twentieth century, Gandhi would put homespun cotton and the image of the spinning wheel at the heart of India's struggle for independence.

This commercial cataclysm is hard to reconcile with Adam Smith's vision of an economic system built on liberty and justice. What did David Ricardo think?

During a debate at the East India Company in London in 1823, ten years after British cottons were allowed into India, Ricardo denied that 'great injury' had been done to Indian weavers. He said:

> 'Undoubtedly some injury was done to that [Indian manufacturing] class; but one would think the Hon. Gent. would have turned his attention to the accompanying good. ... Those [British merchants] who exported must have got a return in something else they had not before had. If we send cotton goods to India, they must be paid for. Our cotton goods were purchased with other manufactures; new branches of trade were thus struck out, and both countries were ultimately

benefited. The one country was employed in making machinery and working it, and the other in fabricating those manufactures by which our cottons were paid for.'[14]

Ricardo had remarkable confidence that British trade with India was mutually beneficial. A year earlier, he said it was 'so clear and self-evident, that he wondered any man could doubt it'.[15] And yet he was noticeably vague on even the most basic details. What were those 'other manufactures' that 'must have' been produced in exchange for British cotton cloth? Ricardo failed to mention that the Indian economy was being transformed into one that exported raw materials such as unspun cotton, indigo, and, increasingly, opium for the Chinese market. He also conveniently ignored the political and colonial context of the trade.

Adam Smith had criticized the 'strange absurdity' of the British East India Company, whose directors were not just traders but 'sovereigns of the countries which they have conquered'.[16] This had been the case for over fifty years when Ricardo spoke. In 1765, amid a string of aggressive military conquests, Robert Clive of the East India Company (whose statue still stands in the political heart of London) had secured the right to collect tax and revenues from the population of Bengal, Indian's richest province.[17] This meant that instead of paying for Indian goods with silver from Britain, the Company 'recycled' a quarter of the tax revenues it collected from the peasants to pay them for their products.[18] The British, effectively, bought the goods for nothing. What's more, the Company used its political and economic might to reorganize the cloth supply chain, removing Indian intermediaries and replacing them with a new bureaucracy staffed with paid Company agents. As Sven Beckert wrote, 'The encroachment of British power on the subcontinent meant that [Indian] weavers increasingly lost their ability to set prices for cloth.'[19] The coercive monopoly and the free merchants conspired together to wreck the Indian economy; Ricardo did not mention it.

The Great Divergence

Aside from India, how strong is the argument that classical economics helped usher in an era in which Britain turned away from imperial conquest and towards free trade? Not very. Instead, there is a strong continuity between the Methuen Treaty and a rash of 'unequal treaties' in the nineteenth century that showed a similar cocktail of naval power, unequal terms, and 'informal empire'. One of the first of those treaties was in 1810 with Brazil.

Ricardo only mentioned Brazil once, in a speech at the East India Company in June 1822. He was pressed to give an example of where free trade was working well. This was not a question of letting France or Spain into Britain's trade in India, he reassured his audience. If they wanted to see the benefits of unrestricted trade, Ricardo said, they should look at how, by 'taking off restrictions, the trade to the Brazils and to the free-states of South America had increased in a wonderful degree'.[20]

We saw in Chapter 5 that the Portuguese royal family fled Lisbon in 1807, guarded by the British Royal Navy. Before leaving the royals had signed a secret deal with the British. When the Portuguese King arrived in South America, he made good on the agreement by declaring the colony's ports open to ships of any country. This ended Portugal's monopoly of Brazilian trade. Two years later, in 1810, the two countries signed a preferential trade deal that reduced import duties on British goods entering Brazil. The British would pay only 15 per cent compared to 16 per cent for the Portuguese and 24 per cent for everyone else. British goods, excluded from Europe due to Napoleon's blockade, flooded into Brazil, including, according to legend, ice skates, shark-fin corsets, and bed-warming pans. In exchange Brazil provided raw materials, produced with enslaved labour, much to the benefit of its White, agricultural elites. (Britain, which had recently outlawed the slave trade, had the Portuguese King sign a separate deal to gradually abolish his country's trade in people, which it did not do.[21])

The British ambassador to Portugal, Viscount Strangford, who negotiated the treaty in Rio, revealed the real power imbalance behind the deal in letters to his boss, the British Foreign Secretary George Canning. He crowed about the 'much greater Concessions' he had extracted from Brazil, to which he said Britain was entitled 'in consequence of Her successful Interference for the Preservation of Portugal'. If Britain encouraged the new country, Brazil could 'become such a powerful Engine in Her hands'.[22] Just as with the Methuen Treaty, the Portuguese royals bought protection for their new home as much as products.

In the year Ricardo offered up Brazil as a 'wonderful' example of free trade, Britain was in the process of prising the country and its South American neighbours free from the Portuguese and Spanish Empires and into its own economic orbit. In September 1822, Prince Pedro (great-great-great-grandson of King Pedro II, who had signed Methuen's Treaty) declared Brazil independent while his father, the King, was back in Portugal. By summer 1823, the Brazilian Navy led by a renowned freelance British admiral, Thomas Cochrane, had chased off the Portuguese Navy.[23] George Canning, back as British Foreign Secretary, in 1824 summed up the mood in London: 'Spanish America is free; and if we do not mismanage our affairs she is English.'[24] By 1850, Britain was South America's leading trading partner. Historians P.J. Cain and A.G. Hopkins write: 'Brazil was Britain's most accommodating and most successful satellite in South America during the first half of the nineteenth century.'[25] It was an important part of Britain's 'informal empire'.

The 1810 commercial deal with Brazil was a template for what was to come. South Korean economist and author Ha-Joon Chang considers it the first of the 'unequal treaties'.[26] The most famous of these was Britain's 1842 Treaty of Nanking with China, signed after the First Opium War. The war began when the British government backed its opium merchants who had been banned from China. Naval superiority gave Britain victory and China was forced to sign a treaty that fixed its import and export tariffs, opened up five ports to British traders, and gave Britain control of Hong Kong. A further ten Chinese ports were opened to foreign trade, and opium legalized, in 1858, in a treaty at the end of the Second Opium War. In the hundred years after the 1842 Treaty—still known as the 'century of humiliation' in China—the country was politically and economically carved up by rival powers.[27]

Britain also signed unequal treaties between the 1820s and 1850s with other nominally independent countries such as Siam (Thailand), Persia, the Ottoman Empire, and Japan. Some did not regain control of their import and export tariffs until the early twentieth century. The first period of economic globalization, Chang writes, was 'made possible, in large part, by military might, rather than market forces'. Merchants, backed by the power and violence of European states, opened up markets.[28]

The question of what happened to these countries' economic development is beyond the scope of this chapter, but we can note some high-level trends. Formal and informal empires helped lock in a division of labour whereby countries in the Global South produced raw materials and those in Europe and North America manufactured products.[29] This contributed to what is known as the Great Divergence: the fork in economic fortunes between the West and the rest that economic historians see in the data from around 1800. The numbers are stark. In 1750, the share of global manufacturing located in Asia, Africa, and South America was 73 per cent, in 1860 it was 37 per cent, and in 1913 only 7.5 per cent. By this date, Europe, North America, and the newly industrialized Japan accounted for 92.5 per cent.[30] This colonial legacy persists: countries that were locked into a specialized economy producing raw materials more than one hundred years ago are more likely to have a less developed and complex economy than those that were not, although there are notable exceptions, such as South Korea.[31]

The idea that Ricardo's 'free trade' was a decisive break from imperialism is a myth. Nineteenth-century free trade was not that different to the imperial dreams of the 'mercantile system'. Merchants and manufacturers remained at the centre of national policy. Their interests just shifted from protecting the home market to opening foreign ones. Manufacturers' interests evolved as Britain's grew in its commercial and its technological lead over its competitors at the end of the Napoleonic Wars. British manufacturers no longer needed protecting from foreign competitors and were tempted by the prospect of expanding sales into overseas markets and bringing in raw materials for factories without paying border tariffs.

In 1820, a prominent group of London merchants lobbied the British parliament to change the trade rules. The Merchants' Petition for Free Trade was presented to the House of Commons in May 1820, arguing that free trade would be 'the best rule for the trade of the whole Nation'.[32] In a letter to a friend from the Stock Exchange that year, David Ricardo wrote, without irony: 'That the merchants should condemn and expose the mercantile system is no unimportant evidence of the progress of liberal opinions.'[33] What did Ricardo mean? Isn't it a contradiction for merchants to tear down their own system? That could only be true if the 'mercantile system' referred to manufacturers pressuring parliament to erect trade barriers to keep out foreign competitors. That did become less common in Britain in the mid-nineteenth century (if only because few other nations could compete). But, if the mercantile system means government supporting the special interests of merchants and manufacturers over the general interest, as Adam Smith had written, the system was in rude health in the decades after the 1820s. It had morphed into something new, not ended.

According to the classic version of Ricardo's theory, both countries and the world become richer if each country exports products in which it has a comparative advantage. It makes no difference if these are raw materials like bananas or high-tech goods like computer chips. (That's why the head of the central bank in Chile's neoliberal government of the late 1970s said: 'If comparative advantage determines that Chile should produce nothing but melons, then we will produce nothing but melons.'[34]) The trouble is this isn't what Ricardo, the MP, told the House of Commons in 1822. Sounding like a classic mercantilist, he stated: 'there would always be a limit to our greatness, while we were growing our own supply of food: but we should always be increasing in wealth and power, whilst we obtained part of it from foreign countries, and devoted our manufactures to the payment of it'.[35]

Small wonder that critics have argued that Ricardo was promoting the special interests of Britain's manufacturers, while claiming that these were in the general interest. These critics include French historian Élie Halévy, who, in a major study, concluded that Ricardo was 'the theorist and the orator of ... the great English manufacturers, who dreamt of making the economic conquest of the world'.[36] Similarly, British economist Joan Robinson wrote: 'When Ricardo set out the case against protection, he was supporting British economic interests. ... Free trade doctrine, in practice, is a more subtle form of Mercantilism [the 'mercantile system']. When Britain was the workshop of the world, universal free trade suited her interests.'[37] The hidden history of English cloth and Portugal wine is part of a broader pattern of deeply unequal trade relationships. A pattern that, as will become clear in Chapter 12, continues today if you replace the 'merchant system' with the 'corporate system'.

Not so dismal science

There is one aspect of the sceptical reader's response I sketched at the beginning of the chapter that has not yet been answered. Britain renounced both the trade in enslaved peoples and later slavery itself in the first third of the 1800s, at the time of the rise to prominence of classical economics. The argument could be made that the previous three chapters misleadingly associate Ricardo and classical economics with slavery, when they helped to end it.

Ricardo has a reputation as an opponent of slavery. In 2021, Sergio Cremaschi, author of a biography of the classical economist, called him 'the West Indian slaves' friend'. The same year, British broadcaster Melvyn Bragg described Ricardo as 'an abolitionist, not just against the slave trade but slavery per se'.[38] The evidence for Ricardo's views comes from a speech he made in March 1823, at a time when Britain had abolished the slave trade but not outlawed owning enslaved people. Ricardo said that the 'question of slavery was one of infinite importance'. It made him blush with shame to think of 'an unfortunate race of men, who were subjected to the horrors of slavery' and he 'ardently desired' that this 'grievous stain would be removed from the national character'.[39]

There is some evidence that the classical economists' vision of organizing society around self-interest and the exchange of products and labour undercut the hierarchical slave system. 'The experience of all ages and nations,' Adam Smith wrote in *The Wealth of Nations*, 'demonstrates that the work done by slaves … is in the end the dearest of any.' People will work harder when pursuing wages rather than when they are compelled by the whip, Smith argued.[40] Some abolitionists preached this economic message. And, the most forceful British pro-slavery group—the West Indian Interest—attacked Ricardo and his school's promotion of free trade in the 1820s for this reason.[41]

Some pro-slavery voices were still attacking economics more than a decade *after* slavery was abolished in the British Empire. Thomas Carlyle, one of Victorian Britain's leading literary figures, took up the fight in a racist essay published in 1849.[42] Carlyle railed against the abolition of slavery, which he claimed had led to rotting, uncut sugar crops in Britain's Caribbean colonies as the formerly enslaved refused to work. Carlyle's text is stuffed with abhorrent racist terms and tropes. British historian David Olusoga describes it as 'a near-hysterical denunciation of the humanity of black people which became an influential assault upon British anti-slavery politics'.[43]

What's most remembered today is not the content of the article but the term Carlyle coined for economics: 'the dismal science'. He blamed the supposed troubles of the former West Indian slaveholders on the marriage of Christian philanthropy and economics led by the 'sacred cause of black emancipation'. He bemoaned that people of different skin colour were 'on a footing of perfect equality, and subject to no law but that of supply and demand according to the Dismal Science'.[44] Popularizers of economic thinking, such as Robert Heilbroner and John Kenneth Galbraith, taught that 'dismal science' relates to the pessimistic vision of the population outstripping the food supply of Malthus and Ricardo.[45] That's not correct. It was first used and popularized in an article calling for slavery to be reinstated. Carlyle's attack was rebutted in print by political economist and philosopher John Stuart Mill.

The tangled relationship between free-trade economists and slavery is much more complex than this brief survey. There is some evidence that the French economic thinkers who first promoted laissez-faire—or leaving the market alone—were inspired by the 'success' of the French deregulating the slave trade in the 1720s.[46] But it is ironic that the verbal jibe 'dismal science' most often thrown at economics actually relates to one of the discipline's finer moments. The story of Ricardo and slavery is not complete, however. Curiously, his anti-slavery comments quoted earlier are the only ones in all 11 volumes of his collected works and correspondence. What's going on?

The context of Ricardo's anti-slavery speech is important. He gave it at the time an 'East and West Indian Sugars' Bill was going through parliament. Slave-grown sugar entering Britain from the Caribbean was taxed at a lower rate than sugar from India. The Bill would have levelled the tariffs. West Indian slaveholders and supporters of the East India Company each hypocritically attacked the other side's barbaric working conditions.[47] Ricardo was talking to the East India Company General Court as he held £1,000 of stock in the company.[48] (We can only wonder if he read Adam Smith on how owning 'India' stock gives you 'a share, though not in the plunder, yet in the appointment of the plunderers of India'.[49]) Ricardo was wealthy enough not to be motivated by money, but he was speaking to an audience who was motivated to tarnish Caribbean slave-grown sugar. By contrast, when Ricardo discussed the same Bill in parliament two months later, he made no mention of abolition, saying only that 'the condition of the slaves, if not improved, would not be injured' by opening the British market to Indian sugar.[50] A year earlier, the economist had even said he 'had no hostility to the West-Indian interest', the campaign group who defended slavery in British colonies. On the contrary, 'he participated in the feelings of regret which their [plantation owners'] sufferings excited' and wished he could 'assist' them and bring them 'relief'.[51]

Ricardo's *Principles* mention cotton 25 times and quote an 'excellent' passage from his follower and political economist, John Ramsay McCulloch, about the 'happy' future state of free trade when 'the raw cotton of Carolina, will be exchanged for the wares of Birmingham'.[52] Ricardo was writing during a boom time for the plantation system in the southern US, driven by the demand of the European textile industry. Between 1800 and 1860, the number of enslaved people in the US quadrupled, from 1 million to 4 million.[53] It's difficult to believe that as a politician and financier he would not have known that South Carolina's cotton was picked by enslaved labourers. Ricardo was no committed opponent of slavery.

A disappearing trick

The final reason I've spent so long breaking down the story of English and Portuguese trade is that it is an analogy for the intellectual tragedy at the centre of today's mainstream economics.

The chasm between the celebrated example of England and Portugal and its real history demonstrates how, despite their reputation for quantified, scientific objectivity, economic models pick out certain aspects of a complicated picture like a spotlight in a theatre. The beam helps direct attention and tell a clean story. But it plunges the rest of the scene into darkness: in this case, the Atlantic slave trade, gold in colonial Brazil and their impact on Britain and the West. For those who see the world through the model the excluded elements effectively disappear.

This disappearing trick is not unique to economics. It happens frequently with history too. Evidence has to be selected and crafted into a narrative, leaving the door open for personal judgement, values, and bias. As we have seen, many of the ways in which John Methuen, Isaac Newton, and David Ricardo were connected to Brazilian slave-mined gold have been ignored by historians. Many of the teachings of Adam Smith have been distorted beyond all recognition by economic theorists of recent decades. Historical knowledge is partial and influenced by our social setting. Misrepresentations should be challenged and neglected global histories told.

Although *Ricardo's Dream* is partly about revising the historical record, it focuses on what is seen or not seen through economics and formal models because of the unprecedented influence of models on government policies in recent decades.[54] Part of this prestige and influence comes from a simple, sweeping vision and the bold claims of leading figures in the field that economics is an objective, value-free science not so different from physics. Its arguments are often cloaked in technical, mathematical language that most of the population cannot understand.

Ricardo pioneered the use of the logical abstract method that later economists would employ and translate into mathematical terms.[55] And there is an analogy, not perfect but still illuminating, between the problems with his classical economics and the mainstream economics of the last two generations. This story, not told in one place before, was perhaps best expressed by economist and economic historian Terence Hutchison in the 1990s:

> Ricardo still is—as he long has been—the Founding Father of 'anything goes' abstractionism; of the contempt for empirical discipline; of the 'unrealism-of-assumptions-doesn't-matter' school of thought ... [whose] ideas, both originally, 170 years ago, and again in recent decades, fell into the hands of people too keen on exploiting them for their own ideological purposes.[56]

To tell this story, we next turn away from international trade and towards Ricardo's other economic theories. We look at the death of Ricardo's reputation and its rebirth as a version of his style of logical, deductive economics became credible again. Then, we will look at how abstract economic theory has proved a dangerous guide for policy makers since the early 1970s in relation to financial markets, globalization, environmental policy, taxes on the wealthy, and corporate power. Along the way we'll consider what a Greek myth, the London Underground, and an African lizard have to do with seeing the world through models.

PART II

Death

7

'Dropped from Another Planet'

How Ricardo bought his way into parliament and later fell out with his best friend, 'Population Malthus'

To appreciate both the praise and scorn Ricardo has generated, it's necessary to shift our gaze from international trade and look at his other economic ideas and their connection with his life. We'll see that the way his comparative advantage theory was constructed was not a one-off. It fits a pattern of guiding real-world policy with abstract theory, which is known as the Ricardian Vice.

This is not the usual picture presented to economics' students today. Greg Mankiw's canonical textbook *Principles of Economics*—the one that explains why the basketball star LeBron James shouldn't mow his lawn—includes a few paragraphs about Ricardo's life. He was 'a millionaire stockbroker' whose economics was 'not a mere academic exercise'. He became a British Member of Parliament and opposed the Corn Laws, which restricted grain imports.[1] The implication is clear: Ricardo's economics emerged from a practical engagement with business and the world. To say that this was only half the story would be generous.

Ricardo's class warfare

Ricardo was, in his own way, a class warrior. As we've seen, in his vision society was neatly divided into three classes: the aristocratic landowners at the top, the stock owners and capitalists in the middle, and farm and factory workers at the bottom. Ricardo saw the members of his class, the industrious middle, as the motor of the economy. Capitalists earned profit that they reinvested constantly in the most productive areas of the economy, pushing it forward and generating more profit and progress. However, in this scheme, the dynamism of his class, the capitalists—on which everyone depended—was threatened both from above and below.[2]

The workers below threatened to eat away at profit if their wages rose too high. This was because Ricardo held that prices reflected the quantity of labour that went into a product. (This potent idea, known as the 'labour theory of value', would be taken up, with a twist, by socialist thinkers, including Karl Marx, to argue that capitalists steal their workers 'surplus labour' as profits.) Ricardo, the arch-capitalist, believed that 'profits would be high or low exactly in proportion as wages were low or high'. In his eyes, progress only came with high profits, meaning low wages were necessary.[3] Attempts to increase workers' wages, in any case, were counterproductive. Due to the competition for labour, he argued, wages would be at the breadline, just high enough to keep the workers alive.[4] This Ricardo presented as an inevitable, natural law drawing on a theory put forward by his friend—and fellow investor in Waterloo stock— Thomas Robert Malthus.

Malthus, six years older than Ricardo, had shot to fame in 1798 with his theory of population, an attack on radical thinking inspired by the French Revolution nine years earlier, particularly the writings of William Godwin (husband of pioneering feminist Mary Wollstonecraft, father of *Frankenstein* author Mary Shelley, and father-in-law of the radical poet Percy Shelley). Malthus—tall, good looking and born with a cleft lip—was not a natural critic of deductive logic. He was a star mathematics student at Cambridge, and the first edition of his breakout success, *An Essay on the Principle of Population*, was heavily deductive. Malthus, an Anglican cleric, argued that population increased geometrically, by doubling every 25 years (1, 2, 4, 8, 16 …) whereas food production increased arithmetically, by addition (1, 2, 3, 4, 5 …). He painted a dismal future of the human race running out of food that in the twentieth century animated concern about the environmental impacts of a growing global population.

In his own day, the main lesson drawn from Malthus' clear, quantified principle was that the poor were poor not because they were exploited, but because there were too many of them for the available resources. The way out of the situation, in his view, was to reduce the population of the poor by fewer of them being born or (less preferably) by them dying from hunger, disease, and war. By this logic any financial aid given to the poor would only cause more misery and suffering in the long run. From this 'Population Malthus' concluded that the existing welfare for the poor, the centuries-old Poor Laws, should be scrapped. Malthus' logical lens was fully adopted by Ricardo. The formula, as its many critics pointed out, neatly absolved the rising middle classes of any responsibility for the miseries of those less fortunate. Poverty, they could say, was a law of nature not the creation of human-made institutions.

Malthus also helped Ricardo explain how the landowners at the top of society threaten the capitalist profit motor in a different way. This was explained with the theory of rent. According to this theory, landowners lived on rent, which Ricardo taught was not invested productively like capitalist profits but wasted on luxuries. More galling still, the landowner did not work for their rent but benefitted from the natural fertility of the soil. The theory held that the most productive land is cultivated first, and then as demand rises, grain is grown in less productive soil. Both more and less productive farmlands require the same investment, according to the theory, and produce grain that sells at the same price. Therefore, the landowners who control the most productive land sell more grain with the same input and receive an excess profit he called rent. Even worse, the landlords' high rent keeps grain prices, and hence wages, high, and that, in Ricardo's theoretical world, undermines the profits of company and stock owners. For Ricardo, economic progress relied on stock owners, as best-selling economic historian Robert Heilbroner explained: 'It was they [the young industrialist class] who drove the economic machine, and the landlord lolling in the back seat who gained all the pleasure.'[5]

This is the bones of Ricardo's domestic economic thinking, which has since been much discussed and disputed. It was a powerful story with immediate political implications. It puts the question of 'who gets what' in the economy at the centre. Once grasped, it was intellectually appealing—especially if it fitted your political views—

as it promised to explain the whole economy using only a few essential variables. And, crucially, Ricardo presented it not as just one viewpoint or theory among others, but as revealing 'the laws which regulate' the distribution of rent, profit, and wages in the economy: laws that aspired to the universality and precision of mathematics and physics.[6] It was both revolutionary and conservative. It sought to overthrow the centuries-old power of aristocratic landowners, but simultaneously, critics argued, it condemned the working classes to toiling poverty. It has influenced, with a few twists, free-market capitalists, socialist thinkers like Karl Marx, and twenty-first-century critics of the concentration of wealth.

Ricardo had 30 years of experience with financial markets and government loans. On these issues his writing is often nourished by conversations and documents from knowledgeable contacts. In some of his later writings, he drew on actual numbers from parliamentary reports.[7] But these are the exceptions. When he wrote about farms and factories, wages and population, and international trade, he had little practical experience to fall back on and did little research. He did not study the history of agriculture, or visit the new factories popping up; he did not assemble and look for patterns in data on wages and population, nor did he travel to Portugal, for example, to research the impacts of trade. His quarry was the general, abstract truth not confined to one country or one time. Ricardo's technique, in three words, was: focus then generalize. It was introspective and imaginative. He separated out in his mind the essential elements of human behaviour and the economy—these principles were often 'self-evident' to him—and stripped away everything else from the picture.[8] Then, working with only these elements deemed essential, he created a consistent, machine-like story about how they fitted together. This was, Robert Heilbroner said, 'the incisive brilliance of the financial trader who saw the world only as a great abstract mechanism'.[9] At some point it would be necessary to compare this conceptual model to reality, but that was rarely a priority for Ricardo.

For some Ricardo was a visionary genius. English writer Thomas De Quincey could barely contain his enthusiasm in his *Confessions of an English Opium-Eater* (1821). 'Thou art the man!' he declared, 'All other writers had been crushed and overlaid by the enormous weight of facts and documents; Mr. Ricardo had deduced, *a priori*, from the understanding itself, laws which first gave a ray of light into the unwieldy chaos of materials.' These were not just the laws of one place or time, De Quincey claimed Ricardo had founded economics 'on an eternal basis'.[10] Economics, it seemed, had found its Newton.

'The rottenest borough I could find'

Ricardo's first published articles on gold had also brought him to the attention of James Mill, a historian, theorist, and father of the philosopher John Stuart Mill. The elder Mill would influence not just Ricardo's writings on economics but would push him to become the public champion of the new 'science' of political economy. Ricardo and Mill's letters still survive. In them, Ricardo told his 'master', Mill, he wanted to 'throw my writing aside'. He argued that he was 'not equal to the task you have assigned me' of writing the *Principles of Political Economy*. In response, James Mill wrote to his 'young beginner': 'I solemnly command and ordain that you proceed, without loss of time.' Mill acted as Ricardo's editor, reading his drafts, suggesting changes, and discussing chapters, order, and title for the book. He pushed Ricardo to concentrate all his efforts on creating 'a work which will gain you immortal honour'.[11]

Mill published his own book, *The History of British India*, in 1817. It is now notorious because its author never set foot in India nor spoke any of its languages but nevertheless wrote a stinging—and influential—critique of Hindu culture as primitive, superstitious, and degenerate.[12] Ricardo told Mill that his book helped 'us to form correct conclusions respecting the civilization of the Hindus'.[13] These conclusions, Ricardo told Malthus approvingly, would help disprove any claims that 'Africa, Mexico, Peru, Persia, and China' also had 'a high state of civilization'.[14] Mill claimed in the preface that the right person 'may attain more knowledge of India, in one year, in his closet in England, than he could obtain during the course of the longest life, by the use of his eyes and ears in India'.[15] As well as propping up his sense of European superiority, Mill pulled Ricardo away from observation as a route to knowledge and towards a priori methods of deduction and logic not anchored in the real world.

Having pushed Ricardo to write his *Principles of Political Economy*, James Mill urged him in October 1816 to join public life: 'You ought indeed to be in parliament.' Ricardo replied that he simply could not stand in a contested election. Mill in reply wrote: 'If I were in your situation, the rottenest borough I could find would be my market, with nothing to do but part with a sum of money.'[16] Ricardo followed his friend's advice to the letter. Ireland's MPs sat in Britain's Houses of Parliament at the time, and the year after Mill's letter Ricardo's land agent identified the Portarlington constituency in Ireland as the ideal seat. The following year Ricardo bought it.[17]

Rotten boroughs, later abolished in the Great Reform of 1832, were electoral districts where a tiny number of voters were controlled by the landowner. They were lampooned by the 1980s British historical comedy TV series *Blackadder*. In one episode, Rowan Atkinson's title character masterminds a cunning plan to get his servant Baldrick elected as MP for the Dunny-on-the-Wold constituency—a half-acre patch, home to a single voter (and 'three rather mangy cows, a dachshund named Colin, and a small hen in its late forties').[18] Blackadder succeeds by becoming the only voter and also the election officer.

Ricardo's seat had not one voter, but 12, controlled by Lord Portarlington, the local landowner.[19] The other 2,800 people living in the constituency, mostly subsistence farmers, did not have a vote. Ricardo paid Lord Portarlington £4,000 (around £640,000 today) and lent him another £25,000 (around £4 million today) at 6 per cent interest.[20] A written contract stipulated that Ricardo would have 'perfect freedom' in the use of his parliamentary vote, and he took his seat in parliament in 1819 (see Figure 7.1).[21] This was, at the time, perfectly legal. He would never visit the constituency.

Ricardo in parliament advocated for what were, in his day, reformist and progressive views. He was strongly in favour of secret voting, more regular elections, and extending the voting franchise, although he stopped short of endorsing universal male suffrage. He supported freedom of religion, as you might imagine from someone with his life history, and opposed clampdowns on political liberty. Ricardo punched up against the aristocratic landlords who still dominated parliament. He was, as the textbooks say, an opponent of the Corn Laws—import tariffs on grains such as wheat and oats introduced in 1815—which kept bread prices high, farmer landlord profits plump, and capitalists' profits low. These effects, he wrote, were 'as certain as the principle of gravitation'.[22] He also used his seat in parliament to punch down on the poorer, working classes.

Figure 7.1: *The House of Commons* by George Hayter, 1833

Source: © National Portrait Gallery, London

The celebrated economist used his maiden speech in parliament in March 1819 to rail against another law. This revealed a much less attractive side. Ricardo was a fierce critic of the social welfare of the day, known as the Poor Laws, provided by parishes. The Bill in discussion proposed stopping relief to adults who were unable to feed and clothe large families even with full-time work. It proposed instead that all but the first two children of such poorer families would be taken from their parents and sent to a workhouse.[23] Ricardo objected to the Bill because it was too lenient.

He wanted gradual abolition of poor relief. If relief were given to 'the children of the poor,' he said, and 'parents felt assured that an asylum would be provided for their children, in which they would be treated with humanity and tenderness, there would then be no check to that increase of population which was so apt to take place among the labouring classes'.[24] The cruelty of the workhouse system would later be attacked in Charles Dickens' 1838 novel *Oliver Twist*. Ricardo, a family man sitting in parliament in a rotten-borough seat, confidently and callously heaped misery on the poor and their children in the name of science. He did this for what he considered to be the greater good, guided by the population principle.

Ricardo's new national prominence attracted the scorn of the fiercest critic of the day, the campaigning journalist William

Cobbett, founder of Hansard, the official report of parliament debates. 'So here we have their pretty notions, then!' Cobbett wrote of Ricardo's comments on the Poor Law debate in his newspaper the *Political Register*. If the Bill were passed, he predicted, whole families will starve: 'The act is one of the most shocking inhumanity; and one that can find no precedent.' Instead of worrying about 'lower orders['] … naughty propensity to breed', Cobbett suggested reducing the population of 'loan and script gentry' living off interest from government debt.[25] It was a reasonable proposal. In Britain, after the Napoleonic Wars, the state spent just 6 per cent of its budget on poor relief, and 53 per cent on payments to bondholders.[26]

Cobbett, more famous at the time than Ricardo, was an unruly voice of the emerging working classes and now a controversial figure.[27] He railed against 'stock jobbers', who traditionally traded from Change Alley, and 'borough-mongers', who bought their seats in parliament. Ricardo was both. Cobbett described Ricardo's *Principles* as 'a heap of senseless, Change-Alley jargon, put upon paper and bound into a book'.[28] Ricardo read Cobbett's work even though he detested the man. In private he castigated Cobbett as a 'mischievous scoundrel'.[29] And some of what Cobbett wrote *was* odious. Mixed in with his attacks on Ricardo is disturbing anti-Semitic and racist language.

Ricardo argued that his opposition to the Poor Laws did not stem from personal prejudice. He supported an almshouse 'for eight poor persons' and created a school for 250 boys and girls near Gatcomb House (although he insisted on no free school meals lest this should encourage overpopulation).[30] His opposition, he said, was based on the principles of the science of political economy. As he wrote in his *Principles*, leaning into Newton's legacy: 'The principle of gravitation is not more certain than the tendency of such [Poor] laws to change wealth and power into misery and weakness.'[31] And to those who argued that workers' wages should rise so that they could support a larger family, Ricardo answered: the wages of a single worker 'would never rise so high as to afford a provision for a man with a family'.[32]

Nowhere in Ricardo's writing does he lay out in detail what he meant by science and scientific. But the way he uses the words suggests that he thought they were synonymous with clear thinking and therefore theory, principles, and doctrines. To study economics 'as a subject of science', he once wrote, meant 'clear and obvious deductions from the known principles of political economy'.[33] Those 'principles' included insights into human nature that came from introspection: looking in rather than looking out.[34] As we saw, he once dismissed one of Malthus' objections as 'a question of fact and not of science'.[35] (This approach, as will be shown in Chapter 8, would create a backlash from the thinkers of the next generation who begun to call themselves scientists.)

'As if he had dropped from another planet'

Ricardo entered parliament when Britain was in an economic depression following the Napoleonic Wars. Discharged soldiers swelled the ranks of agricultural labourers looking for work for subsistence wages. Changes in the climate, triggered by the eruption in 1815 of Mount Tambora in modern-day Indonesia, the largest eruption in human history, contributed to failed harvests and food riots. This was the context for his campaign against the Poor Laws.

His fellow opposition MP, Henry (later Lord) Brougham, was, in general, a great admirer of Ricardo (and supported reform of the Poor Laws). He wrote that Ricardo's 'kindly nature, and his genuine modesty ... won the respect of every party' and that his career in parliament was a 'triumph of reason, intelligence, and integrity'. But, on one point, he found fault with the great economist.

On the floor of the House of Commons in 1820, he complained that Ricardo inhabited a 'Utopian world' of his own creation, deaf to the 'cry of general distress' in the country. Ricardo 'argued as if he had dropped from another planet; as if this were a land of the most perfect liberty of trade'.[36] This is one of the earliest critiques of Ricardo living in a dream world. In a later sketch, Brougham again said that Ricardo put too much confidence in his 'abundantly theoretical' speculations:

> His views were often ... extravagant from his propensity to follow a right principle into all its consequences, without duly taking into account in practice the condition of things to which he was applying it, as if a mechanician were to construct an engine without taking into consideration the resistance of the air in which it was

to work, or the strength and the weight and the friction
of the parts of which it was to be made.[37]

Let me give an example of that tendency from his *Principles*. In
one section, Ricardo wrote about the economics of hunter-gatherer
societies. Reading it horrified me. Ricardo creates a verbal model
set 'in the early stages of society' divided between hunters and
fishermen. In this world, the cost and durability of 'bows and arrows'
and canoes are calculated precisely over a ten-year period, as are
the 'annual labour cost' of labourers and the 'profits'. His point
is to show how the 'natural price' of the fishermen's salmon and
the hunters' deer are 'exactly' and 'entirely' related.[38] There's no
acknowledgement of culture, habit, hierarchy, family, rituals, spiritual
beliefs, reciprocation, or other non-economic beliefs or influences:
only individual self-interest and calculation. It's exactly what you
might expect a veteran stock trader with a fondness for neat theories
to write if he'd never spent a second with Indigenous peoples.

In this fanciful example, the canoes and other fishing implements
cost £100 and the wages of ten fishermen are £100. The same
figures reappear for the bows and arrows and the hunters' salaries.
The deer and salmon in Ricardo's world are sold eventually for £1,
£2, or £3. Like almost every number in the *Principles*, including the
four magic numbers in the famous English–Portugal example, they
have been selected not for realism but to illustrate a point. Ricardo
once admitted, in relation to a table on profit from agriculture:
'It is scarcely necessary to observe the data on which this table is
constructed are assumed, and are probably very far from the truth.
They were fixed on as tending to illustrate the principle.'[39] By
contrast, almost all the numbers in Adam Smith's *Wealth of Nations*
are drawn from documents or history and represent something real.

Ricardo's Indigenous peoples' model also demonstrates the
imperialism of his economic thinking. He strongly implied that his
economic laws hold, or should hold, for all people in all societies at
all times: just as gravity operates whether you believe in it or not.
American economist Wesley Clair Mitchell would later write that
Ricardo saw other non-capitalist societies 'by the light of a capitalist's
reason ... a more deceptive light he could not have had'.[40]

Brougham was far from alone in diagnosing Ricardo's
overconfidence in his own theories. He may have been influenced

by Jean-Baptiste Say (1767–1832), a French classical economist and businessman and correspondent of Ricardo. In 1819, Say complained in print of the English economist's tendency to base his arguments on 'abstract principles which he overly generalises. Once fixed on a hypothesis ... he pushes his reasoning to their remotest consequences, without comparing their results with those of experience.' This meant, Say argued of Ricardo's *Principles*, that 'nothing in the book represents what actually happens in nature'.[41]

Even Ricardo's great friend, Malthus, would make the same point in one of the most celebrated exchange of letters in the history of economics.

'Crude and premature theories'

Malthus and Ricardo became genuine friends as well as fellow economists and delighted in deep conversation. Ricardo's Quaker wife, Priscilla, once dined with Lord Byron's best friend and told him that her husband and Malthus would stay up until 3 am to discuss the definition of rent![42] For more than a decade, they discussed economics in visits, letters, and debates at the Political Economy Club, which was founded in London in 1821 to support a petition of City of London merchants to the House of Commons (and continues to meet to this day).[43] At the start of their correspondence, Ricardo and Malthus expressed the hope they could settle their divergent views on economics in private. It did not work.

David Ricardo and, to a more nuanced degree, Thomas Robert Malthus, represented a new type of intellectual: the theorist in search of general principles.[44] However, Malthus developed his methodological thinking and, in later editions of his *Essay on Population*, he introduced empirical evidence—population data and other real-world facts—to bolster and soften his claims. In Ricardo's lifetime, he was the main force pushing for Ricardo to base his thinking on facts rather than abstract principles.

Ricardo and Malthus' letters show that they cared for each other but their attempts to reach agreement on how economics should be done were in vain. In October 1815, a few months after the Waterloo loan, Ricardo regretted their divergent thinking and suggested an explanation and a self-critique: 'If I am too theoretical (which I really believe is the case), you I think are too practical.' But he then went on to warn his friend of the 'great danger in appealing to experience in favour of a particular doctrine'.[45]

In the midst of the economic depression, in January 1817, Ricardo did not waver in believing that his principles—that the economy should be allowed to self-regulate—were correct, they just needed more time to become apparent. He critiqued Malthus in one letter for paying too much attention to 'the immediate and temporary effects of particular changes—whereas I put these immediate and temporary effects quite aside, and fix my whole attention on the permanent state of things which will result from them'.[46] This allowed Ricardo to say, in effect, it may appear as if my theories are wrong, but I will be proved right in the long run.

In the end, Malthus and Ricardo could not agree. Three years after Ricardo's *Principles of Political Economy*, Malthus published a book with the identical title together with a stinging critique of his friend's thinking. Political economy, Malthus warned, had fallen into a 'serious error' of overconfidence. The 'great general principles' of political economy, he said, can be useful guides but we must not forget the 'passions and propensities of human nature'. This is of 'the highest practical importance' Malthus said, as the conclusions of the science 'will necessarily influence the conduct both of individuals and of governments'.[47]

'To minds of a certain cast there is nothing so captivating as simplification and generalization,' Malthus continued, but this tendency has, 'in almost every science with which we are acquainted, led to crude and premature theories.' In political economy, it led to a mania for attributing complex phenomena to a single cause and to dogma: a 'disinclination to allow of modifications, limitations, and exceptions to any rule'. In his view, this desire for simplification should be balanced with the need to engage with experience and the complexity of the world.

Summing up his attack, with a sting in the tail, Malthus wrote: 'Before the shrine of truth, as discovered by facts and experience, the fairest theories and the most beautiful classifications must fall.' Which beautiful theories? 'There is one modern work, in particular, of very high reputation, some of the fundamental principles of which have appeared to me, after the most mature deliberation, to be erroneous … I allude to Mr. Ricardo's work.'[48]

'I have read your book with great attention,' Ricardo wrote to Malthus by letter in May 1820. Many parts of it, he said, he agreed with: 'I am particularly pleased with your observations on the state of the poor—it cannot be too often stated to them that the most effectual remedy for the inadequacy of their wages is in their own hands.' He was, however, not convinced by his friend's arguments about the correct method of economics. Ricardo considered that their differences came from 'your considering my book as more practical than I intended it to be. My object was to elucidate principles, and to do this I imagined strong cases that I might shew the operation of those principles.'[49] And, yet, time and again, in private and public Ricardo confidently proposed major, practical social reforms based on his economic theories—as have many people since. This is the vice at the heart of Ricardo's Dream.

The pair remained friends and Malthus stayed with Ricardo at Gatcomb House over Christmas in 1820. 'We had plenty of discussion,' Ricardo wrote to James Mill on New Year's Day, but he criticized Malthus' fuzzy thinking: 'Another of his great mistakes is I think this; Political Economy he says is not a strict science like the mathematics.'[50]

'A great light extinguished'

At the end of the Napoleonic Wars, continental Europe opened up to British visitors for the first time in a quarter of a century. Today, the best known of these continental tourists were the poets and writers Lord Byron and Percy and Mary Shelley, who visited Lake Geneva in 1816, where the Frankenstein story was born. Ricardo took a five-month European tour in 1822, with his wife, Priscilla, and servants and trod some of the same paths as the poets. He visited Lake Geneva where he was moved despite himself: 'The spot is an enchanting one, and I, who have not one grain of romance in my composition, was fully sensible of its beauties.'[51]

He travelled to Italy and visited the port city of Livorno in October 1822, where his ancestors had taken refuge after being ejected from Portugal. Ricardo saw the 'very beautiful' synagogue and people working coral into jewellery as his family had done.[52] Three months earlier, a 29-year-old Percy Shelley had drowned in a storm on a sailing trip that left Livorno. Ricardo, aged 50, was also near the end of his life. It was in Italy that he began to complain of earache. He had less than a year to live.

The following September, 1823, Ricardo's acute ear pain returned. He stayed in bed, looked after by his brother, a doctor, and Priscilla and his daughters. A few days later, on 9 September, he 'seemed decidedly better,' wrote James Mill. But it was false hope. The infection spread to his brain and caused, said Mill, 'a period of unspeakable agony'.[53] The family realized, to their shock, that Ricardo was on his deathbed. His brother Moses wrote 'the transition was sudden, from perfect confidence to complete despair'.[54] On Thursday 11 September 1823, around noon, the classical economist, financier, and MP died. He was widely mourned. Lord Brougham, who said that Ricardo had dropped from another planet, wrote of 'a great light extinguished prematurely'.[55]

He was buried and a monument erected by a handsome, yellow Cotswold-stone church, Hardenhuish in Wiltshire, on his daughter's estate. When I visited the grave with my editor in autumn 2022, the church's bird's-egg blue door and clock face were bathed in sunshine. It was difficult not to feel for Ricardo laid to rest here in a family tomb. He was something of a paradox, in John Stuart Mill's words, 'the most modest of men, though firmly convinced of the truth of his doctrines'.[56]

8

'Purely Hypothetical Truths'

*In which the inventor of the word 'scientist' and his
historian friend attempt to destroy Ricardo's economics*

William Whewell (1794–1866) is often described simply as a
polymath. Born to a Lancashire carpenter, Whewell (pronounced
'hyoo-uhl') became long-time Master of Trinity College, Cambridge,
and contributed to mathematics, the study of the oceans, history,
philosophy, poetry, and theology, among other subjects (see
Figure 8.1). His award-winning ocean tides research in the 1830s
saw him co-ordinate a pioneering global project and tabulate tens
of thousands of data points. He may be best remembered today for
having coined the word 'scientist' in 1833, as a replacement for the
terms 'men of science' or 'natural philosophers'. He also introduced
many other scientific terms including 'physicist', 'consilience'
and 'electrode'.[1]

More importantly for this history, Whewell was 'the great enemy
of deductive economics' as the UCLA historian of science Theodore
Porter wrote because he argued that Ricardo and his followers had
'departed too far from the historical pattern of successful scientific
investigation'.[2] He was worried that other sciences would follow
economics' faulty methods and the reputation of all would be
tarnished in the public mind.[3]

While an undergraduate at Cambridge in the 1810s, Whewell
hatched a plan over long conversational breakfasts with his friends to
put science back on the right track. These friends included Charles
Babbage, who went on to invent an early version of the computer;

Figure 8.1:
William Whewell,
lithograph by
E.U. Eddis, 1835

Source: Wellcome
Collection

John Herschel, the astronomer and co-inventor of photography; and Richard Jones, a historian and economist. Laura Snyder, in *The Philosophical Breakfast Club* (2011), shows that the four friends succeeded to a remarkable degree. In addition to their individual work, in the 1830s they were founder members of some of the world's first modern scientific organizations: the British Association for the Advancement of Science as well as the Statistical Society of London. Both institutions, Snyder says, were formed to counter the influence of the Political Economy Club frequented by Ricardo and Mill and friends.[4]

Whewell and Jones had read David Ricardo's *Principles* when it first appeared and were disturbed by what they saw as its dismal conclusions: society doomed to perpetual mass poverty and class conflict. Fear of a general revolt, along the lines of the French Revolution, was commonplace and both men had witnessed local riots and rebellions prompted by the grinding poverty of the day. They also believed that economic knowledge, if it did anything, should help improve the lives of the masses. 'It will be both more easy and more honourable to knock down Ricardo's errors while they are new,' the 28-year-old Cambridge tutor Whewell wrote to his friend Jones in November 1822.[5] They would split the task.

Whewell attacked the logic of Ricardo's theory using mathematics, while Richard Jones took on the heavy lifting of providing the factual evidence that the theories were false by gathering documents and data. But Jones worked slowly, suffering from depression, writer's block, and bad health brought on by heavy drinking. Whewell alternately scolded and encouraged his friend in 'the demolition of the Ricardians', appealing to him as a warrior knight: 'it is a proper adventure for you to set out to kill such a dragon as that system'.[6]

Ricardo, they argued, had based his work on a defective method they called deduction. The orthodox political economists believed they had already captured self-evident, universal truths and so were apt to reason *down* from these general principles to specifics. This is why Whewell once called his opponents 'downwards mad' deductivists.[7] Far better, Whewell and friends argued, to move *up* from a broad survey of facts and evidence and slowly climb the ladder of abstraction towards more general principles, always aware that these principles may be incomplete and later prove to be false. This alternative method they called induction.[8]

The mission of Whewell, Jones and friends was to revive and refresh the teachings of Francis Bacon, the seventeenth-century statesman, lawyer, and essayist known as the father of experimental science. An analogy from Bacon's work most clearly explains the difference between induction and deduction as they saw it.

The ant, the spider, and the bee

Bacon had argued that the 'ill-starred divorce and separation' of reasoning from observation had 'thrown into confusion all the affairs of the human family'.[9] In a famous aphorism, he argued that the researcher should be like the bee, not the spider or the ant. The spider spins 'cobwebs out of their own substance', creating theories without a clear connection to the world outside their mind. Ants 'only collect and use' facts, and fail to create theories to explain the data. The bee combines the best of both as it 'gathers its material from the flowers of the garden and of the field, but transforms and digests it by a power of its own'—using both observation and reasoning to create new scientific theories.[10]

Bacon's vision was of a new age that could come from the 'closer and purer' synthesis of the experimental and the rational known as the inductive method.[11] Thus, Whewell claimed he looked for a 'middle way' between extremes. Whewell and friends saw David Ricardo and his school as a particularly dangerous type of spider: spinning webs of reason disconnected from evidence. Whewell rejected the idea that induction is just the ant's collating of facts. He held there was a role for the 'act of thought' in bringing together these empirical facts by successive steps to more general ideas. But he rejected the belief that scientific laws emerge from 'a loose hap-hazard sort of guessing'.[12] Whewell advocated slow rather than fast science. He also, somewhat ironically, produced one of the first purely mathematical papers on British economics in 1829 as he sought to expose what he saw as the logical fallacies of Ricardo's theory.[13]

Jones focused on economics, searching museums and libraries for old documents and pamphlets that shed light on how economic behaviours had changed over the previous century. His Cambridge friends passed him information on economic conditions from rural Switzerland and the Netherlands. He got economic data on England from parliament. He gathered his own evidence from trips to Wales, Normandy, Paris, and the Rhine.[14] And eventually, in 1831, he published a nearly 400-page book *An Essay on the Distribution of Wealth*. Whewell was delighted.

In the book, Jones marshalled evidence to slay Ricardo's formulation of the theory of land rents. This was the theory, borrowed from Malthus and explained in Chapter 7, that grain sells at the same price but the most productive land was cultivated first, so those who control it get an unmerited profit called rent. Ricardo defined 'rent' narrowly so it only related to the earnings of landowners and not those of capitalists. The theory was underpinned, Jones argued, by one specific type of relationship between the farmer and the landowner, where a capitalist farmer, who in turn employs labourers, pays rent in money to the landlord. This system—which Jones called 'farmers' rents'—was dominant in England and the Netherlands, but globally it was an anomaly. He estimated that the 'farmers' rents' system Ricardo used was present in roughly 1 per cent of globally farmed land in his day.[15] Much more prominent elsewhere were four other types of farmer–landowner relationships, which together Jones termed 'peasant rents'.[16]

What the four 'peasant rents' have in common are relationships underpinned by cultural practices rather than the market competition prevalent in England. In Russia, for example, cultivators paid landowners directly with their labour or with agricultural produce, elsewhere, in much of Central Europe, cultivators and landowners divided the produce between them. In the latter case, when the price of corn was high landlords and cultivators *both* benefitted. In all areas where 'peasant rents' are dominant, Jones argued, Ricardo's laws no longer held. They were a general theory built on a special case; nothing like the universal law of gravity. The broader conclusion of Ricardian economics that the interests of landlords and farmers are always and everywhere in conflict is false, Jones concluded.[17] For this, Jones and Whewell were seen by some as more conservative thinkers, but they were also more compassionate ones.

Richard Jones' exuberant personality comes through in his language. He judged that political economy had so far 'only called itself a science to enforce a dogmatical philosophy of the most pernicious kind'.[18] He called out David Ricardo publicly with a mix of praise and damnation: 'Mr. Ricardo was a man of talent, and he produced a system very ingeniously combined, of purely hypothetical truths; which, however, a single comprehensive glance at the world as it actually exists, is sufficient to shew to be utterly inconsistent with the past and present condition of mankind.'[19] Jones did not get everything right: he did not foresee that the economy could diverge drastically from the historical pattern. But his critique of the orthodox economics for being dangerously unobservant was prescient.

On the strength of his book, Jones lectured on political economy at King's College, London—setting out his method in the plainest terms. If we wish to understand the economy and how revenues are produced and distributed, Jones said, 'I really know of but one way to attain our object, and that is, to look and see.' Views similar to this are sometimes critiqued as 'naive empiricism': believing whatever your senses (or your datasets) tell you and not investigating further. But Jones pointed out that the illusions of the mind are often more beguiling than the illusions of the senses. He warned that if we 'snatch at general principles' and do not take the trouble to study history and statistics we will be 'closet philosophers, [who] take a peep out of our little window, and fashion a world of our own after the pattern of what we see'. That led, he argued, only to ignorance.[20]

In later writings and lectures, some published posthumously by Whewell, Jones attacked other pillars of classical economics. He argued that Malthus' theory of population, an integral part of Ricardo's theoretical machine, was also mistaken. He tracked population changes in England since Elizabethan times and put forward evidence of rapid growth in the food supply from new agricultural techniques and lands coming under cultivation. He argued that the desire for luxuries induced men and women to limit the size of their families.[21]

After Thomas Robert Malthus' death in 1834, Jones took his position as Professor of Political Economy at East India College in Hertfordshire, north of London.[22] Their mutual friend, Maria Edgeworth, who had once described Gatcomb House, imagined the confused pupils who 'must now learn from Jones's lectures the objections he made to Malthus' system!'[23] Jones also attacked Ricardo's principle of the relationship between wages and increasing population. It assumed that the whole population lived on paid wages, which yet again ignored the vast mass of people in his day— including subsistence farmers—who provided their own income.[24]

David Ricardo had been dead for eight years when Richard Jones published his first major critique, so we can only speculate what his reaction would have been. We do know that while the tide of opinion had been turning against Ricardo, his most loyal devotees did not give up on his style of abstract economics. And its chief defender was Ricardo's best friend's son.

'Totally without foundation in fact'

James Mill—who had encouraged Ricardo to write the *Principles* and to enter parliament—gave him one more gift: his eldest son. John Stuart Mill (1806–1873) is now much better known than his father, as a philosopher, humanist, and author of *On Liberty*. He was also an early feminist and was arrested as a 17-year-old for distributing literature on birth control.[25] James Mill is remembered, if at all, as a tyrannical father who set up an intellectual boot camp for his son. John Stuart in his *Autobiography* described how he was taught in Greek at 3, started reading the classical authors in Latin at 8, and was studying political economy by his early teens. One of the main objectives of his father's education, he later wrote, was to show how 'the superior lights of Ricardo' revealed the fallacies and errors in '[Adam] Smith's more superficial view of political economy'.[26] In 1819, James Mill delivered lectures on Ricardo's newly published

Principles to his son who had to submit a written summary the next day, 'which he made me rewrite over and over again until it was clear, precise, and tolerably complete'.[27]

The young J.S. Mill met David Ricardo, liked his 'kindliness of manner', and was invited to Gatcomb House where he learned political economy directly from him during long, country walks.[28] It would turn out to be one of the great trader's best investments. Mill published his first article aged 16, in 1822, a defence of Ricardo's economics, and continued in that vein.[29]

Then, at the age of 20, everything fell apart for John Stuart Mill. He entered into a prolonged period of mental crisis and suicidal thoughts. His education, he later wrote, had made him a mere 'reasoning machine'. The neglect of feeling and emotion left him stranded like someone at sea 'with a well-equipped ship and a rudder, but no sail'.[30] John Stuart only emerged from depression after rejecting the dogmatic narrowness of his father's teaching and opening himself up to the poetry of Wordsworth and Shelley. (Mill now boasted that he could draw on both of the spirits of the age.) He had a brilliant mind, a sharp pen, and an evolving vision. And yet, it is curious, even after his breakdown, how closely John Stuart Mill cleaved to his father's ideas. Decades later, he would publish the leading economics book of the age, in which he skilfully deflected criticisms of David Ricardo's ideas and described him as 'the greatest political economist'.[31]

Emerging from depression, John Stuart Mill wrote a series of essays about economics. They were, he told a friend in 1833, 'in continuation and completion of Ricardo's doctrines'.[32] One of these essays on international trade first associated Adam Smith's theory with *absolute* costs and Ricardo's with *comparative* costs, using a hypothetical example of England and Poland exchanging cloth and corn.[33] Another dealt with the proper method of economics and is still lauded today. It is the first explicit description of 'economic human'—the highly knowledgeable, self-interested, and calculating individual who lives on at the core of so much orthodox economics.[34] Ricardo had rarely been explicit about his method: his views have to be pieced together from asides and correspondence. Mill, by contrast, with rare verve and clarity defends deductive economics. Reading it made my eyes pop: the text claims the highest authority of science and yet subtly cordons off facts from the creation of theories.

Mill, with admirable frankness, writes that political economy is an 'abstract science' that uses 'à priori' methods. He directly states that political economists reason 'from assumptions, not from facts' and that these assumptions may be 'totally without foundation in fact'. Let that sink in. Mill admits that economic laws are only wholly true 'in a case which is purely imaginary'. And yet, here's the rub, he defends this method of 'abstract speculation' as the only legitimate approach to the subject—indeed 'the essence of all science'![35]

Mill argues that the method supported by Jones and Whewell, where you 'look at the facts in the concrete, clothed in all the complexity with which nature has surrounded them', will not lead to the discovery of truths. That's because, he says, political and economic systems are too large, complicated, and intricate. You cannot shrink societies down and experiment on them in the laboratory, as you can with the physical and chemical world. And he's right that it's difficult to pick apart what he called the 'immense multitude of the influencing circumstances'. But it is still a leap to argue, as Mill does, that the deductive method is 'the only certain or scientific mode of investigation'. Having planted his flag, Mill then sets out, with deep insight and skill, sensible rules to avoid many of the pitfalls of his preferred method.[36]

Mill, to his credit, *does* allow facts a role in a theory's verification and reformulation. Economists must be attentive to 'disturbing causes' that inhibit the laws they have identified and make allowances for them. Theories should be cast away, he cautions, if their predictions are incorrect (a position often preached and little practised). And he pre-empts one of the themes of this book—that mainstream economics can make things disappear conceptually—arguing, at one point, for the importance of 'long and accurate observation' and 'the danger of overlooking something'.[37]

Mill's main argument, however, is the necessity of dividing clearly the 'science' of political economy from the 'art' of policy making. The difference between science and art for Mill is this: the science of economics discovers the laws and principles and the art is their practical application.[38] He sensibly argues that there is a difference between investigating society and applying this knowledge to practical affairs, which must involve a broader range of inputs including the values society holds. Hence, Mill claims that his deductive science of economics just investigates what *is*, not what *ought* to be. When it comes to practical politics then, Mill says, political economists should 'have no opinion' or only hold their views with 'extreme modesty'.[39] This is/ought distinction has a long pedigree, going back to Adam Smith's friend the philosopher David Hume, who critiqued the way in which authors shifted without explanation from using *is* to *ought*.[40] As we'll see in Chapter 10, Milton Friedman would make a similar distinction in the 1950s and, under a banner of 'positive economics', usher in an era of speculative model making. But there is one major problem in how Mill (and later Friedman) make use of the is/ought distinction.

The way Mill differentiates between 'science' and 'art' assumes that 'science' is investigating the actual state of society. But he's explicitly said that this is *not* his starting point. His science begins with assumptions that may be 'totally without foundation in fact'. It is based on deductions that start not with *is* but with *if*. Only if his assumptions—for example, that the world is populated with entirely self-interested, calculating individuals—are true will the conclusions be correct. This is basic logic: conclusions are only true if the premises are true. The problem for Mill is what we could call, with apologies to Hume, the if/is problem. By blurring the line between if and is, Mill thickens the confusion between investigating a hypothetical world and investigating the real world in which we breathe.[41]

Too many economists then and now follow Mill into this confusion, while failing to remember his more sensible caveats. Unfortunately, the main impact of Mill's argument in this regard was to shield Ricardo's economics, and other abstract economics in its style, from the criticism that they fail to describe the world. Failure to observe the if/is distinction is endemic in mainstream economics.

Even other economists of the day who disagreed with parts of Ricardo's doctrines frequently supported the deductive method.[42] So, the first Professor of Political Economy at Oxford University, Nassau Senior (1790–1864), often challenged Ricardo and Malthus' theories, yet in 1836 criticized 'the undue importance which many Economists have ascribed to the collection of facts', insisting that the science 'depends more on reasoning than on observation'.[43]

Poor Laws, corn, and famine

The practical impact of this abstract thinking can be seen in a series of legal changes in Britain, notably the 1834 Poor Law and the 1846 Corn Laws.

Poor Law reform is rarely mentioned in today's economic textbooks, but was an issue of the first importance in its day and has some resonance for contemporary debates on social security and the welfare state. The classical economics of Malthus and Ricardo had placed the theory of surplus population at the centre of their system. They had argued, as we have seen in Ricardo's maiden speech in parliament, for the gradual but complete abolition of outdoor relief to the poor, who should be taught self-reliance. Other economists, such as Oxford's Nassau Senior, thought abolition impractical and so favoured drastic reform in assistance made available to the needy. The 1834 Poor Law abolished the old system of relief and legislated that support only be given inside new workhouses, where conditions were intentionally harsh and families were separated. John Stuart Mill went into print to support the legislative changes. By contrast, William Whewell considered the workhouse system evil and wrote of the irony that just as the British parliament (in the wake of the Christmas Rebellion in Jamaica) ended slavery in its colonies in 1833, it enslaved its own poor.[44]

Just a decade after the Poor Laws were passed, numerous abuses and scandals in workhouses burst into public consciousness. In one shocking incident in 1845 in Andover in Hampshire, as Laura Snyder puts it, 'starving inmates were found fighting over the putrid gristle and marrow of animal bones they were engaged in crushing'. Rumours spread that the bones were human. Following a public outcry, within a few years new legislation came into force and relief was once again given outside workhouses.[45]

A much more prominent role in orthodox economic textbooks and history is given to the repeal of the Corn Laws in 1846. These were import tariffs on grains such as wheat and oats that inflated bread prices. As seen in Chapter 7, Ricardo opposed the Corn Laws as a protectionist policy, which held back capitalist profit and, in his scheme, economic development. The repeal did eventually help fuel Britain's industrial development as cheap loaves fed the working classes. But, as with the story of Portuguese and English trade, the political and social context of the repeal is often left out of the picture.

Although the anti-Corn Law movement lasted decades, the immediate spur to abolish the Corn Laws was the Great Famine in Ireland. The problem began in 1845 with an import from South America: this time not gold but fungus. It rotted potato crops while they were in the ground across Europe. In total, around one hundred thousand people died in continental Europe; fearing public revolts governments in many countries, such as Belgium and France, intervened.[46] The British administrators in London— which had governed Ireland directly since the early 1800s—took a different route. The result has been described as the worst peacetime humanitarian disaster in Europe since the Black Death. The Great Famine lasted for seven years in Ireland. It killed 1 million men, women, and children through starvation or related diseases—an eighth of the population. Over a million more fled their homes, many to North America, becoming refugees on the ocean.[47] Even today, the Irish population is below its pre-famine levels.[48]

There were many reasons for the difference between death totals in Ireland and those in continental Europe. Ireland was ruled from afar in London, by a parliament elected by a small tranche of wealthy men. The Irish population had grown sharply and paid rent to landlords, many of whom did not live in the country. Britain's policy towards Ireland was influenced by ethnic and anti-Catholic prejudice and a willingness to blame the famine on a divine plan. But the London elite's belief in laissez-faire economics also played its part.[49] Malthus and Ricardo's ideas that population would inevitably outstrip food production had hardened into a dogma.

The Corn Laws were repealed in 1846 to bring down grain prices, which, it was hoped, would feed more people in Ireland. It was the 1840s version of a market solution to a crisis. Overseeing British relief efforts at the Treasury was Charles Trevelyan, a civil servant and former pupil of Malthus. He worked hard to solve the food crisis but within a political and ideological framework that ruled out the most effective remedy: providing large quantities of unconditional food aid. The starving poor were only given food relief in exchange for work. Many people travelled miles to build roads with their bare hands in the biting cold and slept without shelter.[50] The suffering and death were incalculable.

Trevelyan, who was implementing decisions taken by politicians, deemed that the British government response should proceed, as he said, 'with the least disturbance of private trade and market prices'.[51] Trevelyan described his plan in *The Irish Crisis* (1848) to give 'free scope' to the merchants to provide grain rather than give them the 'discouraging impression that all their calculations might be upset by sudden appearance' of government 'interference'.[52] What this meant in practice was that while people starved, grain and livestock were *exported* from Ireland, often under armed guard. The anthem, 'The Fields of Athenry', now sung at Irish football and rugby matches, is the story of a man who 'stole Trevelyan's corn' and was transported as a criminal to Australia.

The removal of the Corn Laws did little to help the poorest, who were unable to afford the market price. The worst winter of the famine lay ahead: 1846—1847 brought freezing temperatures and even more devastation of the potato crop.[53] Living through it in Ireland was the novelist Maria Edgeworth, who had once described her friend David Ricardo playing charades. Now in her 80s, she wrote to a relief committee asking for help for the '750 desperately shiveringly cold in this weather from the Snow'.[54] Edgeworth wrote about a particularly harrowing incident in 1847. She described a woman 'tottering along' the road near her home 'who seemed too much stupefied by hunger or despair or disease to notice' that on her back, she carried, 'the head bobbing around from side to side without her minding or seeming to feel it a dead child!'[55]

Ricardo's old constituency of Portarlington was not spared by the famine. Shortly before she died, aged 82 in May 1849, Maria Edgeworth wondered what 'our dear deceased friend Mr Ricardo' would have made of affairs in Ireland.[56] The two had exchanged letters in the final years of Ricardo's life about the Irish situation. Ricardo told her that Ireland was a 'great deal of trouble' and expense to Britain but that he wished it would be governed by 'indulgence, kindness and conciliation'. He also expressed his horror at the idea of living through a famine 'I would rather that I had never been born'.[57] But these were remarks in unpublished, private letters. A free-trade dogma, derived in part from his writings, which favoured the interests of capitalist sections of society over rural peasants, had settled in.

New principles and falsified predictions

In 1848, near the height of the Irish Famine and after the repeal of the Corn Laws, John Stuart Mill published his *Principles of Political Economy*, taking the name and the lead from David Ricardo: whom he called 'the true founder of the abstract science of political economy'.[58] It would be the dominant economics text for a generation.[59] It recognized new developments in the field, but insisted that they could be incorporated within Ricardo's framework when properly interpreted.[60]

Mill later wrote that his book's success was because it 'treated Political Economy not as a thing by itself, but as a fragment of a greater whole' whose conclusions are always reliant on causes outside its scope.[61] For this statement, he has been rightly praised. And yet Mill believed, as he explained to a friend, 'I doubt if there will be a single opinion (on pure political economy) in the book' that did not directly follow from Ricardo's 'doctrines'.[62] To balance these two conflicting ideas, he drew on the firewall between the 'strict science' of economics and the art of its application that he'd written about years before.[63] Crucially, the firewall between the abstract and practical went *both* ways: it was designed to insulate society from the application of inappropriate theory, but it also insulated theory from the critique that it failed to fit reality.[64] Mill's book was a reform of Ricardian economics, by which he hoped to forestall its revolutionary overthrow. Later, he would write with pride about how it, 'helped to disarm the enemies of so important a study'.[65]

J.S. Mill included Richard Jones' categorization of the different types of rent in his *Principles*, calling it 'a copious repertory of valuable facts'. Mill included more history and more empirical evidence than in his earlier writings, softening his early views on poor laws and charity in line with Whewell, who received the book more warmly. But Mill continued to promote economics as a deductive science.[66]

Adam Smith was deficient in his understanding of the true theory of economics, Mill wrote, because he was writing when the subject was in its 'infancy'. *The Wealth of Nations*, he remarked, 'is in many parts obsolete, and in all, imperfect'.[67] Smith's unique contribution, which Mill wanted to replicate, was to see economics as part of a larger whole and associate the principles with their applications. But in building this bridge to reality, Mill had a big problem. The statistical evidence that had come to light in the previous decade did not conform to Ricardo's theories.

Ricardo had argued that without free trade in wheat, bread prices would rise. In reality, British wheat prices fell steadily from their high 1818 levels, due in part to improvements in agricultural technology that were overlooked in the model. As we've seen, the theory of rent Ricardo put forward indicated that rents from land would rise (as the landed aristocracy exploited the other two classes in society). In reality, land rents in England rose little, if at all, in the 25 years following Ricardo's death. Workers' wages would remain at a subsistence level, Ricardo had repeated. And, once again, in reality, English labourers' real wages rose slightly between 1823 and the appearance of Mill's book in 1848.[68] Mill acknowledged most of these facts in his *Principles* and yet still taught that Ricardo's theories were the best of science.

Mill explained this divergence by extending the 'temporary' period during which the real-world results might diverge from the supposedly 'permanent' state described by the laws. For example, Mill says that food prices have not risen (as per Ricardo's theory) due to an unexplained 'strong impulse' to 'agricultural improvement' that had appeared in Britain recently.[69] How durable was this anomaly? As the British historian of economics Mark Blaug observes, 'Mill put the Principles through as many as six editions, and with each successive edition it became more and more difficult to deny the refutation of virtually every one of Ricardo's historical predictions.'[70] In 1848, Mill said the divergence between theory and fact had been present in 'the last fifteen or twenty years'. Almost fifteen years later, he was repeating the same line. He increased it to 'twenty or thirty' years by the final edition in 1871.[71] (Which meant at the lower bound that the 'temporary' trend started as late as 1851, after he published the first edition.) Even by the most generous interpretation this was a fudge. Less generously, it might be compared to believers of a sect postponing, time and again, the day of judgement as it fails to appear.

Mill was not alone. Many of the mainstream economic thinkers of his day were unwilling to give facts as much weight as theory. The evidence and statistics were available to show that the whole 'permanent' theoretical structure was faulty, but their arguments usually related to tweaking the assumptions. As Blaug concluded,

'The divorce between theory and facts was probably never more complete than in the heyday of Ricardian economics.'[72]

It would take decades and the work of many others but, within a few years of Whewell's death in 1866, belief in Mill's version of Ricardo's economics and method was on life support.

9

The Fall

A journey through a century of thinking in
which Ricardian economics became a 'vice'

Perhaps the most well-known critics of the orthodox economics of the nineteenth century, a generation after Ricardo's death, were literary figures. Charles Dickens in *A Christmas Carol* (1843) attacked the population theory promoted by Ricardo and Malthus when he made the miser Ebenezer Scrooge wish the poor and destitute would die to 'decrease the surplus population'.[1] Similarly, Dickens exposed the inhumanity of industrial Britain in his 1854 novel *Hard Times* through the hard-hearted Thomas Gradgrind, whose two children were called Adam Smith and Malthus. In the novel, Dickens, has a spirited circus girl, Sissy Jupe, take an eight-week course in political economy. Asked at the end, 'What is the first principle of this science?' Sissy reveals she's learned nothing by replying: 'To do unto others as I would that they should do unto me.'[2]

Arguably more influential than Dickens was *Unto This Last*, a collection of essays published in 1862 by art critic John Ruskin, which tore into orthodox economics and declared 'there is no wealth but life'. It would inspire reformists from the British Labour Party to Mahatma Gandhi.[3] John Stuart Mill referred to figures such as these as 'the numerous sentimental enemies of political economy'. In our time, economist Diane Coyle has called the period 'the Romantic backlash'.[4] Some of this criticism was deeply misguided. Economics is still often called 'the dismal science', which, as we saw, comes from a racist essay by Thomas Carlyle that argued for bringing slavery back to the West Indies.

Less well known than the literary revolt against political economy in the nineteenth century are the challengers of orthodox thinking who saw themselves as part of the discipline. This chapter picks out a few of the milestones in the fall in the prestige of classical economics from the 1860s to the 1950s. This fall is often forgotten or ignored. The story here is focused on those in the UK and US who countered the idea of universal economic laws with the study of history and institutions.[5]

Not a 'science of wealth' but 'a science *for* wealth'

In the generation after Richard Jones and William Whewell, one of the most influential critical economists in the UK was Thomas Cliffe Leslie. Born in south-east Ireland, he graduated from Trinity College Dublin in 1846, the worst year of the Great Famine, and became Professor of Political Economy in Belfast. Leslie studied the impact of the loss of a third of the Irish population through emigration and famine and wrote widely on gold, wages, land, and consumer rights. The work led him to attack the economic dogmas of his day that were masquerading as science.

Cliffe Leslie argued in 1870 that there were two different schools of economics: one that followed the inductive investigation of facts and the other deductive logical reasoning. Cliffe Leslie saw Adam Smith as having used both methods, but he sharply criticized Ricardo, 'the founder,' he said, of the school of economists 'reasoning entirely from hypothetical laws'. Smith had been saved from the 'enormous fallacies into which the school of Ricardo has since been betrayed by their method of pure deduction'. These methods, Cliffe Leslie said, 'greatly thicken the confusion perpetually arising between the real and the ideal, between that which by the assumption ought to be and that which actually is'.[6] He railed against the disappearance in the classical school of the behaviour or motivations of real people, of institutions, and of history. He decried how the 'science' served the established powers in society: 'Instead of a science of wealth, they gave us a science *for* wealth.'[7]

For Cliffe Leslie, to be a real science, economics needed to be far more observational. Deductive logic could only aid in the discovery of economic truths when anchored to the real world. Good economics, he argued, meant 'accepting no assumptions as finally established without proof ... no chains of deduction from hypothetical premises as possessing more than hypothetical truth, until verified by observation'.[8] The old classical economics reached for an 'unreal uniformity and order in the world' that exists only in the mind, Leslie said, and placed in it 'unlimited confidence'. It was 'amazing', he wrote, to have attempted to build economics 'with little or no inspection of the phenomena whose laws it aims to interpret'.[9] He could hardly have been clearer if he had said: economists of the world unite, you have nothing to lose but your chains of deduction. For Cliffe Leslie, this was not just an intellectual argument but related to real economic issues such as wages, land rent, and emigration, impacting millions.

In 1870, J.S. Mill was in his 60s and the last few years of his life. He had continued evolving intellectually and publicly broke with the 'iron law of wages' attributed to Ricardo a year earlier. Mill, in a review of Cliffe Leslie's book, called him 'one of the best living writers on applied political economy', one who studied the subject 'first hand, and on the spot'. Mill criticized people who liked 'to get their thinking done once and for all, and be saved all further trouble except that of referring to a formula'.[10] It was a stark admission of the dogmas created out of orthodox economics.

Ricardo's style of economics was still defended in the mid-nineteenth century but the arguments had become more desperate. Take, for example, John Elliott Cairnes (1823–1875), often called 'the last of the classical economists'.[11] Cairnes wildly asserted: '*The economist starts with a knowledge of ultimate causes. He is already, at the outset of his enterprise, in the position which the physicist only attains after ages of laborious research.*'[12] Those who had launched 'flippant attacks' on David Ricardo for his frequent use of 'hypothetical' reasoning were mistaken. Ricardo's approach, he said, was actually a form of the 'experimental method'.[13] This was not an argument that would hold long.[14]

Other thinkers wanted to stick with the idea of reducing economics to a rigorous mathematical form, but to do it better. Most prominent of those in the UK was William Stanley Jevons (1835–1882), now recognized as one of the leading members of the 'marginal revolution' in economics. In 1879, Jevons wrote of his desire to 'pick up the fragments of a shattered science and to start anew'. The problems stemmed, Jevons said, from 'that able but wrong-headed man, David Ricardo, [who] shunted the car of Economic science on to a wrong line'.[15] The marginalists were a highly influential group of economists who dropped the 'labour theory of value' associated with Ricardo and adopted a view that the value of goods or services comes from the subjective benefit or pleasure created by an extra unit of them. This meant they stopped worrying about tricky questions of the value of things and focused instead on their price. Value was whatever it was worth to you. However new in part, the idea still rested on the same strong assumption of humans as 'calculating machines' that Ricardo held. It paved the way to similar beliefs in today's mainstream neoclassical economics.

Jevons recreated abstract economics in England and pushed it more explicitly towards mathematics as an ideal. He used Newton's laws of motion as a model for his 'law of demand' (which says that as the price of something falls, people will buy more of it).[16] His theories were far from universally accepted in his time, but were celebrated a century later. In 1970, the winner of the first Nobel Memorial Prize in Economics said that modern quantitative economics had realized the 'dream of Stanley Jevons ... not a dream anymore but a reality'.[17] Despite his criticisms of Ricardo, Jevons also shared with the old, classical economist the idea of a theory-first route to knowledge. Responding to Cliffe Leslie's attacks on abstract economics, Jevons admitted that: 'Theory must be invested with the reality and life of fact.' But, he then added, the 'difficulties of this union are immensely great' and so he continued in an almost purely deductive way: 'before we attempt any investigation of facts, we must have correct theoretical notions'.[18]

Britain was in the midst of great social changes. The Second Reform Act of 1867 gave urban working-class men the vote for the first time. In 1871 trade unions were legalized, allowing the working poor to participate more in politics. By the 1880s, blows against Ricardo's economics were coming from all sides. Walter Bagehot, who wrote extensively on politics and economics (as well as race and eugenics) and was editor of *The Economist* for 17 years, wrote a scathing essay—published posthumously in 1880—on Ricardo as the 'true founder of abstract Political Economy'. Despite his genius,

To the end of his days, indeed, he never comprehended what he was doing. He dealt with abstractions without knowing that they were such; he thoroughly believed that he was dealing with real things. He thought that he was considering actual human nature in its actual circumstances, when he was really considering a fictitious nature in fictitious circumstances.

(This is what would later be called the Pygmalion Syndrome.) Spinning out theories, spider-like, had been the easy part, Bagehot suggested, the difficult task ahead for economics was 'comparing the assumptions we have made in it with the facts which we see'.[19]

By 1886, criticism of Ricardo was so mainstream that it even made it into the *Encyclopaedia Britannica*. The entry on Ricardo by John Kells Ingram, an Irish polymath and president of the Statistical and Social Inquiry Society of Ireland, concluded that 'the truth of Ricardo's theorems is now by his warmest admirers admitted to be hypothetical only' and economic science is turning from them 'to real life and men [*sic*] as they actually are or have been'.[20] Those with long enough memories were amazed at the boom and bust of the classical economist's legacy. At one time no name would have better bolstered an opinion than Ricardo's, but by the 1890s the mere suggestion that an idea had been held by him was enough to discredit it.[21]

Cambridge professor Alfred Marshall took up the task of threading these divergent strands of thinking into a harmonious and academically respectable subject (borrowing ideas freely and without acknowledgement from his wife, Mary Paley). Marshall is largely responsible for changing the name of the subject. While Ricardo, Malthus, and J.S. Mill had called their major works *Principles of Political Economy*, Marshall's great book, published in 1890, was *Principles of Economics*. It replaced J.S. Mill's as the standard text in Britain for a generation. Marshall's rationale for ditching 'political economy' and replacing it with 'economics' was his attempt to establish a professional and scientific field that avoided politics and ideology.[22] Stanley Jevons, of the new generation of theorists, could not wait 'to discard, as quickly as possible, the old troublesome double-worded name of our Science'.[23] I once thought this name change marked the point when the discipline forgot that its subject was inextricably bound up with power and society and became overly narrow and abstract. But classical political economy was, in some hands, wildly abstract. I now consider the name change to be a clever exercise in rebranding.

Marshall's book danced nimbly between accepting the criticisms of historical economists, incorporating the new marginalists' theory, and defending Ricardo and classical political economy. He accepted that 'dogmas' mistakenly drawn from classical economics had 'served as an armoury with which partisan disputants (chiefly the capitalist class) have equipped themselves for the fray' and kept 'the working classes in their place'.[24] He argued that Ricardo was a 'genius' but a poor writer who should be generously interpreted. Ricardo's method, he claimed, rightly interpreted was not a dogma but 'an engine for the discovery of concrete truth'.[25] Marshall consistently downplayed and explained away Ricardo's faults and weaknesses and shifted attention from his theories of land rent and wages towards his theories of international trade and money. Like J.S. Mill before him, Marshall kept Ricardo's flag flying from a more defendable position. Historically minded economic thinkers grumbled that Ricardo's economics were being rehabilitated.[26] Joseph Schumpeter wrote on Marshall's *Principles*: 'the rooms of this new house are unnecessarily cluttered up with Ricardian heirlooms'.[27]

The methodology of Marshall's new economics was laid out most fully by his student John Neville Keynes, the father of the great twentieth-century economist, mathematician, and thinker John Maynard Keynes. (Both father and son were known by their middle names.) The older Keynes rejected the criticism from historical economists that economic laws were 'mere fictions of the imagination' produced by the method of 'closing one's eyes to facts, and trying to think out the laws of the economic world in entire neglect of what is actually taking place'. He claimed that Ricardo's writings were 'some of the most brilliant and instructive examples of close deductive reasoning to be found in economic literature ... [but] not free from grave faults'. He sensibly suggested that the deductive method should never be used alone but 'aided and controlled by induction'. The proper method was three steps. Deduction should be sandwiched between the inductive method, which is to be used to identify the premises and to verify the conclusions. The old Keynes put it well: economics 'must both begin with observation and end with observation'.[28]

This chapter is not, and cannot be, a comprehensive history of economic thinking in the late 1800s. It has only looked at the smashing of Ricardo's legacy as a leading thinker and attempts to partially rehabilitate him. The chapter has not considered Karl Marx and other socialist writers, who borrowed from Ricardo his class-based view of society and his theory that the value of goods comes from their labour. Both Ricardo and Marx claimed that there was a section of society—who got more and more of the economic pie—dragging everyone else down. They just disagreed on which section: for Ricardo, it was landowners; for Marx, capitalists. Marx used Ricardo's theory—that goods derive their value from the labour that it takes to create them—to argue that capitalists steal from workers when they sell goods over the price of production and call it 'profit'. Undoubtedly, some of the animosity towards Ricardo was driven by the idea that the arch-capitalist had unwittingly provided a 'scientific' rationale for socialist thinking. Some socially minded writers saw Ricardo's legacy as contributing to dogmatism in the Marxist tradition.[29]

We have also not considered the American institutional economists such as Richard Ely and Thorstein Veblen, who abandoned what Ely called 'the dry bones of orthodox English political economy'.[30] Veblen built a rival theory of economics inspired not by Newton's clockwork universe but the more organic, evolutionary vision of Charles Darwin's *Origin of Species* published in 1859. He was part of a larger 'revolt against formalism' that held sway in American economic, philosophical, and legal thought for 50 years. Members of this progressive movement, its chronicler notes, were 'convinced that logic, abstraction, deduction, mathematics, and mechanics were inadequate to social research and incapable of containing the rich, moving, living current of life'.[31]

This revolt produced some fine thinking in the American democratic tradition. It included writers—such as W.E.B. Du Bois—who worked to dismantle racism. However, some 'progressives'—such as Ely—promoted racist and eugenic policies. It was not until the twentieth-century that the challenge to Eurocentric colonialism, of land and knowledge, came to the fore in the West.

Likewise, we've skipped over the myriad economic and social issues of the age that were the essential backdrop to thought: the rising power of trade unions, the violent repression of striking labourers, the 'robber barons' of the Gilded Age, and also the introduction of state pensions for the elderly, laws to break up corporate monopolies, and progressive income taxes in Britain, France, and the US between 1909 and 1914. We will pause, though, to look at one essential feature of recent economic models first identified in the late 1800s.

Your inner stockbroker

At the centre of so many influential economic models is a curious creature, who we have met already, known as 'economic human'. Economic human is a being with God-like powers. They calculate instantaneously every decision and take the path that will most benefit themselves. They have complete knowledge of the world. Their tastes never change. But, the modeller giveth and the modeller taketh away. Economic human lacks emotions, intimate relationships, a sense of belonging to a place or time or society. They are a replacement of flesh-and-blood humans made for mathematical and conceptual convenience.

It was during the fall of classical political economy towards the end of the nineteenth century that writers first began to use the name *homo economicus* or 'economic human'.[32] Who is this creature? Where did they come from?

Some have argued that their origins are with Adam Smith; as he is claimed to be the founder of economics, this would make sense. Smith does argue that 'the butcher, the brewer, or the baker' provide us with dinner 'from regard to their own interest' rather than humanity or altruism. (Although Smith neglected to mention that his own dinner was provided by his mother, Margaret Douglas, for most of his adult life.[33]) But Smith does not deny the usefulness or power of these other promptings. Indeed, his early work, *The Theory of Moral Sentiments*, is all about the essential role of human sympathy in society: how we are inclined to imaginatively identify with others and feel their sorrows and joys. As Mary Morgan, a historian of economics at the London School of Economics writes, Smith gives us a 'much too well-rounded a portrait [of humans] to work as a model' as it is 'simply too complicated to reason with'. We have to look elsewhere for economic human's birth.[34]

The conventional wisdom, put forward by Mary Morgan and others, is that John Stuart Mill delivered the concept into the world.[35] The evidence for this comes from Mill's 1836 essay where he explains that economics does not study the whole actions of humans in society but 'is concerned with him solely as a being who desires to possess wealth, and who is capable of judging the comparative efficacy of means for obtaining that end. ... It makes entire abstraction of every other human passion or motive.' (It might surprise some to know that Mill went on to claim: 'Not that any political economist was ever so absurd as to suppose that mankind are really thus constituted but because this is the mode in which science must necessary proceed.')[36] Mill did not use the term 'economic human' (or, as it has frequently been known, 'economic man') but the concept can clearly be found in this passage, which was targeted by the critics of the 1870s. But there's good evidence that the idea did not originate with J.S. Mill.

Mill, as we saw in Chapter 8, was raised on Ricardo's economics, which his father saw as the pinnacle of knowledge. When he wrote the 1836 essays, he was deeply under the influence of Ricardo. Mill fleshed out his teacher's ideas. It was Ricardo who wrote in one of his first published article on economics: 'It is self-interest which regulates all speculations of trade ... we should not know where to stop if we admitted any other rule of action.'[37] The true origin of the concept of economic human, I suggest, comes not from Mill, but from Ricardo. And where did Ricardo get the idea from?

Consider again Ricardo in the London Stock Exchange in Chapter 1. He is described as having 'complete knowledge', cool judgement, and an ability to carry out immense calculations with 'surprising quickness'. These were exceptional talents, which he used to become immensely wealthy. These are also the primary characteristics of economic human: self-interest, perfect knowledge, and calculating ability. Ricardo worked in the money markets day after day from the age of 14 until his retirement three decades later. Could it be that the model of economic human was less a window onto the world and more of a mirror reflecting the mind of Ricardo? It makes sense to me that his ideas would have grown out of his everyday experience in the most abstract of business environments, especially as Ricardo often arrived at economic knowledge through introspection. We have lost this insight now, but the origins of economic human on the stock market were well recognized in the 1890s.

Alfred Marshall wrote that Ricardo's fixed idea of humans stemmed from a life spent in London's financial district, known then and now as the City.[38] The people Ricardo 'knew most intimately were city men,' Marshall wrote, which led him to build theories 'on the tacit supposition that the world was made up of city men'.[39] Economic human was, for Marshall, based on the image of the city banker, carrying out 'deliberate and far-reaching calculations … executed with vigour and ability'.[40] Similarly, John Neville Keynes traced Ricardo's assumption of unceasing economic competition to his 'position in the City, and on the Stock Exchange—a market that may be taken as a type of theoretically perfect market, where competition is unceasing, and supply and demand all powerful'.[41] Ricardo overgeneralized from his own experience, Keynes argued, which led his thinking astray.[42] More recently, in 1993, Terry Peach, a historian of economic thought and Ricardo specialist, wrote that 'Ricardo seems to have assumed that there was a stockbroker similar to himself in every man.'[43] That's the origin of economic human.[44]

The contemporary field of behavioural economics provides more supporting evidence that the concept of economic human came from the London trading markets of the early 1800s. Daniel Kahneman, one of its leading authorities, suggests that people become more like economic human by 'thinking like a trader'. Experiments at baseball-card conventions have shown, unsurprisingly, that veteran traders are more calculating and less sentimental about an object they own than a novice trader.[45]

The problem is that too many economic thinkers, even those who are aware of behavioural economics, see acting like an idealized trader or stockbroker as positive and acting like a normal human being as negative.[46] Part of this is due to the mathematical and conceptual convenience. This confusion is thickened by the misuse of the English language. Economic human is often described as 'rational' and any departure from this behaviour as irrational. But in everyday speech rational has the strong emotive meanings of reasonable, intelligent, and sane, while irrational means crazy or foolish. As the common associations of rational are so vivid, it is not enough to occasionally remind students or readers of its technical meaning: one bleeds into the other.[47] The British author and economist John Kay has described the 'impressive feat of marketing' by the economics profession to have twisted the term 'rationality' to mean something quite different.[48] Replacing 'rational' with the more precise word 'calculating', as some already do, would better describe the behaviour of economic human.

The Great Depression

This history now jumps forward from inner stockbrokers to real-life ones on Wall Street in 1929. That year, a meteor slammed into the remains of orthodox economics. In the Great Depression that followed the Wall Street Crash, more than 100,000 businesses went bankrupt in the US and the unemployment rate hit 25 per cent (see Figure 9.1).[49] The depression spread throughout the globe. The orthodox economics of the time held that it would just be a matter of time until the natural forces of the economy righted themselves and that unemployment and overproduction were temporary 'frictions'. The possibility of a lasting depression—or 'general glut' as Ricardo and Malthus called it—was denied.

British economist and philosopher John Maynard Keynes, who, like his father, had been a leading figure in the orthodox Marshall tradition, revolutionized economic thinking in his *General Theory*

Figure 9.1: Detail from Franklin D. Roosevelt Memorial, Washington, DC

Source: Sonder Quest on Unsplash

of Employment, Interest and Money in 1936. Keynesian economic theory, in a nutshell, argued that the modern economy might settle into an unhealthy equilibrium of mass unemployment and that the government, instead of cutting spending in a crisis, should borrow and spend to boost demand for goods. Often overlooked is that Keynes challenged the vision of the economy as a machine and stressed the radical uncertainty of the future, which far enough removed, was immune to calculation.[50]

In 1936, Keynes explained that like 'all contemporary English economists' he had been brought up on Marshall's work, which was ultimately a continuation of Ricardo's.[51] Some saw the title of Keynes' book—*General Theory*—as a play on Einstein's general theory of relativity that had supplanted Newton's laws in the early 1900s. It suggested that Keynes saw himself as the Einstein of economics: exposing the limitations of classical theories.[52] Keynes was much keener on theory than the inductive, historical economists, some of whom had been too like the ant in Francis Bacon's analogy: piling up facts but not connecting them together in theories. But Keynes said explicitly that human society was not like physics. His own originality, he said, was in *not* following the great trader-turned-economist. In a masterful backhanded compliment, he wrote:

> Ricardo offers us the supreme intellectual achievement, unattainable by weaker spirits, of adopting a hypothetical world remote from experience as though it were the world of experience and then living in it consistently. With most of his successors common sense cannot help breaking in—with injury to their logical consistency.[53]

Ricardo's economic world, as we have seen, was not that remote from his lived experience. It reflected, at least in part, the realities of the stock market he lived and breathed for 30 years. It carried the aspirations of his emerging capitalist class who were challenging Britain's feudal aristocracy and wanted to export their manufacturing goods freely around the world. But it was more a dream or vision of how things could be rather than a reflection of the economic reality of most of the world in his own time. Echoing earlier criticism about the confusion between the real and ideal, Keynes wrote that Ricardo's worldview 'represents the way in which we should like our economy to behave. But to assume that it actually does so is to assume our difficulties away.' The intellectual rot, Keynes remarked, was located not in the surface layer of polished logic, but in its foundations; 'not in the superstructure, which has been erected with great care for logical consistency, but in a lack of clearness and of generality in the premises'.[54]

Keynes, with a lucid mix of insight and exaggeration, blamed Ricardo for the widespread idea that a general depression was not possible: 'If only Malthus, instead of Ricardo, had been the parent stem from which nineteenth-century economics proceeded, what a much wiser and richer place the world would be today!'[55] The persistence of Ricardo's ideas had damaged not just the economy, he said, but the standing of economics in society because

> its signal failure for purposes of scientific prediction has greatly impaired, in the course of time, the prestige of its practitioners. For professional economists, after Malthus, were apparently unmoved by the lack of correspondence between the results of their theory and the facts of observation;—a discrepancy which the ordinary man has not failed to observe, with the result of his growing unwillingness to accord to economists that measure of respect which he gives to other groups of scientists whose theoretical results are confirmed by observation when they are applied to the facts.[56]

Keynes took another of Ricardo's ideas and turned it upside down. Ricardo had popularized a theory of rent: the excess, unmerited income that accrues to wealthy property owners or 'rentiers' because of what they own rather than what they earn. Ricardo had said rent, which is by definition a drag on the economy, is only collected by the landlord class. It was not to be confused, he said, with the interest and profit on financial capital.[57] Keynes took the concept of 'rent' and expanded it to include the unmerited income in the finance sector. The *General Theory* called for 'the euthanasia of the rentier, of the functionless investor'.[58] Economic thinkers in recent decades have further expanded the idea of rent—to areas such as patent protection for medicines and digital platforms—to explain the poor performance and inequality of early twenty-first-century economies.

'The Ricardian Vice'

Keynes' new ideas spread through economists aged under 35, it was said, like a virulent disease attacking an isolated tribe. Part of its appeal was that it offered the possibility of preserving the liberal democratic and capitalist world, which, in its current version, had come to be seen as cruel and without remedy for its problems at home and was challenged abroad by totalitarian ideologies of right and left. Keynes' ideas offered a rival system, which could incorporate some of the old classical thinking yet better explain and offer some viable solutions for crises in the modern world.[59]

One of the older economists immune to the charms of Keynes was Joseph Schumpeter (1883–1950), seen as one of the great economic minds of his time and remembered by a column in *The Economist*. Originally from Austria, Schumpeter had crossed the Atlantic and was by the 1930s a professor at Harvard. He is best known for celebrating the 'creative destruction' of capitalism: the idea that economic progress constantly destroys old industries and creates new ones. Often overlooked was Schumpeter's belief that in addition to learning theory and statistics, the economist should be competent in 'economic history—which issues into and includes present-day facts—is by far the most important'. The lack of a sense of history, Schumpeter argued, lay behind 'most of the fundamental errors' of economics.[60]

In his posthumously published, 1,186-page *History of Economic Analysis* (1954), edited by his wife, Schumpeter coined a term some sections of the profession still use to describe a widespread flaw in economics: the Ricardian Vice. Schumpeter argued that Ricardo wanted a 'clear-cut result of direct, practical significance' so, he cut the complex economic system

> to pieces, bundled up as large parts of it as possible, and put them in cold storage—so that as many things as possible should be frozen and 'given'. He then piled one simplifying assumption upon another until, having really settled everything by these assumptions, he was left with only a few aggregative variables between which, given these assumptions, he set up simple one-way relations so that, in the end, the desired results emerged almost as tautologies.[61]

Here Ricardo is like a theoretical Elsa from *Frozen* freezing the world still. Schumpeter in the last part of that quotation points to the power of first principles or assumptions to become conclusions. So, if the assumptions are hollow, so are the conclusions. As an example of a trivial conclusion arrived at in this way, he points to Ricardo's thinking on profit and agriculture:

> a famous Ricardian theory is that profits 'depend upon' the price of wheat. And under his implicit assumptions and in the particular sense in which the terms of the proposition are to be understood, this is not only true, but undeniably, in fact trivially, so. Profits could not possibly depend upon anything else, since everything else is 'given', that is, frozen. It is an excellent theory that can never be refuted and lacks nothing save sense. The habit of applying results of this character to the solution of practical problems we shall call the Ricardian Vice.[62]

The Ricardian Vice lies not in creating highly abstract models but using them to guide real-world actions. Schumpeter's interpretation of Ricardo is not an outlier, it is the summation of a 150-year critical tradition.[63]

By the time Schumpeter's critique of the Ricardian Vice appeared in the mid-1950s, the intellectual tide was turning again. Within two decades, a new classical economics dominated the field and prominent economists would argue that applying abstract models to practical problems was not a vice but a virtue. The great appeal of the 'new classical' economics was in the precision and coherence of the modelling and mathematics that made older theories seem like they were stuck in the Dark Ages.[64] This was a counter-revolution in economics: away from a broad, historical, institutional vision.

The irony is that the person who did more than anyone to spark this counter-revolution was a student of Joseph Schumpeter and a self-described follower of J.M. Keynes.

PART III

Rebirth

10

The Return of Unreality

*How economists learned to stop worrying and
love unreal assumptions during the Cold War*

The theoretical case that government only had a limited role in running the economy, which had been defended since the days of Ricardo, was torpedoed during the Second World War. All the major powers reorganized and directed their economies into warfare states. Then, after the war, faced with the threat of their working populations rallying to communism, it was a short step from a warfare to a welfare state. The US did not go as far down this route as Europe but its economic relations had been revolutionized by the New Deal of the 1930s. The new political order became bipartisan with President Eisenhower in 1953, a new type of Republican. Both major parties signed up to a consensus of greater worker rights, curbs on employer power, and high marginal tax rates for the wealthiest Americans: up to 91 per cent for almost two decades after the war. Laissez-faire had lost its legal, intellectual, and moral hold. Believers in the old market creed lamented that: 'We are all Keynesians now.'[1] The result, in the US and Western Europe, was unprecedented prosperity—at least for White populations—and a 'great redistribution' of wealth.[2]

John Kenneth Galbraith, a Harvard economist in the tradition of American institutionalists and Keynes, had been in charge of fixing prices in the US during the Second World War. His popular 1952 book *American Capitalism* surveyed the astonishing changes of the past two decades. Galbraith began the book with the semi-mythical story of how, according to the rules of aerodynamics and wing loading, the bumblebee should not fly and yet does (see Figure 10.1). The US economy in recent years resembled the bumblebee, he said: 'The present organization and management of the American economy are also in defiance of the rules—rules that derive their ultimate authority from men of such Newtonian stature as Bentham, Ricardo, and Adam Smith. Nevertheless it works, and in the years since World War II quite brilliantly.'[3] The new US economy operated, Galbraith said, on the principle of 'countervailing power'. The concentration of private economic power in the hands of a few corporations had been balanced by the rise of powerful labour unions, consumer groups, and citizen democracy. This countervailing power had forced corporations to share the fruits of commerce more broadly.

Figure 10.1: Bumblebee in flight, Parc Jura Vaudois, Switzerland

Source: Wikimedia Commons CC BY-SA 4.0 (https://creativecommons.org/licenses/by-sa/4.0/). Photo: Giles Laurent

Samuelson's hop and Sraffa's step

Although Galbraith was Professor of Economics at Harvard for over fifty years, he was less an academic than a public intellectual—who coined the term 'conventional wisdom'—and an advisor to presidents. He served as John F. Kennedy's Ambassador to India in the 1960s and was renowned for his glitzy garden parties. While he directed a string of economics books towards the general public, different intellectual trends took hold in US economics' departments.

The person most responsible for shaping modern, academic economics was Paul Samuelson (1915–2009). After studying at the University of Chicago, then at Harvard under Joseph Schumpeter, he produced a PhD that sought to identify the mathematical foundations of economics. In 1948, Samuelson—now at MIT— published *Economics*, one of the best-selling textbooks in history. The extra income was handy when his wife had triplet boys in 1953 and the family, now with six children, went through 350 nappies a week.[4] Samuelson became the dominant figure of early post-war US economics, and other economists occasionally joked (because it's technically impossible) that he had a comparative advantage in every economic specialism. In 1970 he became the first American to win the newly created Nobel Memorial Prize in Economics, for 'raising the level of analysis in economic science'.[5] He was also a follower of John Maynard Keynes and did more to spread Keynesian economics in America than anyone else.

Except it wasn't the economics of Keynes. Samuelson called himself a 'cafeteria Keynesian', picking the parts he liked and leaving the rest.[6] He popularized a version of Keynes' theory that critics said left out many of the novel and interesting parts.[7] Samuelson believed his version was more sophisticated. He even said that Keynes misunderstood his own ideas before others translated them into mathematical models.[8] Samuelson was not alone in his quest to make economics a more mathematical science. Two Dutch mathematical economists—Jan Tinbergen and his student Tjalling Koopmans—also played a leading role. In the 1930s, Tinbergen had transferred the term 'model' from physics to economics to refer to statistical and mathematical objects.[9] In the late 1940s, Koopmans, now in the US, attacked institutionalist economists for 'measurement without theory'. He argued that economics needed to move to the 'Newton stage', where economic theory would be used in the process of observation and measurement in the hope that 'the general theory of gravity described by Newton might find a counterpart in similar discovery of the laws of economic motion'.[10] These views were highly influential. Tinbergen won the new 'Nobel' prize in economics in its first year, followed by Koopmans a few years later.[11]

Samuelson would introduce generations of students to economics as an exact, mathematical science. Samuelson taught that Keynes had shown the limitations of 'the old classical or Euclidean economics', referring to the Greek mathematician, Euclid.[12] For the theorist, the old, classical world was a happy realm where full employment reigned and economic logic mapped onto reality seamlessly. It is model land.[13] But Samuelson flagged to his students what I have called the if/is gap: the importance of keeping in mind the difference between the ideal and the real. While the American economist praised Ricardo's theory of comparative advantage as 'a closely reasoned doctrine which, when properly stated, is unassailable,' he advised it is 'best understood and defended if we agree in advance to apply it only to a Euclidean world where there is substantially full employment'.[14]

Awkwardly, Samuelson had his feet in both camps. He created the field of 'public goods' in economics to analyse commodities or services made available to all members of society such as street lighting and national defence. Classical economics he saw as 'old', recalling a society of raw capitalism that was shown to be too unstable and was replaced by the modern thinking of John Maynard Keynes. While Ricardo and other classical economists appealed to his desire for conceptual clarity, he knew that their clean logic often failed to map onto society. For example, Samuelson wrote that the idea of spontaneous order in the economic system—which he associated with Adam Smith's 'invisible hand'—'has done almost as much harm as good in the past century and a half'.[15] His solution: use the classical theories, imagine the world as neat and logical, but keep in mind that it is unreal. His ideas were taken up by others; the caveats were forgotten.

Joseph Schumpeter might not have been surprised that one of his Harvard pupils helped turn the tide in economics back to unreality. In discussing the Ricardian Vice, Schumpeter wrote: 'The trouble with him [Ricardo] is akin to the trouble I have, in this respect, with my American students.' There is no point in stuffing them with historical material, he continued, because they lack the historical sense to incorporate it: 'This is why it is so much easier to make theorists of them than economists.'[16]

Samuelson had a direct role in updating Ricardo's trade theory for the twentieth century too. Building on work by two Swedish economists Eli Heckscher and Bertil Ohlin, Samuelson created a two-country, two-product model in the 1940s. Ricardo had included only labour as a 'factor of production' in his famous example of English cloth and Portuguese wine. Samuelson's innovation was to introduce capital (essentially money) as a second factor.

The theory predicted that the pattern of global trade is determined by each country's relative 'endowment' of labour and capital. A country such as the US, which was richer in capital than labour, was supposed to export products like cars, which required large quantities of capital, and import products such as textiles, which require lots of labour. However, when Wassily Leontief—one of Samuelson's teachers at Harvard and another future Nobel Prize winner—carried out a detailed, factual study on US trade in 1953, he concluded that the theory was 'wrong' and 'the opposite is true'. Leontief found that the US exported more labour-intensive, rather than capital-intensive products.[17] The curious thing is that few international trade economists abandoned the Heckscher–Ohlin–Samuelson (HOS) theory, as it was known. Instead, some tried to save it using new methods of measurement or new interpretations. The mismatch between theory and empirical study became known as the 'Leontief paradox '. It was a 'paradox' as economists once again began to have more confidence in theory than data.[18]

John Maynard Keynes unintentionally played a central role in rehabilitating David Ricardo. He had brought Piero Sraffa, a shy, Italian economist, to Cambridge in the 1920s. Sraffa had radical socialist leanings: when the Italian Marxist Antonio Gramsci was imprisoned in 1926, it was Sraffa who gave him the journals and pens with which Gramsci would write his influential *Prison Notebooks*.[19] Sraffa disliked lecturing students so Keynes, in the early 1930s, suggested to the British Royal Economic Society that the Italian economist be given the job of collating and publishing the collected works of David Ricardo. The job was due to take a year. Sraffa plunged himself into the role with such diligence, uncovering much of the correspondence on which this and other accounts of Ricardo have drawn, that it took him 20 years to complete![20]

Sraffa's work, especially his introduction to the series, which appeared in 1951, led to a view that the true David Ricardo had been at last revealed underneath more than a hundred years of misinterpretation.[21] Ricardo-style classical economics was reappreciated across the board: from right-leaning George Stigler of the Chicago School to left-leaning Joan Robinson of the Cambridge Keynesians.[22] *The Economist*, reviewing Sraffa's new book, said that it was essential, as 'the classical economists, and Ricardo in particular, discovered something more important than any single economic generalisation; they discovered the technique of economic analysis itself'.[23] Sraffa's volumes were a Ricardian reset. It became easy to argue that all earlier critics were ill-informed and could be ignored.

Sraffa's rehabilitation of Ricardo, in the early Cold War period, led to a fight over his legacy. Sraffa claimed to have identified a 'corn model', drawing on his theorizing related to agriculture. The import of the argument was to claim that Ricardo had stayed true to the labour theory of value and was the ancestor of Karl Marx's socialism, not the capitalist neoclassical school. In reaction, Canadian historian of economic thought Samuel Hollander claimed that Ricardo was a brilliant neoclassical scholar. This has produced decades of dense literature described by Terry Peach in *Interpreting Ricardo* (1993) as 'a bitterly contested paternity suit' of directly contradictory and dogmatic interpretations. Each side, Peach says, created an illusionary Ricardo as the consistent theorist in their own image.[24] Both sides of the highly conceptual dispute have been apt to downplay and dismiss the long tradition of critiquing the unreality of Ricardo's starting point.

Friedman's jump

Samuelson and Sraffa only took economics so far. Warnings about the danger of unrealistic assumptions had been accepted, at least in part, by mainstream economists. In the 1950s, these warnings were still a check on excess idealization in economics. Then, starting in that decade, Milton Friedman (1912–2006)—in the process of building up the right-wing Chicago School of economics—smashed the idea that assumptions had to be realistic in an argument that Samuelson would later call 'a monstrous perversion of science'.[25]

In 1953—the year before Schumpeter's concept of the Ricardian Vice appeared—Friedman published the most influential paper of the twentieth century on how to do economics. His essay, 'The methodology of positive economics', explicitly sought to show why the age-old criticism of the 'unreality' of classical economic theory was baseless.[26] Friedman did not use advanced mathematics himself but for the young, ambitious economic theorist, it was a gift from heaven. Harvard Professor of Economics Dani Rodrik wrote later, Friedman's was 'a wonderfully liberating argument, giving economists licence to develop all kinds of models built on assumptions wildly at variance with actual experience'.[27] It marks the point when speculation once again took priority over the study of the world.

Friedman argued that because some simplification is essential, the assumptions of a theory are never going to reflect the real world. It was necessary and scientific, he therefore argued, to create 'a hypothetical and highly simplified world containing only the forces that the hypothesis asserts to be important'.[28] Friedman's argument cited Alfred Marshall and J.N. Keynes, but abandoned their cautions, writing: 'in general, the more significant the theory, the more unrealistic the assumptions'.[29]

Ricardo's intellectual ghost hovers unacknowledged over this argument. As discussed in Chapter 9, in the 1880s Alfred Marshall sharply criticized Ricardo's overenthusiastic use of theory and his neglect of facts. Marshall had argued that Ricardo's classical economic theory should be thought of as 'an engine' of analysis and not a fixed set of 'dogmas'.[30] Friedman borrowed Marshall's idea of theory as an 'engine', failed to note its origin in Ricardo's work, and, more importantly, twisted its meaning by dropping the warning about dogma. Instead, he contrasted theory as an 'engine' against the idea of it as a 'photographic reproduction' of the world.[31] The crux of Friedman's argument is summed up in the slogan that economic theory is 'an engine and not a camera': that it's assumptions cannot, and need not, match observations of the world.[32] Friedman's twist would lead to new and damaging economic dogmas.[33]

Friedman argued that the *only* criteria on which economic theories should be judged is the quality of their predictions.[34] This rests on a theory of science that presupposes that the social realm is a mechanistic, Newtonian world where precise prediction of the future is possible.[35] In practice, it meant that only theories that produce quantified results were considered scientific, rather than those that had great explanatory power. It would prove almost impossible, with Friedman's method, for empirical evidence to throw out a theory: it led to a mantra that it takes a model to beat a model.[36] When a model failed a predictive test it was described as a 'puzzle' or a 'paradox', as with Samuelson's trade theory. It was easy to argue that the model just needed to be tweaked or that the test was partial or faulty. Friedman's method led to a boom in speculative theory and model making. It helped make the Ricardian Vice (guiding policy by abstract models) into a virtue and unleashed a fierce, decades-long debate.[37] His argument has been the cause of much trouble in what the philosopher Mary Midgley called our collective intellectual plumbing.

On how theories and models are constructed, Friedman is incredibly brief. Only the final 60 words of his 10,000-word article speak to the point. 'On this problem there is little to say on the formal level,' he wrote. Theory formation is more psychology than logic. It is 'a creative act of inspiration, intuition, invention; its essence is the vision of something new'.[38] The gradual asset to more general theories that William Whewell had suggested was out. By making theory creation an afterthought, Friedman also drew a veil on the huge, subjective choice open to the theorists about what should or should not be included in the model. This other 'invisible hand' in economics, that of the model-maker, has too rarely been discussed.

'The principle of unreality'

As an advocate of the return to a rawer capitalism, Friedman was operating on the economic and political fringes in the early post-war period. Almost a decade after his 1953 essay on methodology, the work was still fiercely debated by leading economic thinkers: the debate was particularly intense, in public, at the 75th American Economic Association Meeting. On 29 December 1962 Paul Samuelson spoke on the problems of methodology at the Penn-Sheraton, a grand marble and red-brick-fronted hotel in downtown Pittsburgh.[39] Friedman was not there, but his ideas were centre stage.

Samuelson let rip in the bluntest terms about Friedman's 'twist'. Economists search for laws or regularities in society, according to Samuelson, but they 'must not impose a regularity—or approximate regularity—in the complex facts which is not there'. Sometimes 'unrealistic, abstract models' have a 'psychological usefulness' and can help in the hunt for genuine regularities, Samuelson said, but they can also 'prove misleading to a whole generation'. When abstract models are known to be empirically wrong, 'we must jettison the models, not gloss over their inadequacies'.[40] In a follow-up paper, Samuelson wrote that when he considered the exaggerated claims made in economics for 'the power of deduction and a priori reasoning—by classical [and more modern] writers ... I tremble for the reputation of my subject'.[41] Fortunately, Samuelson added, economists had left deduction behind them. This was wishful thinking.

Alongside Samuelson at the Penn-Sheraton was Herbert Simon (1916–2001), who had already made a name for himself in studying how real, social humans and businesses make decisions; for which he'd win a Nobel Prize in Economics in 1978. He would go on to make major contributions to artificial intelligence and cognitive psychology.[42] Simon argued that assumptions *can* and should be usefully compared to observations in the present. For example, whether a business person acts according to what will maximize profits can be tested. Yes, simplifying is often necessary, but a model can only provide true enough guidance for the real world if it resembles sufficiently that world: 'Unreality of premises is not a virtue in scientific theory; it is a necessary evil.'[43] Simon accused Friedman of setting up economics on the 'principle of unreality'. The purpose was, Simon said, to 'save classical theory in the face of the patent invalidity' of its assumptions.

Paul Samuelson also suggested that the real aim of Friedman's method was to allow economic analysis to support raw capitalism, 'which has been under continuous attack from outside the profession for a century and from within ... [for] thirty years'.[44] Friedman claimed that this was not his motivation and that his work was science. And yet, he and his colleagues at Chicago used the methodology to knock down objections to their ideas, while attacking rival theories as theoretically naive.

Friedman's approach to economic theory—to deny that the realism of assumptions mattered—was critiqued for over a decade but still triumphed. Those in economics arguing that assumptions should be realistic were marginalized and branded 'ultra-empiricists'.[45] Friedman's new–old ideas fit the intellectual times. As the decades ticked by, the memory of the Great Depression faded and the computer revolution fired up. Economists, in order to use the then cutting-edge technology, only available in large institutions, chose to radically simplify the problems they were studying (effectively to substitute them for simpler questions) so as not to overwhelm computer calculating power.[46] Not worrying about the reality of assumptions allowed abstract economists to fully embrace the latest technology and maintain the self-image of scientists.

Mathematical theorizing flourished in economics in these post-war decades. In 1951, only 2 per cent of articles in *American Economic Review*, a leading journal, had included an equation. By the late 1970s, it was 44 per cent.[47] This was driven not just by Friedman and Samuelson, but a whole generation of economic theorists who were themselves part of a larger intellectual movement. By the 1970s, mainstream economics meant mathematical modelling of self-maximizing, calculating agents.[48] This change happened alongside a shift in the meaning of the word 'rigour'. When the influence of historical and institutional economics was strong, economist Roger Backhouse notes, to call a piece of work scientifically rigorous meant 'taking the evidence seriously and providing a thorough, objective account of what was going on in the world'. By the 1960s, rigour meant internal or logical consistency with conclusions derived from assumptions.[49] We are still stuck with this second meaning.

'The economists' hour'

A huge challenge to the mixed economy of the New Deal and welfare state in the West came in the 1970s with the oil crisis, when sky-high petroleum prices linked to war in the Middle East led to slow economic growth and inflation. It was also a crisis for purveyors of economic ideas. Keynesian modellers like Paul Samuelson had sold the US government on a supposedly scientific trade-off they believed they had discovered in the data between inflation and unemployment called the Phillips Curve (that said that when unemployment was lower, inflation was higher and vice versa). He had claimed that the US government could control the economy like a thermostat.[50] But then, when unemployment and prices rose at the same time during the 1970s oil crisis, it was clear that the 'Keynesian' thermostat had stopped working. Faced with this crisis and theoretical vacuum, policy elites turned to the neoliberal ideas that Friedman had kept alive.

The anti-Keynesian revolution was pushed further by the University of Chicago economist Robert Lucas (1937–2023). He was one of Milton Friedman's students, but also learned from Paul Samuelson that mathematical analysis was 'the only way' to do economics, he said: 'Everything else is just pictures and talk.'[51] Lucas, and others, argued that the problem with the macroeconomics of the Keynesians was that they did not include people's expectations in their thinking. But instead of real people, who are tricky to model, Lucas and his followers placed calculating economic human— an idealized stock trader as we saw in Chapter 9—at the centre. This approach became known as 'rational expectations'. And to demonstrate their long intellectual heritage to the founders of economics, the movement called itself new classical economics.

New classical economics was not a rerun of Ricardo's specific ideas, many of which—for example, his theory that the value of a product comes from how much labour it took to create, his class-based view of society, or his theory that the economy could be pulled down by excess income known as 'rent'—remained in the mainstream economics' junk pile. The new classicals took what they found useful and left the rest. Also, while classical economics was axiomatic (or proto-mathematical), the new classicals delighted in showing off their computer-aided mathematical skills. Robert Skidelsky, the biographer of John Maynard Keynes, has said: 'Their "new classical economics" was simply a mathematically souped-up version of the old classical economics, which Keynes had overthrown in the 1930s.'[52] Economic historians Avner Offer and Gabriel Söderberg wrote simply: 'Robert Lucas is well-versed in the Ricardian Vice.'[53]

In important ways the new classicals invoked the seemingly ancient wisdom of Ricardo. One of their most prominent theories was that the traditional Keynesian policy of borrowing money to stimulate the economy could not work because citizens are 'economic humans': calculating individuals with excellent knowledge about government debt. Instead of spending more money when the government stimulates the economy, the theory goes, citizens will save the money instead to pay future tax rises. This idea put forward by physicist-turned-economist Robert Barro, was named 'Ricardian Equivalence' as it resembles something David Ricardo wrote in 1820.[54] While it has been shown time and again that most actual citizens do not act in the way the theory proposed and are not aware of the level of government debt, the idea has continued to be taken seriously.[55] It was, perhaps, Ricardo's posthumous revenge on Keynes.

By the 1980s, Lucas' 'rational expectations' revolution dominated the field. Hypothetical deduction and abstract model building gained incredible prestige.

The Keynesian modellers became self-conscious about their lack of rigour in the newer sense of the term. In that decade, they decided to adopt many of the methods and frame of the new classicals. They became known as New Keynesians.[56] Their plan was to play by the new rules of the game but show that Robert Lucas and his followers did not even understand their own models. So, they brought the new classicals theories a few steps closer to reality by using one or two more realistic assumptions. The New Keynesians would, for example, drop or relax the assumption that agents had perfect knowledge of the economy and see how that affected conclusions. They produced models where wages or prices were 'sticky' and did not move smoothly with market forces (as the empirical evidence shows). They explored well-defined individual 'market failures' or brought new concepts into formal models—that don't need to detain us here—such as the economics of increasing returns to scale in international trade.

The problem was that these small deviations meant essentially putting a little sand in the gears of the new classical economic machinery. Some of the modelling assumptions shared by nearly all mainstream economists were extreme: for example, that all people or 'agents' in an economy were identical, meaning the model could not 'see' rich or poor.[57] (These creations, called 'representative agents', are more honestly described as 'unrepresentative agents'.) Years later, Paul Krugman, a leading New Keynesian modeller, wrote that his side 'mostly accepted the notion that investors and consumers are rational and that markets generally get it right'.[58] The public could be forgiven, like the confused farmyard animals at the end of Orwell's *Animal Farm*, of looking back and forth between the two camps— the new classicals and New Keynesians—unable to tell the difference. They had merged into one school of American economics.

These abstract discussions had real, practical implications for everyday life, as they coincided with the rise in prominence of economists in government policy making in the US.

The four decades between 1969 and 2008 have been described by author Binyamin Appelbaum as *The Economists' Hour*. Before this period, in the 1950s, he notes, the US Federal Reserve was led by lawyers, bankers, and even an Iowa pig farmer, but not one economist. Whereas, almost uninterrupted from 1970 to 2018, the Chair of the Fed has been an economist. Appelbaum tracks the astonishing impact of economic thinking on US society from reducing public spending and taxes on the wealthy, to sidelining judicial curbs on the size and power of large corporations, and paving the way for hyper-globalization.[59] Economists had become, to put it poetically, the unacknowledged legislators of the world.

This new consensus was controversial and criticized within the profession, even by major figures such as Wassily Leontief, the Nobel laureate, who had shown the empirical failure of Samuelson's trade theory. Leontief warned as early as 1970 in a blistering presidential address to the American Economic Association about his colleagues' 'preoccupation with imaginary, hypothetic, rather than observable reality'. They produced precise but meaningless results, he said.[60] Still, the deductive, modelling train kept rolling. Herbert Simon attacked 'armchair economics' marked by 'resistance to looking at the world until you have a theory about it'.[61] But by the mid-1980s anyone not basing their work on people as calculating machines was written off as 'not an economist'. These often included other 'heterodox' economists such as those belonging to feminist, ecological, and dependency schools, who were generally based at less prestigious and less well-funded universities.

Even those plotting to overthrow the current orthodoxy in economics often appear unaware of the history. You can see this in a 1989 piece by feminist economist Barbara Bergmann called 'Why do most economists know so little about the economy?' She wrote: 'After Ricardo, there should have been a turn, at least on the part of some members of the profession, to a more observational style.'[62] The entire history of the revolt against the formalism of classical economics had seemingly been erased from living memory. Ricardo's Dream had once again become the economists' dream.

When the Cold War ended in the early 1990s, everyone knew there would be a revolution in the politics and economics of the former Eastern bloc. Less understood at the time was that the West would have a revolution too. The 1990s, especially Bill Clinton's eight years in the White House from 1993, mark the moment, according to American historian Gary Gerstle, when neoliberalism— today's raw capitalism—replaced the New Deal consensus across the political spectrum. A Democratic president, Clinton accepted in large part the ideas of deregulation, privatization, and globalization of Reagan's Republicans. Although economics is a large and diverse field, there was at the time a striking uniformity and naive faith in the profession about the benefits of trade and financial globalization.[63] Clinton was cheered on by the big beasts of the economics discipline, some of whom, like Larry Summers, held prominent positions in the US government. A solid intellectual consensus upheld 'the virtues of free trade and globalization,' Gerstle writes: 'To attack these policies during the neoliberal heyday was to mark oneself as marginal and irrelevant at best and as dangerously delusional at worst.'[64]

When Milton Friedman died in 2006, Summers, who happens to be the nephew of Paul Samuelson, wrote, 'any honest Democrat will admit that we are now all Friedmanites'.[65] It was a time of unprecedented power for the US, its economists, and their models.

'All models are wrong ...'

When economic modelling is criticized, a quotation from George Box, a twentieth-century British statistician, is often put forward in response: 'All models are wrong, but some are useful.'[66] The idea is that criticizing a model for not exactly matching up to reality is an invalid line of attack as models by their very essence leave some things out. They are not, as Milton Friedman said, a camera. Reducing the complex world into a simpler theory or model, then, is seen as a feature not a bug. And, even though models give only approximately correct answers, they can shine a light on a deep and useful truth and advance knowledge.

This argument for models is often made using an analogy to maps. The essence of a map is that it is a smaller and simpler version of reality. It selects some essential features and ignores the inessential, allowing you to see more clearly and execute the task at hand. Too much complexity—for example, a street map that included the type and location of every flower—is actively unhelpful for most tasks. This is undeniable: some simplification of the world in models and maps can be helpful. A map can sometimes be more useful to its users if it is not geographically accurate. Take the classic example of the London Underground.[67]

The multicoloured spaghetti map does not show the Tube lines and stops in their exact GPS locations. The lines are smoothed out and made straighter and the stops are drawn at more regular intervals. It is stylized but it works. In fact, it is *more* helpful for the millions who use it than a more messy, realistic map. Like a model, the map is 'wrong' in a way, but easier to navigate because what is omitted makes the essential features clearer. It is a good model. This is why, Harvard economist Dani Rodrik says: 'Economic models are relevant and teach us about the world *because* they are simple.'[68]

Too often, though, this argument for *some* simplicity is used to wave away concerns about *all* simplifications. This does not follow. There are many things in life, such as salt in food or chlorine in a pool, which are good in moderation but harmful in excess. This some/all confusion was lampooned by the American philosopher John Dewey as the view that: 'Because a thirsty man gets satisfaction in drinking water, bliss consists in being drowned.'[69] It is easy to imagine a Tube map so simplified, so divorced from reality as to get you lost. The problem with many economic theories is not that they are simple, but that they are oversimple and trusted too much. It is essential, as they say on the London Underground, to 'Mind the Gap' between the model and the world (see Figure 10.2).

Figure 10.2: Mind the Gap sign, Paddington Station, London

The Pygmalion Syndrome

George Box's original paper from 1976, in which he wrote that 'all models are wrong', is not a full-throated defence of simple models. Box wrote that good statisticians were essential to the future of humanity and therefore needed to learn how to be good scientists. The scientist should not ignore what is wrong with a model, he wrote, but focus on what is importantly wrong. Minor errors he called 'mice' and major ones 'tigers'. And the biggest 'tiger' for researchers, he wrote, was falling in love with their models and ignoring their faults.[70]

To make his point, Box drew on a Greek myth used by Francis Bacon, one of the founders of the scientific method and the hero of William Whewell and Richard Jones, as seen in Chapter 8. Box wrote:

> The good scientist must have the flexibility and courage to seek out, recognise, and exploit such errors—especially his own. In particular, using Bacon's analogy, he must not be like Pygmalion and fall in love with his model.[71]

The Pygmalion myth, from Ovid's *Metamorphoses*, is an intriguing story of transformation, which inspired the classic film *My Fair Lady*. Pygmalion is a talented young sculptor from Cyprus who decides that all women are immoral, lustful creatures and chooses to live alone. He practises his art and becomes skilled enough to make up for the lack of a real companion by carving his ideal woman from ivory. The English translation of the text available in Ricardo's time—by leading poets including Alexander Pope—described the statue as: 'a maid, so fair / As nature could not with his art compare.'[72]

Pygmalion knows his model is not real and yet, seduced by his creation, he falls for her. He whispers to her and kisses her cold lips. Pygmalion dresses his fake ivory love in the finest clothes, pearl necklaces, and rings. He lays the statute next to him in bed, puts a soft pillow under her head, and calls her 'wife'. As Ovid's poem puts it:

> He knows 'tis madness, yet he must adore,
> And still the more he knows it, loves the more.[73]

Often retold as a warning about misogyny, the myth in Box's hands is a cautionary tale for model makers.[74] The moral is beware of falling in love with your own representation of reality, however pliable or beautiful, confusing it for the real thing and ignoring its important weaknesses. Box wasn't the first modern scientist to make the analogy. He was beaten to it by Irish mathematician and physicist John Lighton Synge, who wrote in 1970, 'I have invented the name *Pygmalion syndrome* for that disease of the mind which blurs the distinction between R[eal]-world and M[odel]-worlds.' He also confessed: 'I myself suffer from that disease.'[75]

The argument of this book is that a virulent strain of the Pygmalion Syndrome was widespread in the classical economics of Ricardo's time and the neoclassical economics of ours. Only a couple of economists have explicitly used the Pygmalion analogy to explain the methodological problems of their discipline, but many have puzzled about or described the phenomenon in other words.[76] For example, Mary Morgan, Professor of History and Philosophy of Economics at the London School of Economics, wrote about how some economists 'move to a point where they no longer use those models to interpret the world, but they see those models at work in the world'. This 'whole new way of looking and seeing,' Morgan writes, has inspired economists to shape and remake the world we live in to be more like the models.[77] This dream, of the model becoming real, is reflected by the end of Ovid's myth: Pygmalion asks the goddess of love, Aphrodite, for a real woman like his ivory girl. He returns home, kisses the statue, and feels the warmth of her lips. Her skin becomes soft like 'pliant wax'. His flawless model woman has come to life!

The Pygmalion Syndrome can be described as a naive misuse of models. But they can also be misused more cynically. This second misuse of models revolves around a question we've so far ignored: who gets to choose what is essential and included in the model or inessential and excluded, and on what basis? Who benefits if the model's spotlight is shining on cloth and wine, for example, not on naval power and the slave trade?

Cherry-picked assumptions

The idea of cherry picking is well known, selecting data to give a predetermined result that may be misleading or contrary to reality.

Paul Pfleiderer, Professor of Finance at Stanford University, has suggested something similar is going on when theories and models are constructed. He calls it 'theoretical cherry picking'.[78] This is how it works. First, researchers decide on the conclusion they want, then they go back and choose the assumptions that lead to that conclusion.[79] It is a form of reverse engineering. The cherry-picked assumptions are often defended using Friedman's argument that because all models are based on assumptions that are not entirely realistic, no assumptions should be criticized. Pfleiderer's counter implies that the impressive logical or mathematical reasoning of the model may not be an engine for the discovery of a truth but a scientific-looking cover story.

Pfleiderer has noticed that sometimes when his fellow economists are challenged on the realism of their models, they will throw up their hands and admit that their mathematical constructs are purely hypothetical. They are just abstract thought experiments not blueprints to be applied to policy in the real world, they say. However, once the challenge goes away, he notices, that the economists will sometimes revert once again to implying that their model can provide guidance and insight into real-life matters. This behaviour reminds him of chameleons, the colour-changing reptiles found most commonly in Africa. Most of the time they blend into their forest or desert surroundings, but when they want to communicate to a potential mate or rival they change to bright, bold reds, blues, and greens. Chameleons—both reptiles and models—change their colours to suit their purposes. A model is a chameleon, Pfleiderer wrote, when it is 'built on assumptions with dubious connections to the real world but nevertheless has conclusions that are uncritically (or not critically enough) applied to understanding our economy'.[80]

It is an open secret in economics that the output of models can be manipulated easily. (Indeed, one of the arguments in favour of simple models is that they are 'tractable' or easy to control or deal with in mathematics.) This pliability was perhaps best expressed by Yale economist Carlos Diaz-Alejandro, who wrote in the 1970s, 'by now any bright graduate student, by choosing his [sic] assumptions … carefully, can produce a consistent model yielding just about any policy recommendation he [sic] favored at the start'.[81] The high status and easy manipulability of models leaves them open to serving disguised commercial, ideological, or political interests.

One solution Pfleiderer suggests is to apply a 'real-world filter' and compare the model against one's background knowledge of the economy to see if it neglects any factors of first-order importance.[82] In the theatre spotlight analogy, this would equate to turning on the house lights for a while to have a look at the rest of the stage, before focusing in again on the bright beam of light. Dani Rodrik, the Harvard economist, suggests as a solution that economists embrace the diversity of models and be wary of getting stuck looking at the world through one only: the equivalent of using multiple spotlights and deciding which one gives the most useful light.[83] This is a healthy caution against dogma. Models will never perfectly reflect the underlying reality, but the important point for Pfleiderer is to keep our feet on the ground: 'Assumptions may be stylized and unrealistic, but they should capture the essence of something we see on planet Earth. They should not take us into the realm of Complete Fantasy.'[84]

Like other critics in the profession, he is not looking to bury economic modelling but to save it from its worst excesses and promote intellectual honesty: 'We can't pretend to know more than what we know.'[85] For Pfleiderer, 'fantasy' models devalue intellectual currency and 'add noise and contribute to public misunderstanding and confusion about important issues'.[86]

The next four chapters look at the influence of deductive economic models at the national and global levels in the past 50 years, related to finance, globalization, and the living world. We will also look at the emergence in the last decade of more empirical economic thinking challenging low taxes for the top 1 per cent, low wages for the poor, and concentrated private political and economic power. These are vast issues that can only be sketched in outline. They will, I hope, show how much is at stake in these seemingly mazy and abstract debates.

11

Big Finance

*How economic models boosted the
wealth and power of modern finance
and blinded so many to its fragility*

The study of finance in the years after the Second World War, both in the US and elsewhere, was still heavily influenced by institutional and historical approaches to economics. In their textbooks and courses, American students learned about the behaviour of banks and corporations, their legal context, managers, and internal controls. By the 1970s, these management professors had been almost completely replaced. The new generation of professors were financial economists—riding high on the rebirth of deductive approaches—focused more on solving problems in a 'perfect' world where knowledgeable and calculating traders constantly seek to maximize profits. They came, initially, from Friedman's University of Chicago and Samuelson's MIT. This new school saw themselves as applying cutting-edge scientific theory to a backwards area of academia. Their critics saw them as weaving dangerous mathematical fantasies.

The story of the rise of abstract financial economics—and its complicated relationship with empirical reality—has been documented by economic sociologist Donald MacKenzie in his 2006 book *An Engine, Not a Camera*.[1] In the 1950s and 1960s, financial economists used elegant mathematical models built on a foundation of 'perfect markets' to argue that much of the institutional behaviour the older management professors had studied—such as whether a corporation keeps its earnings or distributes them to shareholders—was irrelevant. Other innovators constructed models of optimal share portfolios that led to the development of the now ubiquitous index funds that track the price of all shares on a market such as the FTSE 100 or S&P 500.[2] 'By the late 1960s, the descriptive, institutional study of finance had in the United States been eclipsed by the new, analytical, mathematical approaches,' MacKenzie wrote, 'The financial markets had been captured for economics.'[3]

The pinnace of this intellectual land grab was the efficient market hypothesis developed in the late 1960s by Eugene Fama, a University of Chicago economist. Although it comes in a variety of weaker or stronger forms, its essential idea is that the market is always right. More precisely, the theory claims that market prices reflect instantly all available present and future information about the assets traded, allowing calculating traders to allocate money to the best and most efficient purposes. (This is essentially a substitution of 'value' with 'price'.) The only genuinely new information is that which cannot be predicted and is, therefore, by definition random, leading to limited price fluctuations. Although prominent economists have critiqued the hypothesis repeatedly, it has been hugely influential in business and with politicians and regulators.[4] It underpinned a belief or dogma that Western financial markets were efficient and that the more trades the better.

One of the older institutionalist finance scholars who refused to leave without a fight was David Durand, Professor of Management at MIT. He attacked the new finance theorists for building an intellectual house on the sand. The new theorists had 'lost virtually all contact with terra firma,' he wrote in 1968, and were 'more interested in demonstrating their mathematical prowess than in solving genuine problems'. Diagnosing a case of what others would soon call the Pygmalion Syndrome he wrote: 'When they build models, they often become so infatuated with the product that they will plug in any data, no matter how inappropriate, just to obtain a numerical result.'[5] But within a few years of that broadside Durand had retired and was largely ignored.[6]

In their 1972 textbook, *The Theory of Finance*, Eugene Fama and fellow Chicago financial economist Merton Miller admitted: 'To make the essential theoretical framework of the subject stand out sharply, we have pruned away virtually all institutional and descriptive material.' They also 'assumed throughout that all securities are traded in perfect markets'.[7] These tenuous starting points for analysis would turn out to be catastrophic mistakes, but had enough legitimacy to survive in economics, with its long history of the defence of unreal assumptions. 'Around here,' Merton Miller said in 1999, 'we just sort of take [Friedman's viewpoint] for granted. Of course you don't worry about the assumptions.'[8] He was talking not just about the University of Chicago, but much of the new financial economics.

The new finance theory did not triumph because it fit the facts of the world better. Indeed, it often fit them poorly. Thinkers, however brilliant, who pointed this out were sidelined. One early critical voice was Benoit Mandelbrot (1924–2010), one of the finest mathematical minds of his age. The Polish-born, French-American mathematician and polymath coined the term 'fractals' and sought to understand the 'messiness of everything'.[9] In the 1960s, he began studying the history of cotton prices going back to 1880 and discovered that the swings in prices were much larger and more extreme than the random fluctuations assumed in the theory. The price data did not fit the bell curve (or normal distribution) used in new finance theory. Mandelbrot found the same pattern in data on wheat, railway stock, and interest rates.[10] Real-world market prices, he said, showed 'wild' randomness while the finance models were based on 'mild' randomness. A policy maker relying on the models was like the captain of ship only prepared for the 95 per cent of time when the weather was good, he said, rather than the 5 per cent when there were typhoons. In the orthodox approach, he explained in 1999, 'Typhoons are, in effect, defined out of existence.'[11]

Mandelbrot proposed using an alternative mathematical function to better describe real markets: a type of 'fat-tailed' bell curve known as a Lévy distribution. Financial theorists initially engaged with him; Eugene Fama looked closely at his work. The data were clear. And yet Mandelbrot's ideas were fiercely opposed because his wilder world and mathematics would make vast areas of previous statistical and theoretical work obsolete and meaningless. It would mean, MIT's Paul Cootner said, 'consigning centuries of work to the ash pile'.[12] So, the profession chose to stick by their existing concepts and methods of more well-behaved markets and downplayed the importance of empirical evidence. Fama decided that the standard bell curve he had been using 'was a good working approximation'.[13] Popular books, such as the investment guide *A Random Walk Down Wall Street* (1973) by Princeton economist Burton Malkiel, popularized theories that relied on 'mild' randomness. By the 1970s, Mandelbrot's ideas had been banished from the field.[14]

By the 1990s, Donald MacKenzie wrote, the financial economists had moved to the centre of the economics profession and their victory over the institutional finance professors was total: 'if one walked into almost any large university bookshop in Western Europe or in the United States, one could find shelves of textbooks whose contents had their roots in the [new, abstract] finance scholarship'.[15] In 1999, Edward Lazear, Stanford professor and later George W. Bush's chief economist, delighted that the institutional scholars who had taught finance 'have been replaced by financial economists, almost to the person'. This was all part of economics' invasion of intellectual territories once deemed to be outside its realm. This 'economic imperialism', as Lazear triumphantly called it, was driven by its superior status as a 'genuine science' like 'the physical sciences'.[16] The dream of discovering economic laws of motion, it appeared to many, had come true.

This victory of ideas helped revolutionize trading floors, stock exchanges, and, ultimately, relations between finance and democratic governments. You could think of it as Ricardo's style of economics returning home to the stock exchange.

It's efficient pricing not gambling

For those who only know the current financial markets—where billions zip across borders and through offshore and onshore tax havens with little oversight—the rules-based order that persisted up to the 1970s is a strange, lost world. At the end of the Second World War, the victorious Allied Powers had created a global financial system known as Bretton Woods. It brought international finance under the control of governments. In the Bretton Woods system, exchange rates between currencies like British pounds and American dollars were fixed, as was the price of dollars to gold. These rates could only be changed by government agencies exchanging letters. The US regulated its banks' trading in dollars and the UK did the same for its banks in pound sterling. Both countries had capital

controls—restrictions on the movement of money across borders—
to reduce crises. The power of finance, and banks, was heavily
constrained, but not for long.[17]

Bankers soon discovered a loophole in Bretton Woods. British
banks began accepting US dollars in the 1950s. These currency flows
were not regulated by US authorities because they were outside the
country. And the Bank of England—hoping to revive the City of
London—decided not to regulate them either because they were not
in its own currency.[18] The offshore finance world had been born.
The holdings of these dollars (then called eurodollars) by UK, then
Swiss and Caribbean, banks grew steadily from $200 million in 1959
to $3 billion in 1961.[19] By the end of the 1960s, Bretton Woods,
the rules-based international financial system, was ailing. These
new unregulated dollars coincided with a spike in US government
spending for the Vietnam War and the anti-poverty 'Great Society'
programme, leading to an outflow of gold from the US and a strain
on the fixed dollar-gold price. The US could have decided to reduce
military or welfare spending or rein in its banks and corporations.
Instead, in 1971 President Nixon ended the US's commitment to a
set exchange rate between the dollar and gold, ending the Bretton
Woods system.[20]

After the collapse of Bretton Woods, author and economics
correspondent Ed Conway has written, a 'every single measure of
the size, profitability and leverage of the banking industry began
to increase at unprecedented rates'.[21] The new loosely regulated
offshore financial market boomed in the early 1970s when the
proceeds of oil-price hikes by Middle Eastern countries (then
called petrodollars) were channelled through Western banks.
The new system, now global, grew from $500 billion in 1980 to
$2.6 trillion at the end of the decade. By 1997 it made up 90 per
cent of international loans and had become *the* global financial
market, which exerted enormous pressure for countries to scrap
capital controls and deregulate.[22]

The world of national currencies floating freely against each
other—after the collapse of the Bretton Woods system—meant more
opportunities for traders and greater risks for large corporations
operating in multiple countries. Many worried that fluctuating
prices could cause instability. Global currency trading went from
$150 billion per day in 1985 to $3.3 trillion in 2007.[23] Sudden

changes to the exchange rates between US dollars and Japanese yen, for example, could wreck a corporation's financial planning or investment strategy if they made car parts in one country and sold them in another. What corporations needed was an effective way to reduce, or hedge, these risks in a world where business was increasingly global and currency was national. Economists such as Milton Friedman, who had pushed for the end of Bretton Woods, had a solution for concerns about greater risk: financial derivatives. These are financial contracts, such as options and futures, which give the bearer the right, and sometimes the obligation, to buy or sell an asset at a set price on, or before, a set date. They could give a corporation certainty about the future price of exchanging currencies.

Derivatives had been around since before David Ricardo's days on the trading floor but were eyed with suspicion well into the 1970s, and at times banned, due to their association with gambling.[24] Friedman argued in a 1971 paper that fear of currency speculators was unfounded. In fact, speculating in currency futures markets would help keep costs down and stabilize prices for corporations hedging risks, he claimed: 'The larger the volume of speculative activity, the better the market.'[25] The Chicago Mercantile Exchange—which paid Friedman $5,000 to write his 1971 paper—began trading currency futures the following year.[26] In the same city, in 1973 the Chicago Board Options Exchange began trading stock options.[27]

There was still a problem with these new markets. Unlike pork bellies or bushels of wheat, the products they were trading were abstract: it was difficult to know how much they were worth. Options and futures do not have value in themselves: they are called derivatives because they *derive* their value from other assets. Just as the new Chicago derivatives markets were opening their doors, however, three economic theorists created a formula to price derivatives. Their theory, known as Black–Scholes, provided a lens through which the precise value and worth of derivatives could be seen. While some models can make real things disappear, Black–Scholes did the opposite. It helped transform an abstract financial product into something solid and real enough to be traded in what became a trillion-dollar market.

The initial work on the derivatives theory was done by Fisher Black, a mathematician, and Myron Scholes, an economist trained by Fama and Miller at the University of Chicago, who created an elegant and simple formula. They arrived at this by excluding all unquantifiable values so the formula only had five variables, including the current stock price and the time to maturity.[28] Risk was the most difficult, but they eventually excluded it when they found a formula for creating a portfolio of other financial assets that balanced the risk of the trade. But Black and Scholes' calculations were too slow for the pace of market trading. The final touch came from Robert C. Merton, Paul Samuelson's researcher at MIT. He was inspired by Japanese mathematician Kiyosi Itô, whose 'continuous time' calculus was created to identify the position of rockets second by second.[29] (This is perhaps why early mathematical theorists on Wall Street, see Figure 11.1, now known as 'quants', were once known as 'rocket scientists'.) This allowed Merton to perfectly hedge, or offset, risks, at least in theory. Merton claimed later that with the new maths and the assumption that trading was instantaneous and continuous 'you could get rid of the risk … all the risk'.[30]

The Black–Scholes formula was soon used by traders in Chicago and then worldwide to price and trade options. (Fisher Black for years sold, on subscription, sheets of papers with prices for options calculated by his model.) The formula allowed financial traders to

Figure 11.1: Wall Street sign, New York

Source: Chenyu Guan on Unsplash

calculate a price for an option just by knowing the current price of the asset (whether that was currencies, stocks, or mortgages). It was the most important innovation in financial economics in the late twentieth century. The derivatives market has boomed, going from nothing in 1970 to a notional value of $1,200 trillion in 2010.[31]

The scientific aura of the Black–Scholes model helped the Chicago Board Options Exchange counter the narrative that options were disreputable gambling. The former counsel of the Exchange, Burton Rissman, has said, 'That issue fell away, and I think Black–Scholes made it fall away. It wasn't speculation or gambling, it was efficient pricing.'[32] The model changed what people saw. When gadflies like the global political economist Susan Strange warned in 1986 that the 'Western financial system is rapidly coming to resemble nothing as much as a vast casino' in which 'all of us are involuntarily engaged in the day's play', it was easy enough to dismiss her as scaremongering and not having a real theory.[33] Futures, options, and other derivates were sold as devices to protect clients from risk and uncertainty, but Strange warned presciently: 'it is not so certain that the system as a whole is protected'.[34]

In 1997, Merton and Scholes received the Nobel Memorial Prize in Economics for their 'new method to determine the value of derivatives'. (Black, who died in 1995, was not able to share the award.) Paul Samuelson, at the time, said: 'Bob Merton is the Isaac Newton of his field.'[35] Less than a year after the Nobel prizes, the misnamed hedge fund that Merton and Scholes had helped to create—Long-Term Capital Management (LTCM)—lost $1.9 billion, almost half of its capital, in the month of August 1998. The spark was a contagious financial crisis that spread from East Asia and led Russia to default on its debts. According to LTCM's risk models, the one-month loss was an event so unlikely that it should not happen even once in the entire 14 billion years of the Universe. LTCM was five years old![36] Such is the danger of an idealized vision of finance with no typhoons. In 1998, the US Federal Reserve corralled 14 investment banks to complete a $3.6 billion bailout of LTCM. Without a rescue, regulators feared that the entire financial system would collapse. Traders fluent in the Black–Scholes model talk about delta, gamma, and theta risk, but, as one banker quipped, 'one Greek word that ought to be in there is hubris'.[37]

'We've learned how to do it right'

The romantic, idealized vision of Western finance survived the LTCM collapse and bailout, just as it had survived other crises like the record-breaking bankruptcy of 'too-big-to-fail' Continental Illinois bank in 1984 and Wall Street's Black Monday crash in 1987. In response, most policy makers and regulators were busy *weakening* financial regulation. One exception was Brooksley Born, a lawyer, who headed the Commodity Futures Trading Commission (CFTC). She was concerned about the $25 trillion derivatives market operating without regulation or oversight. In 1998, Born spooked financers by suggesting that bespoke derivatives should be more tightly regulated. She was met with fierce resistance from established economists and bankers in government including the Chair of the Federal Reserve Alan Greenspan, Treasury Secretary (and former Goldman Sachs executive) Robert Rubin, and his deputy the economist Larry Summers. At one point Summers reportedly called Born and said, 'I have thirteen bankers in my office, and they say if you go forward with this [regulation] you will cause the worst financial crisis since World War II.'[38]

Born, head of a small agency, lost the political fight. In October 1998, a month *after* the LTCM collapse, Congress passed a moratorium banning Born's CFTC from regulating derivatives. Another stunning legislative victory for Wall Street, in post-Cold War euphoria, was the 1999 scrapping of Glass–Steagall, the Depression-era Act that banned banks that held deposits for the public from speculative trading. The following year, derivatives were exempted from all government regulation by the Commodity Futures Modernization Act, signed into law by President Clinton.[39] These regulatory victories in Washington showed an aspect of finance that was not lit up in the spotlight of the financial models: politics and power.

That high finance has gained a larger and larger share of national wealth is undeniable. In the US, the share of corporate profits going to the financial sector was less than 16 per cent until the mid-1980s, rising to 30 per cent in the 1990s, and hitting 41 per cent in the 2000s.[40] In the UK, from Victorian times to the 1970s the combined balance sheet of British banks had not risen much higher than half of the size of the country's economy. By 2007, their balance sheets were more than five times the size of the UK economy.[41]

Simon Johnson, an MIT professor and former Chief Economist of the International Monetary Fund (IMF), argued provocatively in 2009 that this wealth has led to the re-emergence of an 'American financial oligarchy'.[42] Johnson's thesis—expanded in a book with law professor James Kwak—is that major Wall Street firms have carried out a 'quiet coup' by translating their economic heft into political power and then 'the new financial oligarchy did what oligarchies do—it cashed in its political power for higher and higher profits'. They 'engineered a regulatory climate,' Johnson and Kwak wrote, to 'generate record-shattering profits for Wall Street'.[43] This political influence is not done through direct, illegal bribery, Johnson said, but through a 'confluence of campaign finance, personal connections, and ideology'.[44] This includes hundreds of millions of dollars spent each year on lobbying and political contributions, and the 'revolving door' between Wall Street and Washington, with major Democratic and Republican figures such as Robert Rubin (Goldman Sachs–US Treasury Secretary–Citigroup) and Hank Paulson (Goldman Sachs–US Treasury) being only the most prominent examples.

It is difficult to recollect just how much faith very smart people had in the Western financial system before the global financial crisis of 2007 and 2008. The conventional wisdom was that it was so sophisticated that a major financial crisis was essentially impossible. Adair Turner, the head of the UK's regulator, the Financial Services Authority (FSA), in 2008 claimed that 'the whole efficient market theory, Washington consensus, free market deregulation system' has become 'like a religion', leading to 'regulatory capture through the intellectual zeitgeist'.[45] These dogmas were underpinned, in part, by the lavish spending of Wall Street on financial economists—in-house and as consultants—who, Simon Johnson wrote, 'gave the stamp of academic legitimacy (and the intimidating aura of intellectual rigor) to the burgeoning world of high finance'.[46] Those who did not sign on to the intellectual consensus were branded Luddites.

The leader of the new classical economists, Robert Lucas, was recognized with the Nobel Memorial Prize in Economics in 1995 as 'the economist who has had the greatest influence on macroeconomic research since 1970'.[47] In February 2007, Lucas was a guest on Russ Roberts' popular *EconTalk* podcast. Roberts praised Lucas' 'extraordinary contributions' to macroeconomics. He also asked his guest whether too much was made of the importance of financial markets in the economy. Lucas couldn't agree more. 'Monetary instability is a very minor source of instability in the modern US, or European or Japanese economies,' he said. 'We've learned how to do it right.' No one experiences economic booms or busts any more, Lucas continued: 'They are such minor wrinkles in the general scheme of things.'[48]

Lucas' timing was atrocious. Within six months, a financial crisis on a scale not seen since the Wall Street Crash of 1929 broke out. As early as August 2007, hedge funds were losing hundreds of millions of dollars a day. In 2008, observers were shocked to see venerated investment banks like Bear Stearns and Lehman Brothers collapse. It seemed possible that financial contagion could freeze up the entire financial and economic system. This was no minor wrinkle. The only thing that prevented a full death spiral was governments and central banks across the world throwing trillions of dollars at other 'too-big-to-fail' banks. The moves worked—to an extent—at an eye-watering cost to public finances and trust. It was, to use Galbraith's analogy of the economy as a bumblebee, like the poor insect, kitted out with all the latest technological flying gear, had crashed to the ground. It could only remain airborne with the artificial gusts of wind generated by governments (through bailouts and other ways of blowing money into the finance sector such as 'quantitative easing' and 'central bank swaps'). The financial chaos discredited, in the eyes of many, the economic system, the economists who had failed to warn of the dangers, and political parties of the left and right who had let the markets get so big and unruly. It contributed to the 2010s being filled with the Tea Party and Occupy protests, house evictions, public-spending cuts, debt crises, and more.[49]

It is important to note that the principal failure of orthodox economics was *not* in failing to predict the crisis. It was in envisioning an idealized financial system that legitimized dangerous risk taking while simultaneously making a crisis unimaginable. The difference is between a seismologist failing to accurately tell you when an earthquake is going to hit and one who tells you that seismology has succeed in solving the problem of earthquakes so you can build your home (or bank) any way you like. Through the lens of the mainstream models a global financial crisis was unseeable.[50]

If financial economists had balanced their interest in models and data from the very near past with a broad historical understanding, it would be difficult to maintain such a starry-eyed view of finance. History is littered with examples of financial crashes and bubbles: when investors' overly exuberant herd behaviour pushes prices so far above their underlying value that no one is willing or able to buy and then prices plummet.

One of the most storied early crises, the South Sea Bubble, occurred in London in 1720. At the close of the War of Spanish Succession, in which John Methuen had yoked Portugal to England's cause, Britain gained the contract to sell enslaved Africans to Spanish colonies in the Americas, the *asiento*, as the diplomat Methuen had hoped. The British government, in turn, gave this slaving contract to the South Sea Company, which was also involved in a plan to reorganize the national debt, and its stock price began to soar to unprecedented levels amid a buying frenzy. Between January and July 1720 its stock rose from £128 to £1,000. One of the investors was Isaac Newton, who by 1720 had 40 per cent of his wealth—derived, as we've seen, in part from coining Brazilian gold—in South Sea stock. Newton sold out before the price got to the top but, astonishingly, bought in again at an even higher price. And then the bubble burst. By the end of September, the stock was worth only £200. Newton had lost a fortune: £20,000 (£7.2 million today).[51] When asked about the fiasco, he is reported to have said: 'I can calculate the motions of heavenly bodies, but not the madness of men.'[52]

Even immediately after 2008, some financial theorists refused to believe in the existence of bubbles. Eugene Fama, one of the founders of financial economics, was interviewed by John Cassidy, a *New Yorker* reporter, in 2010. The reporter asked Fama what he made of the financial bubble. Fama replied: 'I don't even know what a bubble means. These words have become popular. I don't think they have any meaning.' He wasn't joking. Bubbles were, by definition, impossible in his efficient markets hypothesis, as investors were calculating (sometimes mistakenly called 'rational') and the market prices represented real values. Fama stopped subscribing to *The Economist* because he became so tired of reading the word 'bubble' in its pages.[53] This is theory-induced blindness.

For many, however, the experience of the 2008 financial crisis led to a new wave of protest and outcry against the faulty theory. The US broadcaster PBS tracked down the 93-year-old Paul Samuelson in 2008, a year before his death. Samuelson blamed the economic meltdown on 'Fiendish Frankenstein monsters of financial engineering [that] had been created, a lot of them at MIT, some of them by people like me.'[54] The crisis pushed Paul Krugman to be more sceptical of methods he'd previously championed. He put his finger on 'the profession's blindness to the very possibility of catastrophic failures in a market economy'. Economists had fallen in love with a 'romanticized and sanitized vision of the economy,' Krugman explained, and 'as a group, mistook beauty, clad in impressive-looking mathematics, for truth'. He accused Robert Lucas' new classical economists of having led macroeconomics into a new 'Dark Age ... in which hard-won knowledge has been forgotten'.[55] A few years after the crash, Krugman admitted that 'economics is a pretty poor substitute' for Isaac Asimov's psychohistory.[56]

Embrace reality or irrelevance

After the global financial crisis, those who had created the models for financial institutions were also trying to work out what went wrong. One of the most interesting cases is Emanuel Derman, one of the one of the original quants (or quantitative analysts), who worked on derivatives at Goldman Sachs for 17 years.

As a young man in South Africa, Derman said: 'I dreamed of being another Einstein.'[57] The dream led him to a PhD in theoretical physics at Columbia University. Then, in 1985, finding few openings in academia and after a series of disappointing private sector jobs, he surprised himself by agreeing to join Goldman Sachs. Wall Street was fast becoming the biggest, and highest-paying, employer of physicists and mathematicians. Working alongside traders and Fisher Black, of Black–Scholes notoriety, Derman says he 'began to believe it was possible to apply the methods of physics successfully to economics and finance, perhaps even to build a grand unified theory of securities'. He created one of the first models for interest rate derivatives.[58] But 20 years on Wall Street made him 'a disbeliever'.[59] He left finance in the early 2000s and became Professor of Financial Engineering back at Columbia. Financial modelling is not a waste of time, Derman says, and it is not going to disappear. But we do have to understand the limitations of models better.

Derman, an arch-insider and practitioner, makes visible the dirt modellers sweep under the rug in *Models. Behaving. Badly.* (2011).

184

He says pithily—a quotation that's on my pinboard—'Everyone should understand the difference between a model and reality.' Derman especially stresses the difference between physics and finance. The problem when you confuse the two, he writes, is that economists and those who use the models begin to 'ignore the humans behind the equations'. In fact, it's worse. In order to squeeze unruly human psychology into calculable equations, you need to replace those humans with something much simpler. For Derman, the approach that financial economics has taken in the past 50 years can be characterized as 'the naive tendency to attribute the properties of things to human beings'. It is a type of reverse anthropomorphism.[60]

One solution, according to Derman, is to take models much less seriously: 'despite the fancy mathematics, a model is toy'. They can be useful aids to thinking and calculating, and roughly reliable guides as long as the world doesn't change too much. If it does, or if you place too much faith in them, you will be confusing illusion with reality and may end up on the rocks. Derman argues that models should come with a health warning about what has been assumed in their construction and what has been swept out of view.[61] Think about it. If large vehicles on the road have to carry stickers warning 'Blind Spot. Take Care', why not economic models that can cause much larger crashes?

Another fascinating example of a prominent Wall Street economist turned (partial) sceptic is Gary Gorton, now Professor of Finance at Yale. He was a consultant to AIG Financial Products from 1996 to 2008. By the end, he was earning an estimated $1 million per year according to the *Wall Street Journal*.[62] During this time, Gorton helped build the computer models that underpinned AIG's $400 billion trade in financial insurance policies known as credit default swaps. He regularly spoke to investors alongside top AIG executives to reassure them about the robustness of what he described as simple, data-driven models.[63] And then, he was on the AIG trading floor in the 2008 crash describing the 'gut feeling for the size and power' of the financial tidal wave 'so fast and so large that it felt like the economy was coming to end'.[64] AIG lost a world-record $62 billion in the last three months of 2008 and eventually received four bailouts from various arms of the US government totalling $180 billion.[65]

Gorton was targeted with death threats, he later said, yet continued to teach economics at Yale. In 2010, he reflected on the 'astounding' blindness of economists like himself ahead of the financial crisis. Although we cannot abandon computer models, he argued, he noted that 'Economists "see" reality by looking through the lenses of models, which are representations of reality, simplified to highlight certain aspects.' Crises were left out of the models, Gorton says, because economists thought they were a thing of the past. And the history of economics and economic thinking is taught much less in standard economics courses, he noted, and often excluded from view by the focus on recent years where comprehensive data exist. Gorton's powerful conclusion is that economists 'can either embrace reality—through history, institutional details, and measurement—or we can choose to ignore the lessons of the financial crisis, of our failure, and languish in irrelevancy'.[66] These institutional details Gorton wants us to embrace are the same ones consciously 'pruned away' by Eugene Fama and the other creators of financial economics in the 1960s and 1970s.

It was not just financial institutions that were seeing reality through the lens of an oversimplified model, but also central banks. In the 1980s, out of the fusion of New Keynesians and the new classicals, which we looked at in Chapter 10, came a model called DSGE (shorthand for the intimidating sounding 'Dynamic Stochastic General Equilibrium'). These were the so-called workhorse models used by central banks to analyse and forecast movements in the global economy. Unfortunately, they came pre-fitted with blinders. Nearly all DSGE models before 2008 left finance and money out by assumption and gave no warning or guidance regarding a major financial crisis.

Before 2008, some economic researchers were looking into financial bubbles, crises, contagion, and the rest, as Ricardo Caballero, Professor of Economics at MIT explains, but these remained on the periphery of the field. At the centre were DSGE models. Caballero has written about what made these 'irresistible snake-charmer' models 'so attractive, and even plain addictive'.[67] The model's charm lies in its apparent ability to pierce the complexity of the global economy and serve up seemingly precise, scientific answers. But, just like Ricardo two hundred years ago, the researcher pays a big price to get these clear-cut results. The field, Caballero says, 'has become so mesmerized with its own internal logic that it has begun to confuse the precision it has achieved about its own world with the precision that it has about the real one'. This deep confusion means that

> the core of macroeconomics seems to transform things that may have been useful modelling short-cuts into a part of a new artificial 'reality', and now suddenly everyone uses the same language, which in the next iteration gets confused with and eventually replaces, reality.[68]

This describes well of how very smart people can fall in love with an intellectual dream.

Since the crisis, some DSGE models have begun to integrate financial fragility, but this is not universal. In 2013, Bank of England researchers reported that the 'central organising model'—a DSGE model—they use to predict the future of the economy 'does not include a financial sector'. This 'may seem surprising,' they said, but they judged that the benefits of adding finance to the model are outweighed by the added complexity.[69] They have chosen not to embrace reality.

Not 'model dopes'

There's more to the financial crisis than researchers and policy makers mesmerized by models. This was satirized brilliantly in *The Big Short*, a 2015 film adaptation of Michael Lewis' non-fiction book about market rebels who saw the 2008 crisis coming and made millions. A hedge fund manager, played by Steve Carrell, confronts an analyst from the ratings agency Standard & Poor's. The data show that the number of people defaulting on their mortgages is through the roof, Carrell's character says, and yet the agencies are still giving the products made up of those mortgages the safest possible 'AAA' rating. He is swearing and fuming at the 'delusional' ratings. Has the S&P analyst even looked at the data? Of course, she replies, but the joke is on her. In a not-so-subtle metaphor, the analyst is wearing overlarge dark glasses and having trouble with her eyes. 'I can't see a damn thing,' she says (see Figure 11.2). *The Big Short* implies that this blindness may have been wilful, rather than naive: creators of

Figure 11.2: Melissa Leo as a ratings analyst, complete with dark glasses, in the 2015 film *The Big Short*

Source: © Paramount Pictures. Photo by Jaap Buitendijk

the financial products who wanted the highest 'AAA' grade pay the ratings agencies for their services and, if they didn't get them, could take their business elsewhere.[70]

Agencies like S&P made their ratings models for complex financial products derived from mortgage-backed securities (known as CDOs or collateralized debt obligations) available to download. Many investors—such as pension providers—relied on the ratings agencies to indicate if the product was a safe investment. However, finance houses that were manufacturing the financial products 'gamed' the rating agency model: they bought or created optimization programmes to find the most efficient way to combine risky, junk assets into a package that would generate a fat chunk of apparently safe, and lucrative, AAA ratings. This financial alchemy helped produce unprecedented profits for producers of these products while people were buying and then crippling losses when they stopped. Citigroup lost $34 billion on mortgage-backed CDOs alone, AIG $33 billion, and Merrill Lynch $26 billion. Donald MacKenzie, author of *An Engine, Not a Camera*, and co-author Taylor Spears, have written: 'The crisis was caused not by "model dopes", but by creative, resourceful, well informed and reflexive actors quite consciously exploiting the role of models in governance.'[71]

MacKenzie and Spears found that many Wall Street quants mistrusted the most widespread 'Gaussian copula' models in finance even before 2008. The quants continued to use the standard models, however, because they had become a collective way to 'see' and 'talk' about abstract financial products. The standard models were especially popular with traders selling derivatives as they allowed them to get paid quicker. A derivatives deal might be over a five to ten-year period. Rather than wait for the end of the term to receive a sales bonus—by which time the traders may have moved jobs—the standard models allowed them to book the total expected profits on the first day of the deal. To do this, the traders needed to convince accountants and risk managers, who are not specialists in modelling, that the profit was reasonably sure. And the accountants would only sign off on booking the profit on the first day if the industry-standard model showed it was secured.[72] Thus, the model transformed hypothetical future profits into money today. David Li, creator of an influential 'Gaussian copula' model, even told the *Wall Street Journal* in 2005: 'The most dangerous part, is when people believe everything coming out of it.'[73]

Belief that new financial theories, and the products based on them, had got rid of 'all the risk' was not just intellectual hubris but also commercial self-interest. Financial institutions are often restricted in how much they can borrow against the assets they hold by regulators. But, the more they borrow, the greater opportunity for profit (and loss). In so far as banks were able to argue that they had controlled or offloaded financial risks, they were able to convince regulators they should be free to borrow more. This led to major increases in the amount of debt investment banks were allowed to carry by US regulators and an international agreement to allow banks to measure the riskiness of their investments with their own models. LTCM, before it went bust, had $4 billion in capital leveraged to $130 billion in borrowed money.[74] And US investment bank, Bears Stearns, in 2007 was carrying 33 times more debt than it had assets, which meant that only a 3 per cent drop in its assets would make it insolvent.[75] It is perhaps no coincidence that the outcome of these models—often founded on the false assumption that everyone acts as a stockbroker—greatly benefitted Ricardo's modern-day heirs on financial markets.

Models are powerful psychological tools that shape what we see. They play around on the borders between the real and the cognitively ideal, moving objects from one side to the other and back again. They have helped to create the hugely powerful and fragile engine of inequality that is modern finance.

12

Trading Barbarians

How a 'free-trade' dogma diverted attention from the expansion of corporate rights and shocked democracy

In his 1980 TV series *Free to Choose*, Milton Friedman made a powerful case for free trade. In Adam Smith's time, he explained, trade was tightly controlled and consumers paid high prices because merchants had persuaded the government to impose heavy taxes on all foreign imports. 'In every country it is always and must be in the interest of the great body of people to buy whatever they want of those who sell it cheapest,' Friedman said, quoting Adam Smith, and this would be plain to all 'had not the interested sophistry of merchants and manufactures confounded the common sense of mankind. Their interest is in this respect directly opposite to that of the great body of people.' Smith's 'flash of genius' was to recognize that the 'invisible hand' of market prices could produce an orderly and prosperous society, Friedman said, and free trade had made Britain the workshop of the world. The alternative was concentration of power in the state.[1]

Mainstream economists, in the decades since, have overwhelmingly lined up with this strident case for 'free trade'. Often, as we've seen, relying—at least rhetorically—on David Ricardo's theory of comparative advantage, described variously as a 'beautiful proof', 'unshakeable', 'utterly true, immensely sophisticated—and extremely relevant to the modern world'. At the end of the twentieth century, most mainstream economists, whether on the left or right, believed in sweeping away the regulations of the past, which cramped growth and were based on prejudice rather than economic science.[2] One survey of US economists in 2009 found that 93 per cent agreed that border tariffs reduced general economic welfare.[3]

Of course, some were concerned about what global trade meant for jobs, society, and the environment. But these people were often seen as ignorant and small-minded, and perhaps egged on by business interests who did not want foreigners undercutting their profits. Businesses interests pushing for trade protection were seen as rent-seekers; that is, gaining unmerited and socially harmful excess income by manipulating the political environment. Free trade was a cleansing agent. Sometimes the opponents of free trade were called 'barbarians'. In 1996, Paul Krugman—dubbed by the press a 'superstar professor' in his early 40s—said, 'I am tired of having to defend the basics of logic against well-funded barbarians'.[4] The following year, Dani Rodrik, a Turkish-born economist who teaches at Harvard, sent Krugman an advanced copy of his book *Has Globalization Gone Too Far?* It was a nuanced argument that economists had not yet fully understood globalization and needed to do more basic empirical work to analyse how it might impact social stability. Economists had much to bring to the public debate, Rodrik said, but must be more modest and broaden their focus.[5] Krugman replied to Rodrik with a warning: books like his could be dangerous and provide 'ammunition to the barbarians'. Rodrik published his book anyway, but lost sleep over whether he was doing the right thing.[6]

The Western euphoria around the collapse of communism in the 1990s led to a rash of new bilateral, regional, and global 'free-trade' deals. Democratic President Bill Clinton signed the US up to NAFTA (the North American Free Trade Agreement) with Canada and Mexico in 1994. A year later, the US helped to replace the 50-year-old General Agreement on Tariffs and Trade (GATT) with the much more ambitious World Trade Organization (WTO). The new organization's stated aim was to use trade to raise living standards and improve lives. The WTO dealt not just with trade in products—which was the basis for the classical free-trade arguments—but also financial services, foreign investments, and copyright and patent protection. Agreements at the WTO were backed by the most far-reaching enforcement mechanism of any global organization, which included courts able to hand out multi-billion-dollar fines to countries.

The WTO remained for most an obscure global body until 30 November 1999. On that day, the Battle for Seattle, the largest ever protest against a global organization in the US, pitted more than 50,000 protestors—including environmentalists, labour unions, and students—against the Seattle Police and the National Guard. The alter-globalization protests succeeded in shutting down the Seattle WTO meeting, stalling the talks, and raising questions about the legitimacy and future of the 4-year-old organization. A large banner hung from a crane's arm summed up one of the protestors' main messages: 'Democracy' was written in one large arrow and 'WTO' in another, pointing the opposite way.[7]

For the organizers of the Seattle gathering, such as American trade lawyer and campaigner Lori Wallach, they were not protesting closer global ties themselves but the specific set of rules and powers shaping that integration. Alternative paths of globalization were possible, they argued. And the mandate of the WTO, despite its name, went far beyond trade. Negotiators were considering how national laws or rules about how products are manufactured or sold might impede trade. These 'non-tariff barriers' might relate to domestic food safety, to environment and product safety rules, financial regulations, investment policy, patent and copyright rules, and more. The new agreements established by the WTO were, Wallach said, '800-plus pages of one-size-fits-all-rules'.[8] These rules could be used to challenge national laws as 'illegal trade barriers' at the closed-door WTO tribunal. Defenders of globalization, such as renowned economist and author Martin Wolf, often saw health, safety, and environmental regulations as disguised barriers to trade: 'In this sense, then, an assault on regulations was part of the negotiating process.'[9] Just 23 days after the WTO was born, Venezuela challenged US clean-air rules that it claimed discriminated against its oil exports—and won. The US weakened its environmental regulations in 1997 in compliance with the ruling.[10] The system that put trade before all other values led to US environmental rules on dolphin-friendly tuna and endangered species being weakened too. Wallach saw it as a 'slow-motion corporate coup d'état'.[11]

Paul Krugman built his public profile in the 1990s as a straight-talking economic expert. He had made his name in academia by creating models of neglected aspects of trade (such as 'monopolistic competition' and 'returns to scale'), known as new trade theory. But he then turned from advancing the frontier to fighting the enemies of what he saw as of sound economics and free trade. For him, the WTO—the 'bizarrely demonised target of the Seattle protests'—was only a commercial court that made sure countries didn't violate agreements on trade they had made.[12] The protestors were driven by a 'leftist mythology' that was holding poor people in the Global South back from an affluent life.[13] The historian Adam Tooze has called him 'the policeman of orthodoxy of the 1990s'.[14]

Krugman loved using his acerbic pen to expose what he saw as the superficially appealing but shallow arguments of 'pseudo-intellectuals' who should know better. He sprayed insults at John Kenneth Galbraith and Robert Reich at Harvard, among others, who failed to appreciate the win–win nature of global trade, claiming they were 'silly', attention-seeking, media personalities, pedalling 'nonsense' and contributing to 'extremely primitive' debate.[15] What divided the silly from serious economist, Krugman wrote, was the use of models. The critics have 'no sense of the power and importance of economic models in general, or of Ricardo's difficult idea in particular'.[16]

John Kenneth Galbraith was arguably the last mainstream American institutional economist who viewed economic knowledge as a diverse and humanistic system of thought. By the 1990s, he was old and old hat. Although Galbraith did not make the argument, what was happening could be explained using his idea of 'countervailing power'. The market power of big business had been balanced by government, labour unions, and social movements—but these victories had been won at the national level. From the 1970s, although they still relied on state power, corporations began to emancipate themselves from dependence on any one state. There was no countervailing power at the global level: international organizations lacked real heft and global civil society groups were in their infancy. Multinationals expanded into this uncontested space. They moved production to countries where labour was cheap, governments pliable, social and environmental rules weak, and often where independent labour unions were illegal. This would produce a bonanza of corporate profits, of which executives awarded themselves an ever-greater share. But power is not easy to model and Galbraith's ideas were, by the 1990s, often mocked. Paul Krugman called him an 'intellectual dilettante who lacks the patience for hard thinking'.[17]

Dani Rodrik—one of the few mainstream economists to write about the dangers of what he calls 'hyper-globalization'—had not forgotten Krugman's warning that he could be giving 'ammunition to the barbarians'. But he'd been sleeping better since he had an epiphany: the barbarians cannot all be on one side. Anyone who doesn't see that free-trade agreements can get hijacked by big banks and corporations looking to rewrite rules to puff up their profits, he wrote in 2007, 'must have been asleep during the past quarter century'.[18] All industries lobby their governments to tilt the rules in their favour; traditionally economists saw this in the creation of tariffs and quotas to keep out competitors. But industries can also lobby their governments to open markets overseas and secure their interests there through changing the host country's laws, through treaties known as free-trade agreements. It is not so different to Britain's empire of free trade we explored in Chapter 6.

Susan Strange, the pioneer of global political economy, saw in the early 1990s that multinational firms, in working to set the political agenda and develop regulatory frameworks, had created a new type of global diplomacy. Strange (together with John Stopford of the London Business School) called it 'triangular diplomacy'. States were no longer just negotiating among themselves. They had to negotiate with multinational firms, who were also making alliances with each other. The traditional state–state diplomacy was only one side of the new triangle. The game could not be understood without considering the other two sides: state–firm and firm–firm diplomacy.[19] Let me briefly show how triangular diplomacy worked in three areas of global rule making: copyright and patents, the free movement of financial capital, and 'shadow' courts to discipline governments.

'An insurance policy for the structure of the world'

Western corporations had been pushing for increased protection for copyrights and medical patents since the 1970s through a UN body, the World Intellectual Property Organization (WIPO). They had little success as WIPO was dominated by developing countries and lacked means of enforcement. They were also battling the perception that longer and stronger patents and copyrights were forms of monopoly power: the extraction of unmerited profits that dampened innovation. This perception was changing, however, due to the new 'objective' anti-monopoly theory (see Chapter 14). In the 1980s, a core group of 12 American CEOs from the pharmaceutical, entertainment, and software industries created an Intellectual Property Committee, with Pfizer playing a major role. They argued that strong copyright rules provide an incentive for creating new products. Together with counterparts in Europe and Japan, they helped redefine copyright protection as a 'trade-related' issue and shifted discussions to what would become the WTO. This was a brilliant strategic move, as at the WTO the focus was on commerce rather than public health or economic development. A global deal on 'trade-related intellectual property rights' (called TRIPs) came into force in 1995, backed by the WTO's impressive dispute mechanism. The agreement set a precedent for similar provisions in other 'trade' deals.[20]

The WTO agreement required all member countries to change their national laws to adopt 20-year protection of patents, during which time companies had a legal monopoly on production and pricing. This included the US, which increased its long-standing patent term from 17 to 20 years on ratifying the agreement. There were grumbles in Congress but, like most trade deals, representatives could only vote 'yes' or 'no' on the whole package. The most controversial part of the new global copyright regime was related to the AIDS epidemic in Africa. Drugs to treat AIDS, and other diseases, were out of reach of all but a tiny few, not because they cost so much to produce, but because prices were kept high by patent holders. Countries that permitted the use or import of generic low-cost drugs—such as South Africa, Brazil, and Thailand—were challenged by the US both directly and through the WTO. The new rules transferred resources from developing-country consumers to multinational firms and likely had negative impacts on innovation. Activists and developing-country negotiators eventually managed to push through a 2001 WTO declaration stating that the copyright rules should support 'access to medicines for all'.[21] Conflict re-emerged, however, over COVID-19: Pfizer pulled in $37 billion from the vaccine in 2021 alone while developed countries resisted a waiver on WTO pharmaceutical patents that would have increased access to vaccines in the Global South.[22] How strange that a 'free-trade' deal should lead to higher prices and protect monopoly profits.

Let's turn to the second example: finance. At the same time that finance was deregulated in the 1990s at the national level, the industry put its political weight behind new regulations at the global level. In December 1997, over a hundred countries that were part of the WTO sealed a Financial Services Agreement. 'With this agreement, the WTO has completed a golden year,' its Director-General gushed.[23]

It was no secret that the finance industry and major Wall Street executives, many of whom were political donors, had pushed hard for the agreement. They had prompted the US delegation to walk out of negotiations in 1995 in protest against the weak offers on the table from other countries. After meetings at Davos in Switzerland in 1996, US, UK, and European finance firms came together to create a new, unified business lobby: the Financial Leaders Group.[24] And, in the crucial final negotiations, Citicorp, Goldman Sachs, Merrill Lynch, and others, such as the insurance company AIG, established command posts at hotels near the WTO headquarters in Geneva and liaised with the US delegation as it kept seeking greater concessions until 2 am. Business leaders were delighted by the result, which helped guarantee finance could flow across political borders freely. It would bring prosperity to everyone, they told the media. It was another unequal treaty as the *New York Times* told its readers: 'The United States, which already allows unfettered access to its financial markets, conceded nothing in the agreement.'[25] A former top US Treasury officer, who had recently become a Salomon Brothers executive, said that the agreement would 'lock in' global financial liberalization: 'It's like an insurance policy for the structure of the world.'[26]

Another set of provisions included in thousands of trade deals since the 1980s, such as NAFTA, grant corporations the right to sue sovereign governments for changes to the law that hurt their investment or profits.[27] These might include laws to discourage smoking, protect the environment, or raise wages. These provisions—officially known as 'investor–state dispute settlement' (ISDS), and less officially as 'shadow courts'—use a secretive arbitration process, outside national legal systems. These parallel legal systems are intended to give investors greater confidence to put their money into countries with weak rule of law, but have been included in draft agreements between the US and European Union (EU). *The Economist* in 2014 wrote that the secret tribunals could 'convince the public that international trade agreements are a way to let multinational companies get rich at the expense of ordinary people'.[28]

Although little used at first, more than 650 cases were filed between 2000 and 2015.[29] One recent case saw the company behind the overland Keystone Pipeline sue the US government for $15 billion, after President Biden cancelled the project. The complaint, lodged under a NAFTA provision, has yet to be settled.[30]

Global, regional, and bilateral agreements covered more than these three examples—copyright protection, finance, and shadow courts—but these examples show how many trade deals reached deep into national, supposedly democratic, politics. This was the point of the Seattle protest sign showing 'Democracy' and 'WTO' going in opposite directions.

Some of the purest believers in free trade, like the Indian–American economist Jagdish Bhagwati, publicly opposed this mission creep. In 1998, he came out against a powerful network of political and financial elites moving between Washington and New York that he called the 'Wall Street–Treasury complex' that argued that what's good for Wall Street is good for the world. These proponents of free-flowing financial capital have 'hijacked' the ideology and benefits of free trade, he said: 'The pretty face presented to us is, in fact, a mask that hides the warts and wrinkles underneath.'[31] Similarly, Bhagwati explained that including copyright and patent protection in trade negotiations was a result of corporate pharmaceutical and software lobbying which had 'distorted and deformed' the WTO into a 'royalty collection agency'.[32]

In the years after Seattle and before the collapse of Lehman Brothers in 2008, a rash of books, like Bhagwati's *In Defense of Globalization*, were published. Most were not complete without a nod to the stockbroker-turned-economist who died in 1823. Martin Wolf, in *Why Globalisation Works*, called comparative advantage 'perhaps the cleverest [idea] in economics'.[33] Thomas Friedman, in *The World Is Flat*, recalled seeing a stream of educated young Indians arrive at an IT company in Bangalore: 'My mind just kept telling me: "Ricardo is right, Ricardo is right, Ricardo is right".'[34]

Too few academic economists looked in detail at what was actually in the free-trade deals that the profession supported. They had changed. The US's first free-trade agreement with Israel in 1985, for example, included just 22 articles, most of which were devoted to tariffs. By 2004, the US–Singapore free-trade deal was a book-length text with 20 chapters, only seven of which were on conventional trade topics. The others dealt with 'behind-the-border' issues such as labour and environmental rules, financial services, and copyright and patent protection. One 2011 study estimated that 76 per cent of existing trade deals cover some form of investment (which could include limiting governments' ability to control short-term flows of money), 61 per cent covered copyrights and patents, and 46 per cent environmental regulations. It is naive to believe that the special interests of American corporations did not hold the upper hand in trade policy.[35] US trade representatives regularly meet, through a private-sector advisory process, with over thirty committees involving nearly one thousand people from the private sector.[36]

It would be more honest to call free-trade agreements 'treaties'. Just like the Methuen Treaty, they are deeply political as well as economic. They are the result of 'triangular diplomacy'. Often they are unequal. And still they are defended with the convenient facade of the mythical tale of win–win trade in English cloth and Portuguese wine.

'We've got to get this fuckin' show back on the road,' the Director-General of the WTO was reported as saying after the Battle for Seattle, 'We've got to rebrand!'[37] The organization started a fresh round of negotiations. This aimed to turn the page on the years when the WTO promoted rule making in sectors where rich countries were strong, such as finance and pharmaceuticals, and not where they are weak, such as agriculture and textiles. The new Doha Development Round, launched in 2001, was billed as putting the interests of developing countries first. (More than 20 years later these negotiations have been declared dead by most commentators.)

The WTO also published a webpage to explain the basics of open trade. A large part focused on David Ricardo's theory of comparative advantage. The theory, often misunderstood outside the field, is 'arguably the single most powerful insight into economics'.[38] It tells us that prosperity comes from the unrestricted flow of goods and services, the WTO said, where countries can adapt to the needs of the market in a relatively painless way.

Another attempt to change the narrative of the WTO was to revamp their Geneva HQ. When the organization (then GATT) moved into the building in the 1970s they found grand murals, tiles, and paintings celebrating the dignity of workers left by the previous owners, the International Labour Organization. It was not their vibe.

They covered up the artworks with plaster, or rolled up and stashed them in the gardener's cottage. After Seattle, the WTO decided to uncover the images. One of the paintings, revealed behind wood panels, is of a figure at the feet of a naked woman. The image was 'more unusual', one WTO Director-General said; although clearly an allegory, it had 'no apparent link to the world of labour or international organizations'.[39]

The 1925 painting by Spanish artist Eduardo Chicharro y Agüera displays a sculptor's workshop. A person is kneeling, with a half-carved sculpture and a discarded hammer on either side. In front of him is the nude woman, still as a statue, except for her left hand, which seems to be rubbing sleep from one eye. The WTO's hidden painting is of the Greek myth of Pygmalion the sculptor (see Figure 12.1). As we saw in Chapter 10 the Pygmalion myth is a poignant analogy for economists who fall in love with their models

Figure 12.1: *Pygmalion* by Eduardo Chicharro y Agüera, 1925

Source: © WTO

and ignore their faults. The WTO Director-General was wrong: there is a clear link between the painting and his organization. Pygmalion had been behind the walls of the WTO for decades as governments and firms rewrote the global economic and political rulebook guided and legitimated, in part, by too much faith in faulty models.[40]

China Shock

In 1970, the value of goods exported worldwide corresponded to around 9 per cent of global economic output; it rose to 15 per cent by 1990 and 26 per cent by 2008. An important milestone for global trade was the US government permanently granting China 'most favoured nation' status in 2000. All but a handful of countries had this already. It allowed normal trading relations with China and cleared the way for it to join the WTO. Paul Krugman argued that the US–China trade pact was a minor 'procedural' issue and that 'the trade arithmetic suggests that union members as a group would if anything benefit'.[41] Fifteen years later Krugman would admit he'd made a big mistake.

China is one of the great winners from hyper-globalization. Since the early 1990s, it has experienced the largest and most sustained economic growth in history. Hundreds of millions of its citizens have been lifted out of poverty. Between 1991 and 2012, China's share of world manufacturing value added increased sixfold, from 4 per cent to 24 per cent.[42] This has been called the 'Great Convergence', closing the gap created in the 'Great Divergence' (see Chapter 6). Chinese workers' wages have risen dramatically too. So too has inequality inside the country. According to the World Inequality Database, in 1990 the top 10 per cent of earners took home 31 per cent of national income. This had risen to 42 per cent by 2018. In the same period, incomes of the bottom half of earners fell from 22 per cent of national income to 14 per cent.[43]

China embraced the global market but, like South Korea, Taiwan, and Japan before it, its economic miracle was driven by violating Western free-market economics. It explicitly did not choose to focus on its current comparative advantage in low-tech manufacturing such as clothing, but to imitate developed countries and climb up the value chain. China used an aggressive industrial strategy to subsidize home-grown manufacturing and maintained controls on cross-border financial flows. Isabella Weber, a German economist and China expert, explains: 'China grew into global capitalism without losing control over its domestic economy.'[44] Although downturns in its property market and increasing authoritarian control of all aspects of society have reduced economic growth rates in recent years, its economic performance is in stark contrast to many countries in Africa and South America that were incentivized and pressured to follow more orthodox economic policies.

North Carolina has been a centre of the US furniture industry since the 1890s, with its abundant supply of wood from the Blue Ridge Mountains, its railways, and comparatively cheap labour, which helped it out-compete rival firms in New England. In the late twentieth century it had over 5,000 small furniture companies clustered in a rural manufacturing hub employing 90,000 people. Then, in the ten years between 1999 and 2009, more than half these jobs in North Carolina were lost. The culprit was the surge of cheap furniture imports from China, made possible by the US having granted the country favourable trade terms in 2000. Ironically, it was North Carolina's own industrial leaders, who went to Asia in search of low-cost labour and bumper profits, who taught local Chinese manufacturers the tricks of the American furniture trade. By 2016, an estimated 73 per cent of furniture sold in the US was imported, with most coming from China.[45] It is only one of the US industrial sectors upturned by what has become known as the China Shock.

We know this because of MIT labour economist David Autor and his collaborators. Labour economics has been a less prestigious corner of the economics field, which has often retained a more grounded approach. Autor and his collaborators have estimated that 2.4 million American workers lost their jobs due to Chinese imports between 1999 and 2011.[46] The benefits of lower-cost Chinese imports swelled corporate profits and were felt broadly across the economy by consumers, for example, who could afford iPhones made in China by Apple's supplier Foxconn. But the economic pain in America from these new trade flows was often highly concentrated in specific places and industries like furniture, toy manufacturing, and athletic goods. It was worse in rural areas where there were fewer alternative employers. The specific type of globalization created at the end of the Cold War essentially led to decent jobs in America being traded for cheap electronics (and large pay rises for the executive class).[47] As laid-off workers in America reduced their own spending in local restaurants and hairdressers, these businesses often crumbled too, plunging whole communities into regional depressions. This led to deep, long-lasting pain.

Mainstream economists had long known that free trade produced winners and losers in each country. The economics of trade taught to students was more nuanced than the win–win dogma of economists in the media. The Harvard professor Dani Rodrik calls it the gap between what economists 'teach and what they preach'.[48] The feeling among the profession was that the 'crown jewels' of economics—such as market efficiency, comparative advantage, and incentives—Rodrik writes, 'need defending from the ignorant masses'.[49] Economists knew that the losers would be the blue-collar production workers exposed to lower-paid competitors. But, they calculated that the gains of the winners (consumers and firms and workers in highly competitive sectors) would outweigh the losses of the losers. The economic profession was often content to conclude that an agreement made everyone better off if the winners would gain more than the losers lost. That was because the winners could *theoretically* compensate the losers and everyone would win.[50] The problem was the compensation remained theoretical, especially in countries with weak welfare states like the US.[51]

Economists call the economic pains of adjusting to new trade flows 'transition costs', which make them seem fleeting and insubstantial. Laid-off workers should, in theory, move to a more competitive sector. But the real labour market is not the ideal, fluid market of the theory, so while some workers took much lower-paid jobs in retail or fast food, others fell back on social security disability benefits. Programmes designed to help workers retrain are woefully underfunded and sometimes axed by the architects of globalization.[52] Trade theory, at least in the public arena, too often served as an alibi or an easy talking point for political and corporate elites. Other elements disappear in the narrow spotlight of economic theory too: the dignity, sense of purpose, and community that good work can bring.

In 2004, near the height of the China Shock, a journalist asked Greg Mankiw, economics textbook author and Chair of George W. Bush's Presidential Council of Economic Advisers, what he thought about jobs being offshored. Mankiw's response was that it was 'probably a plus for the economy in the long run'.[53] When he faced a political backlash, Mankiw leaned on economics' scientific credentials and 'the basic lessons that economists have understood for more than two centuries', going back to Adam Smith and David Ricardo.[54] A write-up in the *New Yorker* explained that many economists still rely on Ricardo's 'extremely powerful' argument of 'England exchanging its surplus cloth for Portugal's surplus wine, to the benefit of consumers in both places'.[55] Of the real history of that exchange—shown in Chapters 3, 4, and 5—nothing was said.

In 2004, the founder of modern American economics, Paul Samuelson, came out of retirement, aged 89, to challenge his profession's consensus on free trade. He criticized 'economists' oversimple complacencies about globalization', calling out 'Alan Greenspan, Jagdish Bhagwati, Gregory Mankiw, Douglas Irwin and economists John or Jane Doe spread widely throughout academia'.[56] Samuelson foreshadowed some of Autor's arguments, commenting that 'being able to purchase groceries 20 percent cheaper at Wal-Mart does not necessarily make up for the wage losses'.[57] Even the founder of American economics did not rouse the slumber of settled opinion. The tone of the responses to his paper was that perhaps the old man had lost his marbles. Jagdish Bhagwati wrote that Samuelson had got into a muddle; Douglas Irwin called it 'Pretty thin stuff'; Alan Greenspan, whom Samuelson had compared to Marie Antoinette saying 'Let them eat cake' in pre-revolutionary France, did not respond in public.[58] Much of the economics profession—and the political and business class—was in the grip of a self-comforting dogma that only events, not ideas, could break.

Escher models

The intellectual consensus among Western policy makers on free trade still held strong into the early 2010s. President Barack Obama signed into law free-trade agreements with Colombia, Panama, and South Korea that had been negotiated by George W. Bush's administration. Then, even more ambitiously, the Obama administration began negotiating two huge, new, regional trade deals, which would cover two thirds of the global economy.[59] The deals would bind America to allies across the oceans to the east and west and shape globalization. The Transatlantic Trade and Investment

Partnership (TTIP) aimed to set the rules for US and EU trade but has since been abandoned. More controversial, the Trans-Pacific Partnership (TPP)—part of a pivot to Asia and an attempt to isolate China—was agreed in 2016 between America and 11 Asian and Australasian allies.

Politics was changing. It became harder to deny that the economy was not working well for everyone. Workers' pay had stagnated for decades, while CEOs and other top executives had year-on-year double-digit salary increases and generous stock options. For the Western middle classes, the declining cost of consumer goods like flat-screen TVs—the fruit of cheap overseas labour made possible by global trade—has been eaten up by skyrocketing housing, education, health care, energy, and childcare costs.[60] Cracks began appearing in the pro-free-trade agreements consensus. Some, like Greg Mankiw, kept the faith. He argued in 2015 that Congress faced 'an exam in Economics 101' over whether to vote to give the President 'fast-track' authority to negotiate the TPP and TTIP. Voting 'yes' would mean Congress had passed the exam (and, also, that elected officials would not be able to amend any free-trade deals submitted for a vote). The argument for free trade, Mankiw said, had a 'near unanimity' of economists in support. Public scepticism was due to 'irrational' voters who were 'worse than ignorant' about good policy and held onto to 'mistaken beliefs' such as biases against markets or foreigners.[61]

Mankiw's old ally on trade, Paul Krugman, however, came out softly against the TPP. In a world in which tariffs had already fallen so low, there were few economic gains left to be had by cutting them further. Krugman had also woken up to the issue of copyright protection in trade deals in 2013, after more critical voices had been raising the problem loudly for 15 years.[62] The real interest of US negotiators, he now said, had been to push for greater protection for patents and copyrights, which would help mainly Big Pharma and Hollywood but probably not US workers. Economists' 'yay-free-trade sentiment,' Krugman wrote in 2015, stemmed from the fact that Ricardo's comparative advantage was such a classic example of brilliant economic reasoning that 'naturally, economists have always wanted this intellectual victory to be important in the real world too'.[63]

The debate over TPP was informed by detailed economic modelling. Supporters of the agreement lined up behind a study from Peter Petri and Michael Plummer for the Peterson Institute that predicted that the TPP would boost US national income by $131 billion (or half a per cent of GDP) by 2030, with larger proportional rises for other signatories. The authors wrote that the agreement 'is not projected to change US unemployment levels'.[64] It built on decades of academic trade literature and, according to Petri, had '108,000 rows and columns' of equations and variables drawing on '1.18 million data points'.[65] The problem, as ever, was in the assumptions. The Petri and Plummer model assumed the US labour market was highly 'flexible', meaning that job losses would be compensated quickly and fully by job gains. 'Unemployment is ruled out at the get-go,' commented Dani Rodrik, 'the employment "projection" might as well have been made before the computer crunched a single number.'[66]

Opponents of the deal meanwhile praised a model produced by a team led by Jeronim Capaldo at Tufts University. Capaldo built on a UN model and used Petri and Plummer's numbers for projected increased trade flows with the TPP, but critiqued several of their unrealistic assumptions, including the absence of a financial sector and overlooking any impacts on inequality. Capaldo's team used what they considered a more realistic baseline: that increased competition with trade liberalization would reduce wages in the US and that more foreign investment would mean more national income going to investors instead of American workers. It predicted that joining TPP would *reduce* US national income, *increase* its inequality, and lead to 448,000 job losses in the next ten years.[67] Petri and Plummer shot back, saying that Capaldo's assumptions 'simply *predetermine* job losses and a worsening of the income distribution'.[68]

The truth was that each side's results were determined by their assumptions about how an economy works. Each accused the other's model of essentially being like M.C. Escher's impossible *Ascending and Descending* drawing of a circular staircase: each step appears to follow the next but look at the whole picture and you see the end is the beginning. Economists just do not know enough about how trade impacts economies to produce 'time-travel machines' that allow you to see the distant future today.[69] Dani Rodrik has called for his colleagues to show a little more humility and not pretend that 'our cherished standard model has not been severely tarnished by reality'.[70]

The corporate system

Previously heretical views on trade also broke into the much less refined debates of the 2016 presidential election. Donald Trump attacked the Asian TPP deal from the right and Bernie Sanders, using similar language, attacked it from the left. Hillary Clinton, who in 2012 had called TPP 'the gold standard in trade agreements', came out against it.

Trump told upwards of 30,000 lies in office. But he pushed the conventional wisdom to admit one big truth: that international free trade deals can wreck lives and livelihoods, just as it can create them. Three days into his office, Trump withdrew the US from the TPP (which was in any case stalled in Congress), calling the move 'a great thing for the American worker'.[71] That both main political parties, and many others, had not been able to tell that truth for the past 30 years gave Trump power. As he was the first modern president to publicly air the problem, he was able to attach his own solution to it: a highly divisive one of punitive high tariffs and a trade war with China. He used the real, justified complaint against hyper-globalization to shred constitutional protections and serve an elite-friendly agenda. It left Harvard's Dani Rodrik asking: 'Are economists responsible for Donald Trump's shocking victory in the U.S. presidential election?'[72]

Trump gained support for his cultural and anti-immigrant rhetoric as well, of course, but economic populism helped. David Autor, co-author of the China Shock articles, was asking the same question as Rodrik. With colleagues, he studied the connections between manufacturing areas hit by cheap imports from China and political polarization ahead of the 2016 election that brought Donald Trump into the White House. Looking at Fox News' market share, campaign contributions, and voting records, he found strong evidence that voters in areas that lost jobs in the China Shock went increasingly for further right-wing, and sometimes further left-wing, candidates. Trump won nine-tenths of the areas most impacted by China Shock in the 2016 Republican primary.[73] The irony is: in the 1990s, people thought that free trade would make China more democratic; by the 2020s, it appeared to have made the US more authoritarian.

In 2019, several years into the Trump presidency, Paul Krugman admitted in a *Bloomberg* article that his work on globalization had 'missed a crucial part of the story'. With admirable honesty, he said he had a responsibility as one of the shapers of the 1990s pro-globalization consensus to explain what went wrong. His answer was that the consensus 'relied on models' that looked at inequality trends only among broad classes of workers: 'This was, I now believe, a major mistake—one in which I shared a hand.'[74] The important new insight that David Autor had brought was to focus attention not on broad statistical averages but on real industries and communities, where he found large and persistent negative impacts. The return of unreality in economics had made vast swathes of ordinary people effectively invisible.

Where did all this leave Adam Smith's 'flash of genius', as Milton Friedman described it, about the 'invisible hand' of market prices that could produce an orderly and prosperous society? It might shock some to learn that Smith only used the phrase 'invisible hand' once in *The Wealth of Nations* and, even then, it is in praise of buying local. Smith writes—in the gendered language of his time—that an individual 'preferring the support of domestic to that of foreign industry, he intends only his own security' and gain but promotes the public interest as 'he is in this, as in many other cases, led by an invisible hand to promote an end which was no part of his intention'.[75] The line about domestic trade was not a slip of the pen from Adam Smith; he thought that it brought more 'revenue and employment' than foreign trade.[76] However, economics textbooks do not mention this. Paul Samuelson's *Economics* reproduced Smith's 'invisible hand' quotation but omitted, with no ellipses, the part about supporting domestic industry.[77] Today's concept of the 'invisible hand' is largely the product of mid-twentieth-century American economics of Samuelson and Friedman. It was a poetic metaphor for markets ordered by prices with the essential human or institutional contexts ignored. The phrase was ripped from its time and context with few qualms. Friedman was not interested in what Smith meant, Glory Liu wrote in *Adam Smith's America*: he was interested in 'exploiting its rhetorical power for his own message'.[78]

Adam Smith's line, quoted by Milton Friedman in his 1980s TV show, could be read as an apt description of what happened in corporate-led globalization. The 'sophistry of merchants and manufactures confounded the common sense of mankind', as Smith said, and promoted policies 'directly opposite to that of the great body of people'. We know that Adam Smith was a fierce critic of the largest multinational corporation of his time: the British East India Company. He wanted, in part, to free trade from corporate control. The rewriting of the global rules of trade—justified in the name of Adam Smith, David Ricardo and the public interest—was captured by the interests of big, organized, politically connected business.

This has created a twenty-first-century mercantile or corporate system, in which countries compete with each other to lower corporate taxes, deregulate finance, and offer subsidies to attract global capital. These 'tax wars', arguably, have been far more influential and damaging than 'trade wars'.[79] Yet free-trade agreements have never touched the issue of tax competition. Only in 2021 did 135 countries agree a political agreement to introduce a global minimum 15 per cent corporate tax rate. As of 2024, this proposal, even in a weakened form, looked likely to fail amid opposition in the US from Republicans.[80] Rejecting secretive political treaties disguised as 'free-trade agreements' does not necessarily mean a retreat into isolationism. It could mean a safer, freer, fairer global system.

The widespread rejection of 1990s-style globalization in the last few years has been driven by the realization that the social and democratic stability of Western societies can no longer be taken for granted. It is also the realization, as described in the Introduction, that the economic vision, which prioritized 'wealth' over all other values, was inadequate to meet the challenge of fragile supply chains and a resurgent Russia and China. There has been a reappreciation of the value of 'security'. In October 2022, President Biden signed into law sweeping new rules designed to cut China off from the US' more advanced semiconductor technology. We have the opportunity to shape a better globalization, but there is a danger too that Western governments exchange one dogma for another and hand over the running of the global economy to security hawks, which might harm both peace and prosperity.[81]

13

Life: An Externality

*How climate economics helped mislead elite
opinion on the issue of our time*

It is more than 30 years since delegations from around the world
came to Rio de Janeiro—the port city that rose to prominence
with the gold rush of the 1700s—for a historic meeting about the
living world. Rio's 1992 Earth Summit created new international
conventions on climate change and biodiversity to halt the destruction
of 'the Earth, our home' (see Figure 13.1). The convention on
climate change—known by the acronym UNFCCC—agreed to
stabilize 'greenhouse gas concentrations in the atmosphere at a level
that would prevent dangerous anthropogenic interference with

Figure 13.1: View of
the Earth as seen by the
Apollo 17 crew travelling
towards the moon, 1972

Source: NASA on Unsplash

the climate system'.[1] In hindsight, world governments produced a radical document. They collectively recognized the need for fairness between current and future generations (intergenerational equity) and the importance of acting cautiously even when the science is not certain (the precautionary principle). What the new global climate organization lacked, however, was any enforcement mechanisms. Contrast that with the WTO created in the same decade, which has binding rules backed by a supranational court able to impose billion-dollar fines. And, rules without consequences are just good advice.

The world's response to environmental crisis has been profoundly shaped by the vision of orthodox economists. This may be surprising as the living world has been one of the profession's most obvious blind spots. David Ricardo included land in his core model of the economy, but it was seen as a stable backdrop to the action. In 1890, Alfred Marshall celebrated Western 'man's' ability 'to subdue Nature and force her to satisfy our wants'.[2] New, radical voices only gained prominence in the 1960s and 1970s. E.F. Schumacher—who was both an ecological economist and a former coal executive— for example, argued in *Small is Beautiful* that 'It is inherent in the methodology of economics to ignore [hu]mans' dependence on the natural world.'[3] Economists in the mainstream have typically looked down on the heretical ideas of these ecological economists and promoted a solution that leaves their core theories as little changed as possible: externalities.

A negative externality is a damaging impact a market exchange has on someone not directly involved. Atmospheric pollution is a classic example of an unintended side-effect. Abundant energy from the burning of fossil fuels benefits industry and consumers but results in a cost, in ecological damage, not included in the market price. Large parts of the green movement have come to see a focus on externalities as a way of recognizing a host of important things businesses and economics exclude from consideration and responsibility. It aims to put a cost on these excluded elements so people value them and, therefore, create markets that are compatible with a healthy environment. At least, that's the promise.

The economic theory of externalities goes back to Alfred Marshall's protégé Arthur Pigou. Writing in the 1920s, he argued that the social harms of market transactions can be reduced by putting a price on external costs.[4] When set at the right level, the price on carbon emissions should close a loop and send a signal back to producers and users of fossil fuels, making them reduce their use to an optimal level. And here's the clever bit, according to the theory, the 'invisible hand' of the market will seek out the cheapest ways of reducing emissions. That is because *if* everyone is guided by a calculating, self-interested, and knowledgeable internal stockbroker, they will search out and exploit to the maximum every difference in price.

This is the origin of the theory behind fixing the climate crisis by putting a price on carbon. These schemes come in two main forms: cap-and-trade (in which governments set a limit or cap of total emissions and companies can buy and sell permits to emit greenhouse gases) or a carbon tax (in which governments raise the cost of emitting carbon and hence discourage emissions). Many environmentalists in the US have been attempting, unsuccessfully, to make variations of these schemes law since the early 1990s. Economists see putting a price on external harms as the most rational and efficient—in their special technical sense—way to solve the climate crisis. An externality, for an economist, means a missing market. Therefore, we need to build more markets. This vision has been incredibly influential. American economist and former Treasury Secretary Larry Summers suggested in 2021: 'Economists have had a much larger influence on thinking about what we're going to do about pollution than atmospheric scientists.'[5]

Hot air

I got to see at first hand the planning for a new market in environmental commodities while working for Rainforest Foundation UK from 2009 to 2013. It was a scheme to stop the global destruction of forests called REDD (reducing emissions from deforestation and forest degradation). The idea was to pay poorer countries to keep their forests standing through a global market in 'forest carbon' credits, and it was supported by the UN, the World Bank, and the world's richest countries. I worked with civil society groups from Africa, South East Asia, and South America to make their voices heard in the development of the plan. We would support their attendance at climate change summits to meet policy makers directly and to begin discussions in their home countries.[6]

REDD was supposed to work like this. Poor countries would keep more of their forests standing with the carbon in the trees safely locked away. This would allow these countries to generate carbon credits for the emissions avoided. The credits would be sold via a global market to polluting industries in rich countries to 'offset' their emissions. The exact mechanisms were not worked out but the major selling point of the scheme was that the market mechanism would be a cheaper and more efficient way of combatting climate change than polluting industries directly reducing their own emissions. Supporters of REDD often spoke of how it was 'win–win' and the 'low-hanging fruit' of emissions reductions.

From the perspective of forest communities and non-governmental organizations (NGOs) in poorer countries things looked different. Some who heard of REDD were dazzled by the millions and billions of dollars that it promised.[7] But, in reality, who would benefit? Indigenous peoples and forest communities are often marginalized and have little political power. In Africa and South East Asia, few have legal rights to the land on which they live (so do not officially own the carbon in areas they may have lived in for generations). Many forest communities have been removed from their land due to agriculture or a 'guards and guns' approach to conserving nature. As the potential financial windfalls from REDD were talked up, dodgy businessmen—whom we called 'carbon cowboys'—convinced Indigenous peoples in many parts of the world to sign away any rights they had to the carbon in their trees. Environmental and social 'safeguards' for REDD were agreed by the UN in 2010, but there were other fundamental problems with the scheme.

How could anyone be sure that the carbon credits genuinely reduced emissions? This was essential. If the credits were 'hot air' (only emissions on paper) they could lead to an *increase* in global carbon emissions when others used them as 'offsets'. The awkward fact is that too many carbon offsets are hypothetical. They look real on paper, and are especially impressive when accompanied by the right logos and scientific-looking formulas and charts. But, in reality, they are generated by estimating the difference between two projections of the future. One is the 'baseline scenario' of what would happen with no REDD. The other is a scenario of what happens with REDD. The process is wide open to abuse as there is an incentive, for both the creator and buyer of the credits, to exaggerate the difference between the two scenarios.

Let me explain how it can go wrong. A study for the Democratic Republic of Congo, produced by the management consultancy firm McKinsey, suggested a REDD programme that would reduce the intensity of rainforest logging from 15 cubic metres per hectare to 10 cubic metres per hectare by 2030, and that would generate carbon credits due to this difference. This seems fine. The problem was the current legal volume of logging harvest in Congo was only between 3 to 5 cubic metres: the report had conveniently assumed it would increase to 15 so that Congo could be paid to 'reduce' it to 10. Similarly, a REDD plan for Guyana in South America, informed by McKinsey, used an artificially 'inflated baseline' scenario of logging the rainforest at 20 times its current rate so that more carbon credits would be generated for keeping the forest standing.[8] McKinsey disagreed with these findings and said that their work provided a 'fact-base' on potential emissions reductions 'to inform complex national debates'.[9]

In this and other ways the elegant logic of REDD hit messy reality with a bump and the scheme lost momentum. Most attention and money shifted into the voluntary carbon market where corporations pay to offset emissions, leading to slew of false 'carbon-neutral' claims. A 2023 investigation found that more than 90 per cent of forest carbon offsets were 'phantom credits' that do not represent genuine carbon reductions.[10] Despite the good intentions of many, the promise of a forest carbon market has failed. It has fed the idea that corporations and industrialized countries can essentially continue on the same old dirty development path by paying a small fee for someone else to reduce polluting gases.

The father of climate change economics

William Nordhaus, a Yale economist, is known as the father of climate change economics. Now in his 80s, Nordhaus studied under Paul Samuelson—the creator of orthodox American economics—and went on to became a co-author of his *Economics* textbook. From Samuelson, Nordhaus learned that economics was best described using mathematics, which, as he has said, is 'now part of my brain, just as much as the English language is part of my brain'.[11] He thought his mentors had solved most of the big economic problems, so with the oil crisis of the early 1970s, he turned to using then state-of-the-art modelling to forecast oil prices. It impressed a young student, the trade economist Paul Krugman, who became, in his own words, 'Nordhaus' protege'. Krugman emulated his mentor's style of 'small models applied to real problems, blending real-world observation and a little mathematics to cut through to the core of an issue'. And he marvelled at how Nordhaus' 'model transformed everyone's perception of the issue'.[12] Nordhaus' oil-price predictions, according to a 2003 study, 'missed the mark by a considerable margin'. This is not surprising as the long-term future is immune to calculation and Nordhaus had excluded unquantified factors influencing price such as politics and war.[13] But the setback did not put him off long-term scenario planning or sharing his forthright views on the US economy.

In a remarkable 1980 *New York Times* piece, Nordhaus advocated slaughtering economic 'sacred cows' that 'inhibit the play of market forces' and criticized Ronald Reagan's presidential campaign for backsliding. Nordhaus suggested abolishing the minimum wage for young people, cutting social security, and getting the Justice Department to give corporations a break and instead to investigate trade unions for wage fixing. Another concern was that social and environmental policies had been passed into law without considering their economic consequences. He called for a 'thorough overhaul of these rules', such as the landmark 1970 anti-pollution Clean Air Act, which, Nordhaus said, was 'based on a zero-risk philosophy that is neither sensible nor economic in a world of scarcity'.[14]

Nordhaus was still thinking about ecological risk in the early 1990s, when he created a new type of model to integrate economic growth theory and climate science and called it DICE (Dynamic Integrated Climate and the Economy model). His fundamental approach is cost–benefit analysis. One way to explain this vision of climate change is to think of the traditional representation of Justice as a blindfolded woman with a scale in one hand. But, Justice is not needed so her scale is given to Efficiency. On one side of the scale, Nordhaus puts the projected economic benefits of allowing business-as-usual activity without reducing carbon emissions. On the other, he puts estimates of the damage that climate change will do to the economy. Efficiency then weighs the benefits and damages on the scales and plots an optimal path, which is guided by putting a price on carbon emissions.[15] It promises a Goldilocks climate policy: not too much action or risk nor too little. It has been highly influential and used by governments, international agencies, and the IPCC (Intergovernmental Panel on Climate Change) to estimate the costs and benefits of reducing emissions. Nordhaus has said: 'There is basically no alternative to the market solution.'[16]

In December 2018, Nordhaus, dressed in white tie and tails, received the world's most prestigious intellectual prize, a Nobel, from the King of Sweden. 'Your research has given us deep insights into the causes and consequences of climate change,' the Nobel host said, 'the tools you have developed broaden the scope of economic analysis, allowing us to think about the future in new and better ways.'[17] As the King, in a grey sash, gave Nordhaus the Nobel medal a bugle call rang out from the Swedish Philharmonic Orchestra and the bejewelled audience gave him a standing ovation. It was the stuff of dreams. An academic review hailed his visionary work for the benefit of humankind as 'science at its best'.[18] And yet Nordhaus' Nobel Lecture the day before had sparked controversy.

Nordhaus is no climate change sceptic. He compares those who deny human activity is heating the atmosphere to those who refused to believe that smoking causes cancer. He regularly calls for governments to impose new and higher carbon taxes. In the lecture, he used a painting by the Spanish artist Francisco de Goya called *The Colossus* showing a towering giant to demonstrate the scale of the challenge of climate change to economics. He also explained his approach of calculating how the world could reduce greenhouse gases 'most efficiently ... the least costly in the economic sense'. The part of the speech that has generated most buzz since is a graph— Figure 13.2—of temperature trajectories into the future. The graph represents the output of his models, which, he said, are 'based on fundamental scientific theories'.[19]

The UN Climate Conference in Paris in 2015 had agreed to limit temperature rises to 2 °C and aimed to keep them below 1.5 °C. But these targets, Nordhaus has warned, are far too costly and hitting them is 'essentially infeasible'.[20] He plotted an 'optimal' path from an economic point of view—the dotted line with triangles in Figure 13.2—which balances costs and damages. This line would mean an increase in global temperatures *double* that of the Paris

Figure 13.2: Temperature trajectories in different policies by William Nordhaus

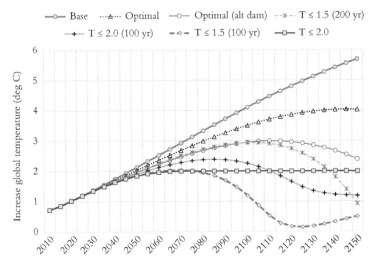

Source: William Nordhaus, Nobel Lecture, 8 December 2018

target to 3 °C by 2080 before levelling off at 4 °C by 2150.[21] Never mind the breathtaking intellectual confidence of drawing a smooth line on a graph for economic and climate impacts for the next 130 years. More controversial is branding a 4 °C average temperature rise as 'optimum' as it is more than double the target agreed by the international community and is likely to transform the Earth from the planet that has cradled the human species.

One outspoken critic, Jason Hickel, an economic anthropologist and author, called Nordhaus and his followers 'the prophets of postponement'. Hickel wrote that 'the failure of the world's governments to pursue aggressive climate action over the past few decades is in large part due to arguments that Nordhaus has advanced'.[22]

The 4 °C optimum is only the most prominent of Nordhaus' questionable statements on atmospheric pollution. He has regularly suggested governments shouldn't try too hard to directly reduce emissions lest it cost them too much. In 1991, in the run-up to the Rio Earth Summit, he published the 'surprising conclusion' that 'for the bulk of the economy—manufacturing, mining, utilities, finance, trade, and most service industries—it is difficult to find major direct impacts of the projected climate changes over the next 50 to 75 years'.[23] He estimated that a 3 °C rise in average temperature might reduce the US economy by a tiny 0.25 per cent or perhaps as high as 1 per cent or 2 per cent if you bring in other 'unmeasured or unmeasurable impacts'. The approach was 'oversimplified', Nordhaus admitted, and 'neglects a number of areas that are either inadequately studied or inherently unquantifiable'.[24] Still, this attempt to quantify economic damage from climate change became a reference point for the field.

When Nordhaus looked again at his 1991 numbers in his 2013 book *The Climate Casino* he had good news: 'one of the central findings of the economics of climate change' is that 'market economies will become increasingly *less* vulnerable to climate change'.[25] That is starkly at odds with the prevailing international or scientific consensus. As Columbia University historian Adam Tooze has written, Nordhaus' 'models acknowledge the climate crisis, but characterise it in such anodyne terms as to cast doubt on whether it's worth doing anything about it'.[26] To understand where Nordhaus' optimistic conclusion comes from, we need take a look at the foundations of his model and what its spotlight illuminates and what it makes invisible.

Illusionary precision

In Nordhaus' model world essentially all markets work perfectly, identifying new opportunities for economic growth. The only exception is the market failure in preventing dangerous greenhouse gas emissions. These baseline assumptions mean that reducing emissions will *always* be a cost, therefore ignoring the possibility that moving to a greener economy will open up new and more dynamic types of economic development.[27] With this as the backdrop, Nordhaus has used two primary means for estimating the future economic damage of climate change.

The first method, which Nordhaus used for over two decades, breaks down the US economy into sectors. How much each sector contributes to the total economic output of the country is calculated along with its vulnerability to climate change. Nordhaus categorized each sector as being at risk of severe, moderate, or negligible impacts. In the severe section, he placed only farming and fishing: a tiny 1 per cent of US economy in 2013. In the moderate category he put coastal real estate and around 9 per cent of the economy, such as construction and transportation, which are 'affected by weather and climate'. Finally, in the negligible impact category he put manufacturing, finance, trade, and more, totalling 90 per cent of the economy. Nordhaus justified excluding from the start nine-tenths of the economy from even moderate impact with the argument that these activities happened in 'highly controlled environments' and are 'likely to experience little or no direct effects from climate change'.[28] This is a sweeping and seemingly arbitrary assumption on which to hang a scientific calculation. It leads to Escher-style circular logic. For heterodox economist Steve Keen, Nordhaus provides a laughably benign version of climate change that can be avoided by stepping indoors. Keen believes that Nordhaus' work 'could soon be exposed as the most significant and dangerous' wrong turn in the history of science.[29]

What is the origin of Nordhaus' 'central finding' in 2013 that developed economies are becoming 'increasingly less vulnerable' to climate? This is based on farming and fishing—the sectors deemed to be at severe risk—having declined as proportion of US GDP while the sectors deemed to be negligibly affected by climate change have risen from 85 per cent of GDP in 1973 to 90 per cent in 2011.[30] Hey presto! The sectors of economy assumed to be 'insulated' from climate are growing faster; therefore, climate is becoming less of a problem. In the real world, extreme weather events can disrupt every type of business and carefully controlled environments have to be continually maintained and restocked from the outside. Also, using money as the universal measuring rod veils the fact that if global fishing and farming were wrecked by ecological damage it would make more than a 1 per cent difference to human welfare. To be fair, Nordhaus has admitted in a technical document in 2013 that this sectoral method is 'outdated and unreliable'.[31]

Unfortunately, the second statistical method Nordhaus used to estimate damages from climate change is not a great improvement. In the search for numbers to plug into the model, researchers have focused on the relationship between average temperature and total economic activity (measured by GDP) in today's world. These two variables are large statistical aggregates that can only 'see' in very broad strokes. On its own, however, that research might have thrown up some interesting insights. Just focusing on the relationship between these two variables—temperature and changes to GDP—and freezing every other factor does provide a weak result, suggesting that higher temperatures are somewhat correlated with lower economic growth in our world today (for example, that France is richer than Central African Republic). But correlation does not mean causation. Nordhaus and other researchers have used this mathematical function to calculate economic damage from future temperature rise. But the changes in temperature across today's world and the dynamic impacts of the climate crisis in the future are two separate things. It is classic substitution; modellers have replaced a difficult question with an easier one and not communicated the swap clearly enough. There are many factors other than temperature—not least political structures, culture, and the history of colonialism—which influence the shape and size of a country's economy. The technique here is reminiscent of Schumpeter's critique of the Ricardian Vice: using highly abstract models that freeze most of reality as a guide to practical problems. Indeed, the Nobel laureate's earlier work on putting a number on potential damages in US agriculture relied on what he called 'the controversial Ricardian method', where perfectly selfish and calculating farmers operate in a world of perfect markets.[32]

This second statistical method generates the numbers behind Nordhaus' claim in his Nobel Lecture that 4 °C average temperature rise is optimum. But climate scientists, let alone economists, have no way of knowing that current dynamics will hold as the climate heats up. Nordhaus' approach assumes one clean global temperature change and ignores the speed of change (so in 'model land' a 4 °C average temperature rise in one year would have the same economic impact as an annual 0.026 °C rise over 150 years), and all costs of adjustment (for example in agriculture, of corn farmers moving to new fields and replacing large items such as grain elevators) are assumed to be zero. Nicholas Stern, who has advocated for bolder action, has complained that far too often climate economics has ignored profound risks and modelled only 'small perturbations'.[33] Stern and Nordhaus have publicly disagreed about what value to give to the 'discount rate': a number that tells the model how important future generations are compared to the present. This discussion has strong ethical aspects but is often carried out behind a technical veneer few can follow. The choice of a number skews the model conclusions one way or the other. Nordhaus uses a higher discount rate—drawn from financial markets—than Stern, which leads his model to suggest that less ambitious action to reduce pollution in the atmosphere is optimal.[34]

Nordhaus has recognized that this second approach still leaves out many essential factors and has compared studying the deep future with models to looking through a 'fuzzy telescope'.[35] And, in the 2013 technical manual for his model, you find this:

> current studies generally omit several important factors (the economic value of losses from biodiversity, ocean acidification, and political reactions), extreme events (sea-level rise, changes in ocean circulation, and accelerated climate change), impacts that are inherently difficult to model (catastrophic events and very long term warming), and uncertainty (of virtually all components from economic growth to damages) … and does not include sharp thresholds or tipping points.[36]

So much has been left out you might question how much of the living world or climate is actually in the model. To compensate for these missing elements, Nordhaus adjusted the expected economic damages upwards by 25 per cent. These types of ad hoc adjustments are often found under the hood of 'state-of-the-art' models. They often stay hidden. In his Nobel Lecture, Nordhaus did not describe the huge aspects of reality that his model cannot see. Not just fellow modellers, but users and the general public, need more information about the dirt swept under the rug.

The counterargument is that the current models are vastly better than they were a few decades ago and are improving all the time. We have no choice but to look through the fuzzy telescope and to keep on trying to make the picture clearer. There has been some progress in the climate economics literature since the 2010s to include more realistic damage functions. This is welcome. Some estimates now suggest a 3 °C increase might reduce GDP by 9–10 per cent.[37] Still, there is the larger issue that the mainstream integrated models are stuck in a very narrow vision of climate and the economy. That approach has 'almost completely failed to be useful to the national policy discourse,' wrote economic commentator Noah Smith in 2021. 'The big conceptual mistake here is to assume that whatever economists can easily measure is the sum total of what's important for the world—that events for which a reliable cost or benefit cannot be easily guessed should simply be ignored in cost–benefit calculations. That is bad science and bad policy advice.'[38]

The most important critical voice within mainstream economics in these debates has been Harvard professor Martin Weitzman. In his first press conference after the Nobel was announced, Nordhaus said he was surprised not to be sharing the prize with Nicholas Stern or Weitzman: 'an extraordinary, brilliant guy'.[39] Weitzman had long argued that Nordhaus should be more upfront about the 'truly extraordinary uncertainty about the aggregate welfare impacts of catastrophic climate change' and the fact that his standard models consist of 'a very long chain of tenuous inferences fraught with big uncertainties in every link'. Weitzman identified an 'artificial infatuation with crispness' of results that pushes researchers to exclude 'the very possibilities that make climate change so grave in the first place'. These critiques are reminiscent of debates within economics since the time of David Ricardo. Weitzman's main message was that the world seen through the standard models presents an illusion of certainty and precision, which could lead to dangerous overconfidence and global catastrophe. His analysis suggested that bolder action was needed.[40] Nordhaus praised his critic's 'radically innovative spirit'. Tragically, Weitzman committed suicide in 2019, aged 77. Colleagues told the *New York Times* that he had grown despondent 'after being passed over for the Nobel Prize in economics last year'.[41]

Climate economics models with 'no climate in them'

Nordhaus is genuinely concerned about climate change. But, what if someone building such models was motivated to put their fingers on the scales, for example, to protect the interests of big corporate polluters? After all, as Robert Pindyck, Professor of Economics at MIT, has warned, climate economics models are 'close to useless' as they can be tweaked 'to obtain almost any result one desires'.[42] Results can be protected from widespread scrutiny by the intimidating aura of scientific rigour. We do not need to speculate thanks to Benjamin Franta, an environmental lawyer at Oxford University with PhDs in applied physics and the history of science.

Franta's 2022 article, 'Weaponizing economics', showed how Big Oil companies funded economic consultants to create models that inflated the costs of reducing emissions while ignoring the benefits. He described the episode as industries attempting to co-opt experts and using 'the language of science to defend their commercial interests'.

This is what happened. In 1991, Charles River Associates, a consulting firm, was paid by the oil industry trade association, the American Petroleum Institute (API) to produce a study. Authored by economist David Montgomery, the study warned of the economic pain that would be caused by reducing emissions by 20 per cent and claimed, putting forward little evidence, that economic damage from global warming would be zero until 2100 and even then not exceed 0.5 per cent of GDP. Montgomery claimed his work was based on 'fundamental economic principles'.[43] In the run-up to the 1992 Rio Earth Summit, an API executive trumpeted the study in the *New York Times* but did not mention they had paid for it. This happened again and again.

Montgomery was joined by co-authors such as Paul Bernstein, another modeller, to produce estimates used to fight off Clinton's attempt at a carbon tax and to keep the US from ratifying the Kyoto Protocol. One of these studies, which Franta says was funded by the American Automobile Manufacturers Association, claimed Kyoto would be the 'single most expensive environmental measure ever adopted by the U.S. government' and could cost up to 500,000 jobs. Similar studies were used in the successful defeat of four cap-and-trade bills in the 2000s. Friendly members of Congress praised Charles River Associates as 'credible' and 'nationally respected'. Another of their studies was lauded by Mobil oil company in the *New York Times* for injecting 'a healthy dose of realism into the climate-change debate'.[44]

When US President Donald Trump pulled out of the Paris Climate Agreement in 2017, he spoke of 'the draconian financial and economic burdens' that would cost the US 'close to $3 trillion in lost GDP and 6.5 million industrial jobs' by 2040.[45] These numbers came from a study published a few months earlier by National Economic Research Associates or NERA. The study had been paid for, and shaped by, the US Chamber of Commerce and the American Council for Capital Formation, a 'pro-growth' think tank, both of which have received funding from oil and gas majors. Its lead authors were the former Charles River consultants Paul Bernstein and David Montgomery.[46]

Bernstein now admits that the models he made were structured to produce one-sided results. 'What bothers me is that our analysis just talked about the costs,' he told Franta, while assuming away economic damages that climate change would bring. The spotlight of the model picked out the parts of the story useful for the industry narrative and—because of the lack of broad understanding of just how malleable models are—too many people swallowed it. 'We could talk about cost effectiveness, but we couldn't actually weigh the costs and benefits. I think it served the API's purpose,' said Bernstein. 'I regret not being in a position where I could tell what I feel is the whole story.'[47]

Although the full models are not public, Franta says that they included unrealistic assumptions that reducing emissions primarily meant reducing energy use (not substituting it with greener power generation) and that any alternative energy would be four to six times more expensive than fossil fuels forever (whereas solar energy has tumbled in cost and is often now cheaper than fossil fuels). Franta points out that the Charles River Associates work shared similarities with other prestigious modelling groups, which have also received fossil fuel funding.[48] Exxon has given money to 82 universities and research institutions in recent years, part of its commitment, the company has said, to finding 'solutions to meet global energy demand and reduce emissions'.[49] We need, Franta writes, 'greater attention on the role of economists and economic paradigms, doctrines, and models in climate policy delay'.[50]

Back in the 1990s, knowledgeable people did try to raise the alarm. One was Robert Repetto, a former Yale economist working for the World Resources Institute (WRI). He testified to the Senate Committee on Foreign Relations on US climate policy in June 1997 after David Montgomery of Charles River Associates. Repetto wanted to clear up confusion about economic models. The models are complicated, he told senators, but they are, nonetheless, 'gross simplifications of how the economy actually works'. It is essential to understand, Repetto said, that 'the predictions that come out of them [climate economics models] are 100 percent determined by the assumptions that are built into them'. These assumptions, Repetto showed in a study of 16 leading climate models—one of which was William Nordhaus'—included whether or not the economy is perfectly competitive, and whether alternative renewable fuels exist and at what price.[51] He warned the committee presciently that 'what modellers leave out influences their predictions as strongly as what they put in'. One of the main things that these climate economics models left out, he said, was ... the climate. 'Most of the models used to analyze this climate policy *have no climate in them* so that there are no potential costs to the economy, no droughts, no floods from climate change.'[52] This was because in their baseline projections the models quietly assumed that climate change would have no effect on the economy. Cherry-picked assumptions produce cherry-picked conclusions.

This is especially disturbing because knowledge generated by models is reputed to be objective and impartial. Much of the public are intimidated by the advanced mathematics, meaning the models are often only intelligible to those with advanced science or maths degrees.[53] The assumptions are rarely questioned or even discussed outside academic seminar rooms.

Economists (and Big Oil) against the Green New Deal

Despite annual conferences, and warning after warning from Earth scientists, concentrations of carbon dioxide in the atmosphere have climbed relentlessly. Carbon dioxide made up 356 ppm (parts per million) when the convention was signed in Rio in 1992 and had risen to 419 ppm by 2022. It is estimated that man-made warming has raised global average temperatures by around 1 °C compared to pre-industrial levels. Summer 2023 smashed temperature records. And polluting the atmosphere is only one part of a much larger ecological crash. The conservation organization WWF estimates that in the last 50 years the Earth has lost on average 69 per cent of its wild bird, mammal, fish, and amphibian populations. The destruction of the living world, on which human civilization rests, has not slowed.[54] No wonder that today's environmental movement has taken on a sharper, more urgent, and boldly political message.

In 2018, Greta Thunberg, a 15-year-old school striker for climate from Sweden, addressed the annual UN Climate Summit. 'We have not come here to beg world leaders to care,' said Thunberg, 'we have come here to let you know that change is coming whether you like it or not. The real power belongs to the people.' (A few years later, when Thunberg told corporate and political leaders at the exclusive Davos meeting to get out of fossil fuel investments, then US Treasury Secretary Steve Mnuchin dismissed her with the line: 'Is she the chief economist? … After she goes and studies economics in college, she can come back and explain that to us.')[55] Also in 2018, a new group, Extinction Rebellion, began a series of mass, non-violent civil disobedience campaigns. In the US, the Sunrise Movement and Congresswoman-elect Alexandria Ocasio-Cortez (AOC) sat in front of then-Speaker of the House Nancy Pelosi's office in November 2018 to push for a Green New Deal: a climate plan that aims to tackle both inequality and reducing emissions.

Once in office, on 7 February 2019, AOC launched a proposal for a Green New Deal together with Democratic Senator Edward Markey. It called for a ten-year mobilization to develop new renewable power, make buildings more energy-efficient, and overhaul public transport and ensure a just transition.[56] This was a turn away from the passive carbon-pricing and market-based approach long advocated by most economists. Justice was being encouraged back onto the stage alongside efficiency (or wealth), although she was not yet given the scales. The political conversation on climate change was changing. The ecological crisis was increasingly being recognized across much of the political spectrum as one of the defining challenges of our time.

On 17 January 2019, three weeks before the Green New Deal was formally introduced, a full-page ad had appeared in the *Wall Street Journal* under the headline 'The economists' statement on carbon dividends'. It was signed by 28 Nobel laureates, every living Chair of the Federal Reserve, and many other big fish such as textbook author Greg Mankiw (but not William Nordhaus). The signature list would grow to 3,649, making it, reportedly, the largest public statement of economists in history.[57] One signer, Larry Summers, called it 'one of the few ideas of economic policy that commands broad, bipartisan support'.[58] The statement declared climate change a serious problem that needed immediate action and announced: 'A carbon tax offers the most cost-effective lever to reduce carbon emissions at the scale and speed that is necessary.' It proposed returning the money raised from the tax to US citizens in a dividend.[59]

Standard economic theory can fix the climate, some argued. In a 2023 book *How Economics Can Save the World*, Stockholm University economist Erik Angner lauded the economists' statement: 'No cause has generated a more robust response from the profession, it seems.'[60] He didn't mention that a 2019 study found only 57 articles related to climate change among 77,000 published in top general interest journals. The study even found that the most-cited journal in the field, the *Quarterly Journal of Economics*, had never published an article on climate economics.[61] Angner also failed to mention the context of the statement or who funded the group behind it.

The 'Economists' statement on carbon dividends' was, in reality, designed to squash the bolder idea of the Green New Deal. This was no secret. The statement itself said that the carbon tax could replace 'various carbon regulations that are less efficient'.[62] Janet Yellen, an American economist who is now Treasury Secretary and had gathered signatures for the statement, told the *Financial Times* that a carbon tax 'is much more efficient and less costly than methods proposed by the proponents of the Green New Deal'. Ted Halstead, the founder of the Climate Leadership Council, which organized the proposal, was just as frank: 'America has two choices, one is the route of the Green New Deal, one is the route recommended by the entire economic establishment, which is the carbon dividend plan.'[63] The message is clear: choose the experts.

But what is the Climate Leadership Council? It had been created in 2017 as a bipartisan organization to push the carbon tax proposal. Founder members include environmental groups like Conservation International and WRI, but also Wall Street giants such as Goldman Sachs, and four of the world's largest publicly traded oil companies—ExxonMobil, Shell, TotalEnergies, and BP. In 2018, ExxonMobil, Shell, and BP gave the Climate Leadership Council's lobbying arm $1 million each and ConocoPhillips—also a founding member—pledged $2 million.[64] The council argues that oil majors have 'the scale, research and development budgets, expertise and infrastructures' needed to reach a low-carbon future.[65]

So, the largest ever public statement by economists was bankrolled by Big Oil and designed to head off a not-yet-announced plan to tackle inequality and reduce pollution. And then it was hailed as evidence that economics can save the world with orthodox theory. The final irony is that to support the 'Economists' statement', the Climate Leadership Council published a study that warned of a huge hit to the US economy of $420 billion by 2036 if governments rejected the carbon-pricing approach and took more direct action (such as increasing fuel-efficiency standards for cars and electricity generation, and subsidizing electric vehicles) . The report, which boasted of its 'state-of-the-art economic model', was produced by NERA. Its lead author was the former head of climate at Charles River Associates.[66]

In 2021, a senior director of ExxonMobil's Washington lobbying team was secretly recorded by Greenpeace saying that his company supports a carbon tax because they needed a policy response and chose one that would never be implemented. 'There is not an appetite for a carbon tax. It's a nonstarter,' the director said, 'But it gives us a talking point.'[67] In response, Exxon said that the comments were 'inaccurate' and 'entirely inconsistent with our commitment to the environment'.[68] That didn't stop the Climate Leadership Council kicking the oil major out of the group later the same year.[69]

Saving the climate or the theory?

For decades, the consensus policy response to climate change has been carbon prices. This faith in the price system now looks like a costly narrowing of vision. Time and again environmentalists in the 1990s and 2000s tried to get cap-and-trade or carbon tax bills passed in Congress. Each time they failed. AOC's Green New Deal plan did not pass Congress either, but to the surprise of many centrists (and despite the warnings of economists) its package of climate investments and regulation was popular in public polling.[70] It helped to change the political weather. US political commentator Ezra Klein explained that Joe Biden's incoming administration in 2021 saw climate as a political problem: 'They view the idea that a carbon tax is the essential answer to the problem of climate change as being so divorced from political reality as to be actively dangerous.'[71]

In 2022, President Biden's administration pushed through the Inflation Reduction Act, which, despite its name, included $369 billion for climate change policies that aim to reduce emissions by 40 per cent by 2030. Although only a fraction of what is needed, it was the largest piece of climate legislation in American history. Al Gore, former Vice President and long-time climate advocate, said, 'I did not for a moment imagine it would take this long.'[72] The Act cast aside the old fixation on the price of carbon and instead gave incentives to businesses and individuals for wind and solar power, batteries, heat pumps, and electric vehicles (and included tax breaks and subsidies for oil companies). It replaced the stick of taxing emissions with a carrot for green energy technology. William Nordhaus was not impressed with the politicians: 'Carbon taxes have proven a toxic mix with politics,' he said, 'Subsidies, by contrast, are catnip to the elected.'[73] Time will tell how well it works.

What looks like a decades-long, unsuccessful policy detour into carbon taxes should prompt us to ask: what use is the idea of 'externalities'? How large and essential can something be and still be considered external? Isn't labelling the entire natural world an externality a clear sign that the intellectual system is not credible? The concept seems to have done a better job of saving standard economic theory than the world. It gave economists a way of explaining why only marginal changes were needed to make our economies compatible with nature. It could all be done with one price. Many now see this as a dangerous dream. As Herman Daly, an ecologist economist looked down on for his views by the mainstream, has said:

> Externalities do represent a recognition of the neglected aspects of concrete experience, but in such a way as to minimise restructuring the basic theory. As long as externalities involve minor details, this is perhaps a reasonable procedure. But when vital issues (e.g. the capacity of the earth to support life) have to be classed as externalities, it is time to restructure basic concepts and start with a different set of abstractions that can embrace what was previously external.[74]

He's right. We cannot get rid of abstractions, but we are not stuck with the ones that we've inherited. Mainstream economists eager to show that they can solve ecological problems are tying themselves into increasingly abstract knots inventing numbers in order to try to put a dollar sign on every living thing on the planet. How much sense does it make to put a dollar value on the pleasure of walking through a flower meadow or on a whale?[75] We need, instead, a broader discussion of what values our societies hold and how institutions and laws might be created to realize these.

We have seen once again in this chapter both the naive and the knowing abuses of modelling. The way that models have altered sophisticated peoples' perception of reality: helping to make hypothetical and often unreal forest carbon credits appear solid enough to be traded on one hand, and the reality of humans' reliance on the natural world slip out of mind on the other.

Remarkably, some of the conceptual traps into which climate economics has fallen were foreseen a century ago by Arthur Pigou, the economist responsible for the idea of externalities. In a eulogy to his mentor Alfred Marshall, he wrote:

> [Marshall] saw that excessive reliance on this instrument [mathematics] might lead us astray in pursuit of intellectual toys, imaginary problems not conforming to the conditions of real life: and further, might distort our sense of proportion by causing us to neglect factors that could not easily be worked up in the mathematical machine.[76]

Meeting the challenge of adapting our industrial and digital civilization to the size and capacity of the Earth will require facing up squarely to the political and economic powers who have a short-term interest in ecological destruction. We will also need new ways of seeing our relationship with the natural world and that requires new stories.

14

New Hope

*New voices in economics that have sprung up to challenge
the concentration of wealth and power in society*

In May 2014, a dense 700-page economics book shot to the top of
US best-seller lists and stayed there. It would go on to sell upwards of
2.5 million copies. This was a surprise in more ways than one. *Capital
in the Twenty-First Century* was by a relatively unknown French
economist Thomas Piketty. Right from the introduction, Piketty did
not hide his violent disagreement with US mainstream economists:

> To put it bluntly, the discipline of economics has yet to get
> over its childish passion for mathematics and for purely
> theoretical and often highly ideological speculation, at
> the expense of historical research. ... This obsession with
> mathematics is an easy way of acquiring the appearance
> of scientificity without having to answer the far more
> complex questions posed by the world we live in. ...
> [Economists] must set aside their contempt for other
> disciplines and their absurd claim to greater scientific
> legitimacy, despite the fact that they know almost nothing
> about anything.[1]

The contents were just as explosive: a detailed, empirical study of the
growth of inequality in the Western world. Mainstream economists
had put their faith in the Kuznets Curve since the 1960s: the theory
that predicted that during industrialization economic inequality

would first increase and—like a projectile pulled down by gravity—naturally decrease. Piketty revealed the neat curve as a 'fairy tale': a snapshot in time that had been overly generalized and used for pro-capitalist propaganda in the Cold War.[2] Piketty's journey to writing his book began in the 1990s when he was hired, in his early 20s, as an economist in the US. He quickly realized 'there had been no significant effort to collect historical data on the dynamics of inequality since Kuznets, yet the profession continued to churn out purely theoretical results without even knowing what facts needed to be explained. And it expected me to do the same.' Instead, he returned to France determined to 'collect the missing data'.[3] His 700-page book, 20 years later, was the result.

Previous inequality researchers had gathered information from household surveys but these tended not to capture the highest incomes. Piketty instead gathered tax records from the US, UK, France, and elsewhere to chronicle the fall and rise of the incomes of the top 1 per cent and bottom 50 per cent of the population over the past century. His results are summed up in a famous U-shaped graph showing the top 1 per cent's income starting high in the 1900s, declining steeply in the mid-century 'great redistribution', and then picking up sharply from the 1980s onwards and returning to Gilded Age levels in the first decades of the twenty-first century (see Figure 14.1). Wealthy elites had used their political power to lobby politicians to get further tax breaks. Democracy, Piketty warned in 2014, was in the balance: 'the risk of a drift toward oligarchy is real'.[4]

Piketty enlisted a surprising ally in his attack on the 1 per cent: David Ricardo. Contemporary economists had sidelined questions of who gets the spoils of economic growth or buried them in aggregated statistics. Piketty praised Ricardo—and other economists of the 1800s—for putting the question of how economic wealth is distributed at the heart of their analysis. He also drew inspiration from Ricardo's attacks on the feudal landlord class, who collect 'unmerited income' in the form of rent and act as a drain on the economy. Ricardo's prediction that rents would rise and rise was wrong, Piketty notes. But the idea still illuminates the 'unmerited income' from the capitalist concentration of wealth in our times. Piketty's argument has seen new interest from heterodox economists into the excess, unmerited incomes in finance, 'intellectual property', and Big Tech platforms.

Figure 14.1: Income share of the richest 1% (before tax), 1913 to 2021

The share of income received by the richest 1% of the population.
Income here is measured before taxes and benefits. The dotted lines
represent extrapolations due to limited data availability.

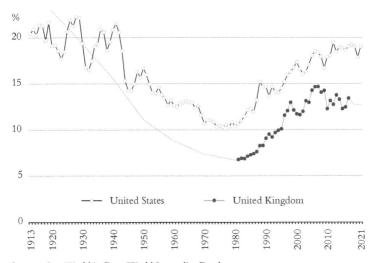

Source: Our World in Data/World Inequality Database

Paul Krugman hailed Piketty's book as perhaps the most important of
the decade with its 'unmatched historical depth' and a new theory of
inequality.[5] Piketty said that when the rate of return (r) on capital is
greater than economic growth (g)—for example, if you can get 5 per
cent interest on an investment but the economy is growing at 3 per
cent—there will be greater concentration of wealth in the long term.
It can be summed up in three symbols: r > g. The theory's spotlight
illuminated things that had been largely in the shadows: inequality
and inherited wealth. He also warned that the formula was not a
forecasting tool and cannot explain the ways in which institutions
and political shocks will continue to shape wealth inequality.[6] Piketty
called for a global annual wealth tax and progressive taxes of 80 per
cent on incomes of $500,000 a year in the US. These were, to put
it mildly, bold proposals that went against the grain of lowering taxes
on the wealthiest. We need to look at conventional economic tax
theory to understand the decisive break of Piketty's work.

Suboptimal tax

The economic theory of 'optimal' tax rates can be traced to a 1971 paper by Scottish-born economist James Mirrlees. A talented mathematician, he was drawn to studying economics at Cambridge because, he said, reducing global poverty 'seemed to me what really mattered in the world'.[7] For a while, he was in the Cambridge circle of Ricardo's left-wing biographer Piero Sraffa. Mirrlees realized that despite the vast literature on taxation, an economic model of tax rates did not exist. Inspired by a conversation with a physics graduate, he set out to create one.[8] The results were a shock to his leftist leanings: 'I must confess that I had expected the rigorous analysis of income-taxation in the utilitarian manner to provide an argument for high tax rates [for the rich]. It has not done so.'[9]

Mirrlees' optimal tax theory, which aimed to raise tax revenue while maximizing the overall size of the economy, suggested a less progressive, flatter tax structure. It concluded that the taxes on top earners should fall steeply and the highest taxes should be levied on the middle classes. Other economists built on his model to 'prove' that the highest-earning person in society—think of Elon Musk or Jeff Bezos—should pay a marginal tax rate of zero or even receive subsidies! In 1996, Mirrlees won a Nobel Prize. In 2015, he took aim at Thomas Piketty's 'big book', suggesting that his focus on wealth inequality was misplaced and that he should 'check his numbers'.[10] On his death, in 2018, the *New York Times* wrote, with understatement, that 'his economic model became a rationale, embraced by many conservatives, for flattening tax rates'.[11]

Let me explain how Mirrlees got to his surprising results. His 1971 paper contains an intimidating 140-plus mathematical equations. But the problems were not, as Keynes once said, in the logical superstructure built with great care but in its foundations. In trying to get a handle on a new and complicated problem, Mirrlees had, in the manner of Ricardo, piled one simplifying assumption on top of another until a clear-cut result emerged.

In the model world imagined by Mirrlees, all humans are extremely simple. Everyone has identical tastes and desires for work and leisure. Everyone decides how much to work solely by calculating their material self-interest (erroneously called 'rational'). There are no other personal or social motivations or rewards from work. Only income is modelled: individual wealth, including property or inherited wealth, does not exist. There is only one type of work available. Mirrlees made these simplifications, he said, 'to render the mathematics more manageable'. In fact, in the model, everyone is identical except in one aspect: their 'innate' skill or ability. The more ability (there is only one type) you have, the more work you can do, and the more you can earn. But here Mirrlees hit a problem: how can the government, which must set tax rates, know each person's ability level or income-earning potential? He presumed it cannot observe the number of hours they work and how productive they are.[12]

Knowing the income-earning potential is important as Mirrlees' aim was to maximize 'social welfare', which is assumed to be everyone's total earnings. The government needs tax revenue, but if it taxes the high-ability people too much, they will 'rationally' decide to work less, reducing the size of the economy. In the 1971 paper, Mirrlees considers how tax authorities can gauge ability levels: 'One might obtain information about a man's income-earning potential from his apparent I.Q., the number of his degrees, his address, age or colour: but the natural, and one would suppose the most reliable, indicator of his income-earning potential is his income.' Amid the multiple prejudices, what Mirrlees did was to replace 'potential earnings' with 'earnings' and thereby abolished from his model world the concept of undeveloped potential. He envisaged society as a perfect meritocracy where everyone's pay—from a teacher to a banker—reflects their ability. This is a fundamentally just world, where the super-rich are simply super-talented and the low paid are low skilled. It is little wonder his model suggested taxing the wealthiest—seen as the most valuable members of society—less.

Mirrlees' model could hardly have been more abstract if it was painted by Piet Mondrian. There is no history, institutions, or social context in the theory. Its values are implicit and not examined. Its results would be utterly transformed by a wider vision or more realistic assumptions. His conclusions are 'only as robust as the assumptions', economic historians Avner Offer and Gabriel Söderberg have written, and 'as in the case of Ricardo, they [the conclusions] were embodied in the assumptions'.[13] Mirrlees did set out a list of assumptions in his paper and even notes that the idea of humans as self-maximizing calculators 'may well be seriously unrealistic'. And yet he concludes that the results of his analysis are 'likely to be relevant to the construction and reform of actual income taxes'.[14]

Although it's impossible to draw a one-to-one relationship between tax theory and practice, actual income tax rates of the highest earners have tumbled since the 1970s. In the US, they were cut by more than half in Reagan's term in office from 70 per cent to 33 per cent. In the UK, Thatcher reduced the top rate of tax from 83 per cent to 40 per cent.[15] The same trend has been seen across rich countries, with average top tax rates having fallen from 67 per cent to 42 per cent between 1981 and 2010.[16] At the least, the work of Mirrlees and other optimal tax theorists provided an argument in scientific dress that these falls were in the general interest. There is no accusation that Mirrlees had ulterior political motives, economic historians Offer and Söderberg wrote: 'What optimal taxation shows is the power of theory alone, with assumptions adopted by convention, to arrive at conclusions that serve the privileged.'[17] It would not be until 2001 that Thomas Piketty's collaborator, Emmanuel Saez, began shifting the theory in a new direction by changing the underlying assumptions of the Mirrlees' model to produce a conclusion that income tax on the wealthiest should be between 50 per cent and 80 per cent.[18]

The tumbling tax rates on the wealthiest gave them more incentive to boost their pay (as they got to keep more) and it exploded. In 1980, in the US, the average CEO was paid 42 times more than the average worker. By 2016, they were paid 347 times more. In the UK, the same ratio rose from 48 to 1 in 1998 to 129 to 1 in 2016.[19] These increases were given intellectual covering fire from American economists such as Michael Jensen who complained in 1990 that CEOs were paid like 'bureaucrats' and promoted the benefits of linking pay to share prices.[20] At the same time, median family income in the US stagnated: after having risen by 3 per cent per year from 1948 to 1973, it has dropped to 0.4 per cent per year since.[21] This toxic inequality has eaten away at the legitimacy of democratic states.

Mirrlees' model only sees income and not wealth. Other economic theorists in the 1980s did look at wealth and 'proved' that it was in the general public interest in the long run—even for those who own no property—for taxes on inheritance, property, corporate profits, and income from capital to be zero. Although few economists supported such radical policies, they remained a reference point in economic teaching and policy discussion.[22] Robert Lucas, in 1990, described this zero-capital-tax result as 'the largest genuinely free lunch I have seen in 25 years in this business, and I believe we would have a better society if we followed their advice'.[23]

In 2006, Mirrlees defended his method of reasoning with 'a very simple model', which is then applied 'directly to real policy issues' (the definition of the Ricardian Vice). He claimed that the only worthwhile conclusion is one that has 'a precise numerical answer'. So, even though he was aware that the modeller has to make 'treacherous' judgements about what is or is not included in the model and, therefore, may have a tenuous hold on reality, he asked: 'What else could one do?'[24] And perhaps he's right. If you aim so high as to aspire to finding physics-like laws of society, you have to make the subject matter conform to the method. But this has the unfortunate effect, as we've seen, of diverting researchers' eyes from this world to another more beautiful realm.

This is the social and intellectual context to Piketty's detailed research into wealth inequality and his undisguised scorn for theoretical speculations without historical data. In Piketty's hands, economics was not attempting to be an exact science like physics: 'this book is as much a work of history as of economics'. We need theories to bring some understanding to the complexity of society, but they should be held lightly: no 'mathematical formula' can tell us what the tax rate should be, he said, only deliberation and democratic experimentation.[25]

Monopoly power

The 2010s saw other challenges to concentrated private economic and political power and to the modern economic theories that justified these. One influential group of reformers were not economists, but legal scholars, activists, and journalists, together known as the New Brandeis movement. The issue in their sights was corporate power.

There is growing concern about the extent of private power in the hands of multinational corporations in the early twenty-first century, from 'too-big-to-fail' banks, to Big Tech, Big Pharma, or

Big Oil. Decades of mergers have consolidated market power across the economy, from supermarkets to mobile phone services, which reduces competition and can lead to excessive 'monopoly profits'. And economic power is often translated into political power through lobbying and campaign contributions.

Johns Hopkins political scientist Lee Drutman estimates lobbying in Washington, DC—the majority of which is corporate lobbying— has increased from $200 million per year in 1983 to $3.3 billion in 2012 (corrected for inflation). In 2012, for every dollar spent by public interest groups and labour unions lobbying the government, businesses and business associations spent $34. If you think about this 34-to-1 ratio divided by time (instead of money), business groups would have the entire calendar year to speak—minus the 11 days allowed for everyone else. Drutman concludes that this has led to corporations becoming more political and politics more corporate.[26]

The monopoly power of corporations today is not unprecedented. In Britain in the eighteenth century economic thinkers railed against the power and influence of wool manufactures and the East India Company. One fierce critic wrote that

> the monopoly which our manufacturers have obtained against us ... [is] like an overgrown standing army, they have become formidable to the government, and, upon many occasions, intimidate the legislature. The member of parliament who supports every proposal for strengthening this monopoly, is sure to acquire not only the reputation of understanding trade, but great popularity and influence.

However, to oppose or thwart their interests leaves parliamentarians open to abuse, insults, and worse.[27] When an industry has succeeded 'in persuading the legislature that the prosperity of the nation depended upon the success and extension of their particular business', they have often 'extorted from the legislature' laws 'written in blood'.[28] This fierce critic was Adam Smith. You can find this view in *The Wealth of Nations* but not in today's economics textbooks.

More recent comparisons of our current situation are made with the businesses who grouped their interests in 'trusts' in the US Gilded Age of the late 1800s: a time of rapid industrial growth, financial crises, political corruption, and a growing gap between rich and poor. The most feared corporation of the time was John D. Rockefeller's Standard Oil, which had aggressively cornered large parts of the petroleum and railroad market. In response, a major political and social anti-monopoly movement—known as 'antitrust'—grew up in the US from the 1880s. The movement secured its first major legislative victory in Congress with the Sherman Antitrust Act of 1890, which criminalized monopolies and those who conspire to rig economies. It was designed not just to protect Americans from being overcharged by corporations, but to give breathing space to small businesses and preserve democracy from over-mighty private power. Senator John Sherman, who sponsored the law, spoke of it squarely in the democratic tradition: 'If we will not endure a king as a political power, we should not endure a king over the production, transportation and sale of any of the necessaries of life.'[29]

In 1911 the US Justice Department used the Sherman Act in court to break Rockefeller's Standard Oil into 34 entities. Over the next 50 years, the US government would pursue monopolists in the courts both at home and, after the Second World War, abroad, in part in a move to preserve democracy.[30] The American historian Richard Hofstadter described the revolt against big business as 'characteristically American'.[31] How did we get from there to today's Second Gilded Age? Much of the story is to do with a clear-eyed strategy of corporate leaders. But, it is also the story of how this strategy was justified by a fundamental change in the vision of antitrust, or competition, law promoted by a well-funded group of economists fixated on prices.

Beginning in the 1950s, University of Chicago Nobel Prize-winning economist George Stigler—who sometimes wore a T-shirt with the message 'Adam Smith's Best Friend'—led the charge.[32] Stigler helped create a school of thought that applied the lessons of economic price theory to legal rules. He worked with legal scholars who wrote influential books in the 1970s claiming to offer a new, more 'rational' way of weighing the pros and cons of business concentration. Richard Posner's *Antitrust Law* in 1976 argued that the law should be judged by its economic efficiency. Robert Bork's *The Antitrust Paradox* in 1978 claimed that the 'consumer welfare standard'—the principle that the price consumers pay is the only measure of monopoly power—was the original goal of antitrust. Bork's claim was against the historical record, but it was accepted by the US Supreme Court in 1979 and has since regularly been cited in court judgements.[33]

Promoters of the 'law and economics' movement achieved this in part by 'training' influential members of the judiciary. They set up residential training programmes for judges in Florida—funded by companies such as ExxonMobil (a descendent of Standard Oil), General Electric, and IBM—where participants learned economic theory from stars such as Paul Samuelson and Milton Friedman. The influence campaign was a stunning success. By 1990, 40 per cent of federal judges had taken the courses and introductory economics became a regular part of law degrees.[34] Although 'law and economics' is seen as a creation of the Chicago School, sociologist Elizabeth Popp Berman shows that the more interventionist left-leaning academics at Harvard also contributed and shared similar beliefs about markets.[35] The John M. Olin Foundation—created by a chemical and munitions magnate—spent $68 million to create law and economics centres named in his honour at Chicago, Harvard, Stanford, Virginia, and Yale among others. John Olin judged, correctly, that if he got the field established at elite universities, others would follow.[36]

The theory helped simplify the judgement of anti-monopoly cases. The new 'consumer welfare standard' meant that corporate mergers, which concentrated the share of the market in fewer hands, were only a problem if customers paid more for their goods. Corporations often grew because they were more efficient and consumers benefitted from this efficiency, the 'law and economics' proponents claimed. Judges could now rely on precise quantified evidence and modelled predictions of price changes to guide their decision-making. Bork lent on the apparently objective standard to boost its authority, arguing that the older, anti-monopoly tradition was 'less a science than an elaborate mythology, that it has operated for years on hearsay and legends rather than on reality'.[37] The future socially liberal US Supreme Court judge Stephen Breyer was overjoyed by the clear and quantified economic theory, saying in 1983 that it 'offers objectivity—*terra firma*—upon which we can base decisions'.[38]

The more corporate-friendly regulatory environment generated by the 'law and economics' movement reduced enforcement of antitrust laws. By the 1990s, a high-profile case against Microsoft collapsed and many others were never brought or were settled out of court. This gave the green light to merger frenzy and consolidation of power on Wall Street and Main Street. In the eight years of Bill Clinton's administration there were over 165,000 mergers valued at $9.8 trillion, more than three times the value of mergers under the 12 years of Reagan and Bush. They spanned almost every industry: hotels, hospitals, banks, defence contractors, IT, and oil. The trend continued, and Clinton's Democrats failed to fight back, anti-monopoly author Matt Stoller wrote, because the party 'had lost the ability even to think about the problem of concentrated economic power'.[39] Similarly, the EU adopted an approach to mergers inspired by 'law and economics' in 2004, leading to steep declines in the percentage of mergers investigated and blocked.[40]

The bright spotlight on consumer prices had thrown into the shadows other crucial issues and values. Just how many was not widely appreciated until a new group of legal scholars and activists appeared in the 2010s, inspired by US Supreme Court judge Louis Brandeis (1856–1941), a stalwart of progressive-era antitrust. Yale legal scholar, Lina Khan, one of the leaders of the New Brandeis movement, wrote an influential 2017 article, 'Amazon's antitrust paradox', about the online retail giant. She argued that the sole focus on consumer price 'disregards the host of other ways that excessive concentration can harm us' across the economy, such as firms squeezing suppliers and producers, systemic risks from too-big-to-fail companies, media concentration, and the dispersal of political power.[41] The views of Khan and others were derided as 'hipster antitrust'. In 2021, Khan, aged 32, was made the youngest ever Chair of the Federal Trade Commission and two years later, with 17 state attorneys, filed a wide-ranging antitrust lawsuit against Amazon, arguing that it is 'exploiting its monopoly power to enrich itself'—in part by hiking fees on sellers in its marketplace and then punishing them if they offer lower-priced goods elsewhere—a charge the company rejects.[42]

Jonathan Kanter, the current antitrust chief at the Department of Justice, gave a remarkable speech in 2022—ironically at the University of Chicago's Stigler Center—summing up the New Brandeis movement. Antitrust in recent decades had lost its way and turned its attention to the 'impossible challenge of quantifying often unquantifiable welfare effects and speculative efficiencies down to the last decimal point'. This led to a vast waste of resources and brainpower, he said, as millions were spent arguing about models of the economy and the tiny hypothetical shifts in outcome they showed. (US consulting firms can hire out top economists specializing in antitrust to corporations at $1,350 per *hour*).[43] This approach introduced a 'technocratic veil' that made regulation of large corporations much less understandable or accessible to the public. In order to recover from this mess, he proposed the protection of open markets and enforcement of the law. He urged his audience to focus 'first on the facts when we examine competitive realities, as opposed to beginning with assumptions embedded in out of date models or cases'.[44]

Barry Lynn, Executive Director of Open Markets Institute and incubator of the New Brandeis movement, put it more bluntly: 'economics is about power and politics, not math'. Our understanding, he continued, 'has been profoundly constrained by an intellectual framework ... built, with the specific intention of exploiting us and then blinding us to the exploitation'. We need new narratives, he said, to promote freedom and democracy.[45] It remains to be seen how permanent or influential the counter-revolution in anti-monopoly thinking will prove.

'Repealing the law of gravity'

Influential economic theories in the late twentieth century, as we've seen, held that slashing taxes on the rich and concentrated corporate power were in the public interest. At the same time, the consensus view among American economists was that minimum wages for the poorest workers did not serve the general good. One survey found 90 per cent of economists believed that increasing minimum wages for low-paid workers would increase unemployment.[46] This was supported by the basic theory of supply and demand: if you raise the price of anything the quantity demanded should reduce. A 1987 *New York Times* editorial declared the 'virtual consensus among economists that the minimum wage is an idea whose time has passed'. The headline was: 'The right minimum wage: $0.00'.[47] Two empirically minded economists from Princeton University— David Card and Alan Krueger—sceptical of the theoretical case and tired of reworking existing databases, went out to gather their own evidence. When they published it, they faced a barrage of criticism from the profession.

In 1992, New Jersey raised its minimum wage from $4.25 to $5.05 while neighbouring Pennsylvania did not. Card and Krueger surveyed over 400 fast-food restaurants on either side of the state border. Their published paper found little to no relation between increases in minimum wages and unemployment: meaning that wages could be increased without hurting the economy.[48]

For sections of the economics profession Card and Krueger's conclusions were blasphemous. The evidence was theoretically impossible and therefore must be wrong. Finis Welch, an economist from Texas A&M University, explicitly drew on the analogy that economic laws were like Isaac Newton's: 'If you drop an apple and it rises, question your experiment before concluding that the laws of gravity have been repealed.' An article in *Forbes* was called 'Repealing the law of gravity'.[49] The most bombastic comment was made by the winner of the 1986 Nobel, James Buchanan: 'Just as no physicist would claim that "water runs uphill", no self-respecting economist would claim that increases in the minimum wage increase employment,' he wrote in the *Wall Street Journal*. 'Fortunately, only a handful of economists are willing to throw over the teaching of two centuries; we have not yet become a bevy of camp-following whores.'[50] Things were little better in private. Angus Deaton, a British economist, wrote that the reception given to Card and Krueger's Princeton colleagues, including himself, when visiting other economics' departments 'was what might be expected by the friends and defenders of child molesters'.[51]

Card and Krueger's conclusions were not definitive and had methodological challenges of their own. They have been challenged by other economists, including some working for a business-funded think tank.[52] But the Princeton pair did manage to shift discussions within some areas of economics helping pave the way to today's push for a $15 minimum wage. Alan Krueger died in 2019. Just two years later, his co-author David Card was recognized with a 2021 Nobel.

Economics, *Fast and Slow*

Behavioural economics is another part of the profession often seen as looking at evidence about what is happening in the world, rather than how we imagine it must work. Inspired by psychology, behavioural economists have constructed ingenious laboratory experiments demonstrating the gap between normal humans and idealized 'economic human' of standard models. Daniel Kahneman, an Israeli-American psychologist and winner of the Nobel in Economics in 2002, is one of the superstars of the field.

In his 2011 best seller *Thinking, Fast and Slow*, Kahneman uses the excellent concepts (which I've borrowed) of 'theory-induced blindness' and 'substitution'. In the book, Kahneman introduces two fictional characters, System 1 and System 2, who between them divide up our thinking. In Kahneman's telling, System 1 does fast, involuntary, non-calculating thinking, which means its conclusions are predictably waylaid by 'biases', 'systematic errors', or mental shortcuts known as 'heuristics'. By contrast, System 2 does slow, conscious, calculating thinking that gets to the correct answer but requires more mental capacity, so it cannot be used all the time. The 'economic human' of classical models only has a System 2. Humans, despite what we sometimes think, go back and forth between the two systems.[53]

This work has systematically laid out the gap between model humans and real ones. But there's a twist. Even if you acknowledge the gap there are two ways to close it: you can decide that the models are wrong or you can decide that the humans are wrong. The discussion within and around behavioural economics contains both approaches. 'I often cringe when my work with Amos [Tversky, his long-time collaborator] is credited with demonstrating that human choices are irrational,' Kahneman wrote, 'when in fact our research only showed that Humans are not well described by the rational-agent model.'[54]

Despite Kahneman's cringe, the fictional System 1 and System 2 frame bears a striking similarity to the American economic orthodoxy that it claims to be correcting. This can be seen in a 1977 paper by two leading University of Chicago figures, George Stigler ('Adam Smith's Best Friend') and Gary Becker. The pair argue that deviations we observe from the calculating 'economic human' hypothesis can be explained because it is often more efficient for people to base decisions on 'habit'—settled ways of thinking and acting—given the mental 'costs of searching for information' involved in a full calculation of their self-interest.[55] Kahneman says something very similar when he claims that we do not use the calculating System 2 thinking all the time because its use is 'effortful' and absorbs much of our 'limited budget of attention'.[56] This shared frame has meant behaviour economics, when it approaches the orthodox 'rational choice' theory, too often pulls its punches. Consider the concepts of substitution and heuristics as Kahneman uses them.

Substitution, you'll remember, is a way to solve problems by replacing a difficult question with an easier, related one. Kahneman *only* discusses how the 'fast' System 1 uses substitution unconsciously. He fails to mention that the 'calculating' System 2 uses substitution all the time (as we saw earlier in this chapter, when using 'income' as a proxy for 'income-earning potential' or using 'consumer price' as a proxy for 'monopoly power').[57] System 2 does this to ensure its calculating method can handle the problem and freezes out broader issues—such as great wealth or politically connected businesses— which threaten to scatter its neat conclusions like a bowling ball scatters pins. Kahneman lets System 2 off too easily.

Kahneman's also teaches that *only* the intuitive System 1 uses simplifying heuristics: mental shortcuts that jump to conclusions that are sometimes good enough but often involve systematic errors. But when System 2 uses substitutions they are, in a way, also heuristics. This is because, in order to make problems tractable or easily managed by computational methods, researchers often ignore the complexity of human behaviour and arrive at an answer that is defended as a good enough approximation even if it has errors (as Eugene Fama did with his 'efficient market hypothesis' in finance). In the 1950s debate around the return of unreality (see Chapter 10), one of Milton Friedman's chief defenders was the Austrian-American economist Fritz Machlup, who called the idealized calculating assumptions a 'heuristic'.[58] System 2 uses substitution and heuristics: it is frequently and systematically error-prone.

It appears to me inaccurate to describe the 'calculating' System 2 as slow thinking. The deductive, quantified method has, in fact, been used to produce quick-and-dirty results and theories. It is fast economics. Often, the speed and cheapness of the method is its great advantage. You can see the critiques of theorists jumping to premature conclusions that have run through this book from Malthus, Whewell, and Susan Strange, among others. The economist and philosopher Piero Mini put it well in 1974: deductive economics 'was able to progress through the social universe with lightning speed ... [with] its aspiration to explain the whole of reality without even looking at it'.[59] Slow economics is the patient, painstaking and often more expensive empirical work needed to arrive at firm conclusions. The downside of slow economics, for some, is that it might trouble settled assumptions.

There are a variety of approaches in behavioural economics. Kahneman, and others, have done incredible work highlighting the differences between humans and models. But in the hands of some, the field ends up as a Dorian Gray-esque flattering portrait of the calculating System 2 and a spotlight on the mistakes of normal people. Alan Greenspan found in behavioural economics the real culprit of the global financial crisis: human irrationality. The implication, then, is to purge the last remnants of the ancient, emotional, social brain in the desire for greater wealth. As Greenspan put it: 'If people acted at the level of rationality presumed in standard economics textbooks, the world's standard of living would be measurably higher.'[60]

Humans are not faulty machines. We need a broader, richer vision.

'Beware of models'

This has been a brief, and incomplete, survey of some of the blind spots in orthodox economics. In the 2010s, there was a wave of economic scholarship, within the mainstream, that sought to shine a light on them and escape overly simple models. Raj Chetty from Harvard has used big data to expose declining social mobility in the US and the racial gaps across generations that are a legacy of enslavement. In 2013, he hailed 'an emerging body of work ... that is transforming economics into a field firmly grounded in fact' (although unfortunately in the context of defending Eugene Fama's Nobel for the 'efficient markets hypothesis').[61] Princeton economists Anne Case and Angus Deaton highlighted 'deaths of despair' in 2015—showing that life expectancy for White Americans without a college degree had been falling due to suicide, alcohol abuse, and addictive opioid use pushed by big pharmaceutical companies.[62] In 2015, Gabriel Zucman, another collaborator of Thomas Piketty, broke new ground in economics by piercing the statistical fog around the trillions held in offshore tax havens in *The Hidden Wealth of*

Nations. Esther Duflo and Abhijit Banerjee of MIT won a Nobel Prize in 2019 for their approach of randomized control trials (RCTs) inspired by medicine that have overturned conventional economic wisdom, especially related to the free distribution of mosquito nets. This approach can narrow vision to small, rather than structural changes. However, in the same year they won the Nobel, Duflo and Banerjee championed 'good economics' that prevails over ignorance and ideology, and warned that

> Bad economics underpinned the grand giveaways to the rich. ... Blinkered economics told us trade was good for everyone. ... Blind economics missed the explosion in inequality all over the world, the increasing social fragmentation that came with it, and the impending environmental disaster, delaying action, perhaps irrevocably. ... Economics is too important to be left to economists.[63]

We may be witnessing the second fall of economic thinking founded on unreality. If so, it's about time. We can hope it's not too late to avoid a much larger social or ecological collapse.

One marker of a shift in elite opinion was a Davos event in 2024 called 'How to Trust Economics'. On the panel was Christine Lagarde, a prominent global economic policy maker for the last two decades as France's Minister of the Economy, the head of the International Monetary Fund, and, most recently, the European Central Bank (ECB). She revealed that she told staff at her first big meeting at the ECB in 2019: 'Beware of models'. Too many of the challenges that Europe faced—fragile supply chains, Russian manipulation of the energy market and aggression in Ukraine, access to rare earth minerals—were just not in models, which therefore proved a poor guide to the future, she said. To see better, she has brought in experts in disease, geology, and ecology. Empirical data, observation, and judgement can reduce what Lagarde called the 'blind faith we had for too many years, I think, in what models can deliver'.[64]

Alongside Lagarde was Michael Sandel, American political philosopher and author of *What Money Can't Buy*. Sandel began by saying that the only way to trust economics was to 'close our eyes and try to forget the follies and failures of models and mainstream economic advice over the past four decades'. But, then he cited some of the new wave of more realistic economic thinkers since the 2010s and said: 'they do not rely primarily on simplified models. They look at the world. They do detailed, empirical studies, animated by a broader social and political set of questions. That's where, I think, the hope for restoring trust in economics lies.'[65]

Conclusion:
Look at the World

In which the argument of the book is concluded

When Isaac Newton died in 1727, Alexander Pope, the most celebrated poet of the Enlightenment, penned this triumphal couplet for his monument in Westminster Abbey:

> Nature and Nature's laws lay hid in night
> God said, Let *Newton* be! and all was light.[1]

In 1802, by contrast, the radical poet and printmaker William Blake—whose bronze bust also stands in the Abbey—wrote: 'May God us keep / From Single vision & Newtons sleep'. One of Blake's most famous prints, produced around this time, shows a naked, muscular Newton bent forwards (see Figure 15.1). Blake drew Newton intently focused on a geometrical drawing, oblivious to the larger, swirling organic forms around him.[2]

These two conflicting visions—of Newtonian mechanics either as the great revealer or great concealer of the truth of the world—have been at the root of arguments in economic thinking over the last few centuries.

Ricardo's Dream has explored this tension between David Ricardo, who promoted the idea that economics was 'a strict science like mathematics', and John Maynard Keynes, who compared Ricardo and his followers to 'Euclidean geometers in a non-Euclidean world'. It has argued that the quest for logical neatness and quantifiable precision has frequently gone too far and led economic theorists like Blake's Newton to disregard the complex, organic world in

Figure 15.1: *Newton* by William Blake (1795–c.1805), colour print with pen, ink, and watercolour

Source: © Tate Photo: Tate

which we live and focus instead on a smaller, simpler model world.[3] Along the way, this book has tried to bring to light numerous substitutions—analogies that forget they are analogies—which have been distorting lenses.

Ricardo is not solely responsible for bringing this quantified fantasy, this dream, into existence or for its continuing power in our time. Long before and after him, people have come to a similar belief. In recent decades, the promise and intellectual thrill of this approach was perhaps best expressed by Paul Krugman. At the height of his championing of hyper-globalization, in 1995, he wrote: 'there is hardly anything I know that is as exciting as finding that the great events that move history, the forces that determine the destiny of empires and the fate of kings, can sometimes be explained, predicted, or even controlled by a few symbols on a printed page'.[4] This belief, one that Krugman now seems to have abandoned, is science fiction.

The first part of the book dug into the history of the iconic story about international trade: the exchange of English cloth and Portuguese wine. The story, inspired by David Ricardo, has been told with 'a few symbols on a page': specifically, four numbers describing how efficient the two countries were at making the two products. The focus on these symbols, however, has overlaid and obscured many of the forces that determine the destiny of empires and the fate of their kings and people. The historical cloth and wine trade cannot be understood without appreciating the might of the English Royal Navy, Lisbon as a gateway to the wealth of Brazil, and the epic gold rush north of Rio de Janeiro. Underpinning it all was the trade in millions of African captives across the Atlantic. We saw how gold mined by enslaved people in Brazil made the real Sir Isaac Newton, figurehead for universal laws, extremely wealthy in his three decades at the Royal Mint.

All of that history is hidden in the simplified world of comparative advantage. It has been hacked off like the toes and heels of the ugly stepsisters' feet so they can squeeze into the beautiful glass slipper of Cinderella. What made it worse is that this narrower, distorted view has been venerated as the pure light of economic science. The danger for those who rely on seeing the world through this model, or who live in a world shaped by it, is the illusion it creates of fair exchange and mutual benefit in all cases, where there may be little or none, and—in the case of England, Portugal, and their colonies—vast exploitation. This history is one thread in the larger story of the links between slavery, colonialism, and Western economic development.

We saw that David Ricardo's approach to economics was profoundly criticized from the beginning, even by friends and colleagues. A succession of historically minded economic thinkers challenged the unreality of his classical economics and the damage done in its name (even though many failed to critique colonialism). By the end of the nineteenth century, there emerged a view even among mainstream figures such as Alfred Marshall that Ricardo's method had grave faults and needed to be supplemented by closely observing the world. It was accepted at this time that the concept of the self-maximizing, calculating 'economic human' began with the false and misleading vision of a stockbroker inside every person. However, Milton Friedman's championing of 'the principle of unreality' as a basis for economic theorizing helped bring deductive methods and the universal inner stockbroker back into intellectual credibility in the 1960s. New classical economics in the 1980s gave us a boom in speculative model making and new economic dogmas dressed as scientific investigation into 'what is'. This became a broadly shared methodology and frame for both the centre-left and right-leaning economists in the US and elsewhere, leading to another 'single vision' of the way to organize society.[5]

The final chapters of this book have focused on the past 50 years when deductive economics has had its greatest popularity and impact. We looked at how financial economics led to a boom in risky derivatives trading and provided a scientific-sounding alibi against the charge that it was socially useless gambling. Looking at the world through these models has left smart people unable to think clearly about the growing instability and political power of finance. We looked at how the intellectual consensus around the benefits of free trade was hijacked by those who supported the granting of new powers and privileges to corporations and Wall Street. The dogmatic boosting of global trade as a win–win blinded too many to the real suffering such trade can cause. We looked at how influential economists produced oversimplified analysis that underestimated the damage climate change may cause and cast markets as the only solution. Finally, we looked at how other economists drastically narrowed the range of thought about the power of large corporations and others who produced a scientific rationale for slashing taxes on the super-rich and, finally, some new mainstream economic thinking, especially since the 2010s, that has pushed back. Economics is much broader and richer than just these examples. However, these models and theories have been among the most prestigious in the field, with proponents of them receiving at least 15 Nobel Memorial Prizes in Economics.[6]

In short, we've looked at financial models with no crashes, global trade models with no state power, anti-monopoly models with no corporate power, climate models with no climate, and all kinds of economic models with no humans in them. All these models have systematically overvalued the power of prices. In this way, too many economists forgot the real world and led us astray. Embracing deduction has gifted us a profound confusion about what is real: made worse by a failure to note the difference between 'if' and 'is'. More people should have taken Robert Lucas, the most influential macroeconomist of recent decades, seriously when he described 'what economists do' in the late 1980s. 'I'm not sure whether you will take this as a confession or a boast,' he said, 'but we are basically story-tellers, creators of make-believe economic systems.' The advantage of 'operating in simplified, fictional worlds,' Lucas added, was the 'clarity' of vision it brought.[7] Lucas did not speak for the whole profession. Economics has turned towards the empirical since then, but not enough. The field has been slow to acknowledge, or apologize for, mistakes stemming from make-believe models.

Imagination and creativity have played central, and often overlooked, roles in the creation of 'rational' economics. It was a huge leap of the imagination for David Ricardo to see the world as if it were populated with stockbrokers minutely scrutinizing the movement of prices.[8] Joseph Schumpeter acknowledged the importance of 'pre-analytic vision': the cognitive act that comes before any analysis and identifies problems worthy of it. Even Milton Friedman described theorizing as 'a creative act of inspiration, intuition, invention; its essence is the vision of something new'.[9] And Mary Morgan, author of *The World in the Model*, wrote that 'model-making is a creative activity' and that the economist plays 'the role of the artist here—responsible for choosing some elements and leaving others behind'.[10] We would understand economics better if we recognized that the great economists were visionaries. 'There is nothing wrong with the fact that our imagination plays a part in shaping our world view,' the philosopher Mary Midgley wrote. 'We need it to do so. But we also need to notice how it is doing it.'[11]

What, concretely, can we do differently? The first task is to see the issues more clearly and ask better questions.

There's a short YouTube video watched over 30 million times of two basketball teams, one in white shirts and the other in black. Viewers are asked to count how many times the white team passes the ball. Midway through someone in a full-body gorilla suit walks into shot, thumps their chest, and strolls off the other side. In tests, half of the viewers failed to see the gorilla.[12] It is the mental focus required for the counting task, psychologist Daniel Kahneman explains, 'that causes the blindness. No one who watches the video without that task would miss the gorilla.'[13] Something similar has happened in too much economic thinking. The intense focus on the closed, machine-like worlds of models has strengthened the belief that there is little alternative to the present system. This 'theory-induced blindness'—as Kahneman calls it—has obscured the great diversity of economic arrangements that can be seen in different times and places, all of which can inspire progressive reform.

There is no shortage of alternative policy ideas for remedying global challenges. Many solutions will be political, rather than purely economic. They need close attention, experimentation, democratic discussion, and oversight. It has become increasingly clear to many, as it was to Adam Smith, that societies must do a better job of reducing the power of great wealth in the political process. A revived anti-monopoly movement in the US and Europe is raising awareness of how concentrated private power is a threat to political liberty and shared prosperity. Pressure is growing for existing bilateral and regional free trade deals to be rebalanced to correct the skew towards corporate powers and privileges. New types of global economic cooperation have already been agreed in principle, such as a provisional agreement to levy a minimum global corporate tax and crack down on offshore tax and secrecy havens. They should be enacted. It is surely only the political power of the financial markets that has prevented the introduction of taxes on speculative financial transactions, such as the 'Tobin tax', to stabilize markets and raise revenue. Much more direct action is possible and necessary to reorientate the economy onto green, circular, and regenerative pathways. Many of these solutions have been invisible, like the gorilla, or seen as radical by the mainstream; that may be changing.

Some of our problems, I've argued, stem from the knowing, rather than the naive, misuse of economics and models. Some economic analyses produced by think tanks in the US and UK that consistently take pro-corporate positions are the product of 'dark money'. There also needs to be more light thrown onto the murky work of funding for academic economists. It is widely reported that many finance economists have received lucrative research contracts from Wall Street firms; anecdotal cases are known but statistics are piecemeal. One antitrust economist is estimated to have made about $100 million through, among other things, writing reports and testifying in favour of dozens of mega-mergers.[14] There is almost zero transparency and I'm not aware of any detailed research into how much funding the finance or other industries have given the discipline and the impact of this. We know that Big Oil funds some prestigious centres of climate and energy modelling. There is also the incredible success of the Olin Foundation, which spent more than $60 million supporting the creation of the 'law and economics' movement in academia that redefined anti-monopoly policy for a generation. We need to direct the spotlight's beam onto these cosy relationships.

But it is too much to discount the whole intellectual trajectory of mainstream economics since the early 1970s as a front for corporate and financial interests.[15] There is something more interesting going on. As we have seen, there is often a mutually reinforcing mix of the naive and knowing misuse of models. My approach has been to take classical and neoclassical economic ideas seriously and engage with their claims to truth. It rests on the assumption that much of economics has been an honest attempt to understand the world over which people in good faith can disagree; that new stories and histories are important; and that ideas—and ways of interpreting the world—have tremendous power. In countries with a democratic heritage the private interests of the rich and powerful are often advanced by packaging these as the interests of all.

Signposts not destinations

It is not feasible to do away with abstraction, in general, or economic models, in particular. One of the best arguments for this comes from Max Weber (1864–1920), author of *The Protestant Ethic and the Spirit of Capitalism* (1905), who is now considered to be one of the founders of sociology but was a professor of political economy. In a 1904 essay, he made a powerful case for the usefulness of abstract concepts, translated as 'ideal-types' in English, to formulate and communicate ideas clearly.[16] (These concepts might be theoretical or mathematical laws or any other abstraction that serves as mental shorthand, for example, the terms 'Protestant' or 'capitalism'.) Such concepts allow the mind to loosen the weight of facts and details that cling to difficult questions and soar into the conceptually pure air. What a thrill! The view can illuminate the world from a new angle, bring order to what would otherwise be an overwhelming mess of details, and make the characteristic features of a system clear and understandable. But Weber was also explicit about the danger of liberating the mind from particulars.

He wrote that the purity of vision that 'ideal-types' (or models) provide is a 'utopia' that 'cannot be found empirically anywhere in reality'. They give a partial, one-sided view on 'an ever changing finite segment of the vast chaotic stream of events, which flows through time'. He continues: 'nothing, however, is more dangerous than the confusion of theory and history'. The confusion leads the researcher to believe that their theoretical construct captures the essence of reality or the force 'which operates behind the passage of events and which works itself out in history'. This results, Weber said, in a misguided attempt to transform the world into the image of the model to prove its truth.[17]

Weber's solution is to hold idealized formal concepts lightly, knowing that they are signposts and not destinations. They only point towards knowledge and suggest areas for empirical work. An understanding of the significance of *concrete historical events and patterns* is exclusively and solely the final end [of knowledge],' Weber argued, to which the creation and criticism of ideal concepts serves.[18] Weber's essay is a gem: a stunning defence of the usefulness of conceptual purity and a warning of its dangers.

Context is crucial. Models work best in fixed, stable environments, with as few moving parts as possible. That's why a billiard ball moving in a straight line is an excellent subject. Models can work very well in contexts in which all the inputs and outputs are controlled, such as a piece of technology or a factory where most of the work is done by robots rather than humans. (For example, for Ocado, the British online food and technology company: 'It is impossible to create a system like this [their Hive packing facility] without modelling.'[19]) It also often works well when the model is based on an experimentally proven scientific theory. Economic models have shown some success in highly structured social contexts such as auctions for mobile telecommunications spectrums (the rights to transmit signals over specific radio frequencies) and the design of mechanisms for donors to swap kidneys. Where it has failed is in trying to capture the dynamics of more complex situations such as ones related to national or global economies that have been covered in the preceding chapters. Roger Backhouse, a British economist and economic historian, sums up:

> economics has proved itself very powerful where problems are sufficiently narrowly defined, where the objectives are very clear, and where it is possible to

change the environment so that it conforms with the assumptions of economic theory. ... When economic ideas are applied to more complex situations, on the other hand, it is arguable that economics, by some criteria, failed, usually by neglecting to take into account dimensions of behaviour that do not fit into the rational-actor, competitive-market paradigm.[20]

At the beginning of the book, I mentioned an apparent paradox: how can Robert Heilbroner say that the 'strength' of Ricardo's economic thinking, and of those who followed his method, lay 'in its very unreality'?[21] Max Weber's analysis shows that unreal models can be a strength when looking at, or communicating about, tricky problems, and a danger if you forget they are just a thought experiments. Abstract, simplified models *can* be used fruitfully for thinking about human society, with some caveats. Those are: (1) remember that some simplicity is a strength, too much is a weakness; (2) don't take the models too seriously; and (3) treat them as signposts rather than destinations. The boosting of model thinking as superior and inherently scientific is misguided.

Venerated thinkers across the centuries have made a point similar to Max Weber's. Francis Bacon, as discussed in Chapter 8, suggested researchers should be neither just fact collectors like the ant nor theory spinners like the spider, but collectors of facts who transform them, like the bee. George Box argued that the good scientist needs to be 'mentally ambidextrous', fascinated equally by tentative hypotheses and 'the practical reality of the real world'.[22] John Maynard Keynes argued that models were useful devices for clarifying thinking, but they needed to be balanced with 'vigilant observation', which he judged was a 'very rare' gift. He gave this excellent advice to a fellow economist in 1938:

> But do not be reluctant to soil your hands, as you call it. I think it is most important. The specialist in the manufacture of models will not be successful unless he is constantly correcting his judgment by intimate and messy acquaintance with the facts to which his model has to be applied.[23]

I would argue that an 'intimate and messy acquaintance with the facts' requires more than the manipulation of computer data. Data can be extremely rich and useful but it can too often be confused for the social reality from which it is extracted. Skilled conjurors of statistics can manipulate it to produce a desired result. Intimate and messy acquaintance must, I think, involve some first-hand contact or personal experience. We need to recapture the original meaning of empiricism: learning about the world through experience derived from the senses. We need more investigative economics, described by author Nicholas Shaxson: 'Get out of your armchairs, recognise those uncertainties, judge where your spreadsheets might help and, crucially, where they won't. Go out and talk to people. Discover the blood and guts of what's going on: who's doing what with whom, how and why.'[24] This is a better way to economic knowledge.

'The apple's motives'

This book has been my attempt to do some philosophical plumbing. Mary Midgley described this, you may remember, as pulling up the floorboards to expose the conceptual pipes that usually go unnoticed to find out where the smell is coming from. One blockage, I'm certain, is caused by a mass of theories of human society created without a thorough investigation into what human beings are. These are theories created on the false assumption that humans act with the regularity of inanimate objects. This mass has grown thanks to another blockage that held that even the most unrealistic assumptions can generate reliable knowledge. That, in turn, seems to be related to an old, leaky connection between experience and theory. Our society's conceptual plumbing, Midgley said, has been built up piecemeal over the centuries and has never been completely replaced. But if we were able to fix some of the pipework we would gain a clearer understanding of how powerful imaginative world pictures have contributed to the exploitation of people and planet. And, perhaps, open the way to new, more helpful visions.

Little of this analysis is new. Part of my purpose has been to gather together the insights of many over the past two hundred years who have seen and said similar things. Often, they have been first-rate economists. One of them, John Maynard Keynes, in the same letter where he wrote about the need for 'vigilant observation', makes a wonderful analogy that brings us back full circle to where *Ricardo's Dream* began: with the 23-year-old Isaac Newton isolated at his family farm during an outbreak of the plague wondering why an apple fell to the ground.

Keynes wrote that the 'pseudo-analogy with the physical sciences leads directly counter to the habit of mind which is most important for an economist proper to acquire'. More specifically, he argued, economics as it deals with humans must engage with 'values ... motives, expectations, psychological uncertainties'. All the awkward stuff. One must not treat humans 'as constant and homogeneous', as the inanimate matter of the physical sciences. People could only be like Newton's apple falling from the tree, if

> the fall of the apple to the ground depended on the apple's motives, on whether it is worth while falling to the ground, and whether the ground wanted the apple to fall, and on mistaken calculations on the part of the apple as to how far it was from the centre of the earth.[25]

Too many venerated ideas in economics are just as absurd as Keynes' fantasy. Only familiarity veils this truth.

When model and world have failed to align, too many have concluded that it was real-world humans who had misbehaved. This tends *not* to happen with physics. If a planet fails to arrive when predicted, the astronomer cannot reprimand it or change its orbit. The only option is to change the theory or model. But people are more pliable than planets.[26] Humans have been seen as faulty machines and goaded and prodded into acting correctly. Great has been the effort to hammer out our irrationality in order to make the crooked timber of humanity straight. Efforts to close the gap between the ideal and the real sometimes involve, as Max Weber saw, 'violence to reality in order to prove the real validity of the construct'.[27] This violence might only intensify in our age of surveillance, artificial intelligence, and synthetic biology.

This is not an argument for abandoning ideals or attempts at improving the human condition. It is an argument that we need to more explicitly notice, and debate, the values that inform those ideals. The most profound substitution in economics has been conceptually replacing human welfare with the universal measuring rod of money. In part, this has been so that the analytical machine can grip onto something firm.[28] Wealth is an important value, but so too are security and freedom and justice. We need to pay more attention to how all these valid and often conflicting values operate. Too often in recent decades all other values have been subsumed under the banner of 'efficiency', another word for wealth. This conceptual shortcut has damaged society, law, democracy, and the natural world.

An intellectual dream—an unhelpful imaginative world picture—has veiled the wonder of what it means to be human, our connection to each other, to the rest of life, and to the Earth. We deserve an economic system with an expansive vision of human dignity at its centre.

The future is not yet written.

Generations to come will have reason to celebrate those who keep their eyes on living humans and the organic world as they fashion new social thinking.

Notes

Note: The reference for each source is given in full the first time it is used in each chapter. For subsequent notes, the author name and excerpt from the title is given.

Introduction: 'As Certain as the Principle of Gravitation'

1   There were several near contemporary accounts of Newton's story of the apple. This one comes from Stukeley, W. (1752) *Memoirs of Sir Isaac Newton's Life*, Available from: www.newtonproject.ox.ac.uk [Accessed 16 May 2024].

2   Fara, P. (2004) *Newton: The Making of Genius*, Picador.

3   Berlin, I. (1998 [1960]) 'The concept of scientific history', in H. Hardy and R. Hausheer (eds) *The Proper Study of Mankind*, Pimlico, pp 17–58, p 36. I do not here pass judgement on the method that Newton followed, which he called inductive reasoning, or his great interest in alchemy, theology, and the like, but on the cultural legacy of the mechanistic vision of the universe that was read into his work.

4   Ricardo to James Mill, Letter 414, 1 January 1821, in P. Sraffa (ed) (2004 [1951–1973]) *The Works and Correspondence of David Ricardo*, 11 Vols, Vol 8, Liberty Fund Inc.

5   Ricardo to Malthus, Letter 87, 27 March 1815, in P. Sraffa (ed), *The Works and Correspondence*, Vol 6. Elsewhere, Ricardo wrote, 'The principle of gravitation is not more certain than the tendency of such [Poor] laws to change wealth and power into misery and weakness', in Ricardo, D. (2004 [1817]) *The Principles of Political Economy and Taxation*, Dover Publications, p 63.

6   Heilbroner, R. (2000 [1953]) *The Worldly Philosophers: The Lives, Times and Ideas of the Great Economic Thinkers* (7th edn), Penguin Books, p 103.

7   Friedman, M. (1953) 'The methodology of positive economics', in Friedman, M., *Essays in Positive Economics*, University of Chicago Press, pp 3–43.

8   Levitt, S. and Dubner S.J. (2005) *Freakonomics: A Rogue Economist Explores the Hidden Side of Everything*, William Morrow.

9   Friedman, 'The methodology', p 4.

10 This term comes from *homo economicus*. It is commonly translated as 'economic man'. I've opted for the more neutral, and more accurate, translation of 'economic human'.

11 Kahneman, D. (2011) *Thinking, Fast and Slow*, Farrar, Straus and Giroux. Kahneman associates substitution with the style of automatic, non-calculating thinking he calls System 1, but he notes that the term comes from George Pólya's book *How to Solve It* where substitution is referred to as a deliberate process for solving difficult questions used by the attentive, calculating thinking he calls System 2.

[12] Schumpeter, J.A. (1954) *History of Economic Analysis*, Routledge, p 448. Edited from a manuscript by Elizabeth Boody Schumpeter.

[13] Berman, E.P. (2022) *Thinking Like an Economist: How Efficiency Replaced Equality in U.S. Public Policy*, Princeton University Press.

[14] Lakoff, G. (2014) *The ALL NEW Don't Think of An Elephant: Know Your Values and Frame the Debate*, Chelsea Green Publishing.

[15] *The Economist* (2009) 'The other-worldly philosophers', 16 July.

[16] Coase, R.H. (1984) 'The new institutional economics', *Zeitschrift für die gesamte Staatswissenschaft/Journal of Institutional and Theoretical Economics*, 140(1): 229–231. Ironically, this was in the context of an article that argued that mainstream economic theory of his time 'floats in the air' with 'no counterpart in real life'—p 230.

[17] Heilbroner, *The Worldly Philosophers*, p 211. The context of the comment is how Alfred Marshall and fellow academicians focused on 'the nice processes of adjustment of a stable textbook society' and failed to respond to the violent changes to the societies in which they lived.

[18] Strange, S. (1970) 'International economics and international relations: a case of mutual neglect', *International Affairs*, 46(2): 304–315.

[19] Dyer, N. (2021) '"Susan Strange saw the financial crisis coming, Your Majesty": the case for the LSE's great global political economist', *Real-World Economics Review*, 98: 92–112.

[20] Strange, S. (1994 [1988]) *States and Markets* (2nd edn), Continuum, p 16.

[21] Brown, C. (1999) 'Susan Strange: a critical appreciation', *Review of International Studies*, 25(3): 531–535, 532.

[22] Hochschild, A. (2006) *King Leopold's Ghost*, Pan Books, p 86.

[23] Global Witness (2016) 'Out of Africa: British offshore secrecy and Congo's missing $1.5 billion', May, Available from: www.globalwitness.org/documents/18357/Out_Of_Africa_final_EN.pdf [Accessed 16 May 2024].

[24] Global Witness (2014) 'Drillers in the mist', September.

[25] Leveson-Gower, H. (2019) 'How fifty years of the "Nobel Prize" in Economics redrew our map of society', *Promoting Economic Pluralism*, 31 August, Available from: https://economicpluralism.org/how-fifty-years-of-the-nobel-prize-in-economics-redrew-our-map-of-society/ [Accessed 16 May 2024].

[26] Midgley, M. (2010) 'Philosophical plumbing', *Royal Institute of Philosophy Supplements*, 33: 139–151.

[27] The analogy comes from Mayer, T. (1993) *Truth versus Precision in Economics*, Edward Elgar. He writes on p 124: 'Like a searchlight a model throws a powerful but narrowly focused beam that plunges everything not caught by it into utter darkness.'

[28] Watson, M. (2015) 'Following in John Methuen's early eighteenth-century footsteps: Ricardo's comparative advantage theory and the false foundations of the competitiveness of nations', Paper for 'Should Nation States Compete?' workshop, City, University of London, June; and Watson, M. (2017) 'Historicising Ricardo's comparative advantage theory, challenging the normative foundations of liberal international political economy', *New Political Economy*, 22(3): 257–272.

[29] Appelbaum, B. (2020) *The Economists' Hour: How the False Prophets of Free Markets Fractured Our Society*, Picador.

[30] David Colander and Craig Freedman put forward an apparently opposite argument. They say that most classical economists, except David Ricardo, understood that economics cannot be a science like physics but a moral science. Ricardo for them is 'an exception rather than the rule' (p 128). I accord Ricardo more influence on later economists such as J.S. Mill and Alfred Marshall. Colander and Freedman

do acknowledge, similar to my position, that 'the same sort of methodology [as David Ricardo's] was adopted in the postwar period' (p 168) with the rise of the Friedmanite Chicago School. See Colander, D. and Freedman, C. (2019) *Where Economics Went Wrong: Chicago's Abandonment of Classical Liberalism*, Princeton University Press.

31 Coyle, D. (2021) *Cogs and Monsters: What Economics Is, and What It Should Be*, Princeton University Press, p 15

32 See, for example, Lawson, T. (1997) *Economics and Reality*, Routledge. Likewise, there are some similarities between my analysis and 'complexity science' and 'complexity economics' that I have not explored here.

33 Kahneman, *Thinking, Fast and Slow*. Alan Blinder quoted in Klamer, A. (1984) *Conversations with Economists*, Rowman & Allanheld, p 157. Romer, P.M. (2015) 'Mathiness in the theory of economic growth', *American Economic Review: Papers & Proceedings*, 105(5): 89–93.

34 Piketty, T. (2021) *Une brève histoire de l'égalité*, Seuil, p 31. Figures for those who reached 1 year of age.

35 BBC (2005) 'Full text of Tony Blair's speech', BBC News, 27 September.

36 UN (2002) 'Secretary-General, accepting Moscow Award, says strength of Russian spirit "is your country's greatest natural asset"', 5 June, Available from: https://press.un.org/en/2002/sgsm8262.doc.htm [Accessed 17 April 2024].

37 Wallach, L. (2012) 'Can a "Dracula strategy" bring trans-Pacific partnership into the sunlight?' *Yes! Magazine*, December.

38 From the French term for the movement: *altermondialisation*.

39 Zumbrun, J. (2022) 'Economic blacklist of Russia marks new blow for globalization', *Wall Street Journal*, 10 March.

40 Sullivan, J. (2023) 'Remarks by National Security Advisor Jake Sullivan on renewing American economic leadership at the Brookings Institution', 27 April, Available from: www.whitehouse.gov/briefing-room/speeches-remarks/2023/04/27/remarks-by-national-security-advisor-jake-sullivan-on-renewing-american-economic-leadership-at-the-brookings-institution/ [Accessed 16 May 2024].

41 Tooze, A. (2022) 'Welcome to the world of the polycrisis', *Financial Times*, 28 October.

Chapter 1: The Other Founding Father of Economics

1 Reagan, R. (1981) 'Reagan talks to the World Bank and IMF', *New York Times*, 30 September, p 22.

2 Liu, G.M. (2022) *Adam Smith's America*, Princeton University Press, pp 247–249.

3 Bownman, S. (2016) 'Coming out as neoliberals', Adam Smith Institute website, 11 October.

4 The starting point for this is often considered to be Winch, D. (1978) *Adam Smith's Politics*, Cambridge University Press. Scholarship on Adam Smith is vast. For a good, accessible recent introduction see Norman, J. (2018) *Adam Smith*, Penguin Books.

5 Blaug, M. (1996) *Economic Theory in Retrospect, Fifth Edition*, Cambridge University Press, p 132.

6 Davis, W.L., Figgins, B.G., Hedengren, D. and Klein, D.B. (2011) 'Economic professors' favorite economic thinkers, journals, and blogs', *Econ Journal Watch*, 8(20): 126–146.

7   As quoted in Episode 1, 'The prophets and promise of classical capitalism', of *The Age of Uncertainty* television series produced by the BBC, CBC, KCET, and OECA in 1977.

8   Ricardo, M. (1824) 'A memoir of David Ricardo', in P. Sraffa (ed) (2004 [1951–1973]) *The Works and Correspondence of David Ricardo*, 11 Vols, Vol 10: *Biographical Miscellany*, Liberty Fund Inc.

9   See Weatherall, D. (1976) *David Ricardo: A Biography*, Martinus Nijhoff; and Heertje, A. (2004) 'The Dutch and Portuguese-Jewish background of David Ricardo', *European Journal of the History of Economic Thought*, 11(2): 281–294.

10   Weatherall, *David Ricardo*, p 33.

11   Mallet, J.L. (1823), diary entry, quoted in Sraffa, *The Works and Correspondence* (Vol 10), p 73. John Lewis Mallet (1775–1861) was a founder member of the Political Economy Club of London.

12   To estimate the contemporary worth of money in the early 1700s, I have used a ratio of £1 to £360 today. For the early 1800s, I have used £1 to £160 today. There are two main ways to measure the relative change in value: either by price (the inflation in the cost of buying products) or average earnings income. They produce very different results. For example, £1 in 1703 is worth £180 by inflation and £2,320 by earnings. For both estimates, I have used approximately twice the inflation figure but far below the earnings figure. All data from www.measuringworth.com/calculators/ukcompare/, created by the Economic History Association.

13   Parys, W. (2020), 'David Ricardo, the Stock Exchange, and the Battle of Waterloo: Samuelsonian legends lack historical evidence', University of Antwerp, Faculty of Business and Economics Research Paper No 2020-009, pp 50 and 67. Parys uses figures from Sraffa, *The Works and Correspondence*, to show that Ricardo traded £6.965 million Consols in the six years between 1798 and 1804. The figure for the average trader of Consols, Parys takes from Patrick O'Brien's 1967 dissertation *Government Revenue, 1793–1815*.

14   Sraffa, *The Works and Correspondence* (Vol 10), and Weatherall, *David Ricardo*.

15   Ricardo to Malthus, Letter 53, 25 July 1814, in Sraffa, *The Works and Correspondence* (Vol 6).

16   Weatherall, *David Ricardo*, p 98.

17   Edgeworth to her sister Lucy Edgeworth, Letter 3 from Gatcomb Park, 12 November 1821, in Sraffa, *The Works and Correspondence* (Vol 10); emphasis in the original.

18   T.W. Hutchison wrote that the contrast of David Ricardo's contribution to the method of economics, refined by J.S. Mill, 'with [Adam Smith's] *The Wealth of Nations* seems sufficiently profound, extreme and consequential, as to justify the adjective "revolutionary". The integration of history with analysis and theory so superbly, and uniquely, achieved in Adam Smith's work was shattered'; see Hutchison, T.W. (1978) *On Revolutions and Progress in Economic Knowledge*, Cambridge University Press, p 54. A counterargument stressing the continuity between Adam Smith and David Ricardo was put forward in Hollander, S. (1979) *The Economics of David Ricardo*, Heinemann Educational Books. Mark Blaug judged that 'Hollander has flagrantly misread Ricardo's message' and the primary themes of Hollander's book are 'false'; see Blaug, M. (1985) 'What Ricardo said and what Ricardo meant', in G.A. Caravale (ed) *The Legacy of Ricardo*, Basil Blackwell, pp 3–10.

19   Sraffa, *The Works and Correspondence* (Vol 10).

20 Sagar, P. (2018) 'The real Adam Smith', AEON, 16 January, Available from: https://aeon.co/essays/we-should-look-closely-at-what-adam-smith-actually-believed [Accessed 16 May 2024].

21 Smith, A. (1999 [1776]) *An Inquiry into the Nature and Causes of the Wealth of Nations*, Penguin Classics. Smith's comment on poverty comes in Book 1, chapter 8. His critique of the British East India Company can be found in Book 4, chapters 5 and 7, and Book 5, chapters 1 and 2.

22 Smith, *Wealth of Nations*, ch 1.

23 Smith, *Wealth of Nations*, Book 5, ch 1. Karl Marx would take up this theme as 'alienation'.

24 Dale, R. (2006) *'Napoleon Is Dead': Lord Cochrane and the Great Stock Exchange Scandal*, Sutton Publishing.

25 Ackermann, R. (1808–1810) *Microcosm of London* (Vol 3), Harrison and Rutter, p 102. The text in volume 3 is by William Combe.

26 Sraffa, *The Works and Correspondence* (Vol 10).

27 Bank of England Archives, G8/7, Bank of England (1797–1832), *Committee of Treasury Report Book*, p 84.

28 The bidding process worked as follows. For every £100 advanced to the government, for example, it would offer to provide £70 of Consols, £70 of Reduced, and an unspecified value of Navys. Consols, Reduced, and Navys were types of government stocks that gave a fixed annual dividend of 3 or 5 per cent. The average price at which the three types of stock traded, that is, the number that everyone focused on, was called the Omnium. Bids were given in sealed envelopes and the government selected the cheapest possibility, which meant the bid with the least number of Navys. See Parys, 'David Ricardo', p 14. He also shows that there were only two consortia for the 1815 loan, not four as other authors have suggested.

29 Parys, 'David Ricardo', p 59, writes: 'Ricardo made some big gains from several Loans, especially from 1812 on, when the Loans were large and profitable for him and for a few other top financiers, who cooperated and made the same bid for the Loans, instead of undergoing hard competition.' Parys notes that financiers began cooperating on bids following the losses on previous loans that contributed to the suicide of Abraham Goldsmid and the rising amounts of money the British government needed. The Prime Minister, Lord Liverpool, was unhappy with the financiers' cooperation but eventually relented.

30 Weatherall, *David Ricardo*, p 15.

31 Michie, R. (2000) *The London Stock Exchange: A History*, Oxford University Press, pp 35–36.

32 Ackermann, *Microcosm of London*.

33 David Ricardo was on the Committee of Proprietors in 1801 when the decision was made to become a subscription-only exchange and move into new buildings. He was also on the General Purposes Committee at various times in 1801 and 1802 as it oversaw the building and opening of the new Stock Exchange. See Weatherall, *David Ricardo*, p 42.

34 Ricardo, 'A memoir of David Ricardo', p 6.

35 Creevey, T. (1904) *The Creevey Papers* (Vol 1, 2nd edn), John Murray, p 236.

36 Parys, 'David Ricardo', p 54, notes that five of the 20 largest up-and-down monthly price shifts in the entire history of Consul trading in London between 1729 and 1959 occurred during the Napoleonic Wars.

37 Ricardo to John Murray, Letter 98, 12 June 1815, in Sraffa, *The Works and Correspondence* (Vol 6).

[38] Parys, 'David Ricardo', pp 28–34.

[39] Malthus to Ricardo, Letter 99, 19 June 1815, in Sraffa, *The Works and Correspondence* (Vol 6).

[40] Parys, 'David Ricardo', p 32.

[41] Samuelson, P.A. (2009) 'An enjoyable life puzzling over modern finance theory', *Annual Review of Financial Economics*, 1: 19–35.

[42] See Parys, 'David Ricardo', and Cathcart, B. (2014) 'Nathan Rothschild and the battle of Waterloo', in *Review of the Year April 2013 to March 2014*, Rothschild Archive.

[43] Parys, 'David Ricardo', Table 2, p 62.

[44] So for the Waterloo loan the first £10 was due on 17 June 1815, and then another £10 each month, with the last on 15 March 1816.

[45] Ricardo to Malthus, Letter 100, 27 June 1815, in Sraffa, *The Works and Correspondence* (Vol 6).

[46] Sraffa, *The Works and Correspondence* (Vol 10).

[47] Ricardo to Malthus, Letter 100, 27 June 1815, in Sraffa, *The Works and Correspondence* (Vol 6).

[48] James Mill to Ricardo, Letter 109, 23 August 1815, in Sraffa, *The Works and Correspondence* (Vol 6); original emphasis.

[49] Bank of England Archives, AC27/2614, Bank of England (1798–1804), *Stock Ledger (Jobbers): 3% Consols, P–R*.

[50] Parys, 'David Ricardo', p 34, notes: Ricardo's 'total profits are unknown, because many of his transactions were not registered'. Time bargains, a type of options trading, were banned by the 1734 Barnard Act.

[51] See Parys, 'David Ricardo', p 51, for the value of Ricardo's estate. Modern equivalents are the author's calculations—see note 12.

[52] Author's calculations. Austen, J. (2022 [1813]) *Pride and Prejudice*, available online via Project Gutenberg, ch 59. Austen describes Mr Darcy as having a 'large estate in Derbyshire'—Pemberley—which, if not included in his £10,000 per year, would increase his wealth.

[53] H. Trower to Ricardo, Letter 102, 23 July 1815, in Sraffa, *The Works and Correspondence* (Vol 6); original emphasis.

[54] The case for Ricardo as an 'empirical economist' is perhaps best made by Timothy Davis. See Davis, T. (2002) 'David Ricardo, financier and empirical economist', *European Journal of the History of Economic Thought*, 9(1): 1–16, and Davis, T. (2005) *Ricardo's Macroeconomics*, Cambridge University Press. Davis shows that Ricardo drew on reports, statistics, and conversations with those in the know to inform his thinking, albeit mainly on subjects close to his business experience such as gold trading, the stock market, and loans. He fails to show that Ricardo engaged empirically in a substantial way on subjects such as rent, land, and corn.

[55] Redman, D.A. (1997) *The Rise of Political Economy as a Science*, MIT Press, p 357. Ricardo's 'method, nevertheless, appears to be the one he had grown accustomed to using as a broker—hence the term *broker's myopia* to indicate its shortcomings'.

[56] Keynes, J.M. (1936) *General Theory of Employment, Interest, and Money*, Macmillan, ch 3.

[57] Keynes, *General Theory*, ch 3.

Chapter 2: 'The Unshakeable Basis for International Trade'

[1] Ricardo, D. (2004 [1817]) *The Principles of Political Economy and Taxation*, Dover Publications, p 1.

2   Peet, R. (2009) 'Ten pages that changed the world: deconstructing Ricardo', *Human Geography*, 2(1): 81–95.

3   Schumacher, R. (2016) *Free Trade and Absolute and Comparative Advantage: A Critical Comparison of Two Major Theories of International Trade*, University of Potsdam.

4   Smith, A. (1999 [1776]) *An Inquiry into the Nature and Causes of the Wealth of Nations*, Penguin Classics, Book 4, ch 2.

5   Smith, *Wealth of Nations*, Book 4, ch 2.

6   Some historians of economic thought argue that Adam Smith did not consider specialization to be the central rule of his international trade theory but believed that trade would lead to a diversification of products. See Schumacher, R. (2017) 'Adam Smith, the patterns of foreign trade and the division of labour: a country as a jack-of-all-trades rather than a specialist', in F. Forman (ed) *The Adam Smith Review: Volume 10*, Routledge, Available from: www.taylorfrancis.com/chapters/edit/10.4324/9781315142043-2/adam-smith-patterns-foreign-trade-division-labour-reinhard-schumacher?context=ubx&refId=856ecc86-ce82-45ec-93ad-c69c76e50acc

7   Smith, *Wealth of Nations*, Book 4, ch 6.

8   Smith, *Wealth of Nations*, Book 4, ch 2.

9   Smith, *Wealth of Nations*, Book 4, ch 5.

10 Smith, *Wealth of Nations*, Book 4, preamble.

11 See Ingram, J.K. (1915 [1888]) *A History of Political Economy*, A.&C. Black.

12 Spiegel, H.W. (1991 [1971]) *The Growth of Economic Thought* (3rd edn), Duke University Press, p 319, points to 'another break with the Adam Smith tradition, indicative of Ricardo's abstract generalizing method, which made him search for economic laws, a term Smith did not employ'.

13 See chapter 7 'On foreign trade' in Ricardo, *The Principles*.

14 Boumans, M. (2005) *How Economists Model the World into Numbers*, Routledge, p 2.

15 Although Ricardo's principle of comparative advantage is the most prominent part of his international trade theory, when it came to grain imports Ricardo often relied on the argument that cheaper imported grain would reduce wages and hence increase profits and capital, which would drive economic growth. This is more dynamic than the one-off gain from comparative advantage.

16 The quote continues by saying: 'Yet, in truth, there is no remedy except to throw over the axiom of parallels and to work out a non-Euclidean geometry. Something similar is required to-day in economics.' From Keynes, J.M. (1936) *The General Theory of Employment, Interest and Money*, Macmillan, ch 2. In a parliamentary debate in 1819, Ricardo said of one of his economic pronouncements: 'no proposition in Euclid was clearer than this'. Ricardo, D. (1819) 'Petition of the merchants of London respecting commercial distress', 24 December, in P. Sraffa (ed) (2004 [1951–1973]) *The Works and Correspondence of David Ricardo*, 11 Vols, Vol 5, Liberty Fund Inc.

17 King, J.E. (2013) *David Ricardo*, Palgrave Macmillan, p 82.

18 Samuelson, P.A. (1968) 'The way of an economist', Presidential Address, Third Congress of the International Economic Association, Montreal.

19 This way of explaining the logic of Ricardo's theory with units was done first by his friend James Mill in 1821.

20 Ricardo, *The Principles*, ch 7.

21 Mankiw, N.G. (2019) 'Reflections of a textbook author', in *Principles of Economics*, Harvard University, p 1: 'I would guess that, including translations, about 4 million copies of my books are in print.'

22 Mankiw, N.G. (2021) *Principles of Economics, Ninth Edition*, Cengage, p 54.

23 Mankiw, *Principles of Economics*, p 51.

24 Boudreaux, D. (nd) 'Comparative advantage', 'Principles of microeconomics', Marginal Revolution University (MRU), George Mason University, Available from: https://mru.org/courses/dictionary-economics/comparative-advantage.

25 The exceptions, which do compare Ricardo's theory to its real-world history, are: Sideri, S. (1970) *Trade and Power: Informal Colonialism in Anglo-Portuguese Relations*, Rotterdam University Press, and Watson, M. (2017) 'Historicising Ricardo's comparative advantage theory: challenging the normative foundations of liberal international political economy', *New Political Economy*, 22(3): 257–272.

26 Historian of economic thought Reinhard Schumacher has written, 'International trade theory, by relying on this theory [of comparative advantage], risks ignoring the most relevant and important elements with regards to international trade.' See Schumacher, R. (2013) 'Deconstructing the theory of comparative advantage', *World Economic Review*, 2: 83–105.

27 Samuelson, P.A. and Nordhaus, W. (1985) *Economics, 12th Edition*, McGraw-Hill, pp 834–835.

28 Hamilton's *Report on the Subject of Manufacturers* was published in 1791, after Adam Smith's writing but before David Ricardo's. Klein, M.C. and Pettis, M. (2020) *Trade Wars are Class Wars*, Yale University Press, p 12: 'It [Hamilton's theory] was a rebuttal to Ricardo before the theory of comparative advantage had even been written.'

29 Quoted in Chang, H.-J. (2008) *Bad Samaritans*, Random House, p 16.

30 Chang, *Bad Samaritans*, p 15.

31 Krugman, P. (2010) 'Who are you calling dense?', *New York Times*, 30 August.

32 The *Contra Krugman* podcast, hosted by libertarian economic writers Robert Murphy and Tom Woods, ran from September 2015 to June 2020; see www.contrakrugman.com.

33 Krugman, P. (1996) 'Ricardo's difficult idea', MIT, Available from: web.mit.edu/krugman/www/ricardo.htm [Accessed on 16 May 2024].

34 Krugman, 'Ricardo's difficult idea'.

35 Krugman, P. (1987) 'Is free trade passé?', *Journal of Economic Perspectives*, 1(2): 131–144.

36 Mankiw, *Principles of Economics*, p 53.

37 *Think Like an Economist* (2021) [podcast] 'A conversation with Greg Mankiw: financial crises, recessions and communicating economics', 2 November, Episode 49, Modulated Media.

38 Rodrik, D. (2017) *Economics Rules*, Oxford University Press, p 52.

39 Rodrik, D. (2011) *The Globalization Paradox*, Oxford University Press, p 65.

40 See McCloskey, D. (1996) 'Ask what the boys in the sandpit will have', (London) *Times Higher Education Supplement*, and McCloskey, D. (2017) 'A punter's guide to a true but non-obvious proposition in economics', Paper prepared for the Institute for Free Trade's Global Trade Summit, 16 October.

41 Ricardo, *The Principles*, p 83.

42 Klein and Pettis, *Trade Wars*, pp 9–11.

43 See Watson, M. (2015) 'Following in John Methuen's early eighteenth-century footsteps', Paper for 'Should Nation States Compete?' workshop at City, University of London, June 2015, and Watson, 'Historicising'.

44 Ricardo, *The Principles*, p 257.

Chapter 3: Unequal Treaty

1   This is why the story is told about 'English cloth' rather than 'British cloth'. Even after the Act of Union, many statistics on trade refer only to England and not to Britain and many later writers use the terms interchangeably. Also, prior to 1752 the Julian calendar used in Britain was ten to 11 days behind the Georgian calendar used in continental Europe. Following convention, all dates stated in this text prior to 1752 are according to the old-style British calendar. The date of the signing of the Methuen Cloth and Wine Treaty in Portugal was 27 December.

2   National Archives, SP 108/393, 'Ratification by Portugal of the treaty of commerce with Great Britain, concluded 1703', Public Record Office, London.

3   Translation from the Latin in Smith, A. (1999 [1776]) *An Inquiry into the Nature and Causes of the Wealth of Nations*, Penguin Classics, Book 4, ch 6, pp 124–125.

4   Fisher, H.E.S. (1971), *The Portugal Trade: A Study of Anglo-Portuguese Commerce 1700–1770*, Methuen & Co, p 16.

5   Costa, L.F., Lains, P. and Miranda, S.M. (2016) *An Economic History of Portugal, 1143–2010*, Cambridge University Press, pp 193–200.

6   Fisher, *The Portugal Trade*, p 16. Portuguese exports to England were estimated at £200,000 per year between 1698 and 1702, £254,000 between 1700 and 1704, and £429,000 between 1741 and 1745.

7   Boswell, J. (2006 [1791]), *Boswell's Life of Johnson*, available online via Project Gutenberg.

8   'International trade and currency markets', *Understand: The Economy*, Series 1, Episode 9, BBC Radio 4.

9   Fisher, *The Portugal Trade*, p 16.

10 See Francis, A.D. (1966) *The Methuens and Portugal, 1691–1708*, Cambridge University Press, pp 202–204. Francis claims the allegations of bribery were 'spread for propaganda purposes by the French', p 202.

11 Francis, *The Methuens and Portugal*.

12 Macky, J.M. (1733) *Memoires of the Secret Services* (2nd edn), Spring Macky, p 143.

13 In Scott, T. (2004 [1902]) *The Prose Works of Jonathan Swift*, Vol 10: Historical Writings: 'Remarks on the Characters of the Court of Queen Anne', available online via Project Gutenberg.

14 Aubrey, J. (2004 [1847]) *The Natural History of Wiltshire*, available online via Project Gutenberg, Part II, ch 12. Aubrey uses an alternative spelling of Methuen: 'Mr. Paul Methwin of Bradford'.

15 Figures from Francis, *The Methuens and Portugal*, p 204.

16 Francis, *The Methuens and Portugal*, pp 203–204: 'Methuen also had some family interest in the wine trade for he had a son-in-law, named Humphrey Simpson, who was an importer.'

17 Shaw, W.A. (ed) (1936) 'Minute book: July 1703', in *Calendar of Treasury Books, Volume 18, 1703*, pp 62–71, British History Online, Available from: www.british-history.ac.uk/cal-treasury-books/vol18/pp62-71 [Accessed 16 May 2024], and Shaw, W.A. and Slingsby, F.A. (eds) (1955) 'Appendix: miscellaneous 1703', in *Calendar of Treasury Books, Volume 28, 1714*, pp 408–420, British History Online, Available from: www.british-history.ac.uk/cal-treasury-books/vol28/pp408-420 [Accessed 16 May 2024].

18 Shaw and Slingsby (eds), *Calendar of Treasury Books*. The entry for 24 November 1703 reads: 'William Methuen, 2,000*l*. [pounds] by her Majesty's command, to enable me to satisfy two bills of exchange of 1,000*l*. each drawn upon me by my brother, John Methuen, Esq., Ambassador to the King of Portugal, both dated

12/23 Oct. 1703, being for her Majesty's service expended by the said Ambassador by her Majesty's particular direction.'

19 Letter from John Methuen to Lord Nottingham, 15 January 1704, British Library, MS 29590, 'Original letters from John and Paul Methuen, envoys at Lisbon, to Charles Montagu, Earl of Manchester, and Daniel Finch, Earl of Nottingham' (1702–1704)', p 403. Methuen reported to the British Secretary of State for the Southern Department, who was responsible for Southern Europe, including Portugal. This position was held by Charles Montague, 4th Earl of Manchester, in early 1702, and then Daniel Finch, 2nd Earl of Nottingham, from May 1702 to April 1704.

20 Francis, *The Methuens and Portugal*, p 202.

21 Letter from John Methuen to the Earl of Manchester, 8 May 1702, British Library, MS 29590.

22 Letters from John Methuen to Manchester, 8 May 1702 and 19 May 1702, British Library, MS 29590.

23 Letter from John Methuen to Nottingham, 16 July 1702, British Library, MS 29590.

24 Letter from John Methuen to Nottingham, 23 September 1702, British Library, MS 29590, pp 128–130. Methuen wrote: 'The great advantage France will make by the arrival of a fleet believed to be so rich. The hopes that the great sums (?) due to the [Portuguese] Cacheo Company here will now be paid. These are all circumstances very disadvantageous to my hopes.' In an earlier letter, in May 1702, Methuen wrote that the French influences in the Portuguese court had persuaded King Pedro II to agree that Portuguese Cacheo Company would take the contract (*asiento*) to furnish the Spanish Empire with enslaved peoples from Africa. Pedro II agreed 'in expectation of great advantage to be deeply concerned as a private person in that Company'. But the contract led to 'a great loose', rather than a gain, which left the king in debt. Methuen suggests that the French had promised to clear Pedro II's debt when the Treasure Fleet arrived from the Americas and that this was a crucial factor keeping Portugal in the alliance with the French—see Letter from John Methuen to Manchester, 5 May 1702, British Library, MS 29590.

25 Rodger, N.A.M. (2004) *Command of the Ocean: A Naval History of Britain, 1649–1815*, W.N. Norton. The battle was on 23 October according to the Georgian calendar used on continental Europe.

26 Letter from the Duke of Ormonde to Admiral Rooke, 17 October 1702, British Library, MS 28925, 'Letters and papers relating to the expedition to Vigo Bay'.

27 Letter from John Methuen to Nottingham, 18 November 1702, British Library, MS 29590.

28 Letter from John Methuen to Nottingham, 29 December 1703, British Library, MS 29590. 'I have now completed the payment of the first five hundred thousand dollars.'

29 Methuen is explicit about using the quid pro quo of using military forces and security as bargaining chips to extract greater trade concessions when writing about a future trade deal with Spain. 'All these will require a force in the West Indyes such as only England can have there and will dispose the Spanyards to depend on her Majesty's assistance and therefore on this occasion no doubt will agree to such terms as may be advantagious to her Majesty in response of the publick charge and to private merchants in respect of the liberty of sending their effects thither in their own names securely.' Letter from John Methuen to Nottingham, 15 January 1704, British Library, MS 29590.

[30] Swift, J. (1989 [c. 1730]) 'On the Irish Club', in P. Rogers (ed) *Jonathan Swift: The Complete Poems*, Penguin, p 409.

[31] Strange, S. (2004 [1988]) *States and Markets* (2nd edn), p 165.

[32] Strange, S. (1986) 'The bondage of liberal economics', *SAIS Review*, 6(1): 25–38.

[33] Benzecry, G.F. (2021) 'Friedrich List and the Methuen Treaty', Norwood University, Available from: https://ssrn.com/abstract=3986358 [Accessed 16 May 2024].

[34] Beckert, S. (2015) *Empire of Cotton: A New History of Global Capitalism*, Penguin.

[35] Letter from John Methuen to Nottingham, 9 December 1703, British Library, MS 29590 (1702–1704).

[36] Beckert, *Empire of Cotton*.

[37] Costa et al, *An Economic History*.

[38] Costa et al, *An Economic History*, p 200.

[39] Palma, N. and Reis, J. (2019) 'From convergence to divergence: Portuguese economic growth, 1527–1850', *Journal of Economic History*, 79(2): 477–506.

[40] Robinson, J. (1974) *Reflections on the Theory of International Trade*, Manchester University Press, p 1.

[41] Birmingham, D. (2018) *A Concise History of Portugal*, Cambridge University Press, p 4. This description of Britain and Portugal's relationship in the early 1700s is disputed by some Portuguese economic historians. Author communication with Leonor Freire Costa, 13 August 2023.

[42] Birmingham, *A Concise History*, p 67.

[43] Lave, J. (2001) 'Getting to be British', in D. Holland and J. Lave (eds) (2001) *History in Person*, School of American Research Press and James Currey Ltd. See also Rodger, *Command of the Ocean*, p 167.

[44] Figueiredo, L. (2011) *Boa Ventura! A corrida do ouro no Brasil, 1697–1810* (5th edn), Editora Record.

[45] Letters from John Methuen to Nottingham, 19 May 1702 and 5 May 1702, British Library, MS 29590.

[46] Rodger, *Command of the Ocean*, p 167.

[47] Letter from John Methuen to Nottingham, 7 November 1703, British Library, MS 29590.

[48] King, C. (1721) *The British Merchant; or, Commerce Preserv'd* (Vol 3), John Darby, p iv. Accessed via HathiTrust.

[49] Fisher, *The Portugal Trade*, p 16. Between 1698 and 1702, England's export surplus with Portugal was £155 k; between 1706 and 1710 it was £413 k; between 1736 and 1740 it was £698 k; and between 1756 and 60 it was £1.04 m.

[50] For my purposes, it matters little. Ricardo spoke of the exchange of cloth and wine, rather than the treaty.

Chapter 4: Black Gold

[1] Freelon, K. (2018) 'The morbid discovery that led to Rio's only museum dedicated to the memory of the slave trade', *Daily Beast*, 5 July.

[2] Phillips, T. (2011) 'Rio's cemetery of new Blacks shed light on horrors of slave trade', *The Guardian*, 20 December.

[3] Data from Voyages: The Transatlantic Slave Trade Database. 'Trans-Atlantic slave trade—estimates', Available from: www.slavevoyages.org/assessment/estimates [Accessed 7 January 2024]. This authoritative database estimates that between 1501 and 1866, a total of 388,747 captives who were embarked in Africa were disembarked in mainland North America and 4,864,373 in Brazil. Updating these

figures with estimates of captives who died in the Middle Passage gives 472,381 embarked for North America and 5,532,118 for Brazil.

4   Malleret, C. (2023) 'Mixed-race people become Brazil's biggest population group', *The Guardian*, 22 December.

5   Thomas, H. (2006) *The Slave Trade: The History of the Atlantic Slave Trade, 1440–1870*, Phoenix, p 318. See also Costa, L.F., Lains, P. and Miranda, S.M. (2016) *An Economic History of Portugal, 1143–2010*, Cambridge University Press, p 195, who wrote: 'The discovery of gold in Brazil and the growth of the colonial market greatly contributed to making Portugal a significant trade partner. Most of the English cloth was re-exported to Portuguese America, partly through the enterprising of English agents who cut off the intermediary role of national ports.'

6   Olusoga, D. (2016) *Black and British: A Forgotten History*, Pan Books, p 47.

7   Letter from Paul Methuen to Secretary Bernon, 4 March 1702, National Archives, SP 89/18/162.

8   A.D. Francis is the historian who has quoted from these letters but overlooked the connections to the African slave trade; see Francis, A.D. (1966) *The Methuens and Portugal, 1691–1708*, Cambridge University Press.

9   Letter from John Methuen to Nottingham, 26 November 1703, British Library, MS 29590, 'Original letters from John and Paul Methuen, envoys at Lisbon, to Charles Montagu, Earl of Manchester, and Daniel Finch, Earl of Nottingham' (1702–1704)', from p 382. Methuen describes the nearly finalized agreement with Portugal as follows: 'It is agreed between us that [Queen Anne] her Majesty agreeing that the dutys on Portugal wines shall by the Pipe or Tunn be always one third part less than those Dutys on French wine the King of Portugal will immediately oblige himself to permitt English cloth.'

10 Letter from John Methuen to Nottingham, 26 November 1703, British Library, MS 29590.

11 All quotations from Letter from John Methuen to Nottingham, 15 January 1704, British Library, MS 29590, from p 403.

12 Data from Voyages: The Transatlantic Slave Trade Database, Available from: www.slavevoyages.org [Accessed 7 May 2022].

13 Data from 'Trans-Atlantic slave trade—estimates', Available from: www.slavevoyages.org/assessment/estimates [Accessed 16 May 2024]. Of the 12.5 million African embarked, 5.8 million were transported by Portugal/Brazil and 3.3 million by Britain. Together this accounts for 73 per cent of the total voyages.

14 See Bank of England Archive, 20A67/4/1/3, 'Humphrey [*sic*] Morice: trading accounts and slave trade volume 3', 1698–1732. The printed receipts from 1727 and 1728 note the place of trade as Annamaboe, later known as Fort William and now as Anomabu, in Ghana.

15 Bank of England Archives, 20A67/3/7, 'Orders and instructions to William Roule of the Portugal galley, fourth voyage'; Morice wrote to William Boyle on 11 May 1724.

16 This account draws on Boxer, C.R. (1995 [1962]) *The Golden Age of Brazil*, Carcanet Press. Also Gomes, L. (2021) *Escravidão* (Vol 2), Globo Livros, p 70, and Figueiredo, L. (2011) *Boa Ventura! A corrida do ouro no Brasil, 1697–1810* (5th edn), Editora Record, p 116.

17 Figueiredo, *Boa Ventura!*, p 124.

18 Boxer, *The Golden Age*, p 59. Author calculations on value of gold as per January 2023 prices.

19 Letter from John Methuen to Mr Tucker, 23–26 May 1706, National Archives, SP 89/19/127.

20 Letter from John Methuen to Nottingham, 15 January 1704, British Library, MS 29590.

21 Boxer, *The Golden Age*, p 47.

22 Boxer, *The Golden Age*, p 41.

23 Gomes, *Escravidão*, p 73.

24 Quoted in Boxer, *The Golden Age*, p 41.

25 Boxer, *The Golden Age*, pp 54–55.

26 Costa et al, *An Economic History*, p 203. 'Mining in Brazil extracted 856.5 metric tons (*toneladas*) of gold during the 1700s, which may represent about 53–61 percent of the total world production.'

27 Cook, J. (1842) *The Voyages of Captain James Cook*, William Smith, p 17. See also Alborn, T. (2019) *All That Glittered: Britain's Most Precious Metal from Adam Smith to the Gold Rush*, Oxford University Press, pp 26 and 163.

28 Boxer, *The Golden Age*.

29 Boxer, *The Golden Age*, p 163. The eyewitness was Simão Ferreira Machado the author of *Triunfo Eucarístico* in 1734.

30 Figures rounded to the nearest thousand. Author's calculations from Voyages, Available from: www.slavevoyages.org [Accessed 16 May 2024].

31 Gomes, *Escravidão*, p 20. 'O impulso decisivo foi dado pela descoberta de pedras e minerais preciosos, primeiro em Minas Gerais, depois em Goiás e Mato Grosso.'

32 See Salgado's collections *Workers* (1993), published by Phaidon Press, and *Gold* (2019), published by Taschen.

33 *Al Jazeera* (2020) 'At least 50 feared dead in DR Congo mine collapse', 12 September.

34 For a recent investigation into African 'conflict gold' and its links to refineries in Dubai and Switzerland see Global Witness (2020), 'Beneath the Shine: A Tale of Two Gold Refiners', July.

35 Author interview, 16 September 2022.

36 French, H.W. (2021) *Born in Blackness*, Liveright Publishing.

37 Quoted by Boxer, *The Golden Age*, p 8.

38 Boxer, *The Golden Age*, p 8.

39 Boxer, *The Golden Age*, p 174.

40 Boxer, *The Golden Age*, p 9.

41 French, *Born in Blackness*, pp 2–3 and 77.

42 French, *Born in Blackness*, p 2.

43 Vilar, P. (1976) *A History of Gold and Money, 1450–1920*, trans J. White, NLB, p 63.

44 Green, T. (2019) *A Fistful of Shells: West Africa from the Rise of the Slave Trade to the Age of Revolution*, University of Chicago Press, p 118: 'For almost the first two centuries of trade in Atlantic Africa, there was no export slave trade on the Gold Coast.' See also Rodney, W. (2018 [1972]) *How Europe Underdeveloped Africa*, Verso, pp 111–122: 'in the seventeenth century, the Portuguese and Dutch actually discouraged the slave trade on the Gold Coast, for they recognised that it would be incompatible with the gold trade. However, by the end of that century, gold had been discovered in Brazil, and the importance of gold supplies from Africa was lessened. ... The above changeover from gold mining to slave raiding took place within a period of a few years between 1700 and 1710.'

45 Author's calculations from Voyages, Available from: www.slavevoyages.org [Accessed 16 May 2024].

[46] French, *Born in Blackness*, p 254. French writes on pp 182–183: 'Less widely noted in accounts of economic change in this era, but also extraordinary in terms of the new wealth that it generated, was a prolonged eighteenth-century boom in gold production in Brazil, centered in the Minas Gerais region.' He notes this boom was 'made possible largely on the basis of African slave labor' and helped 'fuel the Industrial Revolution', but he claims that Brazil's sugar crop generated more income than the gold boom.

[47] Quoted in Thomas, *The Slave Trade*, p 227.

[48] Boxer, *The Golden Age*, pp 44–45.

[49] Boxer, *The Golden Age*, p 45.

[50] Boxer, *The Golden Age*, p 165. Boxer also notes that the discovery of gold in Brazil led to an 'expansion of the slave trade with Guinea' (pp 45–46). Thomas, *The Slave Trade*, p 321, wrote, 'Some of the [West African] slaves bought with Brazilian gold were taken to Brazil to mine that very commodity in Minas Gerais.'

[51] Davies, K.G. (1970) *The Royal African Company*, Atheneum, p 225.

[52] See Rodney, *How Europe Underdeveloped Africa*, p 111, and Green, *A Fistful of Shells*, p 301: 'once the picture reversed in the nineteenth century with the abolition of the slave trade, and gold was exported again by Asante'.

[53] 'John and Paul Methuen', Westminster Abbey, Available from: www.westminster-abbey.org/abbey-commemorations/commemorations/john-and-paul-methuen [Accessed 16 May 2024].

[54] Letter from John Milner to Sir Charles Hedges, 28 August 1706, National Archives, SP89/19/254, p 257.

[55] Costa et al, *An Economic History*, p 195. They note that in 1729, 67 per cent of Portugal's trade deficit was with Britain and 23 per cent with France.

Chapter 5: Newton's Mint

[1] British Library, MS 18763, 'Account of the silver taken at Vigo 1702–3'.

[2] Fara, P. (2021) *Life after Gravity: Isaac Newton's London Career*, Oxford University Press.

[3] Craig, J. (1953) *The Mint*, Cambridge University Press, pp 199–200. Craig wrote that between 1666 and 1770 the Master of the Mint was paid 1 shilling and 10 pence (written as 1/10) for every troy pound (approximately 373 grams) of gold coin issued. During Newton's 27 years at the Mint, Craig states that £12,481,722 of gold was coined in London.

[4] Fara, *Life after Gravity*. All estimates of current values are mine and not Fara's.

[5] It has been overlooked by David Olusoga, other Newton scholars, and the Bank of England's 2022 exhibition 'Slavery & the Bank'. See Olusoga, D. (2016) *Black and British: A Forgotten History*, Pan Books, p 22; Newton scholar Simon Schaffer links Newton at the Mint to gold from West Africa but not Brazil in Schaffer, S. (2002) 'Golden means: assay instruments and the geography of precision in the Guinea trade', in M.N. Bourguet, C. Licoppe and H.O. Sibum (eds) (2002) *Instruments, Travel and Science*, Routledge, pp 20–50. Although the Bank of England's ground-breaking exhibition 'Slavery & the Bank' mentions the Brazilian gold boom in the 1700s it does not link it to the coining of guineas, stating: 'African gold was transported to London by the RAC [Royal African Company], which was then minted into coins for circulation in England'.

[6] Fara, *Life after Gravity*, p xxxi.

[7] Author correspondence with Patricia Fara, 12 July 2023.

8   National Archives, MINT 19/2/604, Isaac Newton's 'Considerations upon trade', *c*.1701; digitized by The Newton Project: https://dev-newtonproject.history.ox.ac.uk/view/texts/diplomatic/MINT00346. [Accessed 16 May 2024].

9   National Archives, MINT 19/2/262, Isaac Newton's 'An account of the moneys coyned annually in the Tower', 6 April 1715; digitized by The Newton Project, Available from: www.newtonproject.ox.ac.uk/view/texts/diplomatic/MINT00571 [Accessed 16 May 2024].

10 Letter from Newton to the Lords Commissioners of the Treasury, including 'Observations upon the state of the coins of gold and silver', Cambridge University Library, MS Add. 9597/2/18/71-78; digitized by The Newton Project, Available from: https://hf-web-newton2.history.ox.ac.uk/view/texts/normalized/NATP00282 [Accessed 16 May 2024].

11 David Ricardo may have been the first to put forward the view that a mismatch in prices explains the adoption of the gold standard in Britain. In 1811, Ricardo noted the role of 'Sir I. Newton in 1717, then master of the Mint' and wrote 'it can, I think, be clearly proved that it [the gold standard] was caused entirely from the circumstance of the market value of silver relatively to gold having become greater than the Mint proportions'. See Ricardo, D. (1811) 'Reply to Mr. Bosanquet', in P. Sraffa (ed) (2004 [1951–1973]) *The Works and Correspondence of David Ricardo*, Vol 3: *Pamphlets and Papers, 1809–1811*, Liberty Fund Inc.

12 It is true that, from around 1700 to 1750, silver was worth more relative to gold in China, the world's largest economy, which sucked vast quantities of silver from Europe and the Americas. Flynn and Giraldez refer to this as the Mexican Silver Cycle. This alone does not explain Britain's tilt towards a de facto gold standard in 1717, as France (allied with the silver-producing Spanish Empire) maintained a bimetallic silver-and-gold monetary system until the late nineteenth century. Flynn and Giraldez note briefly: 'Brazilian gold facilitated England's transition to a bimetallic gold-silver monetary standard after the 1717 reforms of Isaac Newton'; see Flynn, D.O. and Giraldez, A. (2002) 'Cycles of silver: global economic unity through the mid-eighteenth-century', *Journal of World History*, 13(2): 391–427.

13 Vilar, P. (1976) *A History of Gold and Money, 1450–1920*, trans J. White, NLB, pp 220–221. This view was also put forward by British economic historian C.R. Fay, who wrote that Newton based his advice on the price of gold 'on a very precise survey of the European situation'. He remarked on the eighteenth century as 'the age of Brazilian gold' and that England, as the ally of Portugal, 'therefore shared in the gold trade from Brazil … the bulk of it came in British ships and found its way to England'. So that 'England rested her currency on the metal of which she had the first handling.' 'The new traffic helped to make London the monetary centre of Western Europe'; see Fay, C.R. (1935) 'Newton and the gold standard', *Cambridge Historical Journal*, 5(1): 109–117.

14 Alborn, T. (2019) *All That Glittered: Britain's Most Precious Metal from Adam Smith to the Gold Rush*, Oxford University Press, p 15.

15 Fara, *Life after Gravity*, writes that the Mint owned around fifty horses that operated 'the nine deafening presses [that] often started up at five in the morning and continued until midnight'.

16 Vilar, *A History of Gold*, p 230.

17 Palma, N. and Silva, A.C. (2021), 'Spending a windfall', Available from: https://ssrn.com/abstract=3928834 [Accessed 2021] wrote: 'These facts indicate that Brazilian gold may have doubled the stock of gold in Europe.'

18 Costa, L.F., Lains, P. and Miranda, S.M. (2016) *An Economic History of Portugal, 1143–2010*, Cambridge University Press, p 204.

19 Alborn, *All That Glittered*, p 18.

20 Koster, J.T. (1811) *Short Statement of the Trade in Gold Bullion*, available online via Google Books, p 15.

21 Francis, A.D. (1966) *The Methuens and Portugal, 1691–1708*, Cambridge University Press, p 128.

22 Alborn, *All That Glittered*, p 18.

23 Koster, *Short Statement*, p 15.

24 Sutherland, L.S. (1933) *A London Merchant, 1695–1774*, Oxford University Press; and Alborn, *All That Glittered*, pp 18–19.

25 Alborn, *All That Glittered*, p 18.

26 Smith, A. (1999 [1776]) *An Inquiry into the Nature and Causes of the Wealth of Nations*, Penguin Classics, Book 4, ch 6, pp 126–127.

27 Boxer, C.R. (1995 [1962]) *The Golden Age of Brazil*, Carcanet Press, p 304. See also 'National Palace of Mafra', Visit Lisboa: www.visitlisboa.com/en/places/national-palace-of-mafra [Accessed 16 May 2024].

28 Boxer, *The Golden Age*, opposite p 304. The British Gold State Coach—built in the Portuguese style in the 1760s near the height of the Brazilian gold rush—is still used for major royal occasions, most recently to carry the newly crowned King Charles III from Westminster Abbey back to Buckingham Palace.

29 Craig, *The Mint*, p 214.

30 Fisher, H.E.S. (1971) *The Portugal Trade: A Study of Anglo-Portuguese Commerce 1700–1770*, Methuen & Co, p 102.

31 Smith, *Wealth of Nations*, Book 4, ch 6, p 129.

32 Fisher, *The Portugal Trade*, pp 138–139.

33 Black, J. (2020) *A Brief History of Portugal*, Robinson, p 112.

34 This account draws on Weatherall, D. (1976) *David Ricardo: A Biography*, Martinus Nijhoff, p 4. See also British Library, Egerton MS 2227, 'D.M. Da Costa, letter book, 1757–59'. It is not clear from the letters whether the ducats were ever delivered.

35 Sutherland, *A London Merchant*, p 38.

36 Weatherall, *David Ricardo*, p 10, writes: 'For the next year, in October 1773, he [Abraham Ricardo] became what was called a "Jew Broker". It was a rare distinction. By law, all brokers were required to be licensed; by the regulations of the City of London, all brokers were required to be freemen; and since Jews could not take the oath and could not be freemen, 12 brokerships were set aside for them, and the 12 were called "Jew Brokers".'

37 Weatherall, *David Ricardo*, pp 4–7, and Heertje, A. (2004) 'The Dutch and Portuguese-Jewish background of David Ricardo', *European Journal of the History of Economic Thought*, 11(2): 281–294.

38 Bank of England (2019) 'Who is the Old Lady of Threadneedle Street?', www.bankofengland.co.uk/explainers/who-is-the-old-lady-of-threadneedle-street.

39 Koster, *Short Statement*, p 17.

40 Author calculations based on a 2013 database created by L.F. Costa, M.M. Rocha, and R.M. Sousa: O ouro do Brasil, 1700–1807. See especially 'Table II—amounts of gold shipped (1720–1807)', Available from: https://aquila.iseg.ulisboa.pt/aquila/investigacao/ghes/investigacao/bases-de-dados [Accessed 16 May 2024].

41 Braudel, F. (1984) *Civilization and Capitalism, 15th–18th Century*, Vol 3: *The Perspective of the World*, trans S. Reynolds, Harper & Row, p 364.

42 This account, and the anecdote about ladies shaving their hair, is based on Schwarcz, L.M. and Starling, H.M. (2017), *Brazil: A Biography*, Farrar, Straus and Giroux. Translated from Portuguese.

43 Koster, *Short Statement*, p 17.

44 Costa et al, O ouro do Brasil database.

45 Ricardo, D. (1810–1811) 'The high price of bullion', in Sraffa (ed) *The Works and Correspondence* (Vol. 3).

46 Laskaridis, C. (2016) 'A bicentenary review of Ricardo's proposals for an economical and secure currency', *History of Economics Review*, 65(1): 2–14. She writes on p 3: 'Ricardo's plan suggested a means to reinstitute a gold standard which would not rely on gold circulating domestically.'

47 Fetter, F.W. (1965) *Development of British Monetary Orthodoxy, 1797–1875*, Harvard University Press, p 91, said that Ricardo's bullion plan 'showed him at his best as an economist'.

48 Ricardo, 'The high price of bullion'.

49 Ricardo to Malthus, Letter 27, 22 October 1811, in Sraffa, P. (ed) (2004 [1951–1973]) *The Works and Correspondence of David Ricardo*, Vol 6, Liberty Fund Inc.

50 Redman, D.A. (1997) *The Rise of Political Economy as a Science*, MIT Press.

51 Ricardo, 'The high price of bullion'.

52 Ricardo, 'The high price of bullion'.

53 Peach, T. (2009 [1993]) *Interpreting Ricardo*, Cambridge University Press, p 43, wrote: 'Self-interested behaviour, the possession of accurate market knowledge (implicitly credited to the bullion merchants …), and impressively brisk responses to market signals were, and remained, the behavioural characteristics of Ricardo's "economic man".'

54 Watson, M. (2015) 'Following in John Methuen's early eighteenth-century footsteps: Ricardo's comparative advantage theory and the false foundations of the competitiveness of nations', Paper for 'Should Nation States Compete?' workshop, City, University of London, June, p 15.

Chapter 6: The Empire of Free Trade

1 Bernstein, W. (2009) *A Splendid Exchange*, Atlantic Books.

2 Bernhofen, D.M. and Brown, J.C. (2018) 'Retrospectives: on the genius behind David Ricardo's 1817 formulation of comparative advantage', *Journal of Economic Perspectives*, 32(4): 227–240. The authors write that they provide 'further evidence for the continuity of economic thought from the classical economists onward and the decisive break they represented with mercantilist thinking'.

3 Smith, A. (1999 [1776]) *An Inquiry into the Nature and Causes of the Wealth of Nations*, Penguin Classics, Book 4, ch 3.

4 Smith, *Wealth of Nations*, Book 4, ch 4.

5 Pitts, J. (2005) *A Turn to Empire*, Princeton University Press. Pitts documents how eighteenth-century liberals such as Adam Smith and Jeremy Bentham were hostile to European empires, and nineteenth-century liberals such as J.S. Mill much more supportive. She suggests that James Mill was a key figure in this change. In Pitts' analysis the turn towards empire was driven by a belief that colonial peoples were not fully rational and it was in their own best interests for them to be governed by technocratic European experts. Ricardo's thinking on empire can be situated within this shift, although he is not studied by Pitts.

6 Smith, *Wealth of Nations*, Book 4, chs 2 and 3.

7   The exception is seven pages of Ricardo's *Principles*, which make up chapter 25 'On colonial trade', where he acknowledges that colonial powers can benefit from controlling the terms of trade with their colonies and suggests that 'universal free trade' would be in the general benefit. Ricardo, D. (2004 [1817]) *The Principles of Political Economy and Taxation*, Dover Publications.

8   Semmel, B. (1970) *The Rise of Free Trade Imperialism*, Cambridge University Press. Thomas Piketty, citing figures from Kenneth Pomeranz, says that by 1830 British imports of cotton, wood, and sugar from overseas plantations were the product of 10 million hectares, which is between 1.5 and 2 times the total arable land in Britain: Piketty, T. (2021) *Une brève histoire de l'égalité*, Seuil, p 79.

9   Beckert, S. (2015) *Empire of Cotton*, Penguin, pp 48, 65.

10   Robins, N. (2012) *The Corporation That Changed the World* (2nd edn), Pluto Press, pp 181–184.

11   Beckert, *Empire of Cotton*, p 172.

12   Robins, *The Corporation*, p 183.

13   Clingingsmith, D. and Williamson, J.G. (2004) 'India's de-industrialization under British rule: new ideas, new evidence', NBER Working Paper No 10586, June.

14   Ricardo at the General Court of the East India Company, 19 March 1823, in P. Sraffa (ed) (2004 [1951–1973]) *The Works and Correspondence of David Ricardo*, 11 Vols, Vol 5, Liberty Fund Inc.

15   Ricardo at the General Court of the East India Company, 12 June 1822, in Sraffa (ed), *The Works and Correspondence* (Vol 5). The full quotation is: 'It was in vain for the [East India] Company to think of sending their goods to India, unless they could take what India was enabled to afford in return. (Hear, hear!) This position was so clear and self-evident, that he wondered any man could doubt it. If all restrictions were removed from the commerce of the country, and it was left to pursue that course which its own active principle would strike out, it would, most assuredly increase in an almost infinite degree.'

16   Smith, *Wealth of Nations*, Book 4, ch 7.

17   This right to collect taxes in Bengal on behalf of the Mughal Emperor is known as the 'Diwani'. It was formally agreed in the Treaty of Allahabad signed in August 1765 between the Emperor Shah Alam II and Robert Clive after the East India Company's victory (which Clive was not present for) at the Battle of Buxar in October 1764.

18   Hickel, J. (2018) 'How Britain stole $45 trillion from India', *Al Jazeera*, 19 December.

19   Beckert, *Empire of Cotton*, p 44.

20   Ricardo at the General Court of the East India Company, 12 June 1822, in Sraffa (ed), *The Works and Correspondence* (Vol 5).

21   Schwarcz, L.M. and Starling, H.M. (2017), *Brazil: A Biography*, Farrar, Straus and Giroux. Translated from Portuguese.

22   Letter from Strangford to Canning, 28 February 1809, National Archives, FO/63/68, 'Strangford in Brazil', pp 101–102, 124.

23   Cochrane had been convicted for fraud on the London Stock Exchange in 1814, briefly mentioned in Chapter 1, which began when men dressed as French soldiers spread fake news that Napoleon was dead. Many believe that he was wrongly convicted and charged due to his radical democratic advocacy. Cochrane left the UK in disgrace and played a pivotal role with the Chilean and Brazilian Navies in South America's liberation from Spanish and Portugal colonial rule. He was later

rehabilitated in Britain and his body is buried in the central nave of Westminster Abbey at the foot of Isaac Newton's monument.

24 Canning to Granville, 17 December 1824, in P.J.V. Rolo (1965) *George Canning*, Macmillan, p 134.

25 Cain, P.J. and Hopkins, A.G. (2016) *British Imperialism: 1688–2015* (3rd edn), Routledge, pp 270 and 280.

26 Chang, H.-J. (2008) *Bad Samaritans*, Random House, p 24. 'Britain first used unequal treaties in Latin America, starting with Brazil in 1810' (p 225). The term 'unequal treaties' was popularized by Chinese statesman and philosopher Sun Yat-sen in 1924.

27 Bernstein, *A Splendid Exchange*, pp 294–299.

28 Chang, *Bad Samaritans*, p 24.

29 In the twentieth century Argentine economist Raúl Prebisch would call these two poles of the global economy the periphery and the core.

30 Figures cited in Weber, I.M., Semieniuk, G., Westland, T. and Liang, J. (2021) 'What you exported matters', Rebuilding Macroeconomics Working Paper No 41, 11 February, p 6.

31 Weber et al, 'What you exported matters'.

32 Quoted in Semmel, *The Rise of Free Trade Imperialism*, p 135.

33 Ricardo to Trower, Letter 357, 13 March 1820, in Sraffa (ed), *The Works and Correspondence* (Vol 8). The petition was drafted by Thomas Tooke. Ricardo fully supported it and helped found the Political Economy Club in London with Tooke, who became a friend.

34 Álvaro Bardón quoted in Appelbaum, B. (2020) *The Economists' Hour*, Picador, p 269.

35 Ricardo in the House of Commons, 9 May 1822, in Sraffa (ed), *The Works and Correspondence* (Vol 5).

36 Halévy, E. (1934) *The Growth of Philosophical Radicalism*, trans M. Morris, Faber and Faber, p 342.

37 Robinson, J. (1977) 'What are the questions?', *Journal of Economic Literature*, 15(4): 1318–1339, 1336.

38 Cremaschi, S. (2021) *David Ricardo: An Intellectual Biography*, Routledge, and 'In our time: David Ricardo', BBC Radio 4, 25 March 2021.

39 Ricardo at the General Court of the East India Company, 19 March 1823, in Sraffa (ed), *The Works and Correspondence* (Vol 5).

40 Smith, *Wealth of Nations*, Book 3, ch 2.

41 Taylor, M. (2020) *The Interest*, Vintage, ch 8, and McDonnell, A. (1826) *Free Trade*, John Murray.

42 Carlyle, T. (1849) 'Occasional discourse on the Negro question', *Fraser's Magazine for Town and Country*, 40 (February). Earlier, Carlyle, commenting on Malthus' population principle, had called it: 'Dreary, stolid, dismal, without hope for this world or the next'; quoted in Carlyle, T. (1840) *Chartism*, James Fraser, p 109.

43 Olusoga, D. (2016) *Black and British: A Forgotten History*, Pan Books, p 24.

44 Carlyle, 'Occasional discourse'.

45 Heilbroner, R. (2000 [1953]) *The Worldly Philosophers: The Lives, Times and Ideas of the Great Economic Thinkers* (7th edn), Penguin Books, p 78: 'No wonder that after he read Malthus, Carlyle called economics "the dismal science"'; and Galbraith, J.K. (1977) *The Age of Uncertainty*, Houghton Mifflin Company, p 35—'It was with Malthus and Ricardo that economics became the dismal science.'

46 Smith, B. (2016) 'Slavery as free trade', *AEON*, 29 June.

[47] Taylor, *The Interest*, ch 1.

[48] Joseph Marryat (1757–1824), MP for Sandwich, slaveholder, and opponent of abolition, said in reply to Ricardo's speech: 'it was extremely amusing to hear hon. members, proprietors of East-India stock, declaiming in that House on the advantages of a free trade, at the very moment that they themselves were interested in one of the most outrageous monopolies that ever existed in any country in the world'. Ricardo replied 'he had never possessed a shilling more than 1000*l*. East-India stock, and never given a vote in favour of monopoly in his life'. See 'East and West India sugars', 22 May 1823, in Sraffa (ed), *The Works and Correspondence* (Vol 5).

[49] Smith, *Wealth of Nations*, Book 5, ch 1.

[50] Ricardo in the House of Commons on 'East and West India sugars', 22 May 1823, in Sraffa (ed), *The Works and Correspondence* (Vol 5).

[51] Ricardo at the General Court of the East India Company, 12 June 1822, in Sraffa (ed), *The Works and Correspondence* (Vol 5).

[52] Ricardo introduces the passage—an article for the *Encyclopaedia Britannica* written by McCulloch—, noting its 'excellent suggestions and observations'. It first appeared in the second edition of Ricardo's *Principles*. See Sraffa (ed), *The Works and Correspondence* (Vol 1).

[53] Piketty, *Une brève histoire*, pp 86–87.

[54] O'Neil, C. (2016) *Weapons of Math Destruction*, Penguin.

[55] Spiegel, H.W. (1991 [1971]) *The Growth of Economic Thought* (3rd edn), Duke University Press, p 336.

[56] Hutchison, T. (1994) *The Uses and Abuses of Economics*, Routledge, p 99.

Chapter 7: 'Dropped from Another Planet'

[1] Mankiw, N.G. (2021) *Principles of Economics, Ninth Edition*, Cengage.

[2] Ricardo drew on Adam Smith's work here but came to different conclusions. Smith had a more flexible view of classes or 'orders' in society. Smith wrote that the 'produce of the land and labour ... naturally divides itself ... into three parts; the rent of land, the wages of labour, and the profits of stock; and constitutes a revenue to three different orders of people.' Contrary to Ricardo, however, Smith thought that the interests of the capitalists living on profit were often directly opposed to the interests of society as a whole. 'Merchants and master manufacturers are,' Smith wrote, 'an order of men, whose interest is never exactly the same with that of the public, who have generally an interest to deceive and even to oppress the public, and who accordingly have, upon many occasions, both deceived and oppressed it.' Smith, A. (1999 [1776]) *An Inquiry into the Nature and Causes of the Wealth of Nations*, Penguin Classics, Book 1, ch 11.

[3] Ricardo, D. (2004 [1817]) *The Principles of Political Economy and Taxation*, Dover Publications, p 16.

[4] This interpretation is disputed by some scholars who point to Ricardo's occasional reference to wages being influenced by 'habit' or 'customs'. For example, Peach, T. (2003) 'Introduction', in *David Ricardo: Critical Responses*, 4 Vols, Routledge: 'Ricardo also allowed and hoped for an improvement in the material circumstances of labourers through their adoption of better "habits and customs".' My interpretation is that these passages from Ricardo were not incorporated into his theoretical mechanism of society.

[5] Heilbroner, R. (2000 [1953]) *The Worldly Philosophers: The Lives, Times and Ideas of the Great Economic Thinkers* (7th edn), Penguin Books, p 98.

[6] Ricardo, *The Principles*, p 1.

[7] See Davis, T. (2002) 'David Ricardo, financier and empirical economist', *European Journal of the History of Economic Thought*, 9(1): 1–16, and Davis, T. (2005) *Ricardo's Macroeconomics*, Cambridge University Press. Ricardo's 1822 pamphlet 'On protection of agriculture' is often noted as being more empirically based, but even here Ricardo uses imaginary cases and invented round numbers (such as '100,000 loaves') at times. Elsewhere, Davis notes that Ricardo appealed to 'remarkable facts' in making his case, but even this was about fluctuations in the gold price during the Napoleonic Wars and, thus, closely related to his trading work.

[8] For an explanation of classical political economy building deductive models on supposedly 'self-evident' principles see Coleman, W.O. (1996) 'How theory came to the English classical economists', *Scottish Journal of Political Economy*, 43(2): 207–228.

[9] Heilbroner, *The Worldly Philosophers*, p 85.

[10] De Quincey, T. (2000 [1821]) *Confessions of an English Opium-Eater*, available online via Project Gutenberg, Part II.

[11] See Ricardo to James Mill, Letter 173, 8 August 1816; James Mill to Ricardo, Letter 175, 14 August 1816; and James Mill to Ricardo, Letter 192, 18 November 1816, all in P. Sraffa (ed) (2004 [1951–1973]) *The Works and Correspondence of David Ricardo*, Vol 7: *Letters 1816–1818*, Liberty Fund Inc.

[12] David Ricardo praised Mill's book for exposing 'the actual, and past state of Hindustan [India], with a view to ascertain the validity of the claim which has been set up for them for high civilization, [this] appears to me to be most masterly, and cannot I think be refuted', in Ricardo to J.B. Say, Letter 243, 18 December 1817, in Sraffa (ed), *The Works and Correspondence* (Vol 7).

[13] Ricardo to Mill, Letter 242, 18 December 1817, in Sraffa (ed), *The Works and Correspondence* (Vol 7).

[14] Ricardo to Malthus, Letter 240, 16 December 1817, in Sraffa, P. (ed), *The Works and Correspondence* (Vol 7): 'if these in the Hindus are to be deemed marks of a high state of civilization, Africa, Mexico, Peru, Persia, and China, might also lay claim to the same character'.

[15] Mill, J. (1817) *The History of British India*, Vol 1: *Baldwin, Cradock, Joy*, p 6, available online via Google Books.

[16] Ricardo wrote of being 'hurried into all the horrors of a contested election' in Ricardo to James Mill, Letter 193, 2 December 1816. For Mill's comments see James Mill to Ricardo, Letter 186, 23 October 1816, and James Mill to Ricardo, Letter 195, 16 December 1816, both in Sraffa (ed), *The Works and Correspondence* (Vol 7).

[17] Weatherall, D. (1976) *David Ricardo: A Biography*, Martinus Nijhoff & Heertje.

[18] See TV episode 'Dish and dishonesty', *Blackadder the Third*, BBC, 17 September 1987.

[19] See Weatherall, *David Ricardo*, p 137.

[20] Fisher, D.R. (2009), *The History of Parliament: The House of Commons 1820–1832*, Cambridge University Press. Fisher says the population in 1821 was 2,877.

[21] Weatherall, *David Ricardo*, p 137.

[22] Ricardo to Malthus, Letter 87, 27 March 1815, in P. Sraffa (ed) (2004 [1951–1973]) *The Works and Correspondence of David Ricardo*, Vol 6: *Letters 1810–1815*, Liberty Fund Inc.

[23] 'Poor Rates Misapplication Bill. Volume 39: debated on Thursday 25 March 1819', British Parliament, Hansard, Available from: https://hansard.parliament.uk [Accessed 18 April 2024].

[24] David Ricardo 'Speeches in the House of Commons', 'Poor Rates Misapplication Bill', 25 March 1819, in P. Sraffa (ed) (2004 [1951–1973]) *The Works and Correspondence of David Ricardo*, Vol 5: *Speeches and Evidence*, Liberty Fund Inc.

[25] *Cobbett's Weekly Political Register*, 35(4), 11 September 1819, in W. Cobbett (1820) *Cobbett's Political Register* (Vol 35), William Benbow, pp 108–112, available online via Google Books.

[26] Mann, M. (2012 [1993]) *The Sources of Social Power* (Vol 2, new edn), Cambridge University Press, p 521: 'The central government had its priorities clear. During 1820–5, poor relief absorbed 6 percent of its expenditures, whereas cash transfers to bondholders absorbed 53 percent.'

[27] Ingrams, R. (2006) *The Life and Adventures of William Cobbett*, Harper Perennial.

[28] Change Alley, or Exchange Alley, is the street in London where stockbrokers traditionally carried out their business. *Cobbett's Weekly Political Register*, 36(10), 20 May 1820, in W. Cobbett (1820) *Cobbett's Political Register* (Vol 36), William Benbow, p 708, available online at Google Books.

[29] King, J.E. (2013) *David Ricardo*, Palgrave Macmillan, p 46.

[30] Weatherall, *David Ricardo*, p 96.

[31] Ricardo, *The Principles*, p 63.

[32] David Ricardo, 'Poor Rates Misapplication Bill', 25 March 1819, in Sraffa (ed), *The Works and Correspondence* (Vol 5).

[33] David Ricardo, '[ON MR RANDLE JACKSON'S SPEECH] BULLION REPORT To the Editor of the Morning Chronicle', 24 September 1810, in P. Sraffa (ed) (2004 [1951–1973]) *The Works and Correspondence of David Ricardo*, Vol 3: *Pamphlets and Papers 1809–1811*, Liberty Fund Inc.

[34] Coleman, 'How theory came'.

[35] In contrast to this, Ricardo once wrote 'If the facts had been as here stated by Mr Bosanquet, I should have found it difficult to reconcile them with my theory.' The article this comes from is often praised as a high-note of Ricardo as an empirical economist but it is also notable for an early elaboration of theory of 'economic man'. The facts that Ricardo disputes are related to gold trading, a subject close to his financial experience. See Ricardo, D. (1811) 'Reply to Mr. Bosanquet's "Practical observations on the report of the Bullion Committee"', in Sraffa (ed), *The Works and Correspondence* (Vol 3).

[36] 'Agricultural distress. Volume 1: debated on Tuesday 30 May 1820', British Parliament, Hansard, Available from: https://hansard.parliament.uk [Accessed 18 April 2024].

[37] 'Lord Brougham's sketch of Ricardo in parliament', 1839, in Sraffa (ed), *The Works and Correspondence* (Vol 5).

[38] Ricardo, *The Principles*, pp 15–16.

[39] Ricardo, D. (1815) 'An essay on the influence of a low price of corn on the profits of stock', in Sraffa (ed), *The Works and Correspondence* (Vol 4).

[40] Mitchell, W.C. (1929) 'Postulates and preconceptions of Ricardian economics', in T.V. Smith and W.K. Wright (eds) *Essays in Philosophy*, Open Court Publishing, p 52.

[41] Say, J.B. (1819) *Traité d'économie politique* (Vol 1, 4th edn), Deterville, pp lxiv–lxv. Author's translation from the French.

[42] Diary of John Cam Hobhouse, later Baron Broughton (1786–1869), Vol 28, '1819: Don Juan, Westminster, Peterloo', p 606, Available from: https://petercochran. wordpress.com/hobhouses-diary/ [Accessed 18 April 2024]. He writes that after dinner at Brooks's club in London on 22 April 1819: 'Went upstairs to

Mrs Ricardo—she told me that Malthus and her husband would sometimes sit up till three in the morning, defining "rent"!!'

43 'It was to support the principles of the merchants' petition [presented to the House of Commons by Alexander Baring on 8 May 1820] that Tooke, with Ricardo, Malthus, James Mill, and others, founded the Political Economy Club in April 1821.' See G.H. Murray, 'Tooke, William', in *Dictionary of National Biography*, Vol 57: *1885–1900*, Smith, Elder, & Co., p 49.

44 Walter, R. (2021) *Before Method and Models: The Political Economy of Malthus and Ricardo*, Oxford University Press.

45 Ricardo to Malthus, Letter 127, 7 October 1815, in Sraffa (ed), *The Works and Correspondence* (Vol 6).

46 Ricardo to Malthus, Letter 199, 24 January 1817 in Sraffa (ed), *The Works and Correspondence* (Vol 7). Ricardo continues: 'To manage the subject quite right they should be carefully distinguished and mentioned, and the due effects ascribed to each.'

47 Malthus, T.R. (1820) 'Introduction', in *Principles of Political Economy*, John Murray.

48 Malthus (1820).

49 Ricardo to Malthus, Letter 363, 4 May 1820, in P. Sraffa (ed) (2004 [1951–1973]) *The Works and Correspondence of David Ricardo*, Vol 8: *Letters 1819–June 1821*, Liberty Fund Inc.

50 Ricardo to James Mill, Letter 414, 1 January 1821, in Sraffa (ed), *The Works and Correspondence* (Vol 8).

51 Ricardo, D. (1822) 'Journal of a tour on the continent', in P. Sraffa (ed) (2004 [1951–1973]) *The Works and Correspondence of David Ricardo*, Vol 10: *Biographical Miscellany*, Liberty Fund Inc, entry for 19 September 1822. The political economists and poets of early 1800s had numerous interactions that have not been adequately studied.

52 Ricardo, 'Journal of a tour on the continent', entry for 24 October 1822.

53 James Mill to J.R. McCulloch, Letter 555, 19 September 1823, in P. Sraffa (ed) (2004 [1951–1973]) *The Works and Correspondence of David Ricardo*, Vol 9: *Letters 1821–1823*, Liberty Fund Inc.

54 Ricardo, M. (1824) 'A memoir of David Ricardo', in Sraffa (ed), *The Works and Correspondence* (Vol 10).

55 'Lord Brougham's sketch of Ricardo in parliament'. A version of this paragraph appeared in an entry called 'It's 200 years since David Ricardo died—here's why I've written a book about his legacy' on my website—www.natdyer.com—on 11 September 2023.

56 Mill, J.S. (2003 [1873]) *Autobiography*, available online via Project Gutenberg, ch 1.

Chapter 8: 'Purely Hypothetical Truths'

1 Laura J. Snyder, the contemporary expert on William Whewell, sums up his diverse interests by describing him as 'a mathematical-mineralogist-architectural historian-linguist-classicist-physicist-geologist-historian-philosopher-theologian-mountainclimbing-poet'! See Snyder, L.J. (2011) *The Philosophical Breakfast Club*, Broadway Paperbacks, p 366.

2 Porter, T.M. (1995) *Trust in Numbers: The Pursuit of Objectivity in Science and Public Life*, Princeton University Press, p 84.

3 Snyder, *The Philosophical Breakfast Club*, p 101.

4   BAAS is now the British Science Association (BSA) and the Statistical Society of London is now the Royal Statistical Society (RSS). See Snyder, L.J. (2006) *Reforming Philosophy*, University of Chicago Press, p 280.

5   Whewell to Jones, 3 November 1822, cited in Snyder, *The Philosophical Breakfast Club*, p 104.

6   Whewell to Jones, 24 May 1825, cited in Snyder, *The Philosophical Breakfast Club*, p 104.

7   Whewell to Jones, 20 January 1833, cited in Snyder, *Reforming Philosophy*, p 34.

8   Whewell and John Stuart Mill had a long public debate about the definitions and usefulness of 'induction' and 'deduction', which is beyond the scope of this chapter.

9   From Francis Bacon's *The Great Instauration*, reproduced in Sargent, R.M. (1999) *Francis Bacon: Selected Philosophical Works*, Hackett Publishing, p 74.

10   From Francis Bacon's *The New Organon*, Book 1, Aphorism 95, in Sargent, *Francis Bacon*, p 128.

11   From Francis Bacon's *The New Organon*, Book 1, Aphorism 95, in Sargent, *Francis Bacon*, p 128. See also Snyder, *The Philosophical Breakfast Club*, pp 37–41.

12   All cited in Snyder, L.J. (2022) 'William Whewell', in E.N. Zalta and U. Nodelman (eds) *The Stanford Encyclopedia of Philosophy*, Available from https://plato.stanford.edu/entries/whewell/ [Accessed 16 May 2024].

13   Whewell, W. (1829) 'Mathematical exposition of some doctrines of political economy', Paper read to the Cambridge Philosophical Society, 2 and 14 March.

14   Snyder, *The Philosophical Breakfast Club*, pp 104–105.

15   Jones, R. (1831) *An Essay on the Distribution of Wealth and on the Sources of Taxation*, John Murray, p 14: 'In England and in most parts of the Netherlands secondary rents exclusively prevail. ... We shall be making on the whole an extravagant allowance, if we suppose them to occupy one-hundredth part of the cultivated surface of the habitable globe.'

16   Jones, *An Essay*, calls these four types of 'peasant rents': serf, métayer (a type of sharecropping), ryot, and cottier rents. The exact details need not concern us here.

17   Jones, *An Essay*.

18   Jones to Whewell, 27 September 1827, cited in Snyder, *Reforming Philosophy*, p 286.

19   Jones, *An Essay*, p vii.

20   Jones, R. (1833) *An Introductory Lecture on Political Economy*, delivered at King's College, London, 27 February, John Murray, pp 31–32.

21   Whewell, W. (1859) *Literary Remains of the Late Rev. Richard Jones*, John Murray.

22   I went to school at Haileybury College, which occupies the grounds and buildings of what used to be the East India Company College. My politics lessons took place in a building named after Malthus.

23   Snyder, *The Philosophical Breakfast Club*, p 180.

24   Snyder, *The Philosophical Breakfast Club*, pp 124–125.

25   Reeves, R. (2006) 'John Stuart Mill', *Prospect*, 19 May.

26   Mill, J.S. (2003 [1873]) *Autobiography*, available online via Project Gutenberg, ch 1.

27   Mill, *Autobiography*, ch 1. This text became the basis of James Mill's *Elements of Political Economy* (1821), which popularized Ricardian theories.

28   Mill, *Autobiography*, ch 2: 'David Ricardo ... after I became a student of political economy, invited me to his house and to walk with him in order to converse on the subject.'

29   Mill, *Autobiography*, ch 4: 'The first writings of mine which got into print were two letters published towards the end of 1822, in the *Traveller* evening newspaper. ... Colonel Torrens himself wrote much of the political economy of his paper; and

had at this time made an attack upon some opinion of Ricardo and my father, to which, at my father's instigation, I attempted an answer.'

[30] Mill, *Autobiography*, ch 4.

[31] Mill, J.S. (1848) *Principles of Political Economy*, John W. Parker, p 467.

[32] Letter from Mill to William Tait, an Edinburgh publisher, 24 September 1833, in J.M. Robson (ed) (1963–1991), *Collected Works of John Stuart Mill*, Vol 12: *The Early Letters*, University of Toronto Press.

[33] Although written between 1829 and 1833, only one of J.S. Mill's essays was published before 1844. See Mill, J.S. (1844) *Essays on Some Unsettled Questions of Political Economy*, John W. Parker.

[34] Mill, J.S. (1836) 'On the definition of political economy; and on the method of philosophical investigation in that science', *London and Westminster Revue*, October; reprinted in Mill, *Essays on Some Unsettled Questions*.

[35] All from Mill, 'On the definition of political economy'.

[36] Mill, 'On the definition of political economy'.

[37] Mill, 'On the definition of political economy'.

[38] As Mill describes it is the difference 'between the art of gunnery and the theory of projectiles', Mill, 'On the definition of political economy'.

[39] Mill, 'On the definition of political economy'.

[40] Hume, D. (1739) *A Treatise of Human Nature*, Book 3, Part I, Section I.

[41] This formulation in indebted to political economist Thomas Cliffe Leslie (1825–1882), who wrote, as we will see in Chapter 9, that the methods of Ricardo and his followers: 'greatly thicken the confusion perpetually arising between the real and the ideal, between that which by the assumption ought to be and that which actually is'. From Cliffe Leslie, T.E. (1870), 'The political economy of Adam Smith', *Fortnightly Review*, 1 November.

[42] William Coleman explains that English classical economists derived their certainty in the theoretical method from the teachings of Dugald Stewart (1753–1828), Adam Smith's literary agent and popularizer, as well as the French economists of the eighteenth century such as Turgot. See Coleman, W.O. (1996) 'How theory came to English classical economics', *Scottish Journal of Political Economy*, 43(2): 207–228.

[43] Senior, N.W. (1836) *An Outline of the Science of Political Economy*, W. Clowes and Sons. A year later, Senior opposed the proposed Factory Acts, which would limit children and women to ten hours work per day, with an analytical argument that the law would push factory owners to bankruptcy. The law eventually passed in 1847 and the industry did not fold.

[44] William Whewell's 1845 *The Elements of Morality, Including Polity*, cited in Snyder, *The Philosophical Breakfast Club*, pp 105–108. See also Snyder, *Reforming Philosophy*, pp 291–305.

[45] Snyder, *Reforming Philosophy*, p 319.

[46] It is estimated that there were 40–50,000 excess deaths in Belgium, 42,000 in Prussia, and 10,000 in France. See Vanhaute, E., Paping, R. and Ó Gráda, C. (2006) 'The European subsistence crisis of 1845–1850: a comparative perspective', Working Paper, School of Economics, University College Dublin.

[47] Smyth, W.J. (2013) 'The story of the Great Irish Famine 1845–52', in J. Crowley, W.J. Smyth, and M. Murphy (eds) *Atlas of the Great Irish Famine*, New York University Press, pp 4–5.

[48] Carroll, R. (2021) 'Ireland's population passes 5m for first time since C19th famine', *The Guardian*, 31 August. There were an estimated 8 million people in Ireland in

the early 1840s. In 2023, the combined population of the Republic of Ireland and Northern Ireland was 6.9 million, the highest since the mid-nineteenth century.

49 See Trevelyan, C.E. (1848) *The Irish Crisis*, Longmans; and Nally, D. (2013) 'The colonial dimensions of the Great Irish Famine', in Crowley et al (eds), *Atlas*.

50 Trevelyan, *The Irish Crisis*; and Crowley et al (eds), *Atlas*.

51 Trevelyan, *The Irish Crisis*, p 45.

52 Trevelyan, *The Irish Crisis*, p 74.

53 Crowley et al (eds), *Atlas*.

54 Hatton, H.E. (1993) *The Largest Amount of Good: Quaker Relief in Ireland, 1654–1921*, McGill-Queen's University Press, p 142.

55 Letter from Maria Edgeworth to Honora Beaufort, her sister, 8 May 1847. The woman had been seen by Hugh Tuite, a local MP and landowner. 'Maria Edgeworth', Maria Edgeworth Centre, Available from: https://mariaedgeworthcenter.com/meet-the-edgeworths/the-edgeworth-family/maria-edgeworth-5/ [Accessed 16 May 2024].

56 Letter by Maria Edgeworth, April 1849, cited in Castles, I. (1984) 'Economics and anti-economics', Paper presented at the ANZAAS Economics Section, 18 May.

57 Ricardo to Maria Edgeworth, Letter 551, 13 December 1822, in P. Sraffa (ed) (2004 [1951–1973] *The Works and Correspondence of David Ricardo*, Vol 9: *Letters 1821–1823*, Liberty Fund Inc.

58 Mill, J.S. (1845) 'Review of *The Logic of Political Economy* by Thomas De Quincey', June, *Westminster Review*, 43, p 320.

59 Note the continuing discussion among historians of economics on this point. Peach, T. (2003) 'Introduction', in *David Ricardo: Critical Responses*, 4 Vols, Routledge, p 33: 'Just how far this work [Mill's *Principles*] was truly Ricardian is something on which there is no settled opinion among historians of economic thought. It will suffice to observe, first, that Mill's contemporaries identified themes in his *Principles* that are clearly derived from Ricardo …'.

60 Mill, 'Review', p 320, said that new developments such as Richard Jones' *Essay* were not 'contradictions' but rather 'developments' of Ricardo's principles: 'What has been added to the science since Ricardo, does not need to be substituted for his doctrines, but to be incorporated with them. They do not require alteration or correction, so much as fuller exposition and comment.'

61 Mill, *Autobiography*, ch 7.

62 Letter from J.S. Mill to John Austin, 22 February 1848, in J.M. Robson (ed) (1963–1991), *Collected Works of John Stuart Mill*, Vol 13: *The Earlier Letters 1812–1848 Part II*, University of Toronto Press.

63 Mill, *Essays on Some Unsettled Questions*.

64 Mill, *Principles of Political Economy*, Book 3, ch 1: 'Inattention to these distinctions [the gap between theory and reality] has led to improper applications of the abstract principles of political economy, and still oftener to an undue discrediting of those principles through their being compared with a different sort of facts from those which they contemplate, or which can fairly be expected to accord with them.'

65 Mill, *Autobiography*.

66 For Mill's comments on Jones see Mill, *Principles of Political Economy*, Book 3, ch 5. For Whewell's response see Snyder, *Reforming Philosophy*, pp 316, 319–320.

67 Mill, *Principles of Political Economy*, preface.

68 Blaug, M. (1997) *The Methodology of Economics* (2nd edn), Cambridge University Press, p 65.

69 Mill, *Principles of Political Economy*, Book 4, ch 2.

70   Blaug, *The Methodology of Economics*, pp 65–67.
71   Online links to the editions of Mill's *Principles* are on the 'John Stuart Mill' page of the History of Economic Thought website, Available from: www.hetwebsite.net/het/profiles/mill.htm [Accessed 16 May 2024]. Mill's first edition (in 1848) said 15 to 20 years, the fifth edition (in 1862) also said 15 to 20 years, the sixth edition (in 1865) said 20 to 25 years, and the seventh edition (in 1871) said 20 to 30 years.
72   Blaug, M. (1958) *Ricardian Economics*, Yale University Press, pp 187–188. He continues 'the explanation is not, as is sometimes supposed, that a paucity of statistical material in the period made it impossible to entertain any but an abstract and deductive approach to economic reasoning. ... Rather, despite the wealth of evidence, methodological predilections barred the way to a serious consideration of the empirical relevance of theory.'

Chapter 9: The Fall

1   Dickens, C. (2017 [1843]) *A Christmas Carol*, Penguin, p 7.
2   Dickens, C. (1969 [1854]) *Hard Times*, Penguin, ch 9, p 95. Dickens' social criticism jeopardized his reputation. American critic Edwin Percy Whipple, according to Dickens scholar George Ford, considered it immature to oppose: 'the established laws of political economy, which he [Whipple] considered on par with those of the physical universe', cited by D. Craig in 'Introduction', Dickens, *Hard Times*, p 20.
3   Ruskin, J. (2000 [1862]) *Unto This Last: Four Essays on the First Principles of Political Economy*, Hendon Publishing.
4   Mill, J.S. (2003 [1873]) *Autobiography*, available online via Project Gutenberg, ch 7; and Coyle, D. (2021) *Cogs and Monsters: What Economics Is, and What It Should Be*, Princeton University Press, p 20.
5   There is a substantial literature on the *Methodenstreit* or 'battle of methods' in economics between the Austrian School focused on logical deduction and the German Historical School in the 1880s. This chapter focuses on related methodological battles among economists in the UK and US.
6   Cliffe Leslie, T.E. (1870) 'The political economy of Adam Smith', *Fortnightly Review*, 1 November.
7   Cliffe Leslie, T.E. (1870) *Land Systems and Industrial Economy*, Longmans, Green, and Co, p 89; original emphasis.
8   Cliffe Leslie, *Land Systems*, p 358.
9   Cliffe Leslie, *Land Systems*, pp 90 and 357. See also p 379: 'Political economy must be content to take rank as an inductive, instead of a purely deductive science and it will gain in utility, interest, and real truth, far more than a full compensation for the forfeiture of a fictitious title to mathematical exactness and certainty.'
10   Mill, J.S. (1870) 'Professor Leslie on the land question', *Fortnightly Review*, 1 June.
11   Blaug, M. (ed) (1986) *Who's Who in Economics* (2nd edn), Wheatsheaf Books, p 139 (entry for 'Carines, John Elliot').
12   Cairnes, J.E. (1875) *The Character and Logical Method of Political Economy* (2nd edn), Harper & Brothers, p 75; original emphasis.
13   Cairnes, *The Character*, p 81.
14   Cairnes had even abandoned his own method in *The Slave Power*, which helped sway British opinion towards the Union in the American Civil War. Blaug (ed), *Who's Who*, p 139.
15   Jevons, W.S. (1879) *The Theory of Political Economy* (2nd edn), Macmillan, p lvii.
16   Raworth, K. (2018) *Doughnut Economics*, Random House, pp 16–17.

17 Frisch, R. (1970) 'From Utopian theory to practical applications: the case of econometrics', Nobel Lecture, 17 June.

18 Jevons, *The Theory of Political Economy*.

19 Bagehot, W. (1880) *Economic Studies*, Longmans, pp 151–160.

20 Ingram, J.K. (1886) 'Ricardo, David', in *Encyclopaedia Britannica*, A & C Black, (Vol 20, 9th edn), pp 533–535. Ingram makes clear that the criticism of Ricardo's economics do not extend to his work on currency and banking.

21 This is a paraphrase of a comment by E.C.K. Gonner, who wrote in 1890: 'At one time, no name could more effectually guarantee an opinion against contemptuous treatment; at the present, the mere suggestion that such and such a view was held by Ricardo sounds an initial note of discredit.' See Gonner, E.C.K. (1890) 'Ricardo and his critics', *Quarterly Journal of Economics*, 4(3): 276–290.

22 See Marshall, A. (1890) *Principles of Economics*, Macmillan, Book 1; and Backhouse, R.E. and Medema, S.G. (2009) 'Retrospectives: on the definition of economics', *Journal of Economic Perspectives*, 23(1): 225.

23 Jevons, *The Theory of Political Economy*, p xiv.

24 Marshall, *Principles of Economics*, pp 63 and 67.

25 See Marshall, *Principles of Economics*, p 67, and Marshall, A. (1885) *The Present Position of Economics*, Lecture delivered 24 February, Macmillan, p 25.

26 Ashley, W.J. (1891) 'The rehabilitation of Ricardo', *Economic Journal*, 1(3): 474–489.

27 Schumpeter, J.A. (1954) *History of Economic Analysis*, Routledge, p 804.

28 Quotations from Keynes, J.N. (1891) *The Scope and Method of Political Economy*, Macmillan, pp 149, 214, 223; with the exception of the quotation that begins 'closing one's eyes …', which is from Keynes, J.N. (1904) *The Scope and Method of Political Economy* (rev 3rd edn), Macmillan, p 227.

29 Polanyi, K (2001 [1944]) *The Great Transformation*, Beacon Press, p 131: 'From this time onward naturalism haunted the science of man, and the reintegration of society into the human world became the persistently sought aim of the evolution of social thought. Marxian economics—in this line of argument—was an essentially unsuccessful attempt to achieve that aim, a failure due to Marx's too close adherence to Ricardo and the traditions of liberal economics.'

30 'AEA renames annual Richard T. Ely lecture', AEA, 1 October 2020 [online].

31 White, M. (1957) *Social Thought in America: The Revolt against Formalism*, Beacon Press, p 11.

32 Bee, M. and Desmarais-Tremblay, M. (2023). 'The birth of homo œconomicus', *Journal of the History of Economic Thought*, 45(1): 1–26.

33 See Marçal, K. (2018) *Who Cooked Adam Smith's Dinner?*, trans S. Vogel, Granta.

34 Morgan, M. (2012) *The World in the Model*, Cambridge University Press, p 138. See also Norman, J. (2018) *Adam Smith*, Penguin Books, p 186: 'There is no mention of rational economic man or *homo economicus* in his work, and in many ways the idea is foreign to his thinking.'

35 See Morgan, *The World in the Model*, pp 139–141, and Bee and Desmarais-Tremblay, 'The birth'.

36 Mill, J.S. (1836) 'On the definition of political economy; and on the method of philosophical investigation in that science', *London and Westminster Revue*, October.

37 Ricardo, D. (1811) *Observations on some Passages in an Article in the Edinburgh Review, on the Depreciation of the Paper Currency*, John Murray, p 4. Reprinted as an appendix to the fourth edition of Ricardo's 'The high price of bullion', in P. Sraffa (ed) (2004 [1951–1973]) *The Works and Correspondence of David Ricardo*, Vol 3: *Pamphlets and Papers, 1809–1811*, Liberty Fund Inc.

38 Ricardo used 'city' in this way, see for example Ricardo to Malthus, Letter 153, 10 January 1816, in P. Sraffa (ed) (2004 [1951–1973]) *The Works and Correspondence of David Ricardo*, Vol 7: *Letters 1816–1818*, Liberty Fund Inc: 'In the city, at the Stock Exchange, any of my brothers will inform you about me.'

39 Marshall, *Principles of Economics*, Book 1, p 62.

40 Marshall, *Principles of Economics*, p vii.

41 Keynes (1891) *The Scope*, pp 278–279.

42 Keynes (1891) *The Scope*, p 278: 'Ricardo himself never explicitly formulated them [the assumptions on which his reasoning proceeds] probably because they seemed to him in no sense arbitrary abstractions, but patent facts to which it was unnecessary specially to call attention.'

43 Peach, T. (2009 [1993]) *Interpreting Ricardo*, Cambridge University Press, p 141.

44 Mary Morgan's excellent chapter on the development of 'economic man' (or 'human' as I've called them here) shows that different economic men have been created by Stanley Jevons, Carl Menger, Frank Knight, and others. Morgan, *The World in the Model*, ch 4.

45 Kahneman, D. (2011) *Thinking, Fast and Slow*, Farrar, Straus and Giroux, ch 27.

46 Greenspan, A. (2013) 'Never saw it coming', *Foreign Affairs*, November/December, p 90.

47 I am indebted here to Mary Midgley's thinking on technical and general meaning of terms in Midgley, M. (1983) 'Selfish genes and Social Darwinism', *Philosophy*, 58(225): 365–377.

48 Kay, J. (2017), 'Behavioural economics: did Kahneman and Tversky change the world?', *Prospect*, February.

49 Gerstle, G. (2022) *The Rise and Fall of the Neoliberal Order*, Oxford University Press, p 19.

50 Kay, J. and King, M. (2020) *Radical Uncertainty*, Bridge Street Press.

51 Keynes, J.M. (1936) 'Preface to the German Edition' of the General Theory.

52 Pigou, A.C. (1936) 'Mr J.M. Keynes' *General Theory of Employment, Interest and Money*', *Economica*, 3(10): 'Einstein actually did for Physics what Mr. Keynes believes himself to have done for Economics. He developed a far-reaching generalisation, under which Newton's results can be subsumed as a special case.'

53 Keynes, J.M. (1936) *The General Theory of Employment, Interest and Money*, Macmillan, appendix to ch 14.

54 Keynes, *The General Theory*, ch 3 and preface.

55 Keynes, J.M. (1933), *Essays in Biography*, Macmillan, 'Robert Malthus', p 144.

56 Keynes, *The General Theory*, ch 3.

57 Ricardo, D. (2004 [1817]) *The Principles of Political Economy and Taxation*, Dover Publications, ch 2. As usual, this was narrower than Adam Smith's conception of rent.

58 Keynes, *The General Theory*, ch 24.

59 Samuelson, P.A. (1946) 'Lord Keynes and the general theory', *Econometrica*, 14(3): 187–200.

60 Schumpeter, *History of Economic Analysis*, ch 2.

61 Schumpeter, *History of Economic Analysis*, ch 4.

62 Schumpeter, *History of Economic Analysis*, ch 4.

63 Schumpeter accused Keynes also of falling into the Ricardian Vice. Although acknowledging that Keynes and Ricardo came to divergent conclusions their method of 'securing the clear-cut result', he claimed meant they were 'brothers in spirit'. Schumpeter, *History of Economic Analysis*, ch 4.

[64] See, for example, Rodrik, D. (2017) *Economics Rules*, Oxford University Press, p 133.

Chapter 10: The Return of Unreality

[1] Gerstle, G. (2022) *The Rise and Fall of the Neoliberal Order*, Oxford University Press, p 46; see also all of chapter 1.

[2] Piketty, T. (2021) *Une brève histoire de l'égalité*, Seuil, ch 6.

[3] Galbraith, J.K. (1948) *American Capitalism*, Riverside Press, p 1. This story probably comes from a 1934 book *Le vol des insectes* by Antoine Magnan, a French zoologist and aeronautical engineer. Magnan calculated that according to known aviation theory bumblebee flight is impossible. Zoologists have since revealed biological tricks the bumblebee uses that were not used in human flight.

[4] Weinstein, M.M. (2009) 'Paul A. Samuelson, economist, dies at 94', *New York Times*, 13 December, incorrectly suggests that the triplets arrived before *Economics* in 1948. They were born in 1953.

[5] 'Paul A. Samuelson', The Nobel Prize, Available from: www.nobelprize.org/prizes/economic-sciences/1970/samuelson [Accessed 16 May 2024].

[6] Thompson, D. (2009) 'An interview with Paul Samuelson, part one', *The Atlantic*, 17 June.

[7] Leijonhufvud, A. (1968), *On Keynesian Economics and the Economics of Keynes*, Oxford University Press.

[8] Samuelson, P.A. (1946) 'Lord Keynes and the general theory', *Econometrica*, 14(3): 187–200: 'until the appearance of the mathematical models of Meade, Lange, Hicks, and Harrod there is reason to believe that Keynes himself did not truly understand his own analysis'.

[9] Morgan, M.S. (2012) *The World in the Model*, Cambridge University Press, p 10.

[10] Koopmans, T.C. (1947) 'Measurement without theory', *Review of Economics and Statistics*, 29(3): 161–172.

[11] Tinbergen received the prize in 1969 and Koopmans in 1975.

[12] Samuelson, P.A. (1948) *Economics: An Introductory Analysis* (1st edn), McGraw-Hill, p 10.

[13] The term comes from Thompson, E. (2022) *Escape from Model Land*, Basic Books.

[14] Samuelson, *Economics*, ch 23, p 538.

[15] Samuelson, *Economics*, ch 3, p 36.

[16] Schumpeter, J.A. (1954) *History of Economic Analysis*, Routledge, p 447, n2. Edited from a manuscript by Elizabeth Boody Schumpeter.

[17] Leontief, W. (1953) 'Domestic production and foreign trade: the American capital position re-examined', *Proceedings of the American Philosophical Society*, 97(4): 332–349.

[18] Backhouse, R. (2010) *The Puzzle of Modern Economics*, Cambridge University Press, p 122.

[19] Napolitano, G. (1978) 'Our debt to Sraffa', *New Left Review*, 112.

[20] Porta, P.L. (2009) 'How Piero Sraffa took up the editorship of David Ricardo's works and correspondence', *Journal of the History of Economic Thought*, 11 June.

[21] See, for example, John Eatwell, who wrote that Sraffa's work on Ricardo 'penetrated a hundred years of misunderstanding and distortion': Eatwell, J. (1984) 'Piero Sraffa: seminal economic theorist', *Science and Society*, 48(2): 211–216.

[22] Stigler, G.J. (1953) 'Sraffa's Ricardo', *American Economic Review*, 43(4): 586–599.

[23] *The Economist* (1951) 'The scholar's Ricardo', 1 September.

[24] Peach, T. (2009 [1993]) *Interpreting Ricardo*, Cambridge University Press, p 303.

[25] Samuelson, P.A. (1964), 'Theory and realism: a reply', *American Economic Review*, 54(5): 736–739.

[26] Friedman, M. (1953) 'The methodology of positive economics', in *Essays in Positive Economics*, University of Chicago Press, pp 3–43.

[27] Rodrik, D. (2017) *Economics Rules*, Oxford University Press, p 26.

[28] Friedman, 'The methodology', p 40.

[29] Friedman, 'The methodology', p 14.

[30] Marshall, A. (1885) *The Present Position of Economics*, Lecture delivered 24 February, Macmillan, p 25: 'I do not assign any universality to economic dogmas. For the theory, which is the only part of economic doctrine that has any claim to universality has no dogmas. It is not a body of concrete truth, but an engine for the discovery of concrete truth'; and p 19: 'Much as Ricardo and his chief followers are blamed for what they omitted to do ... what they were building up was not universal truth, but a machinery of universal application in the discovery of a certain class of truth.'

[31] Friedman, 'The methodology' p 35: 'Marshall took the world as it is, he sought to construct an "engine" to analyse it, not a photographic reproduction of it.'

[32] See MacKenzie, D. (2006) *An Engine, Not a Camera*, MIT Press.

[33] Hausman, D.M. (2021) 'Philosophy of economics', in E.N. Zalta (ed) *The Stanford Encyclopedia of Philosophy*, Available from: https://plato.stanford.edu/entries/economics [Accessed 16 May 2024]: 'Friedman's methodology ... has been deployed in service of a rigid theoretical orthodoxy.' He says that although its influence had waned due to an empirical turn in economics from the 2000s, the essay still serves 'as a way of avoiding awkward questions concerning simplifications, idealizations, and abstraction in economics rather than responding to them'.

[34] Friedman, 'The methodology'.

[35] The theory of science referenced is Karl Popper's falsification theory, a critique of which is beyond the scope of this chapter.

[36] Hausman, 'Philosophy of economics': Hausman argues that in Friedman's methodology: 'economists need not worry about ever encountering evidence that would strongly disconfirm fundamental theory'.

[37] Blaug, M. (1997) *The Methodology of Economics* (2nd edn), Cambridge University Press.

[38] Friedman, 'The methodology', p 43.

[39] The Allied Social Science Associations panel 'Problems of Methodology' was held in the Aero Room, Pittsburgh, at 2.30 pm on Saturday, 29 December 1962; see www.aeaweb.org/conference/past-annual-meetings.

[40] Archibald, G.C., Simon, H.A. and Samuelson, P.A. (1963), 'Papers and proceedings of the seventy-fifth annual meeting of the American Economic Association', *American Economic Review*, 53(2): 227–236.

[41] Samuelson, 'Theory and realism'.

[42] Simon's aim was to lay the 'foundations for a science of man [*sic*] that will accommodate comfortably his dual nature as a social and as a rational animal'; see Simon, H. (1957) *Models of Man*, John Wiley & Sons, p vii.

[43] Archibald et al, 'Papers and proceedings'.

[44] Samuelson wrote: 'The motivation for the F-Twist, critics say, is to help the case for the perfectly competitive laissez faire model of economics', in Archibald et al, 'Papers and proceedings', p 233.

[45] Machlup, F. (1956) 'Rejoinder to a reluctant ultra-empiricist', *Southern Economic Journal*, 22(4): 483–493.

46 Backhouse, R. and Cherrier, B. (2016) 'Becoming applied: the transformation of economics after 1970', Department of Economics Discussion Paper No 14-11, University of Birmingham.

47 MacKenzie, *An Engine*, p 7.

48 Backhouse and Cherrier, 'Becoming applied', p 10.

49 Backhouse, *The Puzzle*, pp 99–109, 125.

50 Appelbaum, B. (2020) *The Economists' Hour*, Picador, p 49.

51 Lucas quoted in Cassidy, J. (2010) *How Markets Fail*, Penguin, p 98.

52 Skidelsky, R. (2011) 'The relevance of Keynes', *Cambridge Journal of Economics*, 35: 1–13, p 1.

53 Offer, A. and Söderberg, G. (2016) *The Nobel Factor*, Princeton University Press, p 23.

54 Ricardo, D. (1820) 'Funding system', in P. Sraffa (ed) (2004 [1951–1973]) *The Works and Correspondence of David Ricardo*, Vol 4: *Pamphlets and Papers 1815–1823*, Liberty Fund Inc. Ricardo did not take the idea as far as Barro and even pointed out the unfortunate, as he saw it, trait that citizens were not calculators with perfect foresight and willpower: 'In point of economy, there is no real difference in either of the modes [a one-off payment or a series of smaller, longer-term payments] ... but the people who pay the taxes never so estimate them, and therefore do not manage their private affairs accordingly. We are too apt to think, that the war is burdensome only in proportion to what we are at the moment called to pay for it in taxes, without reflecting on the probable duration of such taxes.'

55 See Feldstein, M. (1976) 'Perceived wealth in bonds and social security', *Journal of Political Economy*, 84(2): 331–336, and Barro, R.J. (1989) 'The Ricardian approach to budget deficits', *Journal of Economic Perspectives*, 3(2): 37–54.

56 Backhouse, *The Puzzle*, pp 132–133.

57 Backhouse, *The Puzzle*, p 133.

58 Krugman, P. (2009) 'How did economists get it so wrong?', *New York Times*, 2 September.

59 Appelbaum, *The Economists' Hour*. Appelbaum borrowed the term from historian Thomas McCraw.

60 Leontief, W. (1971) 'Theoretical assumptions and nonobserved facts', *American Economic Review*, 61(1): 1–7, p 3.

61 Simon, H. (1986) 'The failure of armchair economics', *Challenge*, 29(5): 18–25.

62 Bergmann, B. (1989) 'Why do most economists know so little about the economy?', p 36, in S. Bowles, R. Edwards, and W. Shepherd (eds) *Unconventional Wisdom: Essays on Economics in Honor of John Kenneth Galbraith*, Houghton Mifflin, pp 29–37.

63 See Rodrik, *Economics Rules*, ch 5: 'When economists go wrong'.

64 Gerstle, *The Rise and Fall*.

65 Summers, L.H. (2006) 'The great liberator', *New York Times*, 19 November.

66 Box first said 'all models are wrong' in print in Box, G.E.P. (1976), 'Science and statistics', *Journal of the American Statistical Association*, 71(356): 791–799. The full quotation appeared first in Box, G.E.P. (1979), 'Robustness in the strategy of scientific model building', in R.L. Launer and G.N. Wilkinson (eds) *Robustness in Statistics*, Academic Press, pp 201–236, p 202.

67 See, for example, Morgan, *The World*, p 406.

68 Rodrik, *Economics Rules*, p 44.

69 Dewey, J. (1950 [1922]) *Human Nature and Conduct*, The Modern Library Edition, Random House.

70 Box, 'Science and statistics', p 792.

71   Box, 'Science and statistics', pp 791–792.

72   Ovid (1826) *Metamorphoses*, trans Samuel Garth, John Dryden, Alexander Pope, Joseph Addison et al , J.F. Dove, Book 10, Lines 362–363, p 254.

73   Ovid, *Metamorphoses*, Book 10, Lines 374–375, p 255.

74   The story was updated for the AI age in the 2013 Hollywood movie *Her*.

75   Synge, J.L. (1970) *Talking about Relativity*, North Holland Publishing, pp 8 and 148. Synge discusses the syndrome in mathematics and physics, and speculates about its prominence in the consciousness of the general public.

76   The two economists who have explicitly used Pygmalion are, first, Graydon Anderson (1915–2013), Professor of Economics at San Diego State University from 1949 to 1979, in a piece on how the 'tunnel vision fixation' of neoclassical economists has left them unable to respond to contemporary economic, social, and political problems; see Anderson, G.K. (1980) 'On the poverty of economics: the Pygmalion Syndrome', *American Economist*, 24(2): 23–26. Secondly, Ivar Ekeland (b. 1944), a French mathematician and mathematical economist, in a piece about why he rejected a colleague's suggestion of writing a book together on how mathematics had made incredible progress from describing the natural world to describing the social world and creating global financial markets; see Ekeland, I. (2022) 'The Pygmalion Syndrome, or How to fall in love with your model', in J.-M. Morel and B. Teissier (eds) *Mathematics Going Forward*, Springer, pp 429–437.

77   Morgan, *The World*, pp 406, 407.

78   Pfleiderer, P. (2014) 'Chameleons: The Misuse of Theoretical Models in Finance and Economics', Stanford University. This is the March 2014 version of the text published online by Stanford University. Slightly revised versions were published in August 2018 as a Stanford Working Paper (No. 3020) and, later, as Pfleiderer, P. (2020) 'Chameleons: The Misuse of Theoretical Models in Finance and Economics', *Economica*, 87(345): 81–107.

79   Critics have accused Ricardo of this in his theory of international trade. Halévy, E. (1934) *The Growth of Philosophical Radicalism*, trans M. Morris, Faber and Faber, p 328, accuses Ricardo of 'false logic, the logic of men of action and of party men in which the end justifies the means'.

80   Pfleiderer, 'Chameleons', p 1. This is essentially the same definition as the Ricardian Vice, although Pfleiderer was not aware of the term at the time.

81   Cited by Rodrik, D., Naidu, S. and Zucman, G. (2019) 'Economics after Neoliberalism', *Boston Review*, 27 February.

82   Pfleiderer, 'Chameleons', p 14.

83   Rodrik, *Economics Rules*.

84   Pfleiderer, P. (2019) 'Disclosure issues in conducting empirical and theoretical research: a provocative view', PowerPoint presentation, Stanford GSB, August.

85   *EconTalk* (2014) [podcast] 'Paul Pfleiderer on the misuse of economic models', 8 September.

86   Pfleiderer, 'Chameleons', p 10.

Chapter 11: Big Finance

1   MacKenzie, D. (2006) *An Engine, Not a Camera*, MIT Press.

2   The finance theories referred to here are the Modigliani–Miller irrelevance theory and the Capital Asset Pricing Model (CAPM).

3   MacKenzie, *An Engine*, p 67.

4   Adair Turner, Chair of the UK's FSA, said in 2009 that the efficient markets hypothesis 'has been in the DNA of the FSA and securities and banking regulators

throughout the world': Turner, A. (2009) 'How to tame global finance', *Prospect*, September. The theory has been opposed by prominent Nobel Prize-winning economists such as Robert Shiller and Joseph Stiglitz.

5   Durand, D. (1968) 'State of the finance field: further comment', *Journal of Finance*, December, p 1. See also MacKenzie, *An Engine*, p 71.

6   Durand retired in 1973. MIT News (1996) 'Prof. David Durand of MIT dies at 83', Available from: https://news.mit.edu/1996/durand [Accessed 17 May 2024].

7   Fama, E.F. and Merton, H.M. (1972) *The Theory of Finance*, Dryden Press, p vii. They also omitted any discussion of the empirical tests of the theory.

8   MacKenzie, *An Engine*, p 12. MacKenzie adds 'that a model's assumptions were "unrealistic" did not generally count, in the epistemic culture of financial economics, as a valid argument against the model'.

9   See MacKenzie, *An Engine*, p 112.

10   MacKenzie, *An Engine*, p 111.

11   Mandelbrot, B.B. (2008 [1999]) 'How fractals can explain what's wrong with Wall Street', *Scientific American*, September.

12   MacKenzie, *An Engine*, pp 114–115.

13   Fama, E.F. (1976) *Foundations of Finance*, Basic Books; cited in MacKenzie, *An Engine*, p 115.

14   This account draws on MacKenzie, *An Engine*, ch 4.

15   MacKenzie, *An Engine*, p 70.

16   Lazear added: 'Economics succeeds where other social sciences fail because economists are willing to abstract.' But this method leads to a narrowing of analysis, he added. 'Our narrowness allows us to provide concrete solutions, but sometimes prevents us from thinking about the larger features of the problem. This specialization is not a flaw; much can be learned from other social scientists who observe phenomena that we often overlook.' Lazear, E.P. (1999) 'Economic imperialism', NBER Working Paper No 7300, August.

17   See Strange, S. (2016 [1986]) *Casino Capitalism*, Manchester University Press, ch 2.

18   Shaxson, N. (2011) *Treasure Islands*, Bodley Head, ch 5.

19   Shaxson, *Treasure Islands*, p 90.

20   This paragraph draws on Sell, S. (2003) *Private Power, Public Law*, Cambridge University Press, p 18.

21   Conway, E. (2014) *The Summit*, Little, Brown & Co.

22   Shaxson, *Treasure Islands*, p 92.

23   Appelbaum, B. (2020) *The Economists' Hour*, Picador, pp 235–236.

24   De Goede, M. (2005) *Virtue, Fortune and Faith*, University of Minnesota Press, p 129.

25   Friedman, M. (2001 [1971]) 'The need for futures markets in currencies', *Cato Journal*, 31(3): 635–641, 638.

26   MacKenzie, *An Engine* p 147–150.

27   MacKenzie, *An Engine*, p 149.

28   The other three variables are the strike price of the option, the risk-free rate, and the volatility.

29   MacKenzie, *An Engine*, p 135.

30   MacKenzie, *An Engine*, pp 136–139: Paul Samuelson dabbled in financial economics and got close to developing the formula. Samuelson's experience of trading stocks held him back as it taught him that a perfect hedge was not possible. Samuelson said that Black, Scholes, and Merton had the 'courage to take a final step that

I was squeamish about: namely, I was loathe to accept the idealization of truly *instantaneous* rebalancings'.

[31] Coyle, D. (2021) *Cogs and Monsters*, Princeton University Press, p 24.

[32] MacKenzie, *An Engine*, p 158.

[33] Strange, *Casino Capitalism*.

[34] Quoted in Dyer, N. (2021) "'Susan Strange saw the financial crisis coming, Your Majesty": the case for the LSE's great global political economist', *Real-World Economics Review*, 98: 92–112.

[35] Passell, P. (1997) '2 get Nobel for formula at the heart of options trading', *New York Times*, 15 October.

[36] Lowenstein, R. (2002) *When Genius Failed*, Fourth Estate/HarperCollins, p 159.

[37] Quoted in Lowenstein, *When Genius Failed*, p 89. This paragraph drew on my article: Dyer, N. (2019) 'The Nobel bailout', *The Mint Magazine*, 10, Available from: www.themintmagazine.com/the-nobel-bailout [Accessed 17 May 2024].

[38] From Roig-Franzia, M. (2009) 'Brooksley Born, the Cassandra of the derivatives crisis,' *Washington Post*, 26 May. The quotation comes from Michael Greenberger, a University of Maryland law school professor who head up the CFTC's Division of Trading and Markets.

[39] Johnson, S. and Kwak, J. (2011) *13 Bankers*, Vintage Books, pp 9 and 148.

[40] Johnson, S. (2009) 'The quiet coup', *The Atlantic*, May.

[41] Conway, *The Summit*.

[42] Johnson, 'The quiet coup'.

[43] Johnson and Kwak, *13 Bankers*, pp 120–121.

[44] Johnson, 'The quiet coup'.

[45] Turner, 'How to tame global finance'. The phenomenon has also been described as 'cognitive regulatory capture' by Willem Buiter, economist and former member of the Bank of England's Monetary Policy Committee; see Buiter, W. (2009) 'Lessons from the global financial crisis for regulators and supervisors', Discussion Paper No 635, July.

[46] Johnson, 'The quiet coup'.

[47] 'Press release: Robert E. Lucas Jr.', Nobel Prize, 10 October 1995, Available from: www.nobelprize.org/prizes/economic-sciences/1995/press-release/1000/ [Accessed 17 May 2024].

[48] *EconTalk* (2007) [podcast] 'Bob Lucas on growth, poverty and business cycles', 5 February.

[49] Tooze, A. (2018) *Crashed: How a Decade of Financial Crises Changed the World*, Allen Lane.

[50] Watson, M. (2014) 'Re-establishing what went wrong before', *Journal of Critical Globalisation Studies*, 7: 80–101.

[51] Based on the account given by Fara, P. (2021) *Life after Gravity*, Oxford University Press.

[52] The quotation is used widely, see for example: Appelbaum, *The Economists' Hour*, p 3. The earliest version is from 1756, 30 years after Newton's death, and its exact origin and accuracy is unclear.

[53] Cassidy, J. (2010) 'After the blow up', *New Yorker*, 3 January.

[54] PBS (2008) 'Nobel laureates trace how the economy began to fall apart', 26 December.

[55] Krugman, P. (2009) 'How did economists get it so wrong?', *New York Times*, 2 September.

56 Krugman, P. (2012), 'Paul Krugman: Asimov's Foundation novels grounded my economics', *The Guardian*, 4 December.

57 Derman, E. (2004) *My Life as a Quant: Reflections on Physics and Finance*, Wiley, p 20.

58 Derman, E. (2011) *Models. Behaving. Badly*, Wiley, ch 5. The interest rate derivative model is known as the Black–Derman–Toy model.

59 Derman, *Models. Behaving. Badly*, ch 5.

60 Derman, *Models. Behaving. Badly*. He has invented the world for inverse anthropomorphism: 'pragmamorphism' from the Greek word *pragma*, meaning 'a material object'.

61 Derman, *Models. Behaving. Badly*.

62 Mollenkamp, C., Ng, S., Pleven, L. and Smith, R. (2008) 'Behind AIG's fall, risk models failed to pass real-world test', *Wall Street Journal*, 31 October and Osipovich, A. (2018) 'Yale Professor who had controversial role in the crisis now teaches about it', *Wall Street Journal*, 11 May.

63 Mollenkamp et al, 'Behind AIG's fall'.

64 In Garcia, C. (2012) '"Misunderstanding financial crises", a Q&A with Gary Gorton', *Financial Times*, 25 October.

65 Sorkin, A.R. and Walsh, M.W. (2009) 'U.S. is said to offer another $30 billion in funds to A.I.G.', *New York Times*, 1 March, and Johnson, 'The quiet coup'.

66 Gorton, G.B. (2012) *Misunderstanding Financial Crises: Why We Don't See Them Coming*, Oxford University Press, esp pp viii, x, 211.

67 Caballero, R.J. (2010) 'Macroeconomics after the crisis: time to deal with the pretense-of-knowledge syndrome', *Journal of Economic Perspectives*, 24(4): 85–102, p 86.

68 Caballero, 'Macroeconomics after the crisis', pp 85 and 89.

69 Burgess, S., Fernandez-Corugedo, E., Groth, C, Harrison, R., Monti, F., Theodoridis, K. and Waldron, M. (2013) 'The Bank of England's forecasting platform', Bank of England Working Paper No 471, May, p 7.

70 *The Big Short* (2015) [film], directed by Adam McKay, Paramount Pictures.

71 MacKenzie, D. and Spears, T. (2014) '"A device for being able to book P&L": the organizational embedding of the Gaussian copula', *Social Studies of Science*, 44(3): 433–435.

72 MacKenzie and Spears, 'A device'.

73 Whitehouse, M. (2005) 'Slices of risk', *Wall Street Journal*, 12 September.

74 Johnson and Kwak, *13 Bankers*, p 53.

75 Johnson and Kwak, *13 Bankers*, p 140.

Chapter 12: Trading Barbarians

1 Free to Choose Network (1980) 'The tyranny of control', *Free to Choose*, Episode 2.

2 Deaton, A. (2023) *Economics in America*, Princeton University Press, p 231. Angus Deaton says that he shared this view and offers a 'Mea culpa'.

3 Mankiw, G. (2009) 'News flash: economists agree', *Greg Mankiw's Blog*, 14 February, Available from: http://gregmankiw.blogspot.com/2009/02/news-flash-economists-agree.html [Accessed 17 May 2024].

4 Coyle, D. (1996) 'Paul Krugman: keeping the barbarians at bay', *The Independent*, 14 July.

5 Rodrik, D. (1997) *Has Globalization Gone Too Far?*, Institute for International Economics, p 75.

6 Rodrik, D. (2011) *The Globalization Paradox*, Oxford University Press, p 294, Rodrik, *Has Globalization Gone Too Far?*, and 'Barbarians, barbarians everywhere',

Dani Rodrik's Weblog, 9 May, Available from: https://rodrik.typepad.com/dani_rodriks_weblog/2007/05/are_there_barba.html [Accessed 17 May 2024].

[7] Scruggs, G. (2019) 'What the "Battle for Seattle" means 20 years later', *Bloomberg*, 29 November.

[8] Wallach, L. and Woodall, P. (2004) *Whose Trade Organization?* The New Press, Public Citizen, p 1.

[9] Wolf, M. (2005) *Why Globalisation Works*, Yale Nota Bene, p 247.

[10] Burgess, J. (1999) 'Gasoline dispute highlights environmental concerns', *Washington Post*, 28 November.

[11] Wallach, L. (2012) 'Can a "Dracula strategy" bring Trans-Pacific Partnership into the sunlight?' *Yes! Magazine*, December.

[12] Krugman, P. (2000) 'Reckonings: an American pie', *New York Times*, 16 February.

[13] Krugman, P. (1999) 'Enemies of the WTO', *Slate*, 24 November.

[14] Tooze, A. (2021) 'The gatekeeper', *London Review of Books*, 22 April.

[15] Krugman, P. (1993) 'What do undergrads need to know about trade?' *American Economic Review*, 83(2): 23–26.

[16] Krugman, P. (1996) 'Ricardo's difficult idea', MIT, Available from: https://web.mit.edu/krugman/www/ricardo.htm [Accessed 17 May 2024].

[17] Krugman, P. (1996) 'What economists can learn from evolutionary theorists', MIT, November, Available from: www.mit.edu/~krugman/evolute.html [Accessed 17 May 2024].

[18] Rodrik, *Has Globalization Gone Too Far?*

[19] Stopford, J.M. and Strange, S., with Henley, J.S. (1991) *Rival States, Rival Firms*, Cambridge University Press, ch 1.

[20] Sell, S. (2003) *Private Power, Public Law*, Cambridge University Press; and Rodrik, D. (2018) 'What do trade agreements really do?', NBER Working Paper No 24344, February.

[21] Wallach and Woodall, *Whose Trade Organization?*, and Rodrik, 'What do trade agreements really do?'.

[22] Klein, N. (2023) *Doppelganger: A Trip into the Mirror World*, Allen Lane, pp 81–82. A partial vaccine patent waiver was agreed in July 2022.

[23] WTO (1997) 'WTO achieves landmark agreement on financial services', *WTO Focus*, 25. The Director-General was Renato Ruggiero.

[24] Sell, *Private Power*, pp 167–168.

[25] Andrews, E.L. (1997) 'Accord is reached to lower barriers in global finance', *New York Times,* 13 December.

[26] Blustein, P. (1997) 'Nations reach agreement on financial services pact', *Washington Post*, 12 December.

[27] Over the last 50 years, 180 countries have entered into more than 3,000 agreements with investment protections.

[28] *The Economist* (2014) 'The arbitration game', 11 October.

[29] Edwards, H.S. (2016) *Shadow Courts*, Columbia Global Reports.

[30] Reuters (2021) 'TC Energy seeks more than $15 bln in damages from U.S. over Keystone XL', 2 July.

[31] Bhagwati, J. (1998) 'The capital myth', *Foreign Affairs*, 77(3): 7–12, 11.

[32] Bhagwati, J. (2004) *In Defense of Globalization*, Oxford, pp 182–183. Bhagwati, however, said 'the days of gung-ho international financial capitalism are probably past', p 207.

[33] Wolf, *Why Globalisation Works*, p 80.

[34] Friedman, T. (2006) *The World Is Flat*, Penguin, p 261.

35 Rodrik, 'What do trade agreements really do?'

36 Slobodian, Q. (2018) *Globalists*, Harvard University Press, p 280.

37 Quoted in Slobodian, *Globalists*, p 276.

38 WTO (2000) 'Basics: the case for open trade', WTO website, Available from: www.wto.org/english/thewto_e/whatis_e/tif_e/fact3_e.htm [Accessed 17 May 2024].

39 Lamy, P. (2011) 'Foreword', in WTO 'Centre William Rappard: Home of the World Trade Organization', WTO Secretariat.

40 Slobodian, *Globalists*, pp 241 and 281.

41 Krugman, P. (2000) 'Reckonings: a symbol issue', *New York Times*, 10 May.

42 Autor, D. (nd) 'Trade and labor markets: lessons from China's rise', IZA World of Labor website, Available from: https://wol.iza.org/articles/trade-and-labor-makets-lessons-from-chinas-rise/long [Accessed 17 May 2024].

43 China country page on World Inequality Database, Available from: https://wid.world/country/china/ [Accessed 3 March 2024].

44 Weber, I.M. (2021) *How China Escaped Shock Therapy*, Routledge, p 269.

45 Mullin, J. (2020) 'The rise and sudden decline of North Carolina furniture making', *Econ Focus*, Federal Reserve Bank of Richmond, Available from: www.richmondfed.org/publications/research/econ_focus/2020/q4/economic_history [Accessed 17 May 2024].

46 Autor, 'Trade and labor markets'.

47 Appelbaum, B. (2020) *The Economists' Hour*, Picador.

48 Rodrik, *The Globalization Paradox*, p 64.

49 Rodrik, D. (2017) *Economics Rules*, Oxford University Press, p 170.

50 Samuelson, P.A. (1962) 'The gains from international trade once again', *Economic Journal*, 72(288): 820–829, 823: 'Practical men and economic theorists have always known that trade may help some people and hurt others. Our problem is to show that trade lovers are theoretically able to compensate trade haters for the hard done them, thereby making everyone better off.'

51 Rodrik, D. (2018) *Straight Talk on Trade*, Princeton University Press, ch 9.

52 Rodrik, *Straight Talk*, ch 9. Reagan drastically cut the Trade Adjustment Assistance (TAA) programme in 1981.

53 Andrews, E.L. (2004) 'Democrats criticised Bush over job exports', *New York Times*, 11 February.

54 Mankiw, G. (2006) 'Outsourcing Redux', *Greg Mankiw's Blog*, 7 May, Available from: http://gregmankiw.blogspot.com/2006/05/outsourcing-redux.html [Accessed 17 May 2024]. From an op-ed drafted at the time but not published.

55 Cassidy, J. (2004) 'Winners and losers', *New Yorker*, 2 August.

56 Samuelson, P.A. (2004) 'Where Ricardo and Mill rebut and confirm arguments of mainstream economists supporting globalization', *Journal of Economic Perspectives*, 18(3): 135–146.

57 Lohr, S. (2004) 'An elder challenges outsourcing's orthodoxy', *New York Times*, 9 September.

58 Drezner, D.W. (2004) 'Paul Samuelson's outsourcing "bombshell"', *Foreign Policy*, 9 September.

59 Wolf, M. (2015) 'The embattled future of global trade policy', *Financial Times*, 12 May.

60 Klein, E. (2022) 'Why a middle-class lifestyle remains out of reach for so many', *New York Times*, 17 July.

61 Mankiw, N.G. (2015) 'Economists actually agree on this: the wisdom of free trade', *New York Times*, 24 April.

62 Baker, D. (2013) 'Krugman discovers intellectual property', *CEPR Blog*, 19 June, Available from: www.cepr.net/krugman-discovers-intellectual-property-the-1-percent-ar-the-takers/ [Accessed 17 May 2024].

63 Krugman, P. (2015) 'TPP at the NABE', *New York Times*, 11 March.

64 Petri, P.A. and Plummer, M.G. (2016), 'The economic effects of the Trans-Pacific Partnership: new estimates', Peterson Institute for International Economics Working Paper No 16-2, January.

65 Samuelson, T. (2016) 'Modelling the economic impact of the TPP', *Marketplace*, 25 January.

66 Rodrik, *Straight Talk*, p 124. See also DeMartino, G.F. (2022) *The Tragic Science*, University of Chicago Press, ch 6.

67 Capaldo, J., Izurieta, A. and Sundaram, J.K. (2016) 'Trading down: unemployment, inequality and other risks of the Trans-Pacific Partnership Agreement', Global Development and Environment Institute Working Paper No 16-01, Tufts.

68 Petri and Plummer, 'The economic effects', p 8; original emphasis.

69 DeMartino, *The Tragic Science*.

70 Rodrik, *Straight Talk*, p 126.

71 Smith, D. (2017) 'Trump withdraws from Trans-Pacific Partnership amid flurry of orders', *The Guardian*, 23 January.

72 Rodrik, *Straight Talk*, p ix.

73 Research by David Autor et al, cited in Klein, M.C. and Pettis, M. (2020) *Trade Wars Are Class Wars*, Yale University Press, p 2.

74 Krugman, P. (2019) 'What economists (including me) got wrong about globalization', *Bloomberg*, 10 October.

75 Smith, A. (1999 [1776]) *An Inquiry into the Nature and Causes of the Wealth of Nations*, Penguin Classics, Book 4, ch 2, p 32.

76 Smith, *Wealth of Nations*, Book 4, ch 2: 'a capital employed in the home-trade, it has already been shown, necessarily puts into motion a greater quantity of domestic industry, and gives revenue and employment to a greater number of the inhabitants of the country, than an equal capital employed in the foreign trade of consumption'.

77 Schlefer, J. (1998) 'Today's most mischievous misquotation', *The Atlantic*, March.

78 Liu, G.M. (2022) *Adam Smith's America*, Princeton University Press, p 249.

79 Shaxson, N. (2019) *The Finance Curse*, Vintage. The competitive deregulation of finance and lowering of corporation tax are modern forms of beggar-thy-neighbour economic policy.

80 Agyemang, E. and Tamma, P. (2024) 'Global tax deal under threat from US politics and fraying consensus', *Financial Times*, 28 February.

81 Rodrik, D. (2022) 'Don't let geopolitics kill the world economy', *Project Syndicate*, 10 November.

Chapter 13: Life: An Externality

1 UN (1992) Rio Declaration on Environment and Development, June, and UN (1992) UNFCCC, Article 2.

2 Marshall, A. (1890) *Principles of Economics*, Macmillan, Book 5, ch 1, p 138.

3 Schumacher, E.F. (1984 [1973]), *Small is Beautiful*, Abacus, p 36.

4 Pigou, A.C. (1920) *The Economics of Welfare*, Macmillan. This framework was developed by British-American economist Ronald Coase.

5 *Think Like an Economist* (2021) [podcast] 'A conversation with Larry Summers', Modulated Media, 9 November, Episode 50.

6   Accra Caucus on Forests and Climate Change (2010) 'Realising rights, protecting forests', June.

7   Six countries—Australia, France, Japan, Norway, Britain and the US—pledged a combined $3.5 billion to REDD in 2009, some of which were recycled commitments. Reuters (2009) 'U.S. joins $3.5 bln scheme to fight deforestation', 16 December.

8   Dyer, N. and Counsell, S. (2010) 'McREDD: how McKinsey "cost-curves" are distorting REDD', Rainforest Foundation UK, and Greenpeace (2011) 'McKinsey's "bad influence" over rainforest nations around the world', 7 April.

9   Mongabay.com (2011) 'Greenpeace says McKinsey's REDD+ work could encourage deforestation', 7 April, https://news.mongabay.com/2011/04/greenpeace-says-mckinseys-redd-work-could-encourage-deforestation

10 Greenfield, P. (2023) 'Revealed: more than 90% of rainforest carbon offsets by biggest certifier are worthless, analysis shows', *The Guardian*, 18 January.

11 Nordhaus, W.D. (2018) 'Climate change: the ultimate challenge for economics', Prize Lecture, 8 December.

12 Krugman, P. (1995) 'Incidents from my career', Princeton, www.princeton.edu/~pkrugman/incidents.html

13 DeCanio, S.J. (2003) *Economic Models of Climate Change: A Critique*, Palgrave, pp 132–136. See also Nordhaus, W.D. (1979) *The Efficient Use of Energy Resources*, Cowles Foundation Monograph 26, Yale University Press.

14 Nordhaus, W.H. (1980) 'It's time to slay the sacred cows', *New York Times*, 2 November.

15 The 'Justice' analogy is not, of course, used by Nordhaus. He described it this way: 'the optimal degree of reduction of GHGs [greenhouse gases] comes where the current cost of reducing GHG emissions equals the present value of the damage from higher concentrations'; in Nordhaus, W.D. (1991) 'To slow or not to slow: the economics of the greenhouse effect', *Economic Journal*, 101(407): 920–937, 926.

16 Appelbaum, B. (2018) '2018 Nobel in Economics is awarded to William Nordhaus and Paul Romer', *New York Times*, 8 October.

17 Nobel Prize (2018) '2018 Nobel Prize Award Ceremony', YouTube, Available from: www.youtube.com/watch?v=YlQugR7KSKg&list=PLJE9rmV1-0uDA6ib0Ug7gtBteEPKlJqIt&index=6 [Accessed 17 May 2024].

18 Barrage, L. (2019) 'The Nobel Memorial Prize for William D. Nordhaus', *Scandinavian Journal of Economics*, 121(2): 884–924.

19 Nordhaus, 'Climate change'.

20 Nordhaus, 'Climate change'.

21 Nordhaus, W.D. (2018) 'Climate change: the ultimate challenge for economics: lecture slides', p 6. Graph called 'Temperature trajectories in different policies', Available from: www.nobelprize.org/uploads/2018/10/nordhaus-slides.pdf [Accessed 17 May 2024].

22 Hickel, J. (2018) 'The Nobel Prize for Climate Catastrophe', *Foreign Policy*, 6 December.

23 Nordhaus, 'To slow or not to slow'.

24 Nordhaus, 'To slow or not to slow'.

25 Nordhaus, W.D. (2013) *The Climate Casino*, Yale University Press, pp 138–139; emphasis added.

26 Tooze, A. (2021) 'The gatekeeper', *London Review of Books*, 43(8), 22 April.

27 Stern, N., Stiglitz, J.E. and Taylor, C. (2022) 'The economics of immense risk, urgent action and radical change: towards new approaches to the economics of climate change', NBER Working Paper No 28472, February.

28 Nordhaus, *The Climate Casino*; see Table 5: 'Vulnerability of the U.S. economy to climate change by sector, 1948–2011', pp 137–138.

29 Keen, S. (2020) 'The appallingly bad neoclassical economics of climate change', *Globalizations*, 18(7): 1–29, 3.

30 Nordhaus, *The Climate Casino*, p 137, says that fishing and farming reduced from 3.9 per cent of US GDP in 1973 to 1.2 per cent in 2011.

31 Nordhaus, W.D. with Sztorc, P. (2013) 'DICE 2013R: introduction and user's manual' (2nd edn), Yale/William Nordhaus, 31 October, p 11.

32 Nordhaus, W.D. (2018) 'William D. Nordhaus—biographical', Available from: www.nobelprize.org/prizes/economic-sciences/2018/nordhaus/biographical [Accessed 17 May 2024].

33 Oswald, O. and Stern, N. (2019) 'Why does the economics of climate change matter so much, and why has the engagement of economists been so weak?', *Royal Economic Society* [newsletter], October.

34 Pindyck, R.S. (2013) 'Climate change policy: what do the models tell us?' NBER Working Paper No 19244.

35 Nordhaus, *The Climate Casino*, p 101.

36 Nordhaus with Sztorc, 'DICE 2013R', p 11.

37 Howard, P.H. and Sterner, T. (2017) 'Few and not so far between: a meta-analysis of climate damage estimates', *Environmental Resource Economics*, 68: 197–225.

38 Smith, N. (2021) 'Why has climate economics failed us?', Noahpinion, Substack, 13 April, Available from: www.noahpinion.blog/p/why-has-climate-economics-failed [Accessed 17 May 2024].

39 Yale University (2018) 'William Nordhaus, Nobel Prize in Economics Press Conference', 8 October, YouTube, Available from: www.youtube.com/watch?v=zQw-TJxfl-Q [Accessed 17 May 2024].

40 Weitzman, M.L. (2009) 'Reactions to the Nordhaus critique', Harvard Environmental Economics Program Discussion Paper No 09-11.

41 Roberts, S. (2019) 'Martin Weitzman, virtuoso climate change economist, dies at 77', *New York Times*, 4 September.

42 Pindyck, 'Climate change policy'.

43 Franta, B. (2022) 'Weaponizing economics: Big Oil, economic consultants, and climate policy delay', *Environmental Politics*, 31(4): 555–575, 558–559. Franta notes that although corporate 'funding was acknowledged in Charles River Associates' report itself, it often was not in public promotions of the report's results' (p 559).

44 Franta, 'Weaponizing economics'.

45 Trump, D. (2017) 'Statement by President Trump on the Paris Climate Accord', The White House, 1 June.

46 Bernstein, P., Montgomery, W.D., Ramkrishnan, B. and Tuladhar, S.D. (2017) 'Impact of greenhouse gas regulations on the industrial sector', NERA Economic Consulting, March. The authors thank the report sponsors 'for helping with the study design and providing feedback'. Also see Franta, 'Weaponizing economics'.

47 Franta, 'Weaponizing economics'.

48 For example, MIT's Joint Program on the Science and Policy of Global Change and Stanford's Energy Modelling Forum. ExxonMobil supports the 'Negative Emissions Technologies and Hydrogen' project and Shell both the 'Energy at Scale' and 'Quantifying the opportunities for energy transition in hard-to-abate sectors'

projects at MIT Joint Program, according to https://globalchange.mit.edu. A list of Industry Affiliates of Stanford's Energy Modelling Forum, who each pay upwards of $20,000 per year, include BP, Chevron, ExxonMobil, and the API, according to https://emf.stanford.edu/industry-affiliates [Accessed February 2024].

49 ExxonMobil (2020) 'Collaborating with leading universities to meet global energy demand', website article, 17 November, Available from: https://corporate. exxonmobil.com/who-we-are/technology-and-collaborations/university-and-national-labs-partnerships/collaborating-with-leading-universities-to-meet-global-energy-demand [Accessed 17 May 2024]. Author calculations.

50 Franta, 'Weaponizing economics'.

51 Repetto, R. and Austin, D. (1997) 'The Costs of Climate Protection: A Guide for the Perplexed', World Resources Institute.

52 Senate (1997) 'Conditions regarding U.N. Framework Convention on Climate Change', Senate Report No 105-54, US Government Publishing Office. Robert Repetto, Vice President and Senior Economist, World Resources Institute, testified in the Hearing of June 26; emphasis added.

53 See O'Neil, C. (2016) *Weapons of Math Destruction*, Penguin, p 25.

54 Almond, R.E.A., Grooten, M., Juffe Bignoli, D. and Petersen, T. (eds) (2022) 'Living planet report 2022', WWF. The report shows an average 69 per cent decrease in monitored wildlife populations between 1970 and 2018.

55 Reuters (2020) 'DAVOS—Get an economics degree Greta, then let's talk—U.S. Treasury chief', 23 January.

56 Friedman, L. (2019) 'What is the Green New Deal? A climate proposal, explained', *New York Times*, 21 February.

57 Climate Leadership Council (2019) 'Economists' statement on carbon dividends', Available from: https://clcouncil.org/economists-statement/

58 Dlouhy, J.A. (2019) 'From Greenspan to Yellen, economic brain trust backs carbon tax', *Bloomberg*, 17 January.

59 Climate Leadership Council, 'Economists' statement'.

60 Angner, E. (2023) *How Economics Can Save the World*, Penguin Business, ch 3, p 60.

61 Oswald and Stern, 'Why does the economics …?'.

62 Climate Leadership Council, 'Economists' statement'.

63 Hook, L. (2019) 'Surge in US economists' support for carbon tax to tackle emissions', *Financial Times*, 17 February.

64 Dlouhy, J.A. and Natter, A. (2019) 'Oil companies join corporate lobbying push for U.S. carbon tax', *Bloomberg*, 20 May, and Martinez, J. (2018) 'ConocoPhillips pledges $2m to carbon tax group', *Upstream*, 17 December.

65 Lowenstein, A. (2023) 'Meet the DC thinktank giving Big Oil "the opportunity to say they've done something"', *The Guardian*, 9 July.

66 Smith, A.E., Tuladhar, S., Chang, W., Ramkrishnan, B. and Hahm, A. (2020) 'Economic impacts of the Climate Leadership Council's carbon dividends plan compared to regulations achieving equivalent emissions reductions', NERA Economic Consulting, December. Anne E. Smith headed the Climate & Sustainability Group at Charles River Associates before she joined NERA in 2011. Two other authors of the report done for Climate Leadership Council were co-authors of the NERA study cited by President Trump when he took the US out of the Paris Climate Agreement. NERA said, at the time, that Trump had misrepresented their study.

67 Volcovici, V. and Gardner, T. (2021) 'Exxon lobbyist duped by Greenpeace says climate policy was a ploy, CEO condemns statements', Reuters, 1 July.

68   Woods, D.W. (2021) 'Our position on climate policy and carbon pricing' [news release], ExxonMobil, 2 July.

69   Reuters (2021) 'Exxon suspended from climate advocacy group it helped form', 7 August.

70   Meyer, R. (2019) 'It's younger and cooler than a carbon tax', *The Atlantic*, 21 June.

71   Klein, E. (2021) 'Four ways of looking at the radicalism of Joe Biden', *New York Times*, 8 April.

72   Davenport, C. and Friedman, L. (2022) 'Five decades in the making', *New York Times*, 7 August.

73   Davenport and Friedman, 'Five decades'.

74   Daly, H. and Cobb, J. (1989) *For the Common Good: Redirecting the Economy toward Community, the Environment, and a Sustainable Future*, Beacon Press, p 37.

75   Buller, A. (2022) *The Value of a Whale: On the Illusions of Green Capitalism*, Manchester University Press, and Monbiot, G. (2014) 'The pricing of everything', Annual SPERI Lecture, 29 April.

76   Pigou, A.C. (1956 [1925]) 'In memoriam: Alfred Marshall', in A.C. Pigou (ed) *Memorials of Alfred Marshall*, Kelley & Millman Inc., p 84.

Chapter 14: New Hope

1   Piketty, T. (2014) *Capital in the Twenty-First Century*, Belknap Press, p 32.

2   Piketty credits Simon Kuznets with completing the first serious attempt to measure social inequality. Kuznets studied data from US tax records between 1913 and 1948 and saw a real and incontrovertible reduction in income inequality in the US. The problem was that he, and other economists, took this 30-year snapshot as a general rule, ignoring its social and political context. There is some evidence that this rosy interpretation was part of a Cold War mentality of encouraging developing countries to stick with the Western capitalist system. See Piketty, *Capital*, pp 11–15.

3   Piketty, *Capital*, pp 31–32.

4   Piketty, *Capital*, pp 335 and 514.

5   Krugman, P. (2014) 'Why we're in a new Gilded Age', *New York Review of Books*, 8 May.

6   Piketty, T. (2015) 'About capital in the twenty-first century', *American Economic Review*, 105(5): 48–53.

7   Mirrlees, J. (1996) 'James A. Mirrlees: biographical', Nobel Prize website, www.nobelprize.org/prizes/economic-sciences/1996/mirrlees/biographical.

8   Jeffrey Goldstone, the physicist, suggested to Mirrlees that it might be possible to devise a model of optimal taxation in the mid-1960s; see Read, C. (2016) *The Great Financiers*, Palgrave Macmillan, ch 20.

9   Mirrlees, J. (1971) 'An exploration in the theory of optimum income taxation', *Review of Economic Studies*, 38(2): 175–208.

10   Mirrlees suggested instead that inequality is explained by a mathematical 'random walk'. The empirical basis for this was a quantified study of change over time in the Forbes Rich List, done by a research assistant. Mirrlees, J. (2015) 'The causes of economic inequality', Lecture at the Singapore Management University, 6 November, YouTube, Available from: www.youtube.com/watch?v=5REttMOmyBw [Accessed 17 May 2024].

11   Roberts, S. (2018) 'James Mirrlees, whose tax model earned a Nobel, dies at 82', *New York Times*, 4 September.

12   My analysis, based on Mirrlees, 'An exploration'. His theory, therefore, relies on 'asymmetric information', for which he won his Nobel. This approach is often

seen as more 'realistic'. The Mirrlees optimal tax example shows how little reality is gained in models when only one or two strong assumptions are relaxed and a host of others are left intact.

13 Offer, A. and Söderberg, G. (2016) *The Nobel Factor*, Princeton University Press, pp 170–173.

14 Mirrlees, 'An exploration'.

15 From Brewer, M., Saez, E. and Shephard, A. (2010) 'Means-testing and tax rates on earnings', in Institute of Fiscal Studies (ed) *Dimensions of Tax Design: The Mirrlees Review*, Oxford University Press.

16 Bergin, T. (2021) *Free Lunch Thinking*, Random House.

17 Offer and Söderberg, *The Nobel Factor*, pp 170–173.

18 Saez, E. (2001) 'Using elasticities to derive optimal income tax rates', *Review of Economic Studies*, 68: 205–229.

19 Hargreaves, D. (2019) *Are Chief Executives Overpaid?*, Polity Press.

20 Jensen, M.C. and Murphy, K.J. (1990) 'CEO incentives—it's not how much you pay, but how', *Harvard Business Review*, May–June.

21 Based on research by Jason Furman of Harvard University and Peter Orszag of Lazard Frères, quoted in Wolf, M. (2019) 'Martin Wolf: why rigged capitalism is damaging liberal democracy', *Financial Times*, 18 September.

22 Piketty, T. and Saez, E. (2012) 'A theory of optimal capital taxation', NBER Working Paper No 17989, April. The long-run zero-capital tax result was produced by economists Christophe Chamley and Kenneth Judd in the mid-1980s.

23 Lucas, R.E. (1990) 'Supply side economics: an analytical review', *Oxford Economic Papers*, 42(2): 214.

24 Mirrlees, J.A. (2006) 'Preface', in J.A. Mirrlees, *Welfare, Incentives, and Taxation*, Oxford University Press, pp v–vi.

25 Piketty, *Capital*, pp 33 and 513.

26 Drutman, L. (2015) *The Business of America is Lobbying*, Oxford University Press, pp 8 and 13.

27 Smith, A. (1999 [1776]) *An Inquiry into the Nature and Causes of the Wealth of Nations*, Penguin Classics, Book 4, ch 2.

28 Smith, *Wealth of Nations*, Book 4, ch 8. See also Rothschild, E. (2020) 'Adam Smith: the first anti-capitalist?', Engelsberg Ideas, 24 August, Available from: https://engelsbergideas.com/essays/adam-smith-the-first-anti-capitalist [Accessed 17 May 2024].

29 Quoted in Appelbaum, B. (2020) *The Economists' Hour*, Picador, p 133.

30 Stoller, M. (2019) *Goliath*, Simon & Schuster.

31 Hofstadter, R. (1965) 'What happened to the antitrust movement?', in R. Hofstadter, *The Paranoid Style in American Politics and Other Essays*, Alfred A. Knopf, p 195.

32 A picture of George Stigler in his 'Adam Smith's Best Friend' T-shirt and the story of why the T-shirt was made to be can be found in Liu, G.M. (2022) *Adam Smith's America*, Princeton University Press, p 228.

33 Bork, R. (1978) *The Antitrust Paradox*, Free Press, and Appelbaum, *The Economists' Hour*, ch 5.

34 Appelbaum, *The Economists' Hour*, p 149.

35 Berman, E.P. (2022) *Thinking Like an Economist*, Princeton University Press, ch 4.

36 Milner, J.J. (2006) *A Gift of Freedom: How the John M. Olin Foundation Changed America*, Encounter Books, pp 5 and 62.

37 Bork, R. and Bowman, W. (1965), 'The crisis in antitrust', *Columbia Law Review*, 65(3): 363–376, 367.

38 Appelbaum, *The Economists' Hour*, p 150.

39 Figures and quotation from Stoller, *Goliath*.

40 Between 1991 and 2004, 0.7 per cent of mergers in the EU were prevented via prohibitions by the European Commission. New rules inspired by Chicago consumer welfare standard were introduced in 2004. Between 2005 and 2023, only 0.2 per cent of mergers (14 out of 6,462) were prevented by prohibition. The rate of merger investigations went down from 5.3 per cent to 2.5 per cent in the two periods. See Rock, B. (2024) 'Merger intervention rates in the EU', Hertie School Centre for Digital Governance, Student Working Paper Series, 17 January.

41 Khan, L.M. (2017) 'Amazon's antitrust paradox', *Yale Law Journal*, 126(3): 710–805, p 743.

42 Federal Trade Commission (2023) 'FTC sues Amazon for illegally maintaining monopoly power', FTC website, 26 September, Available from: www.ftc.gov/news-events/news/press-releases/2023/09/ftc-sues-amazon-illegally-maintaining-monopoly-power [Accessed 17 May 2024].

43 Eisinger, J. and Elliott, J. (2016) 'These professors make more than a thousand bucks an hour peddling mega-mergers', ProPublica, 16 November.

44 Kanter, J. (2022) 'Antitrust enforcement: the road to recovery', Lecture at the University of Chicago Stigler Center, 21 April.

45 Lynn, B.C. (2002) 'Antimonopoly: a master narrative for democracy?', *Democracy*, Fall.

46 Deaton, A. (2023) *Economics in America*, Princeton University Press, p 7.

47 *New York Times* (1987) 'The right minimum wage: $0.00', Opinion, 14 January.

48 Deaton, *Economics in America*.

49 Both quoted in Deaton, *Economics in America*, pp 8–9.

50 Deaton, *Economics in America*, p 10.

51 Deaton, *Economics in America*, p 8.

52 Deaton, *Economics in America*, p 16. The study looked at what didn't happen—it was counterfactual.

53 Kahneman, D. (2011) *Thinking, Fast and Slow*, Farrar, Straus and Giroux. In ch 25, Kahneman wrote: 'Unlike Econs, [economic humans] the Humans that psychologists know have a System 1.'

54 Kahneman, D. (2011) 'Conclusions', in *Thinking, Fast and Slow*.

55 Stigler, G. and Becker, G. (1977) 'De gustibus non est disputandum', *American Economic Review*, 67(2): 76–90.

56 Kahneman, *Thinking, Fast and Slow*, ch 1.

57 Kahneman, *Thinking, Fast and Slow*. As mentioned, Kahneman takes the term 'substitution' from George Pólya's book *How to Solve It*, where substitution is referred to as a deliberate process for solving difficult questions used by the attentive, calculating thinking Kahneman calls System 2.

58 Machlup, F. (1956) 'Rejoinder to a reluctant ultra-empiricist', *Southern Economic Journal*, 22(4): 483–493, 488.

59 Mini, P.V. (1974), *Philosophy and Economics*, University of Florida Press, p 59.

60 Greenspan, A. (2013) 'Never saw it coming', *Foreign Affairs*, 92(6): 88–96, p 90.

61 Chetty, R. (2013) 'Yes, economics is a science', *New York Times*, 20 October.

62 Deaton, *Economics in America*, p 212.

63 Banerjee, A.B. and Duflo, E. (2019) *Good Economics for Hard Times*, Public Affairs.

64 World Economic Forum (2024) 'Town hall: how to trust economics', YouTube, 17 January, Available from: www.youtube.com/watch?v=xEksn1afRdk [Accessed 17 May 2024].

65 World Economic Forum, 'Town hall'.

Conclusion

1   Pope's lines were not put on the monument. Westminster Abbey (nd), 'Sir Isaac Newton', Available from: www.westminster-abbey.org/abbey-commemorations/commemorations/sir-isaac-newton [Accessed 24 April 2024].

2   William Blake letter to Thomas Butt, 22 November 1802, quoted in Higgs, J. (2021) *William Blake vs the World*, Weidenfeld & Nicolson, pp 23–24 and 63–64, and Fara, P. (2004) *Newton: The Making of Genius*, Picador, ch 6. Blake's *Newton* may have been created in 1795 or 1805. Blake wrote 'Newtons sleep' rather than the more grammatically correct 'Newton's sleep'.

3   Caballero, R.J. (2010) 'Macroeconomics after the crisis: time to deal with the pretense-of-knowledge syndrome', *Journal of Economic Perspectives*, 24(4): 85–102, 100: 'The root cause of the poor state of affairs in the field of macroeconomics lies in a fundamental tension in academic macroeconomics between the enormous complexity of its subject and the micro-theory-like precision to which we aspire.'

4   Krugman, P. (1995) 'Incidents from my career', Princeton, Available from: www.princeton.edu/~pkrugman/incidents.html [Accessed 17 May 2024].

5   The reference is to Blake's short poem quoted earlier in the chapter and the French term for the Washington Consensus: *la pensée unique*, which I translate as the 'single vision' (see Introduction).

6   A non-exhaustive list would include prizes for finance (Modigliani—1985; Markowitz, Miller, and Sharpe—1990; Merton and Scholes 1997, and Fama—2013), law and economics (Stigler—1982), climate economics (Nordhaus—2018, underpinned by Coase—1991), trade theory (Krugman—2008), optimal taxation (Mirrlees—1996), and use of 'calculating' agents in analysis (Friedman—1976, Lucas—1995, Sargent—2011).

7   Lucas, R.E. (1988) 'What economists do', Commencement Address, University of Chicago, 9 December.

8   When he read Thomas Robert Malthus' attack of his economic systems, Ricardo replied: 'My object was to elucidate principles, and to do this I *imagined* strong cases that I might shew the operation of those principles.' Ricardo to Malthus, Letter 363, 4 May 1820, in P. Sraffa (ed) (2004 [1951–1973]) *The Works and Correspondence of David Ricardo*, Vol 8: *Letters 1819–June 1821*, Liberty Fund Inc, emphasis added.

9   Friedman, M. (1953) 'The methodology of positive economics', in M. Friedman, *Essays in Positive Economics*, University of Chicago Press, pp 3–43: p 43.

10 Morgan, M. (2012) *The World in the Model*, Cambridge University Press, pp 157–163.

11 Midgley, M. (2004) *The Myths We Live By*, Routledge, p xiii.

12 Simons, D. and Chabris, C. (2010) 'Selective attention test', YouTube, 10 March, Available from: www.youtube.com/watch?v=vJG698U2Mvo [Accessed 17 May 2024].

13 Kahneman, D. (2011) *Thinking, Fast and Slow*, Farrar, Straus and Giroux, ch 1.

14 Eisinger, J. and Elliott, J. (2016) 'These professors make more than a thousand bucks an hour peddling mega-mergers', ProPublica, 16 November. The $100 million figure is an estimate by ProPublica and includes equity stakes and non-compete payments.

15 I understand this as the message of Simon Clarke, a British Marxist thinker; see Clarke, S. (2005) 'The neoliberal theory of society', in A. Saad-Filho and D. Johnston (eds) *Neoliberalism: A Critical Reader*, Pluto Press, pp 50–59.

16 Weber, M. (1949) '"Objectivity" in social science and social policy', in E.A. Shils and H.A. Finch (eds) *Max Weber on the Methodology of the Social Sciences*, The Free Press, pp 50–112.
17 Weber, '"Objectivity"', pp 90–111.
18 Weber, '"Objectivity"', p 111; original emphasis.
19 Whelan, M. (2019) 'Modelling the Ocado way', The OR Society, YouTube, 1 May, Available from: www.youtube.com/watch?v=o0-N5J6l1nM [Accessed 18 June 2024].
20 Backhouse, R. (2010) *The Puzzle of Modern Economics*, Cambridge University Press, p 181.
21 Heilbroner, R. (2000 [1953]) *The Worldly Philosophers: The Lives, Times and Ideas of the Great Economic Thinkers* (7th edn), Penguin Books, p 103.
22 Box, G.E.P. (1976), 'Science and statistics', *Journal of the American Statistical Association*, 71(356): 791–799, 792.
23 J.M. Keynes to R.F. Harrod, 16 July 1938, in D. Moggridge (ed) (1973) *The Collected Writings of John Maynard Keynes*, Vol. 14: *The General Theory and After*, Macmillan, Part II, pp 299–301.
24 Shaxson, N. (2019) *The Finance Curse*, Vintage, p 261.
25 J.M. Keynes to R.F. Harrod, 16 July 1938, in Moggridge, *The Collected Writings*.
26 The analogy to astronomy and the formulation of this idea are borrowed from Mini, P.V. (1974), *Philosophy and Economics*, University of Florida, p 286: 'But men are more pliable than planets'.
27 Weber, '"Objectivity"', p 103.
28 Pigou, A.C. (1920) *The Economics of Welfare*, Macmillan, p 11.

Index

References to figures appear in *italic* type; those in **bold** type refer to tables. References to endnotes show both the page number and the note number.

Printed and bound by CPI Group (UK) Ltd, Croydon, CR0 4YY

25/03/2025

14647336-0004